Rainbow in the Rock

The People of Rural Greece

Rainbow
in the Rock

···❧[The People of Rural Greece]❧···

IRWIN T. SANDERS

Harvard University Press
Cambridge
1962

Distributed in Great Britain by Oxford University Press, London

Publication of this book has been aided
by a grant from the Ford Foundation

Library of Congress Catalog Card Number: 62–7337
Printed in the United States of America

to
Margaret
Gerda
Rob

··❧[Preface]❧··

When a sabbatical year became due in 1952–53, I inevitably chose the Balkans, picked Greece, and ended up studying village life. The Balkans had interested me since 1929, when I first went as an instructor to The American College of Sofia, where I spent six years (1929–32, 1934–37). There was also a year's tour as Agricultural Attaché in the American Embassy in Belgrade (1945–46).

As for Greece, I had dreamed of getting to know her better ever since the days when I was an undergraduate major in Classical Greek. Two voyages of discovery in 1930 and 1937 made me even more anxious to live there for a spell.

And as for Greek village life, this was a natural subject in view of my training and principal research interest. At first, I expected to study only one or two easily accessible villages, using the same tested techniques in which I had been trained as a sociologist and which I had employed in writing *Balkan Village,* the account of a single community studied in depth. But a thorough survey of the literature in both Greek and other languages, conducted with the help of a competent Greek bibliographer, showed that no general work on Greek village life had been written in over fifty years and that relatively few articles on particular places or regions had appeared. This explains why I was ready to move from the security of precise social-science procedures to the more vulnerable area of personal interpretation, subjecting my conclusions to the scrutiny of at least a score of men and women, each familiar with many aspects of Greek rural life, who agreed to read the rough drafts of this work and test my comments against their experience. A six-week field trip throughout Northern Greece in 1955 and a briefer visit to Attica in 1959 gave me a chance to note the rapid social changes occurring in the places I had come to know well in 1952–53.

The social scientist, if he is to understand the behavior which he studies, not only must observe what is done but also must try to probe the meanings attached by the actors to what they do. Throughout this work, therefore, I have tried to show how the world looks to the Greek villager. I do not necessarily agree with all of his views, but I think that he has the right to be heard. Wherever possible, I have let him speak for himself.

Aside from my research activities of the usual type, I also had approaches to the Greeks through the eyes of my wife Margaret who shopped in the Greek market with her Greek neighbors. Through my twelve-year-old daughter Gerda and my ten-year-old son Robert I shared in the wonders of their daily adventures with Greek friends and playmates. I profited by learning about the vicissitudes and the fortitude of our Greek upper-middle-class landlady, who shared her villa with us. The crises attending the succession of maids and laundresses and their husbands opened up avenues for further exploration. Too much credit cannot be given to Bessie Adossides, my interpreter, who knew the Greek countryside as though it were her own garden and who could translate into idiomatic English the most important nuances of the spoken language. My reading knowledge of modern Greek improved considerably during the year, but time was too brief for me to learn the spoken Greek sufficiently for conducting interviews on my own.

In transliterating Greek terms into Latin letters I have approximated the spelling and have not attempted to follow the pronunciation. Those who speak modern Greek will therefore find the transliteration awkward, but those who have studied ancient Greek will find that many words are familiar.

Prior to May 1953 the value of the dollar was 15,000 drachmas; after that date the dollar was worth 30,000 drachmas. On May 1, 1954, the drachma was revalued at 1 to 1,000, so that 30 drachmas were equivalent to a dollar. For that reason, in using all figures prior to 1954 I have given the 1954 value, moving the decimal point to the left three places.

Thanks should be given to the Social Science Research Council for a grant to help me with my Balkan studies; to the Associates for International Research, Inc., of Cambridge, Massachusetts, for extended research and secretarial assistance; to the University of Kentucky and Harvard University for many courtesies shown; and to the American School for Classical Studies in Athens for giving office space to a nonarchaeologist in their richly endowed Gennadion Library.

Many individuals have helped me in countless ways. I can only name some of them here to acknowledge my great indebtedness to all. Those listed, of course, should not be held accountable for my general interpretations. Special thanks, therefore, go to Mrs. Elle Adossides, Maria Alexandrakis, Constantine Apalodemos, Panos Bardis, Ph. Annino Cavalierato, Angelike Chatzemichali, Ernestine Friedl, D. J. Georgacas, Ann and Charles House, Print Hudson, K. D. Karavides, Lampros Koromelas, Catherine Koumarianou, Bruce Lansdale, Dorothy Lee, Glen Leet, Harry Levy, Spiro Manolas, B. G. Moussouros, Theodora J. Pantos, T. K. Papaspyropoulos, John D. Photiadis, N. D. Rigopoulos, George Sakellopoulos, Theodore Saloutos, Costas Souliotis, William Tait, Chris A. Theodore, Peter Topping, Vasilios G. Valaoras, V. T. Valassis, J. C. Vogel, Clayton E. Whipple, Robert L. Wolff, and Charles Yale.

I. T. S.

Wellesley Hills, Massachusetts
January 1961

ᐧᐧ᠄᠊[Contents]᠊᠄ᐧᐧ

Maps

Tables

Illustrations

·✧[Part One]✧·

Survival

·❀[I]❀·

The People of Greece

THE LEGEND

When God was building the earth, he lavished all goods such as water, pasture, forests, and rich soil on the countries of the world. Then suddenly he remembered that he had forgotten Greece. What could he give to this country since he had given all the riches to the others? He started stroking his beard thoughtfully. All at once an idea struck him when he saw the rainbow hanging over his head. Reaching up, he chopped a piece off, stooped and picked up a little soil and many stones, and kneaded the whole thing together in the palm of his hand. Then, opening his palm, he blew the mixture into the sea, and Greece came into being.[1]

In its symbolic meaning, the rainbow of the legend is the Greek people who are as colorful as the sun-drenched rocks on which their nation grew to greatness.

The fact that the Athenian civilization with its poets, philosophers, dramatists, and sculptors had its origin in a city of less than two hundred thousand people on the rocky Attic plain has been a source of wonder to all who know anything of ancient Greece. But today there is also a miracle of Greece at which to wonder. In our twentieth century we see a land of 51,182 square miles supporting eight million people; that is, an area the size of Alabama supports more than twice that state's population. But Greece has considerably less economic wealth. For instance, only about 25 percent of the land is arable. We see a people which in a fifty-year period has been able to survive five wars, including an exhausting civil war, at least two catastrophic population displacements, several violent earthquakes, and chronic droughts. Although it is a long span between Periclean Athens and the Greece which is the keystone of the Eastern Mediterranean NATO group, the Greeks, despite their repeated crises, seem to have gained in the strength to keep alive their vital spirit.

Every Greek stands out so distinctly as an individual that he defies easy location along the social spectrum. Is it the fierceness of the struggle to survive that has produced the sharply outlined individualism of the Greeks? Despite these marked individual differences, the Greeks can be sorted into three general groupings: the city Greeks, the seafaring Greeks, and the rural Greeks.[2] Each group, though sharing much in common, has a somewhat different orientation in its style of life. Each still depends upon the other two for the realization of its national destiny, and each adds its own color to the rainbow quality of contemporary Greek society.

The largest group, and the one least known, is that of the rural Greeks, the chief subject of this book. But this group cannot be understood out of its social context or without sketching in the outlines of the other two groups — the Greeks who live in cities and the Greeks who live by and on the sea.

THE CITY GREEK

Greek history shows that the Greek has traditionally been a child of the city. In antiquity he developed the city-state and he colonized through cities, not through the homestead on some developing frontier. Today, two thousand years later, Greek peasants coming to America directly from a village take up a trade in a city with much greater alacrity than they take up farming.[3] Behind this feeling at home in the city, which seems to exist in most Greeks (but most strongly, of course, in the settled urban classes), there is a fact of historic importance: the Greeks learned early that the city had a social organization all its own and that from the city radiated lines of economic, political, and religious authority. They knew that those who understood the city could manipulate these lines.[4] Thus armed, they were able to keep in advance of their neighbors to such an extent that, when the semi-nomadic Turks captured the Greek capital (Constantinople) in 1453, the conquered Greeks quickly moved into places of prominence and power in the conqueror's regime. Consequently, the Greeks through the years have become increasingly experienced in the arts of social administration and economic dealing in an urban setting. Every event or possible event had its "angle" to be weighed judiciously and then energetically exploited.

An additional resource of the city Greek after the fall of the Byzantine Empire was the respect which other peoples paid to Greek cultural traditions. The city Greek could rest at times on the laurels of his ancestors, or he could command a situation by assuming superiority based on the glory of his past. Furthermore, when days looked darkest, from late in the eighteenth century on down, he could count on the support of classic-minded benefactors of the Western world. There remained also the implication of the term *barbarian* for the non-Greek; this did not die out with ancient Greece but continued to apply to other Balkan Christian groups which the city Greek assiduously tried to Hellenize. The city was dominant here, too, for this Hellenization proceeded outward from the city. The contact point was usually the Greek priest, with his loyalty to the urban Byzantine tradition, in a Slavic, Vlach, or Albanian village before the rise of national churches in the Balkans during the last century.[5]

This, then, is the proud and rich tradition of the contemporary city Greek — a tradition kept alive by the schools, the church, and by the admiration of many non-Greek scholars seeking to trace the origin of Western democracy to its pristine source in the pre-Christian Greek city-state.

Also helping to keep the tradition alive are the few leisured families, some of whom have highly placed relatives scattered throughout the continent of Europe, as well as the growing intelligentsia and the merchants for whom the city is a natural habitat. Even the urban laborer, whether a skilled worker in a textile plant or an unskilled hod carrier on a construction project, has many of the same traits as the members of the middle and upper classes: in his cafés and *tavernas,* the worker reveals the same zest for life as well as some of the same preoccupations with his daily lot. Yet members of the new intelligentsia, Athenian politicians, and businessmen still have many relatives in the provinces with whom they are in frequent contact and to whom city ways are steadily spreading.

The city Greek's supreme self-confidence, arising out of these traditions of power and glory, is shown in almost any discussion overheard at the cafés where the Greek urbanite meets his friends to argue about anything and everything.[6] His gestures are as eloquent as his words, as Robert P. T. Coffin said so well in his poem, "Greek Hands Are the Greek":

> Greek hands are tongues,
> They are tails of dogs;
> They are also Plato's
> Dialogues.[7]

Completely sure that his ideas on public questions are as sound as those of any cabinet minister or newspaper editor, the city Greek takes great pleasure in expounding these ideas.[8] An incident of half a century ago, at the time of the Russo-Japanese War, is still told with amusement by Athenians. According to the story, a man reading his newspaper at a café table was studying the battle plans and maps of the Russian command. The more he studied the newspaper details of the Russian army lines, the more excited he became, until he finally called out a warning to the Russian general half a world away in these classic words, "More to the right, Koropotkin! More to the right!" This phrase is repeated with a smile by one Athenian to another when he wants to imply that the other is passing judgment on something a little — but only a little — out of his field of competence. As a matter of fact, a multitude of anecdotes told by city Greeks about themselves swarm into memory. One way of gaining an insight into the Greek mind is to listen to these stories.

The Greek shows pride in his intellectual curiosity by relating the tale of the Greek walking along a Paris street with a French friend. The Greek in the excitement of a discussion of nationality traits boasted that he could identify any Greek who came down the street. To the Frenchman this seemed impossible in such a cosmopolitan city as Paris.

"Let us wait here for a few minutes and I will find the Greeks for you," said the Athenian, who thereupon began to twist his cane into a nearby wall as though he were boring a hole. Many people passed by without paying any attention, when all of a sudden one man stopped to observe this strange behavior. He looked at the cane, the small hole, and at the man turning the cane as though trying to figure out the reason for the procedure. The Greek with the cane asked, "Are you Greek?" "Yes, I am," said the inquisitive passerby. "What are you doing with that cane?" The performance with the cane was repeated and after an interval a second man — of course, another Greek — stopped to observe. This was enough to convince the Frenchman of his Greek friend's ability to discover his fellow countrymen by tickling their curiosity.

This intellectual curiosity has its other side, too. One Greek social worker with an objective view of herself and her associates said, "When we Greeks face a crucial problem in social welfare or elsewhere, we are inclined to examine it from all sides. We look at it from so many points of view that we finally convince ourselves that it is not a very serious problem and practically explain it away, with the result that we do not feel the need to take any action about it at all."

It must be obvious by now that city Greeks are never dull. Conversations with them do not merely flow; they roar along. They always have some principles to defend, some causes or organizations to promote, or some absorbing hobbies to share. The mark of the true urbanite, as previously implied, is the regular visit to a favorite café, the modern version of the ancient agora, to transact business or to discuss with friends every conceivable facet of the happenings of the past twenty-four hours, not only in his own social group but in the world at large. It is only fair to point out that a few of the

Athenians know more about the French Riviera than the rural regions of their own country, and others of them live so entirely in an urban world that they take the Greek villager for granted, which in many ways is worse than ignoring him.[9] Yet such city Greeks, once this attitude is pointed out to them, are the first to admit their ignorance and to start another discussion on the novel subject of the Greek village, from which so many of them derive.

But there are somber shades as well to the sparkle and dash of Greek wit. To persuade many of the Greek officials to move from talk to action would have its difficulties and would prove particularly frustrating to an American or Britisher who had a special job to complete in a given period of time. It is also probably true that, given the present state of the Greek economy, almost any official is more interested in holding his job than in pressing toward real accomplishment if this might antagonize those above or below him in the bureaucratic hierarchy. Some of these officials, native sons of the village and not yet sure of themselves in the urban environment, spend disproportionate amounts of time in mending their political fences or in sitting on them, a pose easy for many Greeks to assume while rationalizing their problems away.

The qualities of city Greeks which have been mentioned here — self-confidence, intellectual curiosity, philosophizing a problem away, preoccupation with maintaining and improving one's position, and an awareness of a great cultural tradition — are endearing to some while irritating to others.[10] The urban Greeks who seem best to embody the heritage from the past and to approach with sincerity their problems of today are those who have taken time to know both the city and village Greece of the 1960's. Sharing the difficulties faced by their neighbors in the city, they also understand the grave readjustments occurring in the countryside.

THE ISLAND AND SEAFARING GREEKS

The tradition of the city, ancient but still tremendously significant today, has mingled with the equally ancient traditions of the sea in the formation of modern Greece. Odysseus still lives in the Aegean and Ionian Islands today, not only in the resourcefulness with which he approached his problems but in the extent of his voyages. The seafarers are primarily the islanders, and Greece has many islands.[11] Although the sea, never more than eighty-odd miles distant from any point in Greece, has an indirect influence on the horizons of all Greeks, it is the direct source of livelihood to many islanders. Whether as fishermen or merchant seamen, they must study its moods in the same way that the city merchant studies the market or the peasant the condition of the soil. The seamen become so cosmopolitan through their voyages that they feel at home in many port towns with people speaking many languages. This at-homeness in the world extends to members of their families, who also have a sense of being a part of the wide world.

The true fisherman or merchant seaman looks down upon agricultural pursuits, although many of his fellow islanders living a few miles inland are farmers like their compatriots on the mainland. But even the sons of these island farmers are directed into the navy by law, with the result that the navy fills its requirements from the best of them and leaves the unused balance for the army or air force.

An island, by its very nature, is for its inhabitants a comprehensible universe. Its people supposedly become much alike, giving rise to the belief of Athenians that the people from a certain island make loyal and dependable servants, that the people from another island are petty thieves and deceitful, and those from another island are hard workers. One island, according to Athenians, seemed to be inhabited entirely by delightful "screwballs," because dozens of jokes were supposed to have originated there. The impression of the alikeness of all people on an island is fostered by the fact that islanders away from home tend to stand together with their fellow islanders against all comers.[12] For instance, one of our Greek neighbors, obliged to tell the drunken husband of her maid never to come in her yard again, felt it necessary also to discharge the laundress, "because she comes from the same island as that terrible man and would take his side even though she knew he was in the wrong." The Greek housewife also explained that people from that island were reputed to be "violent and wild" and she was taking no chances, even though the laundress hardly knew the offending man. No Greek servant or neighbor questioned this action as anything but logical and necessary.

Island villages, as later discussion will show, differ architecturally from and are in general much cleaner than the other villages of Greece. While this cleanliness gives the impression of a higher level of living, actually on many of the islands people are close to the poverty line much of the time because of inadequate local resources and the need to buy elsewhere, with what little money they have, those products not available at home. A shipwreck can bring the death of the family head or, if not such tragedy, at least economic ruin.

Despite the fact that each island has its own unique flavor and stands out in popular opinion as a well-defined little social world, there is a way of life common to all of the islands. The beliefs about the sea, the diet, the way ships' crews are formed, the responsibility which the ship captain's wife feels for the families of the crew while the men are at sea, and the varying political alignments would, along with other lesser features, set off the seafarer from his fellow countrymen in degree if not as a distinct type.

To talk at dusk with the fishing-boat crews as they get ready for their long night's work or as they untangle and dry their nets along the beach in the warm morning sunshine, to watch the sailors of the numerous passenger and cargo ships work aboard ship and then relax in the tiny sea-front cafés, and to talk with the families of those whose most energetic sons are away at sea, is an introduction to a world incomprehensible to many peasants in Central and Northern Greece and strange to the inland American. For me, the best hours of all were those spent along the quay of a busy port with a retired sea captain, telling the tales of his misadventures — a 1950 version of the trials of Odysseus. All of these seafarers, fishermen, and merchant seamen, crews and captains and their island-anchored families, are a part of the rainbow in the rock. Yet they, along with the city Greeks, so similar in vitality but different in their life, make up only half of the people of Greece. The other half are rural. It is with this largest single group that we shall concern ourselves.

THE GREEK VILLAGER

Being rural in Greece means living in a village, which is usually a picturesque collection of houses, lanes, gardens, orchards, vineyards, and fields. It also means that one is a peasant, since the Greek terms *choriates, chorikos,* derived from the word *choria* (village), are the closest approximations of *peasant* in the Greek language. But any Westerner, in seeking to understand the rural Greek, needs to divest himself of many false notions about the nature of a peasantry, be these on the romantic side of over-idealization or on the derogatory plane of considering them mere bearers of burdens and dull plodders through life.[13]

In not all countries do peasants always live in villages, but they do in Greece. Therefore, in examining social life throughout the Greek mainland, away from the cities, we can use *villager, peasant,* and *rural population* interchangeably, feeling that if we understand Greek village life, we also shall have gained a point of comparison for the study of peasantries in other countries.

The importance of the small village in Greek life can best be shown by a few figures taken from the 1951 census. For instance, 44.6 percent — or almost half of the Greek people — lived in 5,473 communes, or local political units, of less than 2,000 inhabitants. At the other extreme was Athens, whose population included 18 percent of the nation's total; by 1961 it had reached 22 percent. Since 1940 there has been a definite drift toward Athens and the twenty other towns which in 1940 had a population of over 20,000. Despite this urban trend, one must still recognize that the small village is an imposing aspect of Greek life which deserves far more attention than it has received in the past.

Although rural people today are increasingly drawn to the city, the peasant in years past has been a man of the land, usually suspicious of city ways. And herein lies a question: are these millions of peasants, following a daily

round of activities and so different from the city-dwelling Greek, true heirs
of the classic Greek cultural heritage along with the city dweller? Are they
objects for Hellenization as interpreted by the city Greeks, or are they in
their own right living representatives of Greece, both past and present?

The "racial purity" of the people need not concern us here, since we are
thinking of Greece as a state of mind, a political and cultural ideal, and a
society organized to try to meet the needs of its members. One thing is
quite clear: a sizable minority of the rural folk in Greece today still speak
Albanian, Vlach, Macedonian, or even Turkish as their mother tongue.[14]
Strangely enough, most of these rural families are as Greek in their loyalties, sentiments, and point of view as the Greek whose linguistic and cultural inheritance is unmixed. It might even be shown that the majority of
what we call the Greek villagers, especially outside the Peloponnesos, have
today been assimilated culturally rather than racially into the Greek nation.
Even should this be the case, that would support the view that there is a
Greek cultural reality which has had an unusual persistence through the
centuries.

What does the peasant, whether agriculturist or shepherd, show us about
this culture which the city Greek does not? In the first place, the peasants
have always been the stable population element in the homeland. While
cities rose and fell in prominence, the city Greek went far from his homeland. One hundred years ago Athens, the mother city, was only a run-down
settlement, whereas many villages such as Megara, between Athens and
Corinth, have been lived in continuously and even more vigorously for centuries. No matter what invading people came into Greece to settle on
the land as peasants, they apparently experienced an assimilation into the
Greek traditions, influencing but not imposing their own traditions on the
native group. Thus there has been a cultural, even if not an altogether unmixed racial, continuity.

In the second place, the peasant has remained directly dependent on the
same natural environment. In this respect he is closer to the ancient Greek
than is the modern city Greek whose psychological dependence is more on
the legacy of imperial Byzantium than on the Parthenon, that symbol of
classic simplicity springing from the rock of Greece. It would be rash to
claim that the peasant embodies the true spirit of Greece more exactly than
do his fellow Greeks of city and sea, but it is fair to say that without understanding the peasant one cannot fully understand the roots and substance
of contemporary Greece.

As each color of the rainbow blends into the whole spectrum, so these
three groupings of people — the city dweller, seafarer, and peasant —
blend into each other to form the Greek nation of today. Most of those
who in recent years have increased the city population are of peasant stock;
the children of the wealthy Greeks are often tended from infancy by nurses

from a distant island or an isolated mainland village. On the other hand, almost every village home contains photographs of relatives who have taken on the habits of the city. All islanders are not seafarers, for the majority of those in the larger islands live from the soil as do the peasants of the mainland. There is thus a lively interdependence among the urbanite, the seafarer, and the villager.

This interdependence, not always recognized by the Greeks themselves, has a fascination for the Western observer who is curious about the working of a society other than his own. For him the panorama of Greece is a source of enchantment. Now brilliant, now shadowy, through it the thread of tradition runs. Who are the carriers of this continuity? What has insulated the thread against time? It is doubtful whether the answers can be found in the clear, cold, statistical analysis of the social scientist. But an observer trained in the scientific method, with a background of Greek history and literature and an acquaintance with modern Greece that began with a first visit there thirty years ago, may be able to give interpretations and insights helpful to those interested in contemporary Greece.

Such interpretations may even have a broader implication. The Greeks differ in innumerable ways from Asian peoples and from those of the Middle East and Africa. Nevertheless, most Greeks on the mainland live in villages which are much closer in tempo and quality of life to villages on other continents than to anything one can find in the United States. They work small plots of land, scattered in strips around their villages, as do many rural people throughout the world, in sharp contrast to the mechanized American farm of several hundred acres; they know the meaning of hunger, of poverty, of the catastrophe of war and violence, which most Americans fortunately have not had to experience, but which is all too common in the newly developing countries; they also face many of the same problems of relationship to the central government and its services, of accepting or rejecting national programs of rural change.

To know the rural Greek, therefore, is to know more about rural humanity, most of which lives in a different social world from our own city-dominated society. Village people want to be seen not as cannon fodder, potential customers, religious or political converts, but as parents hoping for a better life for their children, as farmers wishing better yields to feed the family until next harvest, as new citizens — not yet secure in their franchise — learning the rudiments of the political process. Even more important, they want to be seen as individuals, with all the rich color this word conveys.

Mountains, Plains, and the Sea

In a literal sense, the rainbow in the rock is the magical coloring of the Greek landscape, the crystal-clear air, and the intensely blue sea. Anyone who paints the Greek sea as it actually looks runs the risk of skepticism from critics abroad who might well say, "no sea could be so blue, in so many shades," particularly if all they have for comparison is the gray Atlantic. An artist friend told of a young Swedish painter who came to Greece after considerable success in landscape painting in Italy and France.[1] For six weeks he tried to paint, but nothing looked right. It was only after he developed new techniques that he began to catch the spectrum of opalescent colors, the strong variations in light and shadow, and the sharp delicacy of forms visible at a considerable distance. Anywhere in Greece the physical environment is impressive, not as a backdrop to be taken for granted, but as a sensation to be enjoyed in its own right.[2]

Perhaps this is why so many Greeks are ready to accept geographic determinism as an explanation of their difficulties. There, spread out for all to see, are the effects of climate, of differences in terrain, of dwindling or unprotected resources. And the temptation is strong to assume that all troubles would pass away if only the earth were more fertile or if heaven shed its rain more plentifully. But the explanation is not quite so simple. Those turning to the philosophy of history for an answer might be told by someone like Arnold Toynbee that Greece's early greatness grew out of the stern necessity to respond to the challenge of a partly hostile environment and a population growing beyond its means of subsistence.

Although the study of Greece's past shows that the cultural, or man-made, aspects of life have been tremendously important, one must nevertheless give the physical environment its just due. This leads to a consideration of some of the cold, hard facts about the rock that is Greece.

THE REGIONS OF GREECE

Each of the regions of Greece, shown on the accompanying map, has its own assortment of mountains, plains, and a stretch of coastline; each has its own history and traditions; each has its own problems posed by the

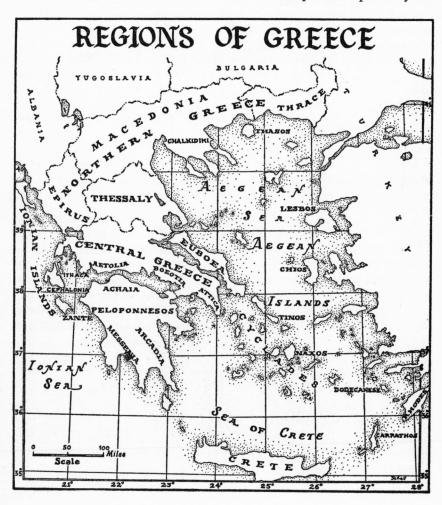

REGIONS OF GREECE

physical environment. To follow the story of village life in Greece as portrayed in this book, one must be able to go imaginatively from one part of Greece to another, since every experience described will be related to the place where it occurred.

Macedonia, linked historically with Alexander the Great and the missionary activities of St. Paul, is a part of the administrative division of Northern Greece. Its northern mountain barrier separates it from Yugoslavia and Bulgaria, each of which has adjoining territory which it too calls Macedonia. The Greeks believe that no area has been more bled over than Macedonia, where Greek and Slav meet.

Thrace, to the east, is also in Northern Greece and is the one area where the Turkish minority still live. Like Macedonia, it is famous for the Oriental kind of tobacco grown there.

Epirus, the northwestern province, is a mountainous land of great beauty and stormy traditions. It borders Albania.

Thessaly, south of Macedonia, boasts Mount Olympus and fertile plains which produce a fifth of the country's wheat.

Central Greece, stretching from the Ionian to the Aegean Seas, holds many tourist attractions such as Thebes, Delphi, and Athens. It also includes the slender island of Euboea along its eastern flank.

The Peloponnesos, separated from the rest of mainland Greece by the Corinth Canal, is an archaeologist's paradise. It is important agriculturally as well as being intimately connected with Greece's liberation from Turkey in 1829.

In addition to these regions on the mainland there are five island groupings in the Greek kingdom:

The Aegean Islands hug the coast of Turkey. Lesbos is the largest, Chios perhaps the best known.

The Dodecanese Islands, to the southeast of the mainland, came under Greek control after World War II with the defeat of the Italians. Rhodes, the chief island, is one of the major tourist attractions of the Eastern Mediterranean.

The Cyclades Islands are also to the southeast of, but nearer to, mainland Greece. Tinos, one of these islands, is the site of a miracle-working shrine visited by thousands of visitors every year on the Day of the Assumption.

Crete stands alone. Its civilization predates that of the mainland. Because of its better soil, more of its people are interested in farming than in fishing or shipping.

The Ionian Islands, on the west coast of Greece, were the hardest hit in the devastating earthquakes of August 1953. They include the beautiful island of Corfu, which was not damaged, as well as Ithaca, home of Odysseus.

These regions, particularly those of the mainland, will be more than names on the map as one becomes familiar with the peasants who dwell in them and with many of the natural features associated with the mountains, the plains, and the sea.

ATTITUDES AND BELIEFS ABOUT NATURE

The Greek people, as one would expect of individuals everywhere, vary considerably in their attitude toward the physical environment.[3] Some, completely oblivious to the beauty about them, nevertheless try to read the weather signs in order to know when they should plow or sow. Some, at the other extreme, show a deep sensitivity to the changing moods of nature, as, for example, the illiterate shepherd in the Boeotian village of Schematari who would take pencil and paper and lovingly draw a tree-filled landscape or the rising sun. Most of the Greek villagers, however, seem to fall between these two extremes; from time to time they, in the words of one peasant, "gain an optimism in life when they see the beauty of a nice slope of the mountain or a lovely dawn." On the whole, the world seems a friendly place and there are few things to fear at the hands of nature.

More than this, the world is in God's hands. The frequent reference to God in popular speech may be a cultural trait handed down from generation to generation, but some of the oft-repeated, time-honored phrases are said with such animation and with such a light in the eye that they must express the individual feeling of those using them. There is no counterpart in English to the common phrase *Chara Theou* (Joy of God), which combines not only rapture and active enjoyment but the sense of the sparkling light God sheds on the earth. During the spectacular Greek spring, this phrase is a most appropriate way of describing one's feeling.

Even those who are not very conscious of their natural surroundings from day to day miss them deeply when distant from them. Over and over again, returned emigrants in Greek villages gave as the reason for their departure from America their need to see the mountains or plains or the sea on which their eyes had rested while they grew up.

Much of this feeling toward nature is based on the sense of intimacy with her.[4] Indeed, one of the first requirements in trying to understand the life of any people is to learn their reaction and adjustment to the natural world. The Greek farmer studies nature for important signs which tell him whether to bring the flock in from the high hillside, whether to start or delay a journey, whether to put out his tobacco plants. Those signs directly relating weather to agriculture are obvious and easily understood by the Westerner, if not always accepted as scientifically valid. But the signs which natural objects and events provide of the supernatural — illness and death, the appearance of ghosts, or even the way the universe was made and is run — all of these stretch the imagination of the scientifically trained specialist, who may be inclined to dismiss them as superstition and therefore unimportant. Nevertheless, they continue to be important to many Greek villagers, young and old alike.

In listening to folk interpretations of nature, one also learns much about the people's attitudes. One must not venture under trees when there is lightning or go to sleep during the day under a walnut tree with its thick foliage (in Central and Southern Greece) or under a fig tree (farther south). A young woman from the Peloponnesos explained that Christ was sitting under a fig tree when he was taken, thus accounting, in her mind at least, for this taboo. As we shall soon see, the idea of fate, destiny, or necessity is strong today, as it was in classical Greece. Natural phenomena are important in helping one learn what is to come or in helping to ward off some impending evil or difficulty.

Plants to some extent aid in knowing what lies ahead. However, most of the blossoms, fragile and fragrant, appear for such a short period in the spring that they are enjoyed primarily for their beauty. Fruit trees in bloom are looked upon as a glorious miracle of color, and one is urged to go out of the way just to see a particularly beautiful tree, especially an almond tree in January. But there are some plants that are appreciated for more than their beauty.

In many parts of Greece belief in the good luck brought by a four-leafed clover is strong. No bullet can affect it, as shown by the following folk story:

Once there was a man who had a silver tobacco case on which he had stuck a four-leafed clover. They put it up as a target and shot bullet after bullet but could not hit it. Afterwards they took away the clover and the case was easily pierced.

If a peasant from Northern Greece comes upon a form of the peony known as "The Holy Virgin's Hand" (*Tes Panagias to cheri*), he may remember that sprigs of it are thrown into the jug from which the water is poured for a woman in travail.[5] The name just as much as the properties of the herb is supposed to relieve the pains of labor. After the birth, the midwife is apt to hang cloves of garlic on the mother and the baby to ward off the Evil Eye. Garlic is so powerful against evil that, when one fears that an envious person will cast a spell upon the animal or baby or any other object of envy, one should say *skortha sta matia sou* (garlic in your eyes).

Anemones, hyacinths, basil, and thyme,[6] as well as the olive tree, the laurel, or the cypress, have stories associated with them which the old people tell to the children. Thus, nature seems intimate since so much of its handiwork carries deep and traditional meaning for the villager.

Animals have an even more special meaning. Both the occasional wild animal and the domestic animals reveal what to expect in the way of catastrophe or changing weather. For example, a man plowing in Central Greece may see a horsefly rest on someone and read into that simple occurrence the coming of a guest. If a person from the island of Spetsai catches a horsefly, he will put it in his wallet for good luck. Or if he is returning from the field and sees two crows quarreling while flying high over a house, he will be reminded of the belief that either the husband or the wife in that house will die soon. If he sees a crow pass in front of him from right to left, he will consider it a good omen; but if from left to right, he will expect bad luck. Should a rabbit or snake be in the path ahead, the peasant knows he must walk on in a straight line; should the road turn to the right or left, then the individual had better return home and start the journey the following day.

A spider walking on you will bring good luck, but if you come upon two snakes fighting and eating each other, a close relation of yours will die. Should you be a shepherd in the Vardousia Mountains of Central Greece, you would probably believe that the wild goats which graze in herds are guarded by the devil and that is why one can hear them make a whistling noise. Furthermore, these wild goats have the same notches cut in their ears as the tame ones kept by the shepherds, which to these mountaineers is proof positive that the devil must be the one who puts the markings there.

Seeing some insect or animal may bring to mind a story learned when a child. The bee, for instance, was once as white as cotton. When Adam and Eve met the devil in the Garden of Eden, it was the bee that saw them first and flew immediately to tell God the news. The devil, who was then holding a burning torch in his hand, ran and tried to catch the bee to keep her from her mission. He could not reach her, but as she was nearing God the devil from afar threw the flaming torch at her. The fire singed her so that she became black. God, who saw all of this, ordered the human beings to burn in the churches only the candles made from beeswax since the bee had proven to be the purest creature of all. I am often asked if these folk beliefs (cited here and in later sections of this book) are widely held or are only the relic in the mind of some aged person. It is safe to say that almost all of them are very much alive at the conversational level. People are aware of them, talk about them. Obviously, many act on them, while others do not. But they are a part of the general atmosphere, as is the belief common in America that a person should not walk under a ladder.

Such beliefs, stories, and personal experiences with many kinds of plants and animals reinforce the rural Greek's sense of intimacy with nature, which develops because of his constant exposure to the elements in the course of his daily life. The Greek peasant, like many farmers elsewhere, moves through a living landscape with which he communicates.

The same holds true for his view of the cosmos and the movement of the heavenly bodies.[7] One of the simplest and clearest descriptions of the latter is taken from an account of a village prepared by a singing master in one of the high schools in Athens. T. K. Papaspyropoulos has written of his native settlement near Kalavryta in the Peloponnesos.[8] A literal translation has been used in order to retain some of the flavor of the village informants.

The sky. Our mother told us that the sky was a big dome which covers the earth like a lid of a cauldron. This dome has for ornaments the sun, the moon, and the stars. High up in this dome God has his throne and sits with Christ, the Virgin, with all the saints and the angels. Near the throne of God is Paradise with the souls of the good people and the saints. Hell is down below in the deepest part of the earth, together with the devils and the sinners. May God protect us!

The sun. The sun is the god of the day. He throws light on the earth and warms the people. The sun brings cereals and all the goods which are upon the earth. Without him we would be dead from cold. The sun does not only warm us but tours the whole world and brings greetings to all those who are away from their home. He also tells us what he sees. We have many songs for the sun, such as those which begin "My sun, three times my sun, and my world-roamer." "The working people watch for him."

Everybody is afraid of the sun. We do not drink water while facing him, neither do we look straight into him because we get blind. In summer time the sun either burns our cereals or our heads. But in winter we beg him to come out and warm us up. We sit there by the sunny spot and he bakes our bodies. We also sing him a song: "Come on out, my sun. Just come out a little bit so that we can take a walk near the threshing floor." Sometimes it rains heavily and the sun is out at the same time. Then we sing to him: "Sun, sun and rain, when the poor get married. Sun, sun and moon, when the donkeys get married. Sun, sun and drizzle, when the female teacher gets married."

The moon. Just as the day has for a king the sun, the night has the moon as its king. The moon is a more agile king than the sun. It takes a walk on the sky shining and chasing the clouds and makes people come out of their homes. With the moon the women spin at night; the children play on the threshing floors; the men water their fields; the muleteers can see and go to their work; and the shepherds enjoy the slopes together with their sheep while playing the flute. But the moon can also harm. The biggest harm is done to the thieves because it throws its light and does not allow them to rob for they can be seen. "The thief enjoys darkness and the wolf the upheaval" [distracting disturbance]. When the moon comes out for the first time we say: "Welcome to the new moon. We are happy to see you. Bring us good." Many seek to find money. They get hold of it and say: "As the moon gets full may my purse get full of coins." When the moon disappears those who are in the mountain and see it set say: "May you fare well and return better and achieve better things." "My moon, my shining moon, and beautifully adorned, did you by any chance see Andrew and his ship?" . . .

The milky way (the priest's straw). Do you see those stars that divide the sky into two? We call them the priest's straw. Once upon a time a priest went to stay for a couple of days in a monastery. When he left, because he couldn't take anything else with him, he took off his cloak and filled it with straw. As he hurried away in his rush and fright the straw bit by bit fell on the road and became stars. When he got to his house his robe was empty and behind him followed the monks. Since then we call these stars the priest's straw.

Rain. When summer has come to an end and fall is there we pick our grapes and harvest our maize and are waiting for God to send rain so that we can sow our wheat. The first rains start in mid-October. . . . They start either with a slow modest rain or sometimes with a strong one. The strong rain starts abruptly and all hell lets loose. The sky meets with the earth. Lightning, thunder, wind, hell. We all run with our hoes to hold the water back from entering our homes; others run to pull their animals out of ravines so that the water does not carry them away. Others gather the things that have remained outside, and others shelter themselves in their homes and gaze at the storm from their windows. When the weather turns good again it is the joy of God. Then we get ready our agricultural equipment for the field; it is time to sow. Rain is our life. Without it nothing grows; we are lost. But the rain can also do harm. When it rains suddenly the rivers come down with a rush carrying things and destroying our fields. It carries many rocks and stones onto the plain; when it rains and blows, it's hell. It throws down the wheat and it does a lot of damage. A good rain is a slow one. . . .

But nature is more than a collection of stars or plants or animals. It represents the forces against which man must contend as he seeks to wrest his living from the soil; nature brings disasters to which man must adjust even though he does not completely reconcile himself to his misfortune.

One type of catastrophe that visits Greece at frequent intervals is the earthquake, which comes usually in the late spring and summer. Wherever a person travels in Central Greece, Thessaly, or the Peloponnesos, he hears of the damage done by tremors. There is today an Old Corinth and a New Corinth, the latter being built after the old city was destroyed in 1858. New Corinth was once more destroyed in 1928 and rebuilt. In one village people still talk with sadness of a quake which occurred in 1875, killing forty-seven women and children inside the church. One of the most damaging earthquakes of recent memory was the August 1953 series of tremors in the Ionian Islands which destroyed so much of Cephalonia, Zante, and Ithaca. In April and May of 1954, more than thirty persons were killed in the quakes of Thessaly, three hundred injured, and thirty-two thousand made homeless.

Nature shows its unkindness in other ways. Sudden hailstorms, drought, and insect pests take their annual toll in many parts of Greece. While on a trip with the inspector of agriculture from Larissa, Thessaly, through some fields recently damaged by a storm, I asked him what the peasants thought of such a devastating rain. He said that they did not feel any enmity against the elements but do say in all seriousness to them "na se pare ho diavolos!" (may the devil take you!)

Kokinya is a village of about one hundred houses not far from Kozane in Western Macedonia. The prefect of Kozane heard that a serious storm had hit the village and went out with his agriculturist to see what damage had been done, taking me along. As the agriculturist got estimates of crop destruction (50 percent of the wheat, 80 percent of the corn), we began to find out the peasants' explanations for this storm. One old man put it simply when he said, "it was God's will." [9] Even though the storm had occurred two days before, the people were still dazed at the thought of so much labor going to waste, to say nothing of the loss of the expected income from the crops. They did not seem bitter, nor altogether resigned. The visit of the nomarch (prefect) and his hour's discussion with the men brought a ray of hope. After many matters had been looked into, the nomarch asked just before he left: "I'm going to write up this report and make request for aid from the proper ministry. What are you people of Kokinya going to do?" They answered: "We are going to go to our fields, work with our vineyards. The rain has made new ravines. We must carry soil and fill in. Now we will have to work harder."

This statement reminded me of a conversation one evening on an apartment terrace halfway up Lykabettos Hill, a hill standing all by itself in the center of Athens. The Acropolis was clearly outlined in the moonlight, and the lights on the sea far in the distance told of the movement of boats in and out of the harbor. There we discussed the Greek peasant's idea of fate with a group of educated Greek friends — one of them the novelist Elias Venezis. As the backdrop for the present point of view we went back to the ancient idea of the three Fates and the classic themes of Greek tragedy.[10]

The Greeks with whom we were talking were careful to distinguish between the passive fatalism of the lands farther to the east and the active fatalism of the Greeks, pointing out that the Greek peasant made no abject surrender to nature or other forces about him. Even though the individual knows the odds are against him, he must stand up and face his destiny with dignity and correctness, whether the forces which would crush him show any mercy or not. We were reminded of the common saying, "syn Athena kai cheira kinei," which means, "with Athena move your own hand too." Thus it was neither incongruous nor contradictory to hear one Kokinya peasant say, "it is God's will," and to hear his neighbor say "now we will have to work harder."

On such a mental adjustment to the mountains, plains, and the sea, which we shall take up in order, is the survival of the Greek people largely based.

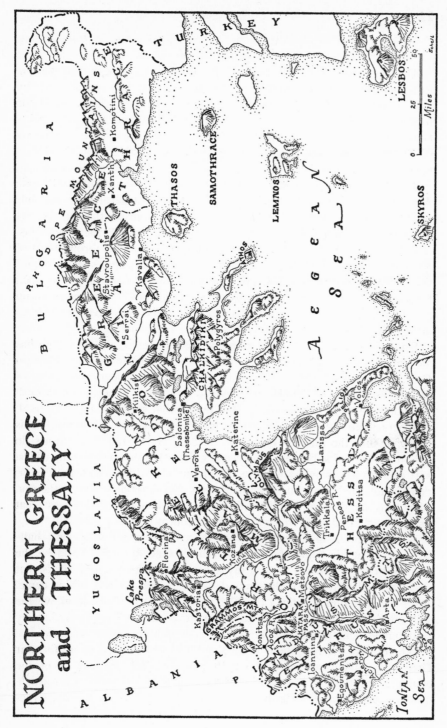

NORTHERN GREECE and THESSALY

ALBANIA

YUGOSLAVIA

BULGARIA

Lake Prespa

Florina

Kastoria

GRAMMOS MT.

Konitsa

Aos R.

Ioannina

PINDUS

Igoumenitsa

METSOVO

Kozane

Larissa

Kardítsa

Trikkala

Peneos R.

THESSALY

Arta

Volos

OSSA

OLYMPUS

Katerine

Veróia

Salonica (Thessaloniki)

Kilkis

Serrai

Stavroupolis

Xanthi

Kavalla

Komotini

THRACE

RHODOPE MOUNTAINS

GREECE

CHALKIDIKI

ATHOS

Polygyros

THASOS

SAMOTHRACE

TURKEY

LEMNOS

AEGEAN SEA

SKYROS

LESBOS

IONIAN SEA

Miles
0   25   50

Scholl

21

THE MOUNTAINS

The legend of the rainbow in the rock does not err in speaking of Greece as a rock. Only one fourth of her area is currently or potentially of any agricultural use and lies mostly in valleys or plains near the coast, at the foot of mountainous slopes. The remaining three fourths of the land consists largely of precipitous mountains, ranging up to a height in Mount Olympus of about 9600 feet.[11] "Beautiful," says the tourist. "Unproductive," says the economic planner.

The Pindus range, reaching its way south as an extension of the Dinaric Alps from Yugoslavia, is most marked in Epirus but nevertheless extends on into Central Greece. A spine of mountains comprises the central part of the Peloponnesos; even Athens is surrounded by gentle Parnes, Hymettus, and Pentele. In Northern Greece the Rhodope Massive cuts through part of Macedonia and Thrace, while Mount Olympus rises majestically out of the Thessalian plain. This means that the rugged topography is not confined to one part of Greece but that peaks can be seen from almost any place on the mainland. Many islands, including Euboea and Crete, have their heights around which legends as well as clouds have gathered.

Since there are no forests on many of the mountains, the landscape has an almost naked look when seen for the first time. But a longer stay in Greece accustoms one to the browns and grays and lavenders in place of the greens often associated with tree-clad mountains. Frequently at dusk the mountains turn to a deep rose and purple that seems magically unreal.

Where there are mountains there should be water to irrigate the fields below or turn the turbines of power projects. Heavy rains and snows do fall on the summits, but since Greece is only 171 miles across at its widest part (Epirus-Thessaly), and since the mountain divide cleaves the center, there is not much space in which rivers can find a gradual slope to the sea. They thus are short and swift, with a torrential character that poses great problems of flood, silt, erosion, and river control.

A village priest in Epirus described the erosion of soil by saying, half-seriously, that his fields grew rocks. When asked how this could be, he replied, "I went out and plowed my field, plowing around two rocks that stood only slightly above the ground. I put in my seed; the rains came. After the first rain I noticed that the rocks had grown farther above the soil; after the second rain they had grown even more. So I knew that my fields grew rocks rather than grain."

Where there are mountains there should be forests. But before the war Greek forests covered only about 19 percent of the total area of the country. Once they were larger in extent. Constantine Nevros, in an article in *Soil Conservation,* holds the goat primarily responsible for the destruction of the forests, but points out that even in classical times portions of Greek forests were felled to provide lumber for the construction of Athenian triremes.[12] He dates the beginning of the serious destruction of Greek forests during the Roman invasion of Macedonia, when the Greeks lost their fields in the fertile plains and took refuge in the mountains where they were forced to become stock breeders. Other writers fix the most serious destruction at the time of the Greek war of independence, beginning in 1821, when large tracts of forest were burned. This form of devastation has continued ever since, either to clear land for cultivation or to encourage the growth of young palatable shoots which are attractive to stock. An example of what warfare can do is the cutting down of the trees on Mount Parnes, near Athens, and other places during World War II by the Germans pursuing guerrillas and by Athenians in need of fuel.

The remaining land area of Greece which is not arable and not in forest, certainly over 50 percent, is either in scrub oak or is open rocky range, a fact which makes sheep and goat raising an important branch of the economy.

Where there are mountains there should be useful minerals. Greece does have a variety of mineral deposits, including some iron ore of high content, iron pyrites, emery, copper, zinc, lead magnesite, chromite, and lignite. An American company is now exploiting a fairly large deposit of asbestos south of Kozane. There is no coal, but much more extensive use could be made of the "brown coal," or lignite, to reduce or eliminate the heavy import of coal. Even if the resources listed here, as well as others not touched upon, were fully utilized, Greece would still compare unfavorably with most other countries.

These barren, colorful mountains modify the climate.[13] We often tend to think of Greece as having a Mediterranean climate, mindful of its similarity to Florida or California. Actually, what is called a Mediterranean climate — a hot, dry, cloudless summer, frequent north winds, and a mild, rainy, cloudy winter — prevails over only a small portion of Greece, such as the eastern coast of the Peloponnesos, Central Greece and Euboea, Crete and the Aegean Islands. The map of rainfall shows this clearly. On the western side of the Peloponnesos there is a modified Mediterranean climate with much heavier rainfall. Much of Greece, however, has a modified Continental climate with cold winters and hot, usually dry, summers. These conditions of extreme alternations in Thessaly, Central and Eastern Macedonia, and Thrace favor the growing of cereals. The dry areas of Eastern Macedonia and Thrace, with soils low in humus, are centers for the growing of the small-leaved Oriental or Turkish tobacco.

What is surprising is the prevalence of an Alpine climate, due to the high altitudes, throughout the Pindus area and the higher parts of the

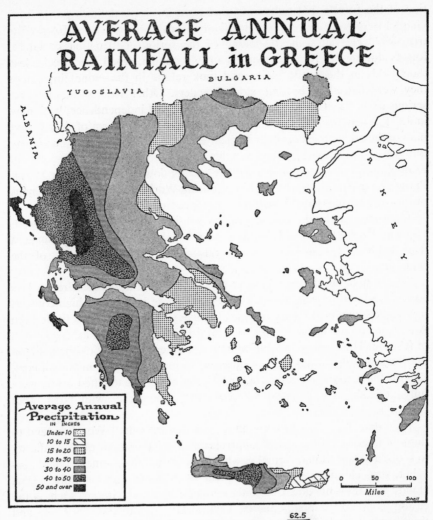

AVERAGE ANNUAL RAINFALL in GREECE

YUGOSLAVIA

BULGARIA

ALBANIA

Average Annual
Precipitation
IN INCHES
Under 10
10 to 15
15 to 20
20 to 30
30 to 40
40 to 50
50 and over

0   50   100
Miles

Scholl

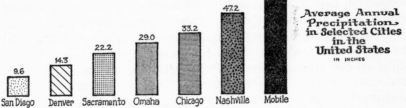

9.6
San Diego

14.3
Denver

22.2
Sacramento

29.0
Omaha

33.2
Chicago

47.2
Nashville

62.5
Mobile

Average Annual
Precipitation
in Selected Cities
in the
United States
IN INCHES

Peloponnesos. Many villages are snowbound for two, three, or even four months. The government has learned the necessity of helping these people stockpile their basic stores of food well in advance of the cold weather to avoid starvation or at least the malnutrition which would otherwise occur in these isolated villages.

Even around Athens, so very near the sea, the mountains take on an Alpine effect. On a January day in 1953, when early jonquils were blooming in the gardens around the villas, a thirty-minute drive took us to the top of Mount Parnes where people were skiing in two feet of snow, which lasted from three to four weeks.

In addition to the climatic role they play, the mountains become places of refuge when invaders overrun the country. Here the revolutionaries against the Turk began to flex their muscles prior to the beginning of the revolution in 1821. The dwellers of the cities and the monks in the monasteries may have kept Greek culture, in the sense of civilization, alive, but the villagers kept the spirit of independence alive. Over and over again those who really know Greece would say, "you have not seen our country until you leave the main highways and go up into the mountains to talk with the hardy peasants there." This tradition of the mountains is a conditioning influence in Greek thought and life along with the tradition of the sea.

What, one wonders, do the peasants think of the rough terrain about them? Do they personify any of the peaks or make their summits the dwelling place of gods, as did the Greeks of old? The old Greek pantheon, it seems, has been liquidated by the Christian God and the collection of saints revered by the Eastern Orthodox Church. "Thou hast conquered, Galilean," Swinburne's classic pagan wept. One does find on most peaks a monastery to St. Elijah, a whitewashed building reflecting the slanting sun in early morning or late afternoon. Students of these matters seem to agree that Elijah (Elias), who disappeared in a chariot of flame, may have superseded Helios and his fiery steeds.[14] The top of the mountain from ancient times has been the place to worship the sun.

Particular mountains, however, do have their own local traditions. One of the peaks of Panaitolikon in Central Greece is called the Mountain of the Old Woman, as the following legend explains.

Once upon a time an old woman had finished pasturing her sheep below for the winter and had moved them up into the mountains for summer grazing. The month of March was almost ended, so the woman said: "March, you can go away; I don't need you any more for I have had a good winter below and will have a good summer here." But March in its anger borrowed one day from February, giving him thirty-one days. On that day there was a heavy storm. The old woman froze and turned into marble and there she now stands. That's why they call those heights the Mountain of the Old Woman.

Despite many difficulties, the rural Greeks continue to like the summits about them, and they settle down in bleak and stony areas with a contentment hard for the outsider to understand. At a point between Lamia and Karpenesi near Tymphrestos Mountain, we passed a peasant woman who was driving a donkey loaded with alfalfa to her village.

"This is a nice place here, isn't it?" we said, to get a conversation started.

"Yes, it's nicely situated."

"Have you got water?"

"Yes, we brought it from afar [made an installation] and now we are all right. The winter is hard but we are prepared to face it. We gather our wood in advance and we sit around our fireplaces, spin, weave, eat chestnuts, while our animals are down below eating their fodder."

A few miles farther on we talked to another woman walking along the road. She remarked in the course of the conversation: "My son wanted to go to America. He went. Now, he's longing for his mountains."

To understand Greece, therefore, one must know not only the geography of her mountains, but the meaning of these mountains to the people who make them their home. The economic struggle in these highland villages is told by Papaspyropoulos in his account of Kleitoria, in the Peloponnesos. Notice his comparison with the lowland villages.

The villagers of my village, like all the others of that area, are farmers. Even the priest is an agriculturist, as well as the teacher, the doctor, and those who own the shops. The shepherds also are farmers; one day they go with their sheep, and the next day they go to their fields. Farming is the basis; livestock and other occupations are secondary. Systematic livestock production is only done by the shepherds of Mount Chelmos. The agricultural life in our village is very hard because the fields are few and divided into strips and the water is scarce. Each owner does not have his fields in one spot; he has one stremma [one-fourth acre] here and another further down; the one on the heights and the other in the plains, the one to the right, the other to the left. Thus in walking "they melt [wear out] their shoes." The same and even worse takes place when it is time for watering. No roads! They walk on stones here and there in the ravines, and to go back to their village after their work, tired as they are, they have to walk for an hour or more. And what sort of road! Abrupt paths and steep climbs. Neither shoes nor clothes can remain undamaged. They roam around in rags. Only on Sundays and on larger holidays can one see them in some way neatly dressed. A hard life without improvement, for the fields are few and not productive. A soft and restful life is led by the lowlanders. They have a good plain, straight road and lots of water, which is supplied by the river there. For this reason they have all kinds of fruit orchards, vegetable gardens, and other kinds of trees.

THE PLAINS

Peasants nowadays live in the plains more willingly than they do in the mountains. Good level land has a scarcity value. The most thorough study of this has been made by A. G. Ogilvie, who prepared a map of population density in Greece for the *Geographical Journal* of May–June 1945. He has identified fifty-nine districts which he regards as plains. These usually contain the regional and local capitals and are widely scattered among and around mountains, including in most cases the slopes facing them. They take up about 30 percent of the mainland, but contain about 52 percent of the nonurban population. Thus, one half of the rural population lives upon plains comprising less than one third of the mainland; but this also means that the remaining one half of the rural population lives in a completely mountainous environment.

In Greece the largest plain — that of Trikkala-Karditsa in Thessaly — is less than five hundred square miles in size, not much larger than many American counties. The roll call of the plains, which are alluvial, would list the major provincial towns, whose location is in part an answer to the need for marketing and transportation services of the villagers located in the surrounding fertile agricultural areas. Whether I was traveling in the Peloponnesos, in Epirus, or elsewhere, it was always a stirring sight to climb some range and find spread out on the other side a fruitful valley, along a river or in some old lake basin whose water drained off long ago.

When Greeks think of the plains, however, they think of the kind around Larissa, the chief city of Thessaly, which has rapidly become the center of mechanized agriculture, or they think of the plain of Thessalonike in Macedonia. These are the most important breadbaskets of Greece. Familiarity with these plains means also familiarity with the sun of Greece, which beats down mercilessly in the summertime. Here, a clump of trees or even a single tree is an oasis of shade for a rest after hours of working the sun-baked fields. Where there is not even one tree, the peasants rig up tentlike shelters for use at noonday or take refuge beneath a battered umbrella. During the agricultural season the plains literally teem with people — seldom are they ever out of sight or sound; but they do become more tired and listless as the day wears on. The peasant men in straw hats become tanned to the color of dark leather, as do many of the women in spite of their free-flowing headkerchiefs. The sun, nevertheless, works wonders with the crops, ripening the grain and bringing sweetness to the magnificent fruits of Greece.

If the plains make one conscious of the sun, they make one even more conscious of water — so much so that a tepid drink from a donkey-borne cask has a refreshing tang to it. On the plains there is usually too much or too little water; never is it "just right." If there is too much, a drainage project must be undertaken to make much-needed land available for cultivation.

reclamation project

The most noteworthy reclamation project before the turn of this century was the draining of Lake Kopais, just north of Thebes in Central Greece.[15] The work was undertaken by a French company in 1886 and completed by an English company in 1887, which continued to operate the agricultural estate of sixty thousand acres down to its purchase by the Greek government prior to the November elections of 1952. At that time, this large holding, along with its complicated drainage system, was turned over to the former tenants, who had worked for the foreign company. Now as owners, or as members of a cooperative, they face the necessity of making their contribution to the over-all maintenance of the drainage channels so that the water may run off adequately and prevent the land from reverting to its once-marshy condition. According to some foreign technicians, the Greeks are doing a good job of managing this operation.

Much of the time, however, there is too little water through the growing season. One answer to this scarcity has been the recent drilling of hundreds of wells, from which water is pumped to the thirsty fields through irrigation ditches. In addition, a number of ambitious water-control projects have led to considerable storage of water and the spread of irrigation.

In villages, usually on the edges of plains watered by streams flowing from a mountain source, the water crier is a unique institution. This individual is encountered, for instance, in the Peloponnesos, where he strides through the streets of the village calling out the name of the person whose patches of land are next in line to receive the flow of water. One of these criers had a voice so powerful that, while standing on the small plain below, he could notify people in the village on the mountainside hundreds of yards away.

A Greek villager, like the Arab, will make much over the merits of the water of his homeplace. To praise the water he will speak of it as *chonephtiko nero,* or "digestive water." He will even fight over it, as the following news item shows.

Athens. The Kentucky mountaineers' storied concept of feudin' justice reached here recently and two girls were killed and four men were critically injured.

Two Greek villages — Kerasovo and Papadates — went to war a few days ago to settle a dispute over water rights, and 400 men, women, and children battled for hours with clubs, hoes, knives and hand grenades.

Two army companies were sent to restore order.

The cause of the trouble was water. Sovereignty over Cold Fountain, a spring irrigating the wheat-fields of Kerasovo, was contested by the farmers of neighboring Papadates.

One night "unknown persons" changed the course of the spring and the water was diverted toward Papadates.

As Kerasovo villagers conferred in the village square, forty villagers from Papadates, armed with stones, assaulted the fringes of Kerasovo.

A general alert was sounded. Hoes were taken from the barns of Kerasovo, knives from the kitchens and hand grenades — relics of the Greek civil war — from various hiding places.

Meanwhile, armed reinforcements arrived from Papadates. Policemen fired into the air to intimidate the enraged villagers, but no one paid any attention.

A few hours later two infantry companies arrived from the nearest town and imposed martial law. Two teen-age girls died from injuries received during the battle. (*New York Times*, September 9, 1954)

The storks like to nest in a village around which there are watered meadows or even marshes. In the village of Almyros, between Lamia and Volos (in Thessaly), a family of storks had built a huge nest of mud and twigs around the cross on the top of the church. "You see," the peasants of Almyros say, "his nest on that spot shows that the stork is a blessed bird." Pharsala, on the main route between Athens and Thessalonike, stands out as a town especially favored by the storks whose coming is considered a good omen. In Epirus and Macedonia and Thrace the evening silence is often broken by the rattlelike noise which this bird makes with his red beak — his white plumage gleaming in the waning sunlight and his long legs silhouetted against the sky. The storks are to the plains what the eagle is to the mountain, one a bird of the lowlands which builds his nests in the chimneys of village homes with people all around, and the other a bird of the heights preferring solitude and willing to pit himself against nature's angriest moods.

MOUNTAINS VERSUS PLAINS

Mountains and plains take on social meaning as people try to gain a living from them. In Greece people frequently speak of "mountain villages" and "plains villages" as though their residents differed from each other. As a matter of fact, both in physical appearance (location, house types, and land use) and in accessibility, the plains and mountain villages are distinct and will be described more fully in a later chapter.

K. D. Karavidas, of the Agricultural Bank of Greece, has for a long time been interested in this problem and points it up by telling an anecdote:

This happened in a mountain village in Central Greece near the Gulf of Corinth. Every year these people would come down to the plains, work fifteen days, and get beans and wheat to carry them through the year. During the German occupation, however, the prices of food went so high that the plains peasants decided to do their own harvesting. They took the produce, which

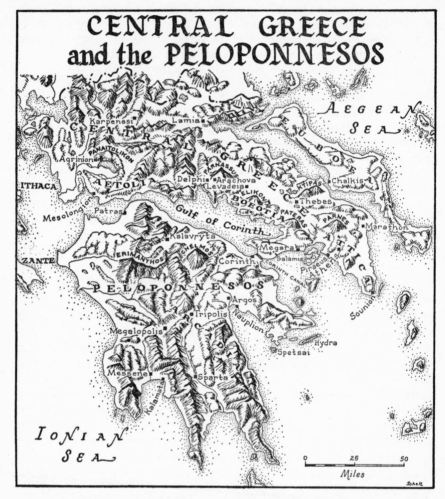

would have normally been paid to the mountain people, to Patras and sold it for
its weight in gold. As a result, the highland villagers faced serious difficulties.

About this time a band of five young guerrillas came by the village and
demanded hospitality. The villagers took them in and killed a lamb so that
they could dine in plenty. After a few months, the same band put in another
appearance, but this time the people could only provide a cock for the dinner.
On the third visit, much later on, a wheat dish had to be the main course. Finally, on a fourth visit, when the members of the band were served only
onions and garlic, they turned to the villagers and said: "You are hungry. Do
you see those villages on the plain below? Why don't you go down there and
take the food away from them, take their land, and let them come up here and
live?"

An old villager answered: "Yes, we may be able to go down there and beat them now and begin to live in their homes. But within a few years they would be strong enough to come down and take all their former fields away from us. Where would we be then? No, we'll get along as best we can."

This story, as did those gathered from many later visits to numerous villages, illustrates the economic distinctions between the mountain and the plains villages. Life in the uplands is more self-subsistent, if for no other reason than the difficulty of getting crops such as figs and apricots to market. Cash crops figure much less prominently. But in spite of the economic disadvantages of the mountain villages, many of their people understand their common cause with the people of the plains.

A group of social-work students at Pierce College near Athens was asked to distinguish between the plains and mountain villages. Since these students came from villages in every region of Greece, the list of characteristics they prepared is of some value in indicating what village people think the distinctions are:

Mountain villagers	*Plains villagers*
Change slowly	Accept change, adapt better
Physically tough	Refined in manners
More hospitable	More sophisticated
Stubborn	Cunning
Happier, more optimistic	Sad (Thessaly)
Have deeper thoughts	
More intermarriage of kin	

An additional observation made by a successful Athens businessman, who was born in a mountain village, highlighted some of the advantages that the plains village has over the place from which he came: "For instance, water has been brought close to the houses in the plains so the people don't have to carry it so far; electricity has come in; new means of communication enable them to travel around; those teaching new methods of agriculture can visit to tell them what to plant and when to plant it."

Despite their isolation, the mountain people are considered by many Greeks to be brighter and more active than those of the plains. Indeed, many mountain villages are thought to have been settled by the more liberal, strongly independent inhabitants of the plain who could not support the indignities of Ottoman rule. According to one commandant of police, they are also less law-abiding. Although many of their young people habitually and successfully migrated elsewhere, most of the mountain people were contented with their simple life until the Communist guerrilla war of the 1940s made them vacate their homes for a temporary stay in market towns or cities on the plains. In spite of this exposure to easier ways, the mountain villagers still are believed to have greater fortitude and a willingness to put up with stark conditions, not simply from resignation but because they take pride in making the best of what they have. Most of the meager sums of money they do have are probably sent in from a son who has a job outside the mountains. Government programs of supplying food are also periodically necessary to support these hardy people.

There are two historical factors accounting for the hardiness assigned to the mountain people over the plains dwellers. Before independence, the plainsmen, particularly in Thessaly and Macedonia, were attached to the estates of absentee Turkish landlords and, according to travelers' accounts, lived in tenancy approaching serfdom, despised by the more independent Greeks of the mountains. Further, the plains villagers suffered for centuries from the terrible malaria of the lowlands; drained of vitality, they were probably actually poorer physical specimens than the peasants of the more healthy uplands.

As various features of the peasant's life unfold, particularly in a later discussion of village ways, we can understand even better the differences between the peoples of the mountains and the plains. Nevertheless, we should not forget that as villagers the two groups hold much in common, such as their shared loyalty to their village and their tendency to be distrustful of the "outside world," particularly of the central-government officials in Athens.

THE SEA

If mountains and plains are disappointing in the resources they contribute to Greece, then surely, one would think, the sea would more than compensate by providing fish in abundance. As a matter of fact, fish are an important source of protein in the Greek diet, but before the Second World War less than half of the total amount of fish eaten (35,000 to 40,000 metric tons) was caught by Greek fishermen in Greek seas. The rest had to be bought from abroad, often from neighboring countries, out of the country's meager store of foreign exchange.[16] Students of the problem seem to believe that the sea around Greece is rich in fish and that the trouble lies in the failure of the authorities to promote and foster a fishing industry. The many fishing boats destroyed during the war are being replaced, though slowly.

The merchant marine of Greece has been through the years a source of national pride. Here is one way the sea has been put to good advantage. Before World War II Greek ships totaled 1,900,000 tons and included 500 ocean-going vessels and a coastal and Mediterranean fleet of 55 large ships and 733 caiques, or small sailing boats. In 1946 there remained 138 miscellaneous ships totaling 501,000 tons. The sale of 100 liberty ships by the United States government to Greek operators at one fourth of the original cost contributed much to the rebuilding of the Greek merchant marine. As of November 1957, the Greek merchant fleet numbered 541 vessels, whose tonnage totaled 1,510,535 tons. By 1961 its 1,110 ships amounted to 5,893,652 tons.

In addition to being a potential economic asset, the sea makes its influence felt in a psychological sense. "The Romans built roads but the Greeks always used the sea" was an observation made to me by a retired Greek admiral. The more one thinks about this simple statement of difference between two great nations of antiquity, the clearer become the varied bases for their greatness. Rome, the conqueror of the European continent and much of the Mediterranean world, held on to her territorial conquests for centuries, but the lasting conquests of ancient Greece were not those of territory, which she also conquered from time to time, but the victory of a superior culture. The Romans were administrators of subject lands; the Greeks became traders and merchants who colonized along the coasts of the whole known world, accumulated their wealth in cities, and maintained a competitive individualism much in evidence even today.

From this tradition of the sea the Greek has gained an outward look, sometimes carried to extremes. "He knows about every country but his own" commented a Westerner who had spent many years in Greece.

An old, old peasant put the way he felt toward the sea and what it meant to him in these words:

"Look over the sea," he said, pointing to the shining water in the distance. "Do you know anything farther than that? Going over the sea means going over to America. In the olden days, under the pressure of need, one stole from the other and the other fought back and killed and so got out of the country. Only the goat thieves and the peasants were left. For us village people, 'farther than the sea' means not just emigrating but also means bringing in. We can use it to improve life. Here near our village we have a waterfall and big water supply; we can have electricity and irrigation but we need scientists from across the sea to tell us how to use what we have. Then more people can live on the land and will not need to emigrate."

There are many Greeks, especially women, in isolated villages who have never seen the sea. Even for them it seems to have a deep emotional meaning, for, as one Greek folklorist explained to me, there is an unconscious worship of water all over Greece. A twenty-one-year-old peasant girl on her way to relatives in Athens rode with us from her village in the heart of the Peloponnesos. This was her first trip away from home. We stopped on the brow of a mountain while she had her first view of the sea. She who had ridden with us for many miles, shy and silent, looked out to the wide indigo horizon and cried, "Thalassa! thalassa!" (The sea! the sea!), and then subsided, wide-eyed. It was obvious to all of us that she was deeply and strangely moved. Not only the majestic view affected her but the knowledge that this same sea had carried off to America many relatives, only a few of whom had returned. To her the actual sight of the sea meant a new horizon; it gave her peasant world a new dimension.

For the islanders the biggest celebration of the year is Epiphany (January 6) when all of the families go down to the sea to participate in "the blessing of the water." The cross is thrown into the sea and boys dive for it, the lucky one obtaining it receiving a gift of money and considering himself fortunate for the coming year. This ceremony represents the baptism of Christ, but its performance — the contact of the cross with the water — supposedly gives the water dipped up at the ceremony a special efficacy in healing sickness. It is treasured holy water. Ethnologists tell us that this blessing of the sea dates from pre-Christian times, another indication of the hold of the sea on these island dwellers. It is still an island habit, when there are big storms at sea, to sweep the church and throw the sweepings into the sea to calm it; or the people may take oil from the lamp in the church and spread it on the water, begging the sea to quiet down.

The sea, like the mountains, has its own folklore. One of the most persistent beliefs among seamen is the presence in the deep of the sister of Alexander the Great, the Gorgon, often called the spirit of the sea.[17] This legend is beautifully told by Elias Venezis, one of Greece's outstanding writers, in his novel *Aeolia*:

Once upon a time in the land of Greece there lived a young king, Alexander the Great. He had a sister called Gorgona. Alexander the Great traveled to distant lands, crossing many mountains and seas, and when he returned he brought back with him the water of immortality. He would have drunk it when his hour of death came, and he would never have died. He would have conquered all the strongholds of the world, and would have reigned forever. But he was not quick enough. His sister saw the water of immortality and, without knowing what it was, drank it. Then Alexander the Great was filled with rage and seized her by the hair and threw her into the sea. Ever since then the Gorgon lives in the sea. Her eyes are very round and she has snakes in her hair. Her arms are of bronze and there are golden wings on her shoulders. From her waist down she is a fish, and she is queen of all the other fish in the sea. She keeps alive the memory of the great king her brother who died when he was young and she always asks seafaring men she meets on her journeys:

"Is Alexander the Great still alive?"

"He is alive, and he reigns," they answer her.

When she hears this, the Gorgon is filled with joy and orders the waves to let the caique pass. But if any seaman does not know this, and tells her that the king is dead, then he has nothing to hope for. The Gorgon raises a typhoon and seizes him and his caique and its crew and drags them down with her. Then she rises high onto the waves again to find another sailor who can reassure her that her brother is living, and that Alexander the Great has never died. . . .[18]

One often hears the expression, "he is alive, and he reigns," in Greece today, for it has become a household adage. When a person is asked how someone is getting along, he may reply, "he is alive, and he reigns."

On the little islands of Greece, on many wild promontories of the mainland, stand the small white churches dedicated to St. Nicholas, the patron saint of the seafaring man. He replaced Poseidon, king of the sea, an important personage in the pagan pantheon, and most of these churches are built as the result of some vow made by the sailors faced with shipwreck who turned for help to the little icon of the saint in the stern or on the mast of the ship. These sailors curse the sea, speaking of it as "that old scoundrel," but they are tied to it with many bonds other than the economic. They tell the story of their patron saint, who found for himself the hold the sea has upon the Greek people. Nicholas suffered so many misfortunes from the sea that he decided to put it behind him forever. He picked up an oar and started walking. Every now and then he would stop someone and ask, "Do you know, stranger, what this is that I am carrying?" He moved higher and higher up into the mountains until he finally found a village where no one could identify what he was carrying and there at last he felt he could settle down, safe from the all-encircling sea.

Thus, it is not at all out of character for the seafarers, like their patron saint, to become thoroughly disgusted with the sea. They will imprecate her and, referring to her in the feminine gender, will imply that there is treachery afoot. They are also aware of her charm and, unlike the monk-like St. Nicholas, find they cannot live apart from her.

The Greek, whether seafarer or peasant, has come to grips with his stern physical environment, and this tough set of mind is just as important to his survival as the resources which he must utilize in his daily life. The tradition of the mountains led to the preservation of an independent villager, proud in his poverty, passionately devoted to his local area, and a worthy perpetuator of the folk legacy of ancient Greece. The tradition of the sea led the seafarer outwards and developed a type of Greek quite different from the mountaineer. The seafarer's commerce supplemented the self-subsistence of the peasant, but both joined together to create the political unit that is Greece today.

···◦][III][◦···

The Village Setting

Part of the story of Greek survival lies in the village form of organization. To be sure, the city has exercised a tremendous sway over the thought and mood of the Greek people in the past and even more so today. But a peasant's tangible world has been his village. We see the village first of all as a place with a focal point, or square, from which emanate streets, lanes, or paths winding in adjustment to the local surface features. As a place, the village has increasing connections with the outside world, since new roads continue to replace donkey tracks which until recently led from the more isolated areas.

But the village is also a service center where the farm family can shop or get some local artisan to make or repair household or farm equipment. In the rural areas of Greece, as elsewhere, these village services do not extend to waste disposal, this being the responsibility of the individual family. Viewed from another point, the village is a collection of houses, yards, and gardens, which also deserve a brief description if one is to see the backdrop against which so much of the peasant's daily life occurs.

In the village the rural Greek has found a pattern of life which gives him the many advantages of a close-knit community and at the same time allows him to farm his land, exchange work and implements with his relatives or neighbors, sell his crops, and care for his animals in a common pasture, frequently under the care of a common swineherd or shepherd. Agricultural experts are rightly questioning some of the obvious economic difficulties of trying to farm several scattered strips from a village home base, but they sometimes forget the social efficiencies found in a village in contrast to the isolated farmstead. Some of this social efficiency becomes apparent as soon as one arrives in the *plateia,* the village square.

THE PLATEIA

Any visitor from outside is expected by the villagers to make his identity and business known as soon as possible, not to conform to any legal or police requirements but to satisfy the lively, usually friendly village curiosity. The plateia is the stage for this performance. Upon entering the village, one heads toward the most imposing coffeehouse in the plateia. A reception committee springs apparently from nowhere in the person of the local village president or some other dignitary. By the time the coffeehouse is reached, the visitor becomes the honored guest and is asked what refreshment he prefers — coffee or something stronger. Meanwhile, four or five other men, who consider themselves important enough locally to display such forwardness, join the reception committee at the table. Others stand around to watch what the strangers do and to listen to the conversation. Such situations call to mind the observation of a traveler through the Balkans and Eastern Europe half a century ago, who pointed out that when the Russian or the Turk had no business to occupy him, he went home; but when the Greek or the Jew had nothing to do, he stood on the corner of the square hoping something would turn up.[1] After the newcomers have observed the formalities and explained the purpose of the visit, everyone can then sit back and relax to drink the sirupy coffee or to give one's throat a chance to cool after each swallow of the fiery *ouzo.* Only then can the visitor really devote his attention to what the people who pass through the square are doing or wearing.

First there are the children, some of them startled as they suddenly see their reflection in the shiny chromium automobile bumper; other youngsters settle down to some simple game after the visitor becomes monopolized by the older people. Next comes a man carrying pottery jars to the fountain at the edge of the square, getting water for his coffeeshop around the corner. Peasants on their way from the fields ride their carts through the square, with a spare horse used for plowing led along behind. The animals as well as the very small children shy away from the automobile. Women look from the windows of the nearby houses at the group at the tables under the trees in front of the coffeehouse, but only very few ever venture close enough to hear what the men are talking about. A bus from the city pulls in with a roar and a clatter and quickly becomes the center of attention.

As the sights and sounds of the people and the animals become familiar, the buildings around the plateia catch the eye. The church with its bell tower and dome is easily spotted. The cemetery is at the edge of the village, we are told, "back there where you passed the row of tall cypress trees." The school is usually nearby. If school is in session, then the noise of children at recess can be distinctly heard, as can the bell which calls them indoors. A sign rather than the size of the building announces the headquarters of the local village council. Many villages have a cooperative society, identified by a sign on its office near the plateia. Other coffeehouses and one or two small grocery stores account for the rest of the buildings on the square.[2] The universality of these coffeehouses and small shops is shown in Table 1, presenting the services provided in eight villages of more than a thousand in population, in the early 1950s.[3] Some of the items deserve fuller explanation.

The flour mills. In the case of the Xanthe village, four of the flour mills were built during the occupation, the other two long before then. These mills operate not more than a total of thirty days each during the year because local grain production is very limited and also because local people get their ration flour ready-ground from the government.

The one flour mill in the Mesolongi village has an old engine which uses charcoal for fuel and which hardly works more than two days a week. Most of the time it is under repair. Many of the villagers are therefore obliged to take their grain to the mills of neighboring villages.

The bakeries. In the larger villages these find sufficient business to stay open not only to sell their goods but to bake throughout the day for the village housewives, who bring in either unbaked loaves of bread or some dish for the ovens. With fuel so scarce in many parts of the country, it is much more economical at times for a family to take an uncooked casserole to the commercial baker than to try to bake it at home.

The village stores. In one of the Macedonian villages the yearly gross sales of the seven stores run from just less than $700 for the smallest one to $3330 for the two largest. These same two largest ones extend over $1000 of credit each year, while the smallest one gives no credit.

The owners of these stores purchase their goods directly from wholesale dealers in Salonica and bring them to the village with trucks or horsecarts. They do not hire any outside laborers, but use their sons or family members for the work. All stores sell for cash, credit, or take different farm products as payment. The credit extended to farmers by the different shopkeepers depends on the financial situation and the economic standing of the customers. More credit is given to farmers who own livestock because they are able to pay back their debts at more frequent intervals than ordinary farmers, who can pay back their debts only once a year after harvest. No direct interest is charged on credit goods, but their price is usually such as to include the interest.

The studies cited contain much more information about these village stores. The stock carried may include food, clothing, and farm implements.

TABLE 1. BUSINESSES AND SERVICES IN EIGHT GREEK VILLAGES*

	Tobacco village near Xanthe	Village A near Mesolongi	Village B near Mesolongi	Village in Central Greece	Mountain village near Lamia	Village near Agrinion	Village A in Macedonia	Village B in Macedonia
Population	1145	1062	2030	1372	1060	2915	1654	2493
Flour mills	6	1			2	3	2	
Bakeries	1		3	1		3		
Groceries	6	8	3	7	6	21	7	8
Barbershops	3	2	3	3	2	5		
Coffeeshops	6	8	5	5	1	7	3	3
Carpenters	5				2			
Masons	12			4	4			
Shoemakers	5	1		2	1	4	1	1
Saddlemakers	1		1	2				
Tinsmiths	1					1		
Blacksmiths	2	1	2	3				
Butchers	2	5		4	3	6		
Tailors	1	1		3	1	1	2	3
Dressmakers	3	6		10	2			
Carriagemakers						2	1	
Yardgoods shops				2		1		
Tobacco-news			2			2		
Restaurants			6			4		

* Includes those services mentioned for two or more villages.

Source: Village studies by Near East Foundation, Greek Ministry of Agriculture, and United States Mission to Greece (mimeographed).

Now and then we find mention of a shop grossing over $5000 a year, but this is exceptional and means that the proprietor has to extend a great deal of credit to take in that amount. Mention could be made here of the yardgoods shops which have come into existence because of the women's desire for the factory-made cotton goods, often of inferior quality. Often they sell beautiful handmade woolen fabrics at ridiculously low prices just to buy the cotton goods which they take to a local dressmaker in order to have a frock in the modern style.

The artisans ply their crafts in small shops, often in full view of those passing on the street. By working near the door or window they take advantage of the daylight and thus use less electricity in their dim ateliers. The list of these artisans for a village in Central Greece reveals much about them and about the Greek village itself:

Two saddlemakers — who are also part-time farmers.

Two blacksmiths — both well-trained skilled laborers owning their own shops.

Two shoemakers — one only repairs shoes, while the other also makes new shoes.

Three tailors — one is exceptionally good, but the others are considered poor in their work.

Four butchers — all have out-of-door shops and kill animals only as needed. Usually one or two sheep are butchered each week. The owners cook the intestines which they sell very readily.

Ten seamstresses — some farm in addition.

Three barbers — one popular, the other two fair. All are located in the coffeehouses.

One horseshoe maker — owns twenty-five stremmas of land, which he farms. (One stremma is one fourth of an acre.)

Four masons — one owns eight stremmas of land which he farms, while the rest own no land. Two of these men are in the small village musical group which plays at all weddings and festivals.

Five cart owners — who earn a living by transporting products.

This random presentation of the services found in eight Greek villages scattered over Central and Northern Greece provides a quick introduction to, rather than any conclusive statement about, the business activity going on around the village square.

Telephone and electric poles indicate whether these two utilities are available locally. There is usually only one telephone, either in the office of the gendarmerie, the local community council, or a centrally located café. Should the village be one of those favored with electricity, the peasants proudly inform the visitor of that fact. When we asked what the advantages of electricity are, we got various replies: "Electricity brings cleanliness. We used to have smelly kerosene lamps." "Now we can light the streets and see where we walk in the evening." "We can have radios and learn what is going on in the world." "A few of us get small cooking stoves and others electric irons." Some also add, with a twinkle in their eyes, that since they can see after dark they do not have to go to bed so early and that the birth rate will probably drop.

Where there is no electricity there may be radio sets run by batteries. In one mountain village we found that five of the eight coffeehouses had battery receiving sets which they always turned on to the newscasts. "Why," we wanted to know, "are you villagers so interested in newscasts?" "Oh, we like to hear farm prices over the radio, but most of all we like news about what is going on in foreign countries because that is what enlightens us." In some of the most out-of-the-way villages we found receiving sets run by gas motors supplied by the United States Mission. Thus the air waves are reaching the village plateia and the villagers' sense of isolation gives way to a growing demand for more of the benefits enjoyed outside the village.

The water supply in the village is quickly identified by the procession of people to and from the springs, artesian well, or street faucets. A local gendarme in his trim gray uniform, who joins our group, and a field guard on his way to leave the rifle slung over his shoulder at the community-council office are expressions of services from the national or local government, as is the mailman who comes from the next largest center once a day, or perhaps three times a week.

Our observations of the people, public buildings, and available utilities are constantly interrupted by the liveliness of the eager conversation around the café table. Although the American visitor is not directly engaged, the topics sound so interesting and so close to the facts he is trying to collect that he cannot remain entirely aloof. For instance, the young officer in charge of some people recently resettled in the Greek-Albanian border area under his control says that the peasants are complaining because their land allotment is too small and the soil too sandy, so they go into the forbidden no-man's-land to cultivate even if they do place their lives in jeopardy; a man who prides himself on knowing local history affects a learned air when he tells the history of the local church, built on the site of an ancient pagan shrine; a child, bolder than the rest, comes up to ask the woman interpreter, who is wearing slacks, whether she is a man or a woman.

Again, in a low voice, a local official inquires politely: "Who is this American professor? What is he doing in our village?" When he is told that the professor is interested in understanding the Greek people, and in telling Americans about them, he finds it hard to believe. "You mean," someone asks, "that he has come all the way from America to visit our village? Please tell the professor that we are greatly honored." One man adds, "I've lived here sixty-seven years and during none of that time has a Greek professor ever come to visit us." A woman related to the coffeehouse proprietor has edged her way into the group and asks, "But isn't he young to be a professor?" It is at this point that one pulls out the impressive credentials, beribboned and sealed, from the university authorities back in America. Though it is written in English, no one questions the authenticity of such an imposing document. Everyone is then delighted to supply any information at his command, even going so far as to ask: "What would the professor like to know about our village?" "Let's begin at the beginning. How did your village get started?"

LOCATION

Almost every village has some tradition about its origin; it may be legendary or historical. The following account by a native of a Peloponnesian village illustrates the legendary:

In the old days my village was built more to the west in a place now called Palaiochori [Old Village]. My forefathers left Palaiochori and built the village where it is nowadays because a great epidemic had caused the death of many people. It is said that all of those who had danced at a wedding on a particular day died, for the evil was caused by a spook in the form of a dog which jumped from one shoulder to another. Wherever it stopped, that guest became sick and died. Those who survived the evil came and built the village of today. In the beginning they put up huts and later on houses. The country was wild and full of trees. In order to choose a good spot they took three pieces of meat and put them in three possible sites. They then noticed which piece of meat spoiled last and chose that site; they were glad that the North Wind blew upon the spot selected.[4]

Many Greek villages are of relatively recent origin and do not need to rely upon legend for an explanation of their location. Particularly in Macedonia and Thrace, scores of new villages were built to accommodate the approximately 150,000 rural refugee families coming from Asia Minor in the 1920s, although as many as two thirds of the rest of these new arrivals were installed in old villages in temporary huts or in houses vacated by the Bulgarians and Turks exchanged for the Greeks. As a rule, these villages were located near a road and on cultivable land, so that they were much more accessible than the older mountain villages.

There was some discussion at the time of resettlement about the advisability of establishing the farmers on independent farmsteads rather than in villages. Some serious disadvantages to the village system from the standpoint of efficient use of time have been set forth in various reports. Frequently not less than two or more hours each day is spent by several members of the family in traveling between their home and their fields. It is also necessary to transport all food supplies, the grain, grapes, beans, hay, and other crops, as well as all fuel, by donkey or mule over long distances, an expenditure of labor which would be unnecessary if the people lived on the land they farmed.[5] Despite these economic disadvantages, the Greek peasants, in the 1960s as well as in the 1920s, kept on living in villages. The talk of "saving time" has little appeal, since the villagers move in a time sequence quite unrelated to the concept of the industrialized West. They ask, "Save time for what?" As an aside, it is of interest to note that whereas the Greek villager becomes bored when one talks of saving time, he listens intently when one suggests ways of increasing his income, adding to his food supply, or helping him meet his taxes.

Another deterrent to the settlement on the independent farmsteads was noted by Henry Morgenthau, who had been United States Ambassador to Turkey (1913–16) before serving as Chairman of the Greek Refugee Settlement Commission, established by the League of Nations. He called it the "hiving" habit of Greek families, which led those coming from one village in Asia Minor to try to relocate together in a new community in Greece. His observations, though couched in superlatives, are well worth repeating:

The Greek character has special qualities that had to be taken into account [in resettlement]. Like his ancestors, the modern Greek is an intense individualist. Interference with his personal independence, or his freedom to order his life in his own way, is sharply resented. Every Greek has his own ideas about everything and hesitates neither to express them nor to act upon them. He would be quite impossible to manage were not this disintegrating characteristic counterbalanced by his equally intense social instinct. He is the most gregarious of human beings and will not live where he cannot foregather in the evening with his fellows. The daily gatherings in the local café are as dear to the heart of the Greek as were the weekly gatherings at the meeting house to the Puritans of old — and for many of the same reasons. . . .[6]

Furthermore, as Morgenthau also pointed out, new houses could be provided much more quickly and inexpensively in a village setting than if each house had to be constructed all by itself at considerable distance from all other houses.

Reconstruction also had to be carried out after World War II and the close of the guerrilla war. Along with this there was some relocation of villages because the old sites were considered too inaccessible or the means of livelihood too precarious. One such place was Menithi, on the seacoast of Western Greece, where three hundred families were settled between 1949 and 1951. They had come from two communities in the mountains about five or six hours' walk away. Their home villages had been destroyed three times: by the Italians, then by the Germans, and finally by the Communist Antartes. The peasants were primarily agricultural and livestock producers but knew nothing of the sea. As we talked with them in the plateia, within a stone's throw of the sea, some of the men asked, "What do we shepherds know about fishing?" and others, with disgust in their voices, questioned: "Just how would a fisherman know how to guard livestock?" The new site had been chosen because it was sheltered, near the water, and on the road. The houses had been provided free by the Ministry of Reconstruction, each being set in a plot of four hundred square meters in which a small vegetable garden was possible. As the surrounding cropland was insufficient to support all of these families, the men had to go far away in search of jobs while leaving the women and children behind.

In the beginning of the reconstruction period, private contractors were given the task of rebuilding the destroyed villages and in some cases put up shoddy dwellings in a location where people did not want to live. Some of these stand today between Lamia and Volos abandoned, mute testimony to the failure of projects carried out without consulting those supposed to benefit from them. But most of the postwar villages are now inhabited and contrast, because of their straight streets and their houses in a perfect line, with the older villages where the streets wander and each individual put up his house on his lot as it pleased him.

Location, however, is more complex than some of the peasants' explanations or the contractors' choices would imply. It usually represents over a long period of time an adjustment to the resources which people need for their livelihood. First of all, there must be water available for drinking and washing. Should a spring upon which everyone depended dry up, the people of the village would move, ghosts or no ghosts, particularly if the women got tired of carrying water from some unreasonable distance. Over a period of time, also, the peasants locate their settlements as a compromise between the requirements for wood and pastures on heights above the village and the need for daily travel to their fields lying below. That is why villages are so frequently perched on a hillside instead of on the level land beneath. Of course, if the plain is large and the hills distant from land owned by the peasants, they will build a village on the plain and make long trips for their wood. Another factor affecting location in the days of Turkish rule was the villager's desire to be off the main road and thus less subject to taxation by officials and to requisition of foodstuffs by passing troops. He valued his freedom. Those old villages are now suffering from the isolation which was once a blessing. But many of the people still cling to residence in the old village in preference to separate farms because of the protection a village gives against wild animals and predatory armies, and because neighbors help each other to cultivate the earth. A further reason for the long survival of the village was its suitability to the system of large landholdings prevalent through much of Greece before the liberation from the Turks. Estate owners or managers could better control and supervise the rural workers whose houses were conveniently grouped together. Nowadays, according to those engaged in community development, better provisions for schools, roads, medical services, mail, and other public facilities can also be provided where the people are concentrated in villages.

Students of village life, in addition to deciding why settlements are found where they are, also try to describe the different shapes which the settlements assume. In Greece one finds a great many compact (nucleated) villages in which the lanes move in all directions from the central square and houses are built along these lanes. Another type, found, for instance, in the northern Peloponnesos between Corinth and Patras, is the line village which extends like a ribbon along some main highway and has little depth in either direction. Sometimes these line villages also follow a narrow river valley. In any event, the lay of the land contributes to the shape of the settlement, as well as to its aesthetic effect upon the passerby.

THE IMPORTANCE OF ROADS

One need not sit in the village square or around a fire in the main room of a peasant's house very long before learning that roads are important topics of conversation.[7] They loom large in the peasant's consciousness, revealing a growing desire on the part of the villagers for a rapid link with the outside. Their isolated world is breaking down, much to their joy, and they are feeling more and more a part of the body politic of Greece.

Today one can travel to most of the major towns of Greece on relatively narrow but high-speed, black-topped roads. Every few miles an all-weather gravel road leads off from these highways to serve a number of villages through which it winds; it also serves an even greater number connected with it by a road passable only in good weather or by a donkey track over which no motor vehicle can travel. Many familiar with the contribution of the American aid program to Greece maintain that, aside from the turning of the tide against the Communist guerrillas, the most lasting reminder of American help will be the greatly expanded road system. In Northern Greece, in particular, military roads are being constructed through areas which formerly were hours away from any contact with trucks or buses; and in all parts of Greece villagers through the "personal labor" program are building roads to connect their communities with some good highway not too far away.

Sensing the stress placed upon roads, we began to talk to people about the difference that a new road made to the villages it reached. Everywhere the testimony was much the same. One nomarch (or prefect) gave this explanation: "With a new road the state functions can be more immediately brought to the people. The new agricultural extension program can be taken to a village on a road and people can go to the center to talk to the officials. But there are more gradual changes as well: the peasant wants to improve his home because his wider travel helps him see a better life; he wants to keep his home cleaner."

At times, one comes across an unusually good road system in what would at first seem to be an isolated area and learns, as in the case of the area south of Volos, that emigrants from these communities, who went to Egypt, sent back large sums of money for the construction of these roads, which were built at heavy cost per kilometer because of the great amount of masonry work needed. Near Xourichti, in this same area, we came across a small unpadlocked building on the main road connected by a path with the village seen in the distance. We learned that this was the place where villagers left their money and orders for purchases desired from Volos. When a truck driver passed that way he would stop, pick up the money and the orders, and do the necessary shopping in Volos. When he came back he would leave the purchases in the little house, perhaps toot his horn or flash his lights, and people from the village would come to get their new possessions. There were no thefts, no shortchanging, in this area of mutual trust where, before World War II, it was safe for a young woman to walk anywhere through the mountains at night unattended.

In Epirus, across Greece from this Volos area, life is lived in a different historical and physical setting. In order to learn what effect a new road had upon village people there, we went to the village of Tsepelovo. On August 20, 1952 — only a few months prior to our visit — the first automobile had arrived at the village, using the road that had been built to open up a large forest to be exploited for the people's benefit. As we sat in the office of the community council and talked to the village secretary, we learned what the road had already accomplished for this village. The first advantage mentioned was the lowered transportation costs, for the hauling charges per oka (2.8 pounds) by truck are only one fifth or one fourth of those by donkey. When pressed to give other results, the secretary put it this way:

Now we can build homes with sand and cement; formerly it was too expensive to carry these in by animals. Formerly we built our stone houses with lime and mud as mortar, and that is why they tend to crumble so quickly. Here we produce about 14,000 okas (about 20 tons) of walnuts each year. We received little for them because of the transportation charges; now the merchant comes here in a truck and pays us cash and gives a higher price. Today we can also sell our lumber because, before the road came, we couldn't very well strap long boards to the donkeys.

We used to spend twelve-and-a-half hours going by animal to Ioannina, the only large city nearby. Now we do it in two-and-a-half hours by car. The grocer can sell fresh goods, whereas formerly he had only staples. Although we had great riches here, we also had great poverty so that beggars would go from house to house. The road reduces this inequality. Many of our men who had no other income earned much money working on the construction.

In case we get sick we can be carried down by car and not have to ride a donkey. Now we can get the Athens newspapers on the same day they are published, whereas before they would always be at least two days late and frequently more. We have no illiterates here, so many subscribe to these papers.

Considerable insight into what living on a good road means was gained from talking with mountain people who had been resettled in the lowlands away from their destroyed villages. One woman mentioned the advantages with little hesitation, beginning with the access to medical treatment mentioned above: "Here medical care is available because of the road. If a child gets appendicitis, he can get to a doctor in time; in our village up above he would have died. Also woman's work is lighter here. The children are better off. They can go to the school right here in the village whereas in our location up above they had to walk from two to three hours every day."

A commandant of police brought out some interesting examples of what a road means to a village by comparing his community, which got a road ten years before, with another community not far away which was not yet on a road:

The road brought many economic changes. For instance, my father had three hundred cherry trees which he had never bothered to fence in, prune, or tend in any way. Anybody could come and eat the fruit; they would break the branches. But when the road was built, my father fenced in the land and sold the cherries. The income began coming in. Also, it was a disgrace in our village to sell a chicken, but when the road came the women began to sell both eggs and chickens. This meant more income. Eggs in the village without a road sell for half the price obtained by the women in my village. This holds true for all products.

In the village without a road you would have a hard time finding a man with enough cash to buy a candle to light in church, while in my village people always seem to have some cash. In the other village each farmer needs a donkey for transportation and will spend about two thousand drachmas a year just for the upkeep of the donkey; in our village we do not need donkeys because we can use the trucks at much less expense.

Politically, too, roads make a difference. The candidates for parliament seldom get to the villages off the road but try to visit the rest; the same holds true for government officials in position to help in agriculture or other ways. They stick pretty much to the villages which they can easily reach.

The roads that lead into and out of the plateia do more than bring in the welcome buses, trucks, and occasional private cars; they bring in new services, new ideas, better teachers, and increased economic opportunities. People begin to feel that their village has moved from the shadow of isolation into the Greek sunlight.

VILLAGE HYGIENE

This closer contact with the ideas and the services of the city is helping overcome one of the negative aspects of village life from the survival standpoint, namely, its lack of adequate hygienic provisions. When Greek villages are judged in terms of what one finds in many rural settlements throughout the United States and Western Europe, they measure up fairly well. They have their expected quota of flies, their problems of sewage disposal, and the difficulties of obtaining pure drinking water, but these concerns are common to farm people in other parts of the world.

When, however, one measures the Greek village by scientific standards of public hygiene — and these should be the goal in the interest of better health for its people — then there are obvious shortcomings. According to *Medical and Sanitary Data on Greece*:

many of the rural sections depend on small springs and hand-dug wells for their water supplies. These are usually isolated from inhabited areas and the water is not piped to the villages. It is quite common to see women carrying water in earthenware containers from sources as far as a mile from their homes.

In semi-rural communities, particularly in the lowlands where underground water is more common, public wells, springs and private wells are often in use. Many private wells exist all over Greece and are sometimes the preferred sources of supply, even where safe piped supplies are provided. In some of the smaller Ionian and Aegean Islands and in a few villages in the northeastern Peloponnese and eastern Crete, the complete lack of any surface or underground water has compelled the population to depend on rain water collected from the roofs of their homes.

Many private and public wells and many rural springs are open and unprotected from contamination which may be introduced by the human or animal population which it serves. . . . Even after collection, the water is frequently subject to contamination in containers. . . .[8]

The urban water supplies are more apt to be adequate with proper precautions taken for filtration and chlorination.[9]

A description of waste disposal is also contained in the report quoted above:

For the disposal of human excreta in the rural areas of Greece either the pit privy or bored-hole latrines are utilized. Defecation on the ground is still widely practiced due to lack of sanitary facilities in residences and schools. However, the sanitary type of bored-hole latrine and pit privy has been installed under various programs at low cost to villagers in rural areas mainly as demonstration projects.[10]

In addition to the obvious visible signs of sanitation progress, one can learn much from the list of causes of death for Greece as a whole. Table 2 shows the first fifteen general causes of death for 1950. Some of the

TABLE 2. CAUSES OF DEATH IN GREECE, 1950,
BY NUMBER AND RATE

Cause of death	Number	Death rate (per 1000 people)
Heart disease	3270	.427
Cancer	2730	.358
Cerebral hemorrhage	2679	.352
Tuberculosis (respiratory)	2214	.293
Senility	1954	.258
Pneumonia	1523	.201
Nephritis	1284	.168
Violent accidents	1259	.165
Causes unknown	1166	.154
Congenital debility	998	.132
Diarrhea, enteritis	973	.128
Other tuberculosis	634	.083
Other diseases of digestive system	629	.082
Other infectious diseases	621	.081
Diseases of the liver	511	.067

Source: Mutual Security Agency Mission to Greece, *Medical and Sanitary Data on Greece* (Athens, 1952), p. 62 (mimeographed).

diseases which give the health authorities most cause for concern are tuberculosis, dysentery, typhoid and paratyphoid, venereal diseases, smallpox, various intestinal parasites, and particularly infectious hepatitis.

Of these causes of death, tuberculosis creates the greatest problem for those interested in preventive medicine, for it is commonly recognized that the reported death rate, 29.3 per 100,000 people, is probably less than half of the true figures. Greek peasants can therefore take small comfort in the fact that tuberculosis death rates in the urban areas are more than twice as high as those for rural districts, since this still means relatively high rates in the villages. Although the government is attacking tuberculosis with considerable vigor, the public response is only half-hearted. One of the first jobs of the UNRRA–World Health Organization mission after the war was to try to persuade the tuberculous to recognize their illness, to take treatment, and to realize that it was no disgrace to be ill.

However, in most families it is still considered a shame to have the disease, so much so that cases are hidden and doctors are even paid for not reporting cases to the public-health authorities. Although undernourishment is frequently associated with the high incidence of the disease, in Greece malaria has been a contributory cause by undermining resistance to the tuberculosis bacillus.

Where tuberculosis presents a dark picture, the reduction of malaria is a story of great progress. Prior to World War II, the annual rate of malaria among the civilian population was estimated at one million to two million cases, or from 15 to 30 percent of all of the people. The heaviest incidence came in the years of very heavy rainfall, sometimes reaching three million cases. One indication of the magnitude of the problem before 1946 was the annual expenditure by Greece of $1 million just for quinine, found in almost all village stores. From 1946 to 1950, according to an official report, an average of 5,000 villages were residually treated with DDT and an average of 900,000 acres of potential breeding places such as lakes and swamp land were sprayed each year, the latter operation requiring an average of ten airplanes per season. Now the once-dreaded disease of malaria is no longer a major public-health problem in Greece, a result achieved at the equivalent sum of $7.6 million during the 1946–51 period.

Hygienic improvement depends just as much upon attitude change as it does upon the installation of proper facilities. And favorable attitudes are developing. Whenever the matter was brought up in discussion at the coffee-houses or elsewhere, the local village dignitaries would tell of the project they had formulated and submitted to the *nomos* (prefecture) authorities, in which they applied for funds to better their situation. In Arachova, on the way to Delphi, the project dealt with improving the water supply; the same held true for Vouno in the Arcadian part of the Peloponnesos, Karpenesi in Eurytania, Konstantinia near Kavalla, Myrodation in Thrace, and on to a list of communities too lengthy to include. Other communities give priority to the construction of community latrines, school baths, or a general sanitation program.

THE VILLAGE HOUSE

As a convenient starting point for typing the village houses, one can associate the stone house with the mountain village, the mud-walled house with the plains village, and the white, squarish house with the islands. Each is well adapted to the resources at hand, and each has its own historical development.[11] Many of the island homes with their thick walls took on a fortress character as a defense against pirates who, for many years, plagued this part of the world. Furthermore, the thick walls have been necessary in the mountain areas where the only possible defense lay in the hands of the villagers themselves. As already noted, down on the plain, particularly in Turkish times, the farms were for the most part estates of Turkish beys, and the villagers were little more than serfs dependent upon the bey for protection. He was not concerned about their shelter and they had less incentive to go to the trouble of building the more durable stone houses, even if there had been building stone at hand.

When walking through a mountain village, one often looks from an upper lane down upon several tiers of houses beneath, since the buildings compactly hug the slope vertically rather than stretch in a narrow row at the same level. This gives a good opportunity to observe the roof types, one of the simplest ways used by Greek folklorists in the classification of village homes. There are, in general, two main types of roof: the sloping, which predominates on the mainland, and in which the slopes from either side of the central roof beam may or may not be of equal length. If they are equal, one has the eagle type or saddle-back type. The second general type is the flat roof, called *doma,* found chiefly on the islands and characteristically Mediterranean. The houses with a sloping roof can be further divided into two types: the one-story house of the plains and the two-story house of the mountains. These types have been well described by George A. Megas and Angelike Chatzemichale, as well as by other students of Greek architecture.

The peasant, of course, will not tell you that his house is of the two-story, sloping-roof type. Instead, he will want to show you where he carries on his daily activities after he has served you some refreshment in the part of the house reserved for such honors. He will introduce you to some of the domestic animals almost as though they were members of the family; he will show you how his wife makes bread and will call to her, "Helene, come out here and show our guest how you put the loaves into the oven." He will want you to see the few tools he uses in repairing a wagon, an implement, or a piece of harness. Now and then, if the scenery warrants it, he will stop and show you the view and ask you if you ever gazed upon a more beautiful sight. He will apologize for the mud in the yard, reminding you, "we are just village folk and this is just a village home." When he tells his daughter to get busy at the homemade loom to show you how she weaves the coarse cloth, he will casually ask, "Do women in America weave as pretty cloth as our women in Greece?"

Should his house be one of the few with a flush toilet or with a homemade privy superior to the others in the village, this may be the first wonder he will proudly display. There is no rhyme or reason to the tour of the small farm, nor should there be. Somewhere en route, perhaps while one is still enjoying the sweets offered upon arrival, the family photographs will be passed around, special attention being centered upon the young man living in Chicago, Los Angeles, or Pittsburgh, who regularly sends remittances back to his family — or at least he did until he married an American wife. One is immediately aware that this is a home, a place where people live rather than merely a house consisting of building materials fashioned into some kind of suitable pattern.

Nevertheless, anyone interested in carrying away some lasting impression of a Greek home needs to pay attention to the house itself. I was fortunate enough to find a description already written by a man of village origin which presents in nontechnical terms the typical house of the central Peloponnesos:

The houses are usually storeyed. The animals are kept in the ground floor and the people live above. The houses are made from stones taken by the *mastora* [master builder] either from the mountain or the river. Nowadays most of the houses have replaced slate with tiles. Most of the houses have no ceiling but the room extends up to the beams, so one can see the whole wooden construction of the roof.

Each house has its *liakoto,* or balcony, which faces toward the mountains. Windows of the houses are small and in many houses you can still see the holes in the wall through which guns were fired at outsiders. The older people used to say that they made windows small so as not to pay a high tax to the Turks [before 1829]. The smaller the window, the lower the taxes you paid. From outside you see on the balconies and window sill pots full of carnations, basil, zinnias, and other flowers. The plans of the houses follow the regular mountain pattern. Each man tries to make his home nicer than his neighbor's. The space and the slope regulate the shape. The height of the house is regulated by the slope. Many times the tiles on the top part of the house touch the soil. To avoid having the goats climb on the roof, the upper wall is built higher [than the roof] so that each house has its own design, but altogether they form a beautiful pattern.

Outside each house next to the wall is the oven. Our oven is not round and made out of earth as they are in Megara [a village near Athens] and the islands. It is built with stones. To protect people from getting wet when it rains, they have built a roof on top. This place is called *phournario.* During the summer time the people also do their cooking near the oven, and throughout the year light it every other day or once a week, depending upon how much baking they have to do.

Each house has its own courtyard. It is fenced with stones and holm oak bushes, which have been cut and put in place so as to prevent the animals from entering. Most of the courtyards have a grape arbor or some trees such as fig, mulberry, pomegranate, almond, or olive.[12]

Now and then one comes across villages where the houses are perpendicular rather than parallel to the slope on which they are built. This is due, according to George Megas, to the difficulty of blasting out sufficient rock to form the foundation of the house. Much less of the precious gunpowder is needed to blast out the narrow part rather than the long part. The house thus extends out from the slope, affording considerable room for the basement where the animals, agricultural implements, fodder, and fruit are stored. Sometimes there is a direct stairway from the basement to the upper story, consisting chiefly of the main living room; often the stairway is outside the house, usually built in front of the house and ending on a wide landing.

Variations of this two-story, sloping-roof house occur in all the mountain areas of Greece, which includes most of Epirus, western Macedonia, much of Central Greece, and the Peloponnesos. There is much snow in this region, and the sloping roof keeps it from accumulating on the housetops. The one-story, sloping-roof house can be found in Attica around Athens as well as on the plains of Thessaly, Macedonia, and Thrace. This house usually has a stone foundation of twenty inches or less on which walls of sun-dried, home-made mud brick are built. The roof is covered with tiles:

In their original and simplest form, these houses consist of one rectangular room, including under one roof the family, their cattle and corn. . . .

The most ancient and the most closely related to the original form of Greek house is the simple narrow-front house, belonging to the type known as "megaron." It has the entrance on one of its narrow sides, having usually in front of it a "prostoon," or wide portico. . . .

The wide-front house, however, is found more frequently in the Greek countryside. This house has its entrance and its "prostoon" on the long side of the rectangular plan.[18]

In many parts of Greece the one-room house has gone through a development which gives a separate space for the family, the stabling of the cattle, and the storage of the cereals. A final development is the separation of the stables from the house proper, leaving two rooms in addition to the granary often located between them. Where these two rooms have been provided, one is kept as a guest room, one as a storage place. In the winter the family moves into one room heated by the hearth or small stove on which the meals are prepared. The hearth, which can still be seen today in the center of some village homes, was moved in course of time to one of the walls — usually the middle wall separating the rooms of the two-room house — or to one of the inner corners of the room where a chimney was built.

These village homes, though simple in structure, call for considerable investment of time, money, and thought on the part of the family building a new house. Just what is involved is shown in the following conversation with a peasant woman, whose remarks hold generally true for all of the Greek mainland. Her husband had invited us to his house but had to leave for a short while to take care of his sheep. The woman, bright-eyed and wearing a scarf over her braided hair, moved her head quickly as she talked.

This home had one room, with wooden floors. Unlike some of their fellow villagers, this couple had wooden beds and did not have to make use of sleeping platforms, ordinarily found at one end of the room. There was a storeroom underneath the main room. To enter, one came directly into the yard from the street, then into the house after passing under the portico.

"Are most of the houses in this village like this one?"

"Yes, only the priest and the teacher have two rooms in their homes, but people here are beginning to think about building bigger houses."

"How do you go about building a house such as this?"

"Oh, we get all the materials together and then call one of the builders who lives here in the village. It may take us quite a while to collect the material, depending upon the prices we get paid for our crops. We have to pay the master builder fifty drachmas a day; it usually takes him about fifteen days, since members of the family help him. We need him because he knows best how to place the stone in the walls so they will be firm."

The woman showed little interest in the actual details of construction, but quickly passed to the ceremonies connected with a new house. She pointed out that when the cornerstone was laid the family and relatives came together, cut the throat of a cock, and let the blood spill on the four corners of the house, selecting the eastern corner first. Just prior to this ceremony, money was thrown out to the workers. Customs vary, as we discovered, as to just what was buried in the cornerstone, but in this Peloponnesian village the family buried earth from a sacred place near the village where they had found a treasured ikon; they also included a small wooden cross and an ikon of the Holy Virgin. If the house is built as a dowry for the daughter, then some of her personal possessions such as a dress or a shoe are also included in the cornerstone. Usually a big dinner of roast lamb follows the laying of the cornerstone.

A second ceremony occurs when the topmost beam of the house is in place. The roof has not yet been laid, but this is the time for the family to bring presents to the workmen, who upon receiving a gift call out the name of the donor and wish him many years and a happy life. Later on, when the house is finished, the priest is called. He must be the first person to enter, after which he blesses the house and departs. Thereupon, for good luck, a young boy must be the first to step in.

Now the furniture can be installed and the family can settle down. The dowry chests, containing valuables saved up for the unmarried daughter, will be placed along a wall and the dowry blankets piled on top. "And unmarried girls must never sit on this chest or they will never get married," declared our informant.

Other furniture includes a small table along the wall over which is hung a large mirror. The family photographs are stuck into the edges of the mirror frame. Pictures also decorate the walls, as do pots and pans and other cooking utensils. Two or three chairs complete the roll call of furniture.

In other visits to village homes our attention was directed more to the court than to the interior. The weather would be warm and balmy and the vines in leaf. The family had in reality moved out of doors for the season, even to the extent of sleeping on the portico, on the roof balcony, or any-where else where they found it comfortable. As a matter of fact, some students of the Greek house think the court the basic element, and the other parts of the house an adaptation to it and to the other needs con-nected with the individual peasant's kind of agriculture. Where the court is covered with flagstones, it serves for a longer season than do those that turn to mud after the fall or spring rains begin.

The court is separated from the street by some kind of wall or a fence of holm-oak branches. In the plains villages these walls, like the houses, are of mud brick. They too are white-washed a brilliant white on the Mon-day of Holy Week before Easter. Later on, when the rains come and the white-wash wears away, the walls take on a drabness that made travelers from early times on down to our day describe these plains villages as un-attractive. Where the walls are well kept, where there are attractive tiled gateways — as in Macedonia — large enough for the wagon to drive through, the yards behind have a mysterious and richer look.

The village setting is part of the Greek peasant's physical adjustment to the land. Throughout Greece there are many variations in the appearances of the settlements due to differences in terrain, location, and communica-tion. Villages set in the shadow of a towering mountain and surrounded by a forest of firs have a snug look; those whose green trees and vines are the only cool color in a vast stretch of hot brown fields invite one to stop and rest; those which stand proudly on the brow of a hill seem to be keeping a watchful eye on the farmlands lying around. Others, perched on some airy height, dare you to climb and visit them, and anyone doing so will be sur-prised to find that behind the village there is a broad shoulder of the moun-tain which provides good farmland to those willing to live there on the heights. For many villages the dark blue sea is part of the setting, even though none of the villagers may be able to swim a stroke. Whatever the location, the villager has the deep belief that his village site is the best possi-ble one. The water of his village is the best-tasting in the world, and in mo-ments of homesickness when he is away from his native place he would give anything for a drink of that water again and for a chance to see the incomparable view from his village.

·•◦❏ Part Two ❏◦•·

Land

·∘⟦ IV ⟧∘·

Land as a Birthright

Grandfather slipped his hand underneath and drew out a little bundle which had lain over his heart.

"It is nothing. . . . A handful of earth. . . ."

"A handful of earth! . . ."

"Yes, a handful of earth from our fields so we can plant a root of basil in our land of exile, to remind us. . . ."

Elias Venezis, Aeolia, p. 259

A HANDFUL OF EARTH

To some readers, this passage will reveal a poetic insight into the mystic attachment which not only the refugees portrayed but people in many parts of the world have for the land which is theirs, which they revere, and for which they will endure bloody encounters. To other readers, this will seem an overromanticized stereotyping of the peasant. Which reaction is more justifiable in considering the Greek villages today?

Seeking an answer to this question brought me face to face with the dramatic social changes which have been occurring in Greece, with all their marked regional differences. Facts and figures are a good starting point for trying to resolve a debated question. Certainly, in Greece today, with the population increase, good land is at a very high premium. The "handful of

earth" is a term really descriptive of the average peasant holding of less
than 10 acres, too small an area to support the average family of 5 people
who try to live from its products. Put another way, 37 percent of the
farms have an area of less than 2.5 acres, and 51 percent comprise from
2.5 to 12.5 acres.[1]

As peasants come more and more into the orbit of the city, as they substitute commercial values for their traditional agrarian values, the bond
with the land loosens and their attitude toward the land undergoes a
change.[2] Where it once was a sacred heritage to be preserved and passed on
intact to posterity, the land tends to become a commodity to be bought and
sold; and the peasant becomes a farmer, whom one approaches differently
from a peasant, for his attitudes and values are different. Such differences
are described more fully later as part of the summing up of social changes
noted in Greece.

There was no way of finding out what changes were occurring among
the villagers in the various regions of Greece except to talk with them and
with those who work with them. Few studies had been made. People in
Athens, both Greek and American, guessed and speculated, sometimes
shrewdly, but no one could do more than point out that change was occurring. So I had to go into the provinces and see for myself, being careful
to visit areas which Greeks generally agreed differed markedly from each
other. Some areas have become much more like the city than other areas,
more farmer than peasant. Others are much more in the classic peasant
mold of Hesiod's day.[3]

Far in the northwest corner of Greece, in Epirus, the director of agriculture said:

The rural people here do not part willingly with their land. On the contrary,
because the plots are small, they are always trying to increase the size of their
holdings. At the same time, the people here have a strong trait of localism.
They may be offered a larger tract in another part of Greece in keeping with
some of our current resettlement programs, but the Epirote is reluctant to leave.
He prefers to live on a poverty margin in the area that he knows and loves
rather than to follow the promise of a better existence elsewhere.

One clue to the importance of land to the Epirote is the quarrels that
families and even villages have about it. Within one hour of Ioannina there are
three villages which have been arguing over a tiny bit of land for three months.
Although the land is so rocky that it is useful only for pasture, a representative
had to be sent to Constantinople to search the old records to see to whom the
land really belonged.

It also happens quite frequently that Epirotes who move to Athens, and even
settle there permanently, becoming quite prosperous, won't relinquish the fields
that they own back here. They, too, still sense a certain security in the possession
of land.

Moving eastward across Northern Greece, I learned from the agricultural officials of Serrai (in Macedonia) that more and more unwilling people there were being forced to get rid of their farms and go down to the cities. This is not because of any lack of love for the soil but because the yields in the mountainous areas make it impossible to earn a living. Economic necessity has forced a change of location, but not yet a change in attitude. One official compared Macedonia and Thessaly, with respect to attachment for the land: "I would say that there has been much greater security through the years in Thessaly, which has led to more fondness for their fields; here in Northern Greece the constant uprooting of families has created an uneasiness and therefore a tendency for people to part with their land."

In Thrace, farther eastward, the peasant is still attached to the soil but "he is not stuck to it absolutely body and soul," as one peasant expressed it. These areas of Macedonia and parts of Thrace depend largely on growing Oriental tobacco, a commodity sometimes moving slowly on world markets, with agricultural depression a serious consequence. Here the man-land bond is loosening.

The peasants living at the head of the Chalkidike peninsula (central Macedonia) around Polygyros, the capital of the prefecture, enjoy relative prosperity and are not willing to leave their land. Nor is there any desire to emigrate, although five or six families have sent sons to Italy to study agriculture and veterinary science in the expectation that they would return better prepared to improve agriculture and kindred pursuits.

In the rich plains of Thessaly, south from Macedonia, the mechanization of agriculture is apparent everywhere. When harvests are good, people are optimistic about the future, secure about their food supply. Peasants there have invested heavily in tractors, which have had an interesting effect on attitudes toward the land. In this area of good soil, where scientific farming is increasingly practiced, the basis of the attachment is changing from the traditional idea of land ownership as a sacred trust closely bound in with the fortune of one's immediate family to a view of land as a source of financial gain. Here in Thessaly the rural man is changing from peasant to farmer, in contrast to the hard-pressed people in the northern mountains who are forced to move to cities for bread and, far away from their land, still cling to peasant values.

When a peasant in Central Greece was asked what a family from his village would do if it received $500 from America, he said: " A man would be more apt to buy fields rather than improve his home; of course, if his house leaks and he has enough land, he would start with the house but, generally speaking, a peasant from my village thinks it more important to own more land than to build a big house. Of course, we do have another type among us — the 'chewer' who would squander the $500 right and left in the hope that the next year the cousin in the United States would send some more money in answer to a plea of distress!"

Here, then, is what one might call an illustration of a normal process of change in attitude, the peasant becoming the farmer. When the house rather than the accumulation of more land begins to be stressed, the farmer is moving to "city ways." Throughout the south, in the Peloponnesos, the younger people seem more ready to move cityward than do their elders, who still insist that one should hold onto the land.

In Northern Greece when there is a shift from the land the whole family, young and old, moves together, whereas in the Peloponnesos the young people make the move on their own. This seems to indicate that when the traditional attitude toward land changes, another basic change in peasant life is occurring — in family relationships.[4] However, everywhere in the southern villages, as elsewhere in the country, the village shopkeeper, barber, shoemaker, and other artisans, as well as the priest, all own land which they farm if they can find the time; if not, some member of their family works it instead.

On the basis, then, of dozens of interviews — only a small sampling has been quoted — carried out in thirteen thousand miles of travel in the provinces, some generalizations may be attempted. Wide regional variations are apparent. One may generalize, though conscious of many exceptions, that peasants on fairly good soil which they work with their time-honored methods by hand and not by machines hold strongly to the belief that the earth and the earth alone is their treasure and their great security. On the other hand, where peasants in Northern Greece and elsewhere live in areas frequently troubled by war, or on marginal land, they will reluctantly accept a chance to move away from their family fields — even to the cities. But those who sold their land before the war and lost all of their money because of devaluation now appreciate the worth of land even more. In the fertile plains where mechanization has come, the attitude toward land corresponds more to that in Western Europe and the United States: it becomes a commodity rather than a part of the family heritage. In areas of high education and of long-time contact with the city, such as in much of the Peloponnesos or in Attica, the urban values and attitudes as to land and family have so permeated the thinking of the young that they prefer nonfarm work when this can be found, abandoning the emphasis their elders still place upon " the good earth " as treasure, security, and heritage.[5]

THE CYCLE OF LAND OWNERSHIP (ATTICA)

Whatever the quality of the villager's attachment to his fields is now, he always has had, and still has, an intimacy with his fields that the city dweller can seldom appreciate. Many a villager may curse the land or bless it, as the seafarer does the sea, but he does it as though he were speaking of a part of his own body. In this he resembles his forebears of three thousand years ago. Legally, however, land ownership in Greece has gone a full cycle in the past three millenniums.[6]

A good vantage point from which to view this cycle of land ownership is Attica, the area around Athens. The average tourist to Greece speeds down the road from Athens on his way through the Attic countryside to Sounion, where Poseidon's temple overlooks the sea; or he drives a few miles north to Marathon to climb the memorial mound; he moves through Attica for forty or fifty miles on his way to Megara and Corinth, ancient places to be seen and photographed. On all of these trips he will see peasants everywhere. In the spring and summer they are bringing loads of vegetables — carrots, tomatoes, squash — into the city; in the fall they are taking grapes from the vineyards to be pressed by foot in the large wooden vats or, as winter comes, carrying the dead branches of the vines home to burn in their small, cold houses. Their slow-moving animals delay the tourist bus, their sheep respond erratically to the auto horn, but the peasants themselves seem unconcerned about the traffic. And the land, the dusty countryside, dotted with the gray-green olive groves, and the dark points of the cypress, surrounded by heights incredibly changing from silver to rose to violet and purple in the dusk, must look very much the same as it did when travelers or Athenians described it long ago.

In the sixth century B.C. most of the soil of Attica was in the hands of individual proprietors. It was "cultivated, as far as it was cultivable at all, by peasant proprietors, who appear to have been, if not prosperous, at least independent and contented until the devastation of Attica in the Peloponnesian War brought with it widespread unsettlement and ruin and inaugurated a period of hardship and struggle for the rural population." [7] Today peasant proprietors again work their own land, independent and moderately content, on the Attic plain and up the rocky slopes where crops, vineyards or olive trees can be made to grow.

The story of what happened between the Golden Age's peasant proprietors and the return of the land to peasant owners in the Atomic Age not only reveals much about the past of Greece but helps explain the contemporary peasant's concern for land.[8] The individual property holder, sometimes medium and sometimes small, persisted, although with difficulty, from classic times down to the Byzantine period. Then some villages, called *kephalochoria,* did manage even under Byzantium to preserve the private peasant holdings, and many more settlements possessed communal property to serve the needs of the commune. But most of the individual holdings yielded to the large estate which belonged to the crown, the nobles, or the clergy.[9] After the end of Byzantium in 1453, the Turkish authorities continued the existing forms of land ownership as long as they controlled Attica and the rest of Greece.

There were, for four centuries, four ways in which agricultural and forest land was held during the Turkish occupation. First of all, much land (the old Byzantine estates) belonged to the Turkish state; that is, it was the property of the Sultan who owned it by right of sovereignty. He could not give it away irrevocably, but he could award it as grants to Turks or to Christians adopting Islam. Such grants included the fiefs (or estates called *tsiflikia* in Turkish) over which the new owners had all property rights. These holdings were found chiefly in the richest parts of Attica.[10]

A second form of property in land was that owned by the communes, which had full property rights. The Turkish occupation, for reasons of general policy, preserved the communes existing prior to the occupation together with their administrative institutions. Also, every city, town, and village preserved its magistrates who, elected for the most part by the Christians, were called *demogerontes* (village elders). The occupying Turks also respected the communal property reserved for the needs of the commune (pastures, woodlots), which was administered by the demogerontes. As the later description of local government will show, these elders, in addition, had the right to impose taxes, enforce civil law, exercise police and other powers, with the result that they became the natural protectors and councilors of every inhabitant in the commune. This institution of demogerontes was the incentive which maintained and helped develop national sentiment during the years of occupation, and it was found in those communes which had been *kephalochoria* (head or independent villages) in the Byzantine period.

A third form of landed property was that owned individually by the inhabitants of these kephalochoria, the villages which had the communal land mentioned above. These were settlements usually in the mountain or hill regions. Because their poor or mediocre soil was of little economic interest to the Turks, and because of their inaccessible location, they were not completely subjected economically. They preserved the regime of small holdings: either small holdings already existing in Byzantine times or those which their inhabitants had begun to acquire around the places where they lived, some by purchase of the right of limited tenure, some by grant on the part of landlords. These small holdings frequently were planted with olive trees, vineyards, and fruit trees, as they had been for generations.

The fourth form of property was that which belonged to monasteries and to religious foundations. The Turks, under the system of the Waqf, deeded land to mosques or hospitals in keeping with Koranic law in much the same way as Christians had given land to monasteries in the Byzantine era. In this way, large estates came into being under the control of these religious and philanthropic foundations, reinforcing the system of large rural estates in private hands. The convents of Pentele and Petraki in Attica became very rich as the result of gifts and bequests from Christians who did not want their land to pass into the hands of the Turks.

These four forms of land ownership began to change in the nineteenth century with the coming of Greek independence and the Treaty of Constantinople in 1832, setting the boundaries between Greece and Turkey. While the communal land and the peasant holdings of the kephalochoria remained much as before, as did the monastery properties, the great estates of the beys changed hands, going to Greeks with the departure of their Turkish owners from Greece. They remained intact, worked by tenants under Greek landlords for another century — the peasants were legally landless. The land reform legislation of 1917 changed the last two forms by expropriating large estates and turning back the land once again to private cultivators. The cycle of land ownership in Attica was complete. As P. J. Iliopoulos has put it in his excellent study of Attica:

This audacious agrarian policy of expropriation, which allowed in general each proprietor to keep only 30 hectares of cultivable land, has permitted landless inhabitants of Attica to become owners. This right was acquired on condition of complete payment of the value of the plots acquired and with the obligation of cultivation under penalty of forfeiture. The total amount of land alienated amounted to about 17,000 hectares.[11]

When one realizes that the total cropland of Attica was 33,000 hectares, this 17,000 hectares becomes a very significant figure. By 1948 the croplands of Attica totaled 63,640 hectares, with 36,249 hectares in cereals and the rest in other crops.

The fact that the peasant in Attica now owns his land has much to do with the increased interest which he takes in its improvement. As one would expect, working the land around Athens, though still performed in part according to ancient methods, is moving more and more into the commercialized sphere. There are now, for instance, modern poultry houses with large flocks which are the pride of the men, who formerly would not do the " woman's work " with chickens; truck farming is increasing, greatly dependent upon water now available for irrigation. There is a definite shift from olives to vineyards, since a vine matures in three to five years, whereas an olive tree will not bear for twelve years and does not reach full maturity until twenty years.

On the farm, which is now his own, the peasant is also adding to his plantation of fruit trees and vines, for the strong insolation and clear sky of Attica make them produce well. His venturing into dairying, dependent upon forage crops and vegetables, will be limited to the irrigation he can manage. The chances are, however, that cereals will continue to be the main crop because the peasant can harvest them before the great heat of summer descends and the countryside lies parched and torpid under the blazing sun.

LAND REFORM (THESSALY)

Attica was selected as the best illustration of land ownership in Greece, but Thessaly, with the richest land in Greece, almost selects itself to illustrate modern Greek land reform.[12] The size of the farm holding in Thessaly averages just over eleven acres, which is the highest of any province: the figure is less than ten acres in Macedonia, Thrace, and Central Greece; just over five acres in Epirus and the Peloponnesos; and less than five acres on the islands. No wonder that now and then I encountered what can best be termed "land-hungry peasants," particularly where they thought that the government, through its program of land redistribution, was in a position to turn over to them at a reasonable figure the fields of some estate not yet fully reduced to the proper size set by the land-reform law.

This was the case in 1953 in Thomai, a village not far from Larissa, the capital city of Thessaly. I was driving the director of agriculture in Larissa out on his inspection trip through the neighboring area where a severe rainstorm had damaged the nearly ripe wheat. The road, stretching for miles between grain fields, was headed in the direction of Trikkala and passed the Larissa Forest Nursery, whose sign linked it with the Marshall Plan. Farther on, in recently harvested grain fields, a few gleaners were bending over the golden stubble in the hot sun, gathering their winter's bread supply like Ruth who gleaned in the fields of Boaz. In rich Thessaly, there are few gleaners now, but the unwritten law permitting gleaning still exists for those poor villagers who need it.

During the drive the discussion centered about the problem of land reform. The director was reluctant to visit Thomai because he had not yet received any final instructions from Athens to help him answer the questions he knew the villagers would ask about some promised increase in their land. The Land Reform Law of 1917 had boldly attacked the problem of the big estates, and its gradual application had eliminated tenancy throughout most of Greece by 1930. Around 1922 the influx of refugees, with their desperate need for land, speeded up the redistribution. This law still permitted certain classes of landlords to hold up to 500 acres although requiring them to dispose of acreages above that amount. As the result of further government action in 1952, the archbishop of the national church had agreed to the sale of the monastery estates, which accounted for a little more than one fourth of the 1.5 million acres to be turned over to private proprietors in this new redistribution program. Another type of landlord living in Larissa had formerly owned about half of the rich Thessaly plain; he had given up most of the land, keeping the 500-acre maximum holding.

But he was being forced to surrender even this by the provisions of the 1952 constitution which sought to put in the hands of all the remaining peasant tenants the land which they tilled.

It was some of this land the Thomai peasants were waiting for. Thomai was a village of refugees from near Konya, Turkey, who had settled there in 1926 and 1927. Each had been given approximately fifteen acres of land, much of it quite fertile in comparison with land elsewhere in Greece, but still not enough for their needs.

Arriving in the village, the director of agriculture questioned the men, gathered in the coffeehouse, on the extent of the damage done by the rain and they agreed with him that the loss was not nearly so great as the Athens papers had stated in their morning editions. One of them was even frank enough to say, " Oh, you know how farmers are inclined to exaggerate their losses."

"But what about our pasture land?" one of the more aggressive peasants wanted to know. "We are supposed to get some from one of the Hadjilazaros estates. When will the government give it to us? We need it for our flocks."

Patiently the director explained that they would definitely receive this land but that it would take time. He said he felt the matter would be settled fairly soon since the expropriation — the most difficult part of the transaction — had already been completed. One peasant asked: "How could the owner manage to sell some of the estates to be expropriated before the government took them over? This gives the government less to distribute."

The director pointed out that in any sweeping law like the land reform there were often legal loopholes. These were being closed, but the landowner had been able to use them to his advantage. "Remember," he added, "the present government is really interested in enforcing the law and you will get your pasture land." [13]

The land hunger so vigorously expressed by these villagers in the middle of some of the best land of Greece was due partly to their social origins. Added to the conservatism, the moderate pessimism, and longing for land common to most rural people, there was another factor: when they had lived in Turkey, deep in the interior, they had had all the land they could use. Turkey is less densely populated than Greece. Some Thomai peasants even longed to return to Turkey, so much had they idealized the earlier years before their forced exodus. Yet they admitted that in the 1920s in Turkey they had used primitive methods, plowing with a wooden rather than a steel plowshare; many had lived in caves. Significantly, they admitted also that in this part of Greece they had found agriculture more advanced, but it was an admission of a fact to which they could not adjust. Compared to the more flexible peasants of the refugee villages of Northern Greece, these Thomai villagers were reluctant to change; their nostalgia for the past and discontent with the present was a compensation for their feeling of inferiority to the other villagers about them. Their slowness to adopt anything new showed up in small ways. Noting that the flies were bad at the café, I asked them what they thought of DDT. "Oh, that's wonderful," they said. "The English brought in DDT just at the end of the war and for two years we weren't bothered with flies at all. But now the flies are back and I guess we'll have to put up with them." Flies, of course, were only a minor irritation. They complained of many greater difficulties.

"We are becoming overpopulated. We are increasing. A person with seven children can't feed them properly on fifteen acres. If we tried to stop children from coming someone would say that we were being anti-religious."

And then another added, "If we only get our pasture land, we will be content."

"Are you sure of that?" someone asked. "If you had one hundred fifty acres instead of fifteen, wouldn't you still think that too little? Isn't that human nature?"

The director, perhaps to even up the score of what was a trying experience for him, sent a parting shot which made the men grin sheepishly: "Really, now, this talk of your getting the pasture land is a little beside the point. Actually, you are already profiting from this land, since — contrary to the law — you are now letting your animals pasture there during the night in the belief that nobody knows what you are doing. But let us hope that soon the land will be yours and you won't have to try to be so clever." The frank, rather acrid discussion ended, as most Greek café arguments do, with at least the appearance of good humor.

Thomai in Thessaly pointed up one aspect of land reform — land redistribution. However, no matter how disturbed the Thomai peasant became about it, the crucial aspect of land reform in Greece today is not redistribution. The government has scraped bottom in its search for more land for the peasants. What is more desperately needed, from the standpoint of efficient farm management, is the concentration of an owner's scattered strips into one compact holding which can be worked as a unit.[14] One traditional way of decreasing the disadvantages of the divided holdings is the *domka* system of Thessaly, Macedonia, and Thrace under which the entire area of the community is divided into three sections.[15] In any given year all of the land owned by the various families of the community in one section is planted with the predominant crop, a second section lies fallow for a year, and the third section is kept fallow for a longer period and is used for pasture. Obviously the abandonment of the fallow part of the rotation cycle and the increasing use of cover crops or fertilized commercial crops makes the domka system outmoded.

Another village in Thessaly tackled this crucial problem of strip holdings in its own way. This village, Nees Karyes, south of Larissa on the main road to Lamia, was another place the director of agriculture wished to visit. On our way there we picked up the agriculturist who, like a county agent, had been the chief adviser to the peasants while they were planning their successful scheme. He recounted the development of the program as we drove to the village. The people of Nees Karyes, like those of Thomai, were also refugees, but they had come to Greece much earlier, in 1907, from Eastern Roumelia, now a part of Bulgaria. Otherwise, they were ordinary villagers, some with more land, some with less. It was the peasants with less who devised a plan.

After World War II, they realized that they could no longer make ends meet with what they had. In May 1952 twenty-three of the men with the smallest holdings in the village came together to talk about what would happen if they pooled their farms and other resources. The land of these 23 families totaled about 575 acres, showing an average per family below that for the other 200 families in the village, but well above the figure for Thessaly. They talked and talked, swapped ideas and contacted the agricultural-extension agent in Larissa. In October 1952 they held their first assembly. They decided to buy a tractor and to follow the advice of the agricultural specialist as to improved methods, type of seed, kind of equipment needed. They decided to combine the 575 acres for production purposes into one farm. The various types of soil are now used to best advantage. Fortunately, the first year had been a good crop year and successes far outstripped expectations. The cooperative into which they organized themselves bought a combine for 60,000 drachmas ($4,000 at the rate of exchange in 1952). But since they would have had to pay out five sixths of that to others as charges for harvesting their grain, they are in reality only 10,000 drachmas ($667) in debt, and sure of the future.

Since this idea of pooling land sounded so much like a collective farm on the Communist model, the government carefully investigated to be sure no subversive influences were at work before it granted any loans. The planners proved to be far from subversive, merely independent peasants with a common-sense approach to an old, old problem.

Our first stop in the village was at a big brick-walled granary almost completed by the cooperative. There we talked with the villager who was the cooperative's secretary. He paid great tribute to the part the government agricultural worker had played in the success of their undertaking. While we fingered the heaped golden grain on the cement floor of the impressive building, I asked, "What made you begin this cooperative in the first place?" The answer was a single eloquent word: "Necessity."

The founders of this cooperative, the twenty-three village families with the smallest holdings, must have found sweet consolation in knowing that now many of their more advantaged village neighbors wish to join the cooperative pool. But this poses a problem. "How," the secretary asked anxiously, "can we calculate what arrangement to make with these people? How can we know what to charge them for the risk we took, the major expenses we bore? Certainly, now that we have succeeded, it would not be fair for them to come in and benefit free of cost from the pioneering work that we have done."

As these cooperative members talked of their plans, their eyes glowed with happiness and enthusiasm. The men had concrete proposals to solve other problems. They expect to shift from sole concentration upon grain production to more diversified farming, including livestock and poultry production, the raising of dry legumes and other crops that tend to give employment to the able-bodied members of the cooperating families.

International recognition as well as scientific farming is coming to Nees Karyes. Today there are people from Yugoslavia and Israel, as well as touring Americans, who have seen the way some of the peasant families in this village of Thessaly set about solving their problem of too little land in too many strips cultivated in unscientific ways. The secret of this undertaking, in great part at least, lies in the feeling of responsibility on the part of those who participate, since they originated and now conduct and plan for the cooperative which they jointly own.

Pressure on the Land

Most rural Greeks, however, struggle along with insufficient resources and with no cooperative venture such as Nees Karyes to give them hope. A village cobbler from Karpenesi in Central Greece explained the matter in this way: "There has been such an increase in population that the fields are no longer sufficient. The village child today lives more poorly than did his father as a child, because there are more mouths to feed and no added resources."

A well-informed Greek official put the problem in excellent perspective: "Today there is less income per family, less food, and the land values go up. Those that have more land become better off, leading to totally new economic and social distinctions in the villages. Many of our farmers are trying to make a living on such small farms that all they produce is hate. The main problem of the Greek farm family is the population problem. There are too many people. The villager with nothing to do has no place to go in search of work. That is why you see here in Athens many strong, healthy men selling matches. They have no work to do either in their villages or here in the city."

What the Greek villagers are up against in one part of the Peloponnesos is revealed in *Greece, Ripe for Improvement:*

Like many of the older agricultural areas of the world, this area is densely populated and now has far more people than its depleted resources can adequately
support. . . . At the present time, nearly 10,000 people are attempting to support themselves on 25,000 hectares (62,500 acres) of land, some of it water-
logged, most of it eroded, and all of it reduced in productivity.[16]

Yet this population pressure is of relatively recent occurrence. One
writer in 1842 described the large amount of land then available in the
Greece which at that time consisted of the Peloponnesos and Central
Greece:

The industry of the 100,000 persons engaged in agriculture is almost completely lost to view in the extensive wilds of Greece; and the universal remark
of tourists is, "What a pity that the cultivation of the soil is so neglected! what
a rich and fertile country! what myriads of colonists might prosper here!" [17]

What happened between 1842 and 1952 to change the population
picture so drastically? The population of Greece grew not only by natural
increase but by the acquisition of new territory. The story can be told
most simply by figures contained in the United Nations' *Demographic
Yearbook* for 1952; in 1861 there were 60 people per square mile in what
was then Greece; in 1951 there were 149 people per square mile in what
is Greece today.

Students of population remind us quite properly that mere density per
square mile is not a safe guide to the actual or the potential standard of
living. The highly industrialized areas of Western Europe support several
times the density of Greece and their people have many more modern conveniences. In a rural country, the density in terms of arable land is a more
revealing indication of living conditions.

In the United States there are 17 acres of arable land for each farm person, but in both Greece and India there are only 1.3 acres. Our major farm
problems come from surpluses; Greece, too, has her surpluses, although,
like most countries moving away from a peasant economy, she is deficient in
certain food supplies. One ray of hope for the less-privileged countries is
the possibility that they may increase production per acre from 13 to 14
bushels (the present grain yields in Greece) closer to 30 bushels, a figure
surpassed by the United Kingdom, Denmark, and the Netherlands, where
scientific agriculture is practiced. But even here basic soil types set certain
limits.

The present situation seems likely to become even more acute. In Greece
between 1951 and 1961 there was a population increase of 9 percent, a
figure which may grow larger if death rates are lowered faster than birth
rates. Without a rapidly expanding economy to absorb these added people
into productive jobs, the Greeks will feel their economic limitations even

more acutely and will find it harder to raise the level of living in many of the depressed areas of the country.

LAND USE IN GREECE

What each peasant does with his own birthright of land adds up to the use Greece as a whole makes of her soil resources.[18] We may not be able to spot the patterns of ownership from observing the countryside, but we can see what is being grown and can check casual impressions against the official figures. Of 100 acres, 25 are used for agriculture, 15 are in forest, and the remaining 60 are in scrub, settlements, poor natural pasture, or just plain rock, gravel, or swamp. Roads, however, tend to take the observer through the areas where the land is cultivated and where many fields lie close together. In such areas, if we look only at the agricultural land, out of every 100 acres we would see 46 acres in grain, 5 in other food crops, 4 in industrial crops (cotton, tobacco, and so on), 25 in orchards and gardens, and 20 acres lying fallow. In the farm areas of the United States we would not find so high a proportion of fallow land, nor so much in orchards and gardens; instead, there would be more land in temporary meadows and in forage crops, because of our greater emphasis on livestock even though we have only about 27 acres out of each 100 in agricultural land, close to the Greek figure of 25. Our forest area takes up 32 acres (double that of Greece) and all other uses, 41 acres.

When we think of the land hunger of many Greeks, and the insufficient diet they get from their harvests, we wonder if there is any way to change these statistics. Is there more arable land available than 25 out of each 100 acres? Is there possibility of better use? Two studies, one Greek and one American, supply partial answers for those concerned about the peasant and his handful of earth.

Greece Today, a publication of the National Bank of Greece and Athens, in a 1954 article on Greek agriculture, points out that the available land is inadequately exploited owing to lack of funds. Only 7.8 percent of the agricultural land is irrigated; 11.5 percent is under mechanized cultivation; and chemical fertilizers, although used in twice the quantity of a few years ago, still cover not more than 25 percent of the cultivated land. Furthermore, when Greece is compared with 14 other European countries, the yield of Greek agriculture, expressed in gross income per unit of area, is 63 percent below, livestock production is 44 percent below, and the productivity of the labor of the Greek farmer is 48 percent below the respective average for these countries.

A study made by the American Mission for Aid to Greece indicates that much more efficient use could be made of the so-called idle lands, most of which are owned or administered by the state.[19] They were obtained in the population exchange of 1922–24, and from the Chams (*Tsamides* is the Greek for this Albanian Moslem minority) and Communists when they fled Greece, from Italian reparations and the relinquishment of some lands by the royal family. These government-controlled lands total from one fourth to one third of all of the agricultural land in the country, and many of them are so inefficiently administered that they are not producing at anywhere near their full capacity. Some of the abuses often cited are:

Tenants have not been able to get title to land they have been working for thirty years.

Land and orchards have been auctioned for a one-year period to nonoperating individuals who sublet to peasants on crop-sharing basis, with both parties having little interest in maintaining soil fertility.

Large tracts of fertile farmland have been leased year after year for grazing purposes, either because of political pressure by stock owners or simply because of inefficient and shortsighted administration.

Other lands, idle for years, have suffered devasting damage from flood, for dikes and drainage ditches have not been maintained.

Orchards containing hundreds of thousands of olive and fruit trees have gone untended and unpruned for years.

Whether the problem lies in the lack of funds, as the National Bank claims, or in poor administrative practices, as the American Mission claims, or in both, it is obvious that there is much work ahead for those planning the more complete use of the Greek birthright in land and wanting to satisfy the peasant's desperate need for life-sustaining work.

The significance of land is shown in the importance of agricultural products in the total economy of the country. Let us look at the export figures for 1956–57. Out of the $213 million of exports, about $187.5 million, or 88 percent, was in agricultural products (cotton, tobacco, grapes, raisins, apples, and so on). The balance of $25.5 million represented mainly exports of chemicals, textiles, ores, and industrial raw materials.[20] These figures show that land is important not merely to the peasant but to all Greece as she today seeks to find markets abroad in order to get foreign exchange to import raw materials and finished products not available within her borders.

The rural Greeks, quite unconsciously on their part, remind us that one of life's basic relationships is that of man to the land.[21] In many studies I have made of rural people, I have found that this is a crucial focus, which many specialists from industrialized societies are apt to minimize or overlook, much to their disadvantage. To some peasants, still steeped in tradition, the earth is holy and is not treated in the light of modern knowledge to make it more productive; other peasants are taking up scientific agriculture and in doing so tend to think of the soil as a commodity. If tradition holds too tightly, which it probably will not do among the energetic Greek villagers, then conservatism and lack of progress will handicap the peasant; if, on the other hand, the man-land bond becomes too abruptly broken, a rural proletariat will come into existence and will make demands beyond the capacity of the country to provide.

The golden mean would call for such a balancing of forces that Greek villagers, proud of their rural heritage but aware of steps necessary to improve their economic and educational position, would grow stronger with the passing of time. For some the answer to greater economic stability would lie in higher yields per acre through fertilization and better farming practices; in other cases mechanization may prove an aid, as would more efficient irrigation or marketing facilities and lower interest rates. Along with the economic remedies, whatever they prove to be, a sense of psychological security will develop in the peasant if he thinks of himself as a landowner and gets prestige and satisfaction from the intelligent way he treats his land. Linked to this, however, must be the feeling that he — the villager — is not Greece's forgotten or neglected man, but that those engaged in agriculture are viewed by policy makers as an important segment of national life. Individually and collectively, no people can afford the costly luxury of taking lightly their birthright of land.

··❦[V]❦··

The Peasant at Work

A description of how the land is owned and what it grows gives only one side of the agricultural picture. To round out the chapter just concluded, one needs to see the peasants at work, to follow them from tobacco field to olive orchard, to see how they plow and harvest, and what they do to the part of the earth they own. As they live and work in their small fields, the peasants develop their own way of looking at man and the world. This sets them off from the city dweller or the seafarer, for certain basic rural attitudes prevail all over Greece whether the farmer's energy goes into producing citrus fruits and olives in the south or tobacco and hardy grains in the north. Closeness to the land in the physical and often in the spiritual sense is one such attitude already described. Matching this is the villager's closeness to the changing seasons and weather and his dependence on them. For a truly genuine account we rely again upon T. K. Papaspyropoulos, who has vividly described contemporary life in Kleitoria. The entire following section on the seasons is a translation of his words.

THE CYCLE OF THE SEASONS IN THE PELOPONNESOS

Winter. During winter we have finished all our tasks and we gather in our homes. We have sown, we have gathered our maize, beans, and what other goods God has given us — onions, garlic, potatoes, quince, pome-granates, and so on. We have put our cheese to age; we have rendered our lard; we have bought our oil, our kerosene, salt; we have made *trachanas* [wheat coarsely cut, cooked in milk, dried, and then recooked into a soup or porridge]; our wood is gathered for the fireplace and the oven. In winter we get up before the light. The nights are long and we get our full sleep. We go to bed as soon as it darkens. The older people go to bed with the chickens. For that reason we get up when it is still dark with the third crowing of the rooster, who wakes us all up. The fireplace is going night and day. In one corner sleep grandpa and grandma. In another corner the wife and husband. All around sleep the children. It is the house of the poor. The first to waken up is grandma, who puts the water on the fire for the trachanas; she next wakes grandpa and the housewife, and when the trachanas is ready we all get up. The trachanas is poured by the mother into the deep soup plates and we all eat it hot around the fire. With the trachanas we eat olives, cheese, and we also drink some wine. Wine is never missing. When the children are many, the mother makes breadcrumbs, throws them into the saucepan, gives a spoon to each child and they all eat the trachanas. When the trachanas is nearly finished then it is a madhouse. The children each try to eat the biggest crumb; the crust of the trachanas is around the edges of the pan and at the bottom. Great laughter is heard when the crust is snatched away from one spoon to another.

The children who go to school go out to the fountain, wash a bit their faces, and when they hear the bell, pick up their booksacks and go to school. Whoever's turn it is to light the stove in the school has to go before the others; each child has to take a log. Thus the stove gets fed and all the children keep warm. Those who remain in the house do the housework. The women spin, look after the animals, even weave. The men turn a little around in circles, do some small jobs and go to the shops. Whoever has a gun takes his dog and goes rabbit hunting. The children who are too small to go to school roll themselves on the floor, sit by the fire which they feed. What jobs could they do anyhow? Only damage can they do and then they are spanked. The winter is for women's tasks. Then the women have time to weave, to darn, to spin. When it rains and snows it is a calamity. Mud! Nobody can get dried out; it's nice in winter when the sun appears. Then all of us like foxes try to catch a sunny spot. There we sit and talk of our own affairs. The children play with snowballs. When the sun sets we all snuggle near the fireplace whilst others go to the shops. If anybody has a task he first finishes it and then sits down.

In the shops we gather and play cards. We talk to each other, we tease each other, we quarrel and we shout a bit. From the cigarette smoke one cannot see another; when the *dodekaïmera* [December 25 to January 6 holidays] start, the women stop weaving and the other tasks and start baking *christopsoma* [Christmas bread], ring cookies, St. Basil's cake, put the house in order, and whatever other tasks belong to the dodekaïmera. The children stop going to school and they get together to prepare for their caroling. When they have sung, then they divide what they have gathered as gifts. If it's a nice day, they play outside and go also to the flocks. The man follows his regular schedule from home to the coffeehouse. They also go to church. When the weather becomes clear, even if it's February, slowly the tasks start. One goes plowing, the other prunes, another carries fodder or wood; others plant trees. Those who need to plant vineyards start preparing the branches. The women continue weaving and darning; they still do not undertake outside jobs. They start these when the men need hands. To the shops the man will go only in the evening. There the teacher comes; they all sit together, while he reads the paper. Everybody listens but few understand. The teacher finishes with the paper, then the shopowner, not wishing to waste kerosene on a group ordering no drinks, bangs a piece of wood on a bench and turns down the light. If we haven't gone he puts it out completely. As we go out it's pitch dark. Some fall in the mud; others curse, and some go here and there. As winter comes to an end we have Carnival. Then we kill the pig, then we have our dances near the church, then we enjoy ourselves in the houses.

Spring. When spring comes other tasks start. Then women start to help outside too. They go to the gardens and plant potatoes, spring onions, beans, tomatoes and vegetable marrows, cucumbers, and so on. When some damage has been done during the winter to our hedges or homes then is the time for repairs. And when we want to build then is the time because the weather improves. The children go to school and can play their games; in spring the fireplace does not burn during daytime. We light a fire in the evening when we come back from our work and we can rest and get warmed up. The fireplace burns in the evenings up to Easter. From then onwards, summer starts. Up to Holy Tuesday we must have finished our work; on Holy Wednesday we do not work; on Holy Thursday we may do something; after that we prepare ourselves for Easter.

Then we slaughter our lambs, we hold the big dance near the church; then the girls show their beauty and their charms, and the men their manliness. During those days we also visit the chapels and, after the local mass, we start dancing. We dance and we are merry. After Easter we start our tasks in the fields and in vineyards, as we have mentioned previously. Then the women help too. And they do the same type of work as the men. If we have to leave somebody in the house it's all right. Otherwise, if the children return from school they get hold of a piece of bread and sit to eat it by themselves. You can imagine what happens. When the children are many, it's topsy-turvy; when the mother comes back in the evening she pulls her hair; she doesn't know where to start. She starts beating them and murmurs to herself. The men who like the coffeehouse go there as soon as they return; some to hear some news, others to buy a cigarette. Many have their evening meals before and go afterwards.

Summer. As soon as *Theristes* [June: the Harvester] begins we start preparing ourselves for harvesting. One looks for an extra workman, others prepare their sickles, we all mix ourselves into the harvest tasks. Nobody remains at home. The children come and help too in the carrying. During summertime school is closed. They have their examinations in the presence of the entire village; they recite poems and give dramatic sketches. This is done on a Sunday after church inside the school.

When we have good harvests we start threshing; then we winnow; then we sack the wheat and put it in our storerooms. The straw we carry into our storage huts. After these jobs are finished we go to the mountains to cut wood and we water the maize. During summer the big festival of St. Elias takes place. All the village is in an upheaval. When we have returned from the Church of St. Elias we all start dancing and are merry. Lots of people come from other villages. The musicians play all day and night. During the summer evenings under the moonlight the women gather with the girls and the children on the threshing floors, in courtyards, and where-ever there is an opening. And they "nightspin." There they sing songs, tell jokes, ask riddles, say tongue twisters. The small children and girls play all kinds of games and end with dancing.

Fall. As fall starts, the big festival of Panagia, the 8th of *Trygetes* [September: the Grape Gatherer] comes. The dance and merriment last until dawn. Music does not stop for one minute. After our festival follows that of Mazeika [a nearby town]. There we buy what we need: livestock, wool, clothes, equipment for the house, agricultural implements, and whatever else. But in order to buy we have to sell. For that reason we sell walnuts and wheat. What else can we sell? We haven't got anything. The walnuts we gathered before the festival. When the festival has come to an end we start our work again. Then we gather our beans, we pick our grapes, we press them, we put our wines to ferment, harvest our maize and husk it and place it in wooden cases, and we get ready to sow our wheat. We prepare our agricultural equipment and our seed and we wait for rain. When it has rained we start sowing up to Christmas. In fall also we open our wines and down there in our basement a great merriment goes on.

The life in our village is all work and a hard lot. If God wants us and our animals to eat we do so; if it rains we will sow; if there is *Livas* [hot south wind] our crops are scorched; if God throws sickness on our vineyards we do not eat grapes; if the grasshopper comes we have a disaster; if we have little water during the summer our maize doesn't grow. God is regulating our lives, and if you dare to, don't believe in Him and don't bow to Him. Our tasks are heavy ones and most of the time we live a miserable life. What holds us in life is when we come back at night to our homes and we find our children. What holds us are our festivals, our customs, our holidays, the joys of our children and the love we bear our animals, our birthplace where we have also grown up. To drink water and to eat bread here is better than all the goods we find in the cities. Here we pass each season differently. It is different in winter, different in summer, and different in spring and fall.[1]

YANNES NEEDS A HORSE; ALEKOS BUYS A TRACTOR

To work their land to get their bread, the peasants need tools and equipment, draft power and seeds. I had not fully realized the severe limitations under which most Greek peasants tried to carry on in the early 1950s until I talked to Yannes in the shade of a tree just outside of Alistrate (in Macedonia). Yannes, aged twenty-nine years and dressed like most peasants of that area in brown shapeless garments, quickly came over to start a conversation with us when he saw the car come to a stop. During the few preliminaries he played with his small mustache and finally asked:

Did you see me standing over there? It's not because I don't want to work. My animal is there in the team of the man plowing in that field below. He uses mine while he does his work and then I use his animal when I do my plowing. I have my own fields in 13 plots. This man using my horse works on shares; the owner of the field in which he is plowing is a tobacco commission merchant who has altogether 25 acres of good land. The owner in 1950 got 125,000 drachmas [$8,333] to build a poultry house from the government but we haven't seen a sign of a poultry house around here. Had that money been given to the people of Alistrate to get farm animals then we all would have been much better off. Five years ago 200 of us petitioned the Agricultural Bank for draft animals but only 6 people got any.

We did not challenge his poultry-house figure or try to dispel the deep gloom in which he was immersed. But we were willing to listen. He complained about the way American aid was being spent but, when pressed for details, said that this was his impression because "he couldn't see anything being done." Perhaps those who travel around, he pointed out, might see factories going up, dams being built, but he and his people did not believe it because they had nothing tangible, such as animals or equipment. Reflecting the peasants' attitude toward urban life, he said, "Money is for the cities." During the long wait in the refreshing shade, Yannes talked about his family.

"I have eight members in my family. Now we have only yogurt thinned with water for these eight people to eat. For forty-three months I was a soldier and came home thinking things would be better, but the Bulgarians before they left had cleaned us out and we had nothing with which to do our farming. I tried to get into a technical school, for there isn't enough work for me to do here; I also tried to get into a factory in Salonica but the same favoritism worked there."

He looked bitter and tired.

"Did you sell your tobacco for a good price?"

"Yes, I did get 7,000 drachmas for my tobacco but I was already 5,500 drachmas in debt. And for the crop I am now putting in I'm already heavily in debt. What does the price of tobacco matter when sugar is going up from 16 to 20 drachmas an oka? Today there is not an oka of sugar in Alistrate for use in case of sickness. There is unemployment, not enough fields; we can't rent any more land, for soil is too expensive. How can I live? If I could, I would emigrate anywhere. I don't care where. It would be a better life."

This young peasant's dark view of his world in 1953 was due to much more than the fact that he had only one horse and had to wait restlessly while a neighbor was using it in a team. He was representative of the young village people who are uprooted because of lack of economic opportunity at home or elsewhere and who become psychologically dispossessed. No matter how willing they are to work, or how hard they do work, they have neither enough bread nor enough security.

Not far down the road we stopped to talk to an elderly couple who, with one of their three unmarried daughters, were chopping out the weeds from around the anise plants (anise is used for flavoring ouzo, a popular and potent alcoholic drink in Greece). They were using short-handled hoes, a fact that led to a discussion of their farming methods which more nearly resembled those of their ancient forebears than those of the twentieth century. The description of a Greek village in an UNRRA publication just after World War II might well have been describing them, although the old couple got most of their income from tobacco rather than grain:

Plows are the major implements used. Crops are cultivated by hand with hoes and harvested with the sickle or corn knife. Grain is threshed by driving livestock over it and the chaff is separated by tossing in the wind. The method of seeding is to plow the land, scatter the seed and plow again. Sometimes the seed is dropped in the furrow and covered by the succeeding furrow. The rate of seeding is very high and at least one-third more seed than necessary is sown.

Primitive methods of cultivation result in many long days being spent in the fields by the women and children — an average of 250 days per year. Often the women carry their babies and small children to the fields and watch over them while working.[2]

Although this old couple complained about not having enough food, showing us that they had only bread and water in their bag, nevertheless they had a resilience that kept them going. When asked how their tobacco crop was doing, they broke into broad smiles, and the man said:

"This year our tobacco is just like basil." (By this they meant that it was nice, thick, and round.)

The woman was quick to add, "ho Theos na dosi" (may God grant it).

In a book of interpretations there is a temptation to linger with a couple like this, to record in detail their simple ways which contrast so markedly with the complicated life in the West. The temptation is even stronger when one encounters throughout Greece peasants who are as far removed from mechanization as the Acropolis is removed from the Empire State Building. The late Robert P. T. Coffin, during a year in Greece, caught their spirit in "The Golden Age," which begins:

> High in the back mountains of old Greece
> I came upon incredible peace;
> A wife with a distaff twisting wool
> A boy who filled wool breeches full,
> Riding together on a burro
> Ahead of a bronze man running a furrow
> On a steep acre mostly rocks,
> Twenty red hens, and two bronze cocks.[3]

Yet there is a spirit of change stirring in Greece that cannot be ignored no matter how strongly one may be drawn to the simplicity of the past. To drive along the road just south of Corinth and to see a new bright orange tractor plowing in the shadow of Akrokorinthos, with its lofty crown of crenelated medieval ruins on the summit, is a startling sensation; or between Levadeia and Lamia in Central Greece, to come suddenly upon a combine efficiently working its way through a wheat field with Mount Parnassus, the home of the Muses, as a backdrop, is to be jolted momentarily by the incongruities of an invasion by the machines into an ancient world which for ages had moved in the pattern of man, land, and animals.

The swiftly changing techniques are illustrated vividly on almost any day's tour through the countryside. At threshing time, for instance, I have seen peasants threshing grain by putting it into a bag and pounding it with sticks; not far away will be several threshing floors on the edge of the village with many teams of horses tramping out the grain; elsewhere there will be the slow-moving oxen pulling a little platform with metal teeth fixed underneath to separate the grain from the stalk; and around the next bend may be a big cooperatively owned threshing machine operated by a long belt turned by a tractor. Tired women, faces veiled with white scarves against the scorching heat and dust, stand feeding the broken sheaves into the thresher; other women sack the grain for the sweating men to carry away in trucks. In the memory of the traveler the impression of fierce heat and exhaustion hangs over the incessant labor of these peasants through the fields of Greece at threshing time. And when the onlooker finally sees the combine doing all of the operations at once, he experiences a feeling of relief. It is as if the accumulated work and sweat of centuries begins to be removed from the people who struggle for their bread.

Mechanization has begun to do miracles in the waste lands of Greece as well. One of the agricultural achievements since the war has been the drainage of marshlands by gigantic earth-moving machinery and dredges, thus putting large acreages under rice cultivation for the first time. Here the machine is a mixed blessing, for where rice growing has come with its promise of higher income for the people, it has also meant much heavier burdens for the women to whose lot falls the new task of planting the rice and cultivating it while the men give the orders and manipulate the flow of water.

The machine age has also brought pumps: not the kind powered by blindfolded donkeys or by tired human feet, but the kind that are run by gas engines or, in some places, by electricity. First, heavy drills operated by a semigovernment agency reach down for the water and, when it is found, the pumps are installed. The water is channeled into thirsty cotton fields and vegetable gardens to help raise the agricultural production of Greece up to as much as 37 percent over prewar figures.

Around Larissa, in Thessaly, on the trip with the director of agriculture and on other trips through that area, I had seen the great concentration of mechanized equipment which contrasted sharply with many other areas of Greece where peasants found it hard to get even iron plowshares or new hoes or sickles. In this mechanized area I talked with a man who bought a tractor. Alekos was his name. This is what he told me: "Three years ago I bought a tractor on the installment plan. The first year I did very well, for I could do work for my neighbors after I finished my own work and they paid me a good income. Now six of my neighbors have tractors; owning one is like a craze and I do not have so much work to do for others."

Alekos went on to describe how the wheat of his village had been threshed by machinery since 1925, each farmer bringing his grain to the place where the thresher had been set up, but nobody locally had owned a tractor and the thresher had come in from outside. Since the war, however, tractors had become so popular that they were symbols of social prestige. We told Alekos that we had been much amused by the sight of the peasants going to market in town with their families aboard the tractors and wondered if the higher the tractor the greater the prestige. He smiled and said:

That is partly true but in the beginning only those who had 250 acres of land could buy a tractor and they needed a medium rather than a small tractor. Now anybody can buy a tractor who can afford one and will try to get one as good as his neighbor's.

At first I had to hire a driver for the tractor but my boy rode around with him, asked a few questions, and learned how to drive. So the second season I turned the tractor over to my son. Unfortunately, some people start driving before they know how and that is why an inexperienced person killed two men the other day not far from here.

Alekos estimated that only 30 percent of the tractor owners hired drivers and that the rest of the owners drove themselves or had members of their family who could drive. He thought that this shift away from hiring drivers would mean a trend from the bigger tractors to smaller tractors for, as he put it, "If you are going to pay for a driver you might as well get a larger tractor and get your money's worth out of the driver. If you are going to do the work yourself, a small tractor is sufficient." Not many of them who now drove, he thought, were very skillful at repairs; they were dependent on the tractor shops in town or upon the traveling automobile-borne shops which came out to the village when necessary.

In the midst of our conversation on tractors, Alekos interrupted to say, much to the amusement of the three other men who had gathered around the stone wall where we sat, that he had at first been suspicious of us: "Some of us thought you were either tax collectors or officials from the Agricultural Bank. We were ready to run away until we heard somebody cry out, 'Americans!' "

That reminded one of the bystanders of a good story he had heard from an acquaintance in the Peloponnesos who lived near Messenia. It seems that while a funeral procession was under way there, those participating saw a car with a policeman and other officials thought to be tax collectors. In perfect unison the pallbearers rested the coffin in the middle of the road and disappeared as though into thin air, leaving the officials confronting the lonely coffin.

After a laugh all around the circle, we steered Alekos back onto the subject of his tractor in order to find out why he had bought a Lantz tractor instead of an American tractor. He thought the latter much more complicated. Diesel tractors, both German and American-made, are preferred to the gas-driven type.

"Has the tractor made much difference in your life?"

Alekos furrowed his brows and thought a moment. "Yes, it has made me work much harder to pay off the debt I owe because of the tractor." He agreed that the machine had probably not lightened his wife's work very much, but a shrug of the shoulders seemed to imply, "why should it?"

Throughout the plains area of Greece I met many men like Alekos who, in one financial plunge, had leaped from the peasant farming of their fathers into the machine farming of the Western world.[4] Unlike Alekos, some of them seemed to think that the work of the women as well as that of the men had been considerably lightened. One man from Schematari, near Thebes in Central Greece, had this to say: "The coming of a tractor will 'rest a family.' They will have better yields due to more systematic treatment and better plowing. Before, people had to work ten hours a day while with a tractor they need to work from five to six hours at a maximum. The fact that they have to work less brings joy to the house, for a person who is rested has more of a mood for gaiety than one who is tired. The women certainly are helped for they do not have to be in the fields and can occupy themselves more with housework, with clothes, and can have more time for amusement."

Elsewhere I asked, "What difference does the machine make?" The director of the Larissa agricultural school answered this way:

Twenty years ago this area around Larissa was in large *tsiflikia,* or estates, belonging to a very few families, which produced chiefly sheep. With the expropriation and redistribution of land there was a trend toward wheat, corn, alfalfa, so much so that even the slopes where the sheep once grazed are now cultivated.

Today Thessaly is the most mechanized area of Greece. In 1940 the plain around Larissa had 160 tractors; now the number is well over 1300. [Greece in 1952 had 5400 tractors and in 1956 over 12,000 compared with 1700 in 1938.] [5]

The war, the occupation, and the guerrilla conflict brought an equality in that everyone lost their animals. Then, those who were able to buy tractors — chiefly those who had had the animals before the war — gained an economic advantage. Before mechanization the peasant used to toil and sweat over his land and get very little from it; now with mechanization people become more attached to the land since they see that they can make a profit from it. Those who before would have sold now hold on to it. The merchants in town complain that there is a crisis, but there is none really, for the peasant is putting all of his spare money into fields and more equipment. Now he is farming in a scientific way.

At this point his wife, who had been sitting in the living room with us, began to speak. She owned some land which she had not visited for three years because of illness. When she did visit the peasants who worked this land for her, she found that they were telling her all kinds of things that she needed to do — to use fertilizer, which they had formerly thought unnecessary, and machinery, with which they had been unacquainted before. She attributed much of the recent adoption of machinery to the great movement of people during the war.

Her husband then pointed out that today there was a greater and finer spirit of competition among the farmers than formerly, for they try to see who can get a greater yield. Mechanization leaves them more time for education and learning about new practices. It used to take a whole day for a peasant to plow less than an acre with two horses but now he can do ten acres a day with a tractor. "Before the war," he went on to say, "a peasant who tried something new was considered an amusing person with a loose screw in his head. Even the agriculturists were received with 'what have those educated people got to tell us who have callouses from working?' Also, the agriculturist has learned more about agriculture and more about people, changing for the better."

The director's wife agreed with what we had learned from Alekos about the effect of mechanization upon woman's work. She did point out that machine harvesting and threshing had relieved the housewife of an old burden of feeding many people for long periods of time when the work was done by hand. However, the women still plant tobacco and cultivate cotton. Men are helping out a little more, but this hard field work in Thessaly is still a woman's job. Here again there is some compensation for the women. Although they have as much work now as before, they have more money. They will change into better dresses in the evening and go for a walk on a weekday, something much less common before the last war. Finally, the director's wife pointed out, those families who own twenty to twenty-five acres of land have acquired ease and prosperity and are becoming a well-to-do peasantry.

Elsewhere around Larissa we inquired about the spread of mechanization. The tractor dealers in the town put Alekos' problems in a somewhat different light. We learned, for example, that a 46-horsepower tractor, with starter and pneumatic tire wheels, cost 55,000 drachmas ($3,667); the purchaser had to pay 40 percent in cash and could sign a bill for the remaining 60 percent, payable after 18 months to the Bank of Greece at the rate of 16 percent interest. Dealers and some of the local government officials considered this rate most oppressive.

A second problem was that of spare parts, most of which had to be imported. Foreign-exchange difficulties and import restrictions make this difficult; when the parts were not available, the owner of the tractor was greatly inconvenienced, to put it mildly. We got some idea of the problem of spare parts when we learned that there were 25 dealers of tractors of different makes in Larissa alone. The dealers attempted to teach the purchasers how to use the machine and, a year or so before, the government had set up traveling schools which instructed in the operation and care of the tractor and afterwards gave examinations for licenses. That year, out of 1,200 farm workers examined, only 700 were given a license.

Dealers also indicated that the buyer of a tractor usually ordered a plow and a disk-harrow, with many requesting grain drills. This equipment adds greatly to the total cost. Most of the tractors were bought by individuals or by a group of three to five peasants, with only twenty to twenty-five tractors belonging to cooperatives.

In the tractor land of Larissa everything seems fine now. As in the case of Alekos, the first few owners get good income from custom plowing, but with many tractors there is not very much supplementary income to go around. These steel horses in Greece plow more deeply, give more leisure, help spread scientific farming throughout the plains, and service an increasingly larger proportion of the 950,000 farms of the land. But with one tractor to every 70–80 farms, it is not surprising that Yannes, the tobacco grower from Alistrate, still waits for his horse so that he will not have to stand idly by while another finishes plowing a field.

THE HARVESTERS OF CHALKIDIKE (MACEDONIA)

Social changes, and especially those connected with mechanization, frequently wear two faces — one bright, the other dark. In Athens I had heard from fellow Americans about the growing use of machinery, the previously mentioned over-all increase in agricultural production to more than 37 percent above the prewar figure, and the steps being taken to rationalize agriculture to an even greater degree. These programs represented not only heavy investments of dollars and drachmas, but also considerable self-sacrifice on the part of American and Greek staff members with a missionary zeal for their work and a willingness to work overtime. There was no question of the need for Greece to become a part of the scientific revolution in farming, but it was at times perplexing to find that little thought was being given to the social effects of this revolution on the people in the rural areas.

Once out in the provinces, away from the bright programs of Athens, I saw the dark face of mechanization. While riding with the director of agriculture of Larissa on the drive previously mentioned, I was somewhat shocked to hear him say that he was glad the recent storm had visited the area.

"Why is that?" I asked. "Doesn't it make it harder to harvest the grain?"

"Yes, that's the point," he replied. "Now it will have to be done by hand in many places, giving work to some of the people from the mountain villages in this area who depend upon the harvesting to earn their supply of wheat for much of the year. Without the bread from this wheat they cannot live."

Again, a nomarch of Thessalonike talked to me of the people displaced by mechanization. He tried to see the good as well as the bad, indicating that machines without any question had raised the yields by putting more land under cultivation and by making better farming methods possible. He, too, however, used much the same words as had the official in Larissa, pointing out that he was glad to see the rains in Macedonia since it meant that harvesting would be done by hand.[6]

One bright June morning found us in Niketas, a small coastal village in Chalkidike where mechanical threshing was in progress on the edge of the village. We hired a caique, with both sails and motor, to take us on the three-hour trip to Neos Marmaras, a picturesque refugee village. Hardly were we aboard when a group of excited peasants came to ask if they could go with us. Our one crewman seemed to have no objection so we told them to join us.

Almost at once these lively individuals explained that they were from the village of Parthenon. They had been spending the past twenty-five days helping the peasants around Niketas harvest their grain and were no longer needed now that threshing had begun. Before talking about their work, however, we had to exchange the rites of hospitality. We had spread out a blanket on which we placed a large piece of bread bought just before departure and a portion of white cheese given me by the teacher in the village. Although the peasants looked thin and hungry, they refused our food. One man, carefully eyeing our bread, said, "Here, take some of my bread; yours isn't well done."

Six or seven of the people of Parthenon, sprawled around the blanket while we ate, tried politely to hide their curiosity. Our lunch finished and the purpose of our trip explained to them several times, it became our turn to ask them questions. We started with a woman in her thirties, a widow. She was dressed in a poor cotton dress, was barefoot, wore a kerchief on her head, but her proud look and direct answers were those of an independent spirit. She was obviously very anxious to get back to Parthenon and several times expressed her gratitude for the lift. "Thank you very much. You have saved us four or five hours of walking on this warm day." She had had to leave her four children at home twenty-five days ago and had had no word from them since then, even though her village was only a relatively few kilometers away. Apparently she had gone on working in the harvest fields for winter bread, clinging to the belief that "no news was good news," but her drawn face showed her long concern: "I left them with only a piece of bread to eat. I don't know how they made out."

"How old are your children?"

"My eldest child is fifteen, the next is eleven, and the other two quite young."

"Does the fifteen-year-old take care of the rest while you are away?"

"He would if he could, but he must look after the cows of my brother who is a soldier, and so the eleven-year-old takes care of the younger two."

We learned that there were some relatives living in the village who probably kept an eye on the youngsters but did not assume full responsibility for them.

We were told that these villagers did not look forward to this trip. It is a trial, an ordeal that must be endured if they are to have any bread, for the men cannot find work in Parthenon that will provide them with money to buy bread.

"You ought to come harvesting and stay with us for a week and you would have plenty of material for your book," said one of the men good-naturedly. "When working in the wheat we sleep in the fields with only a blanket for a bed. It has been raining and we have been wet through and through. We can't wash ourselves, we can't even wash our plates — we are so busy."

"Where do you get your food?"

"The person for whom we work feeds us. He gives us garlic, olives, bread, salted fish, and sometimes a bean soup or potatoes. We all lose weight during this period and wish we didn't have to work this way."

"Are you well paid for your work?"

One of the men, unshaven and tired, but gay throughout the conversation, said that the average pay was about 10 okas of grain for 1 stremma of land (28 pounds for one fourth of an acre). A man might get 14 okas and a woman as low as 7 okas, but the average ran about 10. There was no explanation for this different treatment of the sexes except that the bargaining position of the woman was lower. (I compared this figure of 10 okas with the 20 okas that the farmers of Thessaly paid a combine owner for each stremma of land harvested, while they had to pay 30 okas per stremma when the harvesting was done by hand, losing about 10 okas through this less efficient way. Out of the total yield of 150 to 200 okas per stremma in Thessaly, the cost amounted to 7 to 10 percent of the crop in the case of the machine and 15 to 20 percent in the case of hand harvesting.)

"Do you get enough wheat during the harvesting period to see you through the year?"

"It all depends. Some years we do and some years we don't. Bread is our only food. It is our milk, cheese, butter, honey, sugar, all in one. What the grass is to the animal, bread is to us. Otherwise we live on air and water."

Then, as though carried away with some of their troubles, one of the men asked, "Do you know what we say about our village of Parthenon? We say that when Christ walked by our village he left us a curse, for we have only stones there." Another added a variation, "Yes, when Christ passed he blessed what was on his right, but on his left he threw stones." Even this rationalization had no trace of bitterness, but a matter-of-factness that was supposed to help the foreigner understand why they were having difficulties with food. Other villages down on the plains had an easier time of it, but Parthenon, high on its rocks, had to make a living the hard way.

Coming back to the question of harvesting, we asked them when they would get their wheat, for they were carrying nothing but a woven handbag or a spare jacket. In about a month they would return, for then the grain would be threshed and ready to distribute. Each person had carried his own tape to measure just how much he had harvested so there was little likelihood that they would be short-changed. "But don't you often work as a group in a field? How do you measure the individual share in that case?" "Then the owner will say that the field is twenty stremmas in size and that he will give so much per person per stremma for doing that field. An agreement is reached and we all get to work." When they return for their wheat they will have to find some way — by donkey and by caique — of getting it back to their village on the heights overlooking the sea.

It seems that the people of Parthenon do not follow any set pattern in late May or early June when they go to help with the harvest. Individuals or small family groups are independently "on their own"; they go wherever there seems to be a demand for their services; and each individual, a woman as well as a man, is entitled to keep or dispose of the grain earned as he sees fit. In some mountain villages where there are many unmarried girls they often are sent by the families to do this work and are expected to bring back their earnings to the family. Groups of such young people always have a festival air lacking when the middle-aged people have to leave their home village and put in long hours in the field. "We also work with the moon," interjected one of the women who had said little up to that point, indicating that working hours were not from sun to sun but went on far into the night as long as people could see. And light was necessary, for there was danger of accident when wielding the razor-sharp sickles which each worker provided for himself.

There was a crescendo of excitement as we approached Neos Marmaras, our destination. The peasants could see their village of Parthenon far away on the slopes above. They pointed it out to us, asked us to come and visit them and, when we were forced to decline, thanked us profusely for the wonderful favor we had done them. As usual, they had no idea of the help they had rendered me in trying to understand the economic significance to them of this annual trek to the plain to help with the harvest. When mechanization runs its full course and the bulk of the grain is harvested by combines, these people will face the problem that now confronts many thousands of village families in the mountains bordering Thessaly where their services are no longer needed.

Social change is inevitable in the face of an ever-expanding industrial revolution that reaches even to the isolated mountain valleys of ancient Greece. We can only hope that along with the spread of mechanization there will be imaginative social policies to keep man the master rather than the victim of the machine, taking into account the inevitable shifts in type of labor and sources of income in areas where hand labor is no longer needed. The peasants of Greece, with their readiness to tackle whatever is new, would be the last to want to turn back the clock, but they do have a right to wonder where they are to get their bread.

TOBACCO GROWING IN THRACE

During an interview with some peasants in the office of the commune secretary of Toxotae in Thrace during May 1955, I was surprised to see some of the men pull out pink cigarette paper in which they expertly rolled cigarettes for a leisurely smoke.

"But why the pink paper?" I wanted to know.

"We are tobacco producers," they answered with an air of distinct pride. "We can keep some of the crop for our own use, but must use pink paper to distinguish our cigarettes from those that are bought."

"Yes," a gendarme added. "Any time I see a person smoking a pink cigarette I can go up to ask for a certificate showing that he is a tobacco grower and thus entitled to 'roll his own'!"

This conversation, which lasted for more than four hours, gave me an even better understanding of tobacco farming than I had gained on previous trips, as did frequent visits in the fields with the peasants who were transferring the plants from the seedbeds to the carefully prepared land or hauling barrels of water in their oxcart from a spring or well to the place where the planting was going on. What was most helpful of all, however, was the intimate story of one tobacco village, as described in the Near East Foundation study mentioned earlier. It gave me a deeper realization of the problems that the people there continue to face.[7]

Dafnon, a village of 1145 people in 1952, is northwest of the city of Xanthe. This community, like so many in Northern Greece, was settled by Greek refugees from Asia Minor and the Pontus following the departure of 127 Turkish families in 1924. By 1935, 294 families had moved in, attracted as they were by the rich vegetation, the good climate of this semi-mountainous area, and the possibility of raising a high-priced product such as tobacco. When the first official land redistribution was carried out in 1935, and a second in 1938, it became apparent that the allotments were too small for the support of a family, and so people began to leave. Today there are 255 families.

The village, covering slightly over 70 acres, sprawls over a hill. Two former Turkish mosques have been converted into Greek Orthodox churches; six grocery shops have total assets of less than $1700; three of the six coffeehouses attract the young men because each has a gramophone and a battery radio; the village school, destroyed along with many of the houses during the guerrilla war in 1948, was rebuilt in 1950. Outside the village is an athletic field on which 30 young men, members of the sports club, practice faithfully in an effort to uphold their reputation as the best football (soccer) team in the area. In the evening, the streets are dark, for Dafnon has no electricity and its people must rely upon kerosene lamps.

Of the 255 families previously mentioned, 220 own land; 32 own no land but work rented land or as farm laborers; and three are in business (baker, coffeehouse proprietor, and dressmaker). Some of these land-owners, in addition to farming, run a local business, or practice a trade such as carpentering and smithing, but their basic orientation is toward the land.

Being farmers, one might assume that they could grow some of their own food. A few manage to do this. Of the 589 acres of cultivated land belonging to the village people, 338 acres are in tobacco. This cash crop, therefore, takes up about 57 percent of all arable land. Corn accounts for 187 acres, vegetable gardens 25 acres, potatoes 20 acres, alfalfa 6 acres, and other crops 13 acres. But no matter what methods one uses in Dafnon, it is impossible to grow enough food for 1145 people on the shallow land. There are two ways out: first, grow a cash crop such as tobacco, sell it, and use the income to buy food and other necessities; the second is for a large number of families to be resettled elsewhere and thus provide suffi-cient land for those that remain. The latter suggestion is impossible, since other rural areas are also overcrowded and the opportunities in the cities are not yet equal to the demand of those making the exodus from the rural areas. Indeed, cities have been discouraging the influx of new families in search of work.

This leaves only the other possibility of getting most of the family income from tobacco alone. Here, again, the tobacco producer is caught at the mercy of the market or in the "price scissors." Without food of his own production, he has to sell his tobacco at any price offered simply in order to have bread for his children. The producer, according to this study of Dafnon, knew that tobacco prices, including the premium paid by the state, had risen over prewar prices 260 times. This was small consolation for, in reading *Vema,* an Athenian newspaper dated December 14, 1951, he also learned that costs of foodstuffs had risen 425 times, clothing 554 times, fuel 394 times, sundries 367 times, manufactured goods 467 times, and im-ported supplies 416 times.

It is difficult to grow tobacco, particularly the Oriental type (Basmas variety) that requires so much manipulation, leaf by leaf, with an average leaf being four inches long and two and one-half inches wide. The first plowing is usually done in February or March. Seedbeds are heavily man-ured, and the seed is well mixed with sand and ashes, then sown. The beds are pressed down by foot for better germination; sieved manure is scattered over them; and the beds are watered. This watering is continued, usually morning and evening, until the end of May when the plants are ready to be transplanted. Because of this need for water, the beds are always located near some accessible water supply.

The tobacco fields are usually plowed under three times before the to-bacco plants are set out. The same fields are used for tobacco year after year, since there is not sufficient land to permit crop rotation. This means that extensive use has to be made of costly chemical fertilizers, about 260 pounds to the acre. Formerly, when fewer Turkish families lived in the village, they were able to keep more animals and had plenty of animal manure which, according to old-time residents of the area, gave a 40 percent higher yield. Since then the land has become more worn out, and more reliance must be placed on chemical fertilizers.

The transplanting of the young tobacco plants from the seedbed to the regular fields is done in rows which have been marked in the field by straight lines, drawn by a hoe, about a foot apart. For each row the peasant uses a stick to make holes three inches apart, into which he puts the plants and presses the soil firmly down around the plant. He waters them immediately but is careful not to get any water on the tobacco leaves themselves. Ten days later he hoes around the plants and follows this with a second hoeing ten to fifteen days later.

Usually tobacco-leaf collectors start about July 15 and continue their work until the end of October. They are up by 2 A.M. to gather the leaves before sunrise, and gather only once in a while in the evening. There are four or five collections from each plant during the season, with each leaf picked just at its maturity. During the daytime the members of the family string these leaves into long strands which are then hung up to dry in the sun. Once dried, they are hung in dry sheds or on the rafters of the house.

In November, after the first dews fall, the village home manipulation starts and continues until the middle of March. The purpose of this manipulation is to sort out the leaves into three categories: the first category includes the best small leaves; the second includes the larger sound leaves; and the third includes all those that do not meet the previous qualifications and yet are sound. This last class is called *refouzia*. Any broken leaves are thrown away or else made into pipe tobacco. The leaves of each class are made into bales of from 55 to 70 pounds and then stored in a dry, protected place for the merchant. By the time the baling has been completed, the family must begin once more the cycle of preparing and sowing the seedbed to start the next year's crop. The tobacco farmer, whether from Macedonia, Thrace, or Central Greece, largely because of the traditional pattern of manipulation, is on a twelve-month work year somewhat like the American dairy farmer. His year contrasts markedly with that of the Peloponnesian villager whose seasonal change was described at the opening of this chapter, or with the wheat farmer of Thessaly. Furthermore, what he grows he cannot eat but must sell as best he can to buy his food.

HARVESTING OLIVES IN SOUTHERN GREECE

During my travels in Greece I have passed countless olive trees, for they hug the coasts, crowd the islands, and thrive inland where the climate is mild enough. But I never really understood the significance of the olive tree until I visited an estate in Southern Greece where three thousand trees of about seven varieties provided the only income.

I had already learned that over 12 percent of the caloric intake of the Greek people came from olives or olive oil; that Greece produced in 1948–1950 an annual average of 47,000 metric tons of table olives, chiefly in Thessaly and Central Greece; that the smaller oil olives, grown elsewhere in the country, accounted for 103,000 metric tons annually of this precious oil, which was bought and stored as a financial reserve whenever the currency became the least bit shaky. The oil olives also produced another 12,000 tons of residue oil. Friends had said that olive growing was a story of "from rags to riches," since one year might bring an outstanding crop and the next a disastrously poor one,* but that this was one of the accepted features of growing olives.

Some inquiring students think the olive was in Greece before the goddess Athena, with whom it is so closely associated in myth, and was originally associated with the cult of Erechtheus. Be that as it may, the olive — the "All-Dewy One" — has held a special place in the tradition of the Greek people. They have also come to know that olive growing is much more than storytelling or the writing of descriptive poetry; it is hard work. In Thessaly, around the Gulf of Volos, it was interesting to watch men plow underneath the trees and fertilize the soil to increase the olive crop; to see on the western coast of Greece and in the Peloponnesos how the peasants irrigated the fifteen to twenty trees that each might own, thereby adding to the quality and the size of the fruit. In Attica one could watch the men expertly trimming the tree so that it would bunch as it grew, making harvesting a simpler task. In the Ionian Islands, where the air is humid and growth more lush, the trees reached much higher, causing the people there to wait for the olives to fall after ripening rather than pick them directly from the tree. "A lazy man's way," said a mainland peasant.

Like many things of importance, the olive harvest has a slow beginning. In October, walking through the olive groves of this estate, one could see the table varieties beginning to ripen. The Kalamata olive was one. At first, the few workers on the estate gather the olives falling to the ground, but within a week's time they begin to gather some from the trees. It is then that the girls from the surrounding villages make their gay appearance. Not many are married, for this would show that their husbands were

---

* Compared to the 1959–60 figure of 156,000 tons of oil, 1960–61 showed 75,000 tons.

not supporting them. But for the unmarried this is a rare opportunity to earn some money for the family budget, or even more important, to get money for the dowry that each would-be bride must accumulate.

To follow the workers through their daily round of labor, one gets up long before sunrise and walks with them in the darkness from their village homes to the grove. Each girl carried a little bundle of food with her to last her through the day. Later repasts showed that the bundles contained a variety of foods, such as fried *marida* (small fish), cheese, bread, an onion, or brined olives. A very few had meat balls, but only once a week. A donkey brayed as it heard the people going by; the air was chilly and bracing, and birds were beginning to wake up in a nervous twitter. Once at the grove, the mild-mannered foreman assigned the girls to their tasks for the day. They put their bundles down in a place where inquisitive dogs would not molest them and set off in twos either to gather the olives that had fallen during the night or else to pick them from the tree. When they could reach no higher in "cleaning the tree," as they called it, they took long-handled rakes and "combed" the tree.

"Why do you use rakes instead of the reeds such as people in other villages use? Aren't the reeds much lighter?" The foreman explained that those who used reeds really beat down the olives, and in doing so broke many more twigs than those who used the rakes. This would endanger the next year's crop, since the new olives would grow on the sprig which extended beyond the olives formed for harvesting this year.

The girls all wore bags around their waists which they filled and left for the men to collect that day. From time to time, as the young men came to collect the sacks, they would banter good-naturedly with the girls. One could trace the path of the boys by hearing the interruption they caused in the girls' singing and the self-conscious giggles that took the place of the songs. Under many of the trees burlap cloth placed there facilitated the gathering and kept the olives which fell from getting dusty and lowering the quality of the oil.

About 9:30 the whistle from the olive mill announced that time had come for a break. During this half-hour rest period, the harvesters ate a small snack from their bundles, usually staying together in partners as they had been assigned. Apparently the foreman knew the girls very well, since he was able to assign a slow picker to work with a fast picker; he also took into account the way the girls got along with each other, but gave efficiency in picking the first consideration. After another two hours of work, between ten o'clock and noon, the hour-long lunch period began. At this time, each girl gathered with her closest friends in intimate groups to exchange gossip about family affairs, to tell about their dreams, or to express an opinion about some eligible bachelor in the village.

Lunch out of the way, the original work partners got busy again. Fast hands moved busily to fill more sacks as the afternoon wore on. At five o'clock, when it was getting chilly once more with the setting of the sun, the girls would collect their brightly colored jackets and bundles from a tree where they hung and move down toward the mill to wait for next day's instructions and, incidentally, to have a further chat with friends.

"How many sacks did you fill today?"

"Oh, Maria and I picked 70 okas," which we learned was a fair average for medium-sized olives for two pickers.

"Yes, you picked larger olives today but we had to pick the small ones. That's why we got only 40 okas."

After hearing about the work for the following day the girls formed in groups and headed back home for a well-earned rest. This daily round lasts well into January in Southern Greece, with February being the end of the harvest farther north.

When the day's harvesting is done, the focus of attention shifts to the mill. Somewhat against their will, the men who have been working in the warm air inside are asked to go out and gather the sacks the girls have left under the trees. These are tied onto pack animals and brought into the mill, each sack having been identified by the girl filling it as to whether its olives were from the tree or from the ground.

The peasants, whose womenfolk have been harvesting their own trees during the day, bring their olives to the mill, weigh them in, empty the bags into the place allotted each person, and then hang around for a chat with the mill workers and with the other peasants who show up. Here the day's news is exchanged to the accompaniment of barking dogs, the noisy impatience of donkeys and horses, and the cries of a small child perched precariously on a wooden saddle which formerly had been carrying the bags of olives. If the men in the mill have stopped for their evening meal, the peasant may have a drink with them. Eventually he will ask: "When do you think you'll get to my batch of olives?"

"About one o'clock tomorrow, for we have some real ripe olives that Panagiotes just brought in which must be pressed before they turn rancid. Hey, Panagiotes, why didn't you bring these olives two days ago? They are already beginning to turn." In reply to the foreman, now running the mill instead of directing the work of the girls, Panagiotes gives some lame excuse about having to use his donkey to do some other kind of work, but agrees to be more careful in the days ahead.

The peasant who learns that his olives will have been pressed by one o'clock on the next day will probably arrive about noon and wait; he does not consider it good etiquette for him to watch the olives go through the various stages: the grinding into pulp by the big millstone, the putting of the pulp into the goat hair or jute "folders," the pressing of these folders under 150 pounds of pressure, the pulling out of the folders and their replacement in a stack one at a time after three gallons of boiling water have been poured over each, and the final subjection of the stack to 200 pounds of pressure. If the peasant carefully watched this while his olives were being processed, it would show lack of trust in the honesty of the millowner, to whom he must give 10 percent of the oil before he takes the rest home to be stored in earthenware jars for later use or sale. When he comes for his olives, the peasant will probably bring a gallon of wine to the workmen who drink to his health, saying "Kalaphagoto" (May it be well eaten). Later, in visiting the homes of the villagers, I asked about the storage of the oil and found that the big jars were kept in the storeroom with the hay and fodder. These jars were covered with a wooden lid. When I removed the lid I noticed a rancid odor quite different from the oil I had sampled during the pressing at the mill. "This oil has spoiled," I said, in my ignorance. "No, that is just right," I was told. "We want our oil to smell like oil," which was another way of saying that a certain degree of rancidness was considered most desirable.

And seeing in the home one of the young women who had been engaged in the harvesting a few weeks before, I asked how much she had earned. Since she was a good worker, she had been given 1.5 okas (4.2 pounds) of oil per day for 42 days. When told how many dollars such an amount of pure olive oil would bring in America, her eyes opened wide and she said, "If only I had all of my oil in that many dollars I could start to build that house in Athens that I want for my dowry." The six or seven men that work through the season in the mill are even better off, for they receive 2.5 okas of oil per day as wages, and the foreman gets 3 okas; in addition, their food is usually provided by either the millowner or the peasant producers who bring their crop to be pressed.

The description of the distribution and utilization of arable land and these encounters with the peasant at work show that the peasant is not so self-subsistent as he used to be. He is more than a producer who uses only what he grows; he must also market his products to pay off his loan from the agricultural bank, which he incurred in order to get more equipment, good seed, or better livestock. He needs money for taxes, clothing, many food items, and other necessities such as kerosene and hardware. What he gets for the work he has done depends upon government credit and price policies, world markets, his adoption of efficient farm practices, and the marketing facilities set up near him.

The Changing Life of the Shepherd

A year in Greece puts one on intimate terms with sheep and goats. They are everywhere. They dart across the highway before a speeding car and raise their tails in a contemptuous gesture as they leap to safety across the ditch into a field; they form a fitting part of almost every landscape one wants to photograph; and they provide the country's chief meat supply as well as the white *feta,* or soft cheese. Their wool and hides are also important sources of income to the shepherds.

There is nothing particularly glamorous about the Balkan sheep of which those in Greece are typical. They have a narrow, long tail and wool mixed with hair. C. S. Stephanides in his article, "Sheep — Man's Best Friend in Greece," writes: "The Greek sheep has a small skeleton; narrow body; short but strong legs, well-fitted for long journeys; the ability to feed on poor roughage, to withstand hardship; and early maturity." There are eleven leading breeds, seven of these being island sheep, which give much more milk, meat, and wool than the mainland sheep.[1] This is explained by the isolation of the islands, the comparative small acreage of some, and the poverty of the farmers there which forces them to keep but a few sheep and to select out the very best. The superiority of their livestock has come about through centuries of such selection. As a matter of fact, those mainlanders undertaking scientific improvement of their flocks import the island sheep for breeding purposes.

Land

Although before the war Greece had over 8 million sheep and almost 4.5 million goats, these were still insufficient to meet local needs, and additional animals had to be imported each year. The war brought a reduction of about 2 million sheep and over a million goats, but by 1954 the numbers had risen to more than the prewar figures, and by 1957 sheep were estimated at 9.3 million and goats at 4.9 million.[2] From 1922 to 1937, with the resettlement of the 1.5 million refugees from Asia Minor, the pasture area in Greece decreased but the number of sheep rose from 6 million to well over 8 million. It takes little stretch of the imagination to see what this has meant in terms of overpasturing and in accentuating the competition for grazing land.

The chief concentrations of sheep and goats are found in Thessaly and through the western part of the country (Epirus, Roumele, and the Peloponnesos). Even in Attica, according to P. J. Iliopoulos, a region where numbers are not so dense, the small livestock make the best adaptation to the natural conditions; they provide the peasants with some income to offset farms that are too small or harvests that are insufficient; and they require less capital investment than do large cattle.[3]

There are three different systems of sheep management in Greece.[4] The first is that used by the so-called Vlachs, an interesting nomadic group to be discussed in detail later on. This group of grazers controls about 15 percent of the sheep. They are landless and rent grazing land from private landholders, the church, or the state. It is customary for them to graze their herds in the plains during the rainy winter months, while the lowland pastures are lush, and then drive their flocks into the mountains as spring and summer advance.

The second type of management is that practiced by the village ranchers, who control about 70 percent of the small animals. They own land in the plains, where they singly or cooperatively graze their flocks in the winter; they send them to the mountains in summer, as do the Vlachs. In some instances, farmers in this group will arrange with a Vlach to include their animals in his flock during the summer grazing in the mountains.

The third type is connected with settled agriculture. Village farmers control the remaining 15 percent of the sheep and goats and keep them on the plains at all times. Usually, the animals of these farmers are combined under the care of Greek shepherds, whose responsibility is to prevent the animals from damaging the crops by restricting their grazing to the rougher foothills or the fallow or idle areas in the plains.

The best way, however, to describe the changing life of the shepherd is not to talk about sheep and goats, but to look him up wherever he is and try to view the world through his eyes. We will do this by visiting him in the Peloponnesos and in Epirus, by which time facts and figures on sheep and goats should have much more meaning.

TRANSHUMANCE IN THE PELOPONNESOS

We were on our way to Tripolis, the chief interior city of the Peloponnesos. Earlier we had crossed the Corinth Canal, had stopped for gas at Corinth, and gone on to Argos, perhaps the most ancient city of Greece. Oranges were ripe on the trees in the square around the cathedral, where buses pulled up to let their through passengers have a bite to eat. Turkeys and chickens tied by the leg to the top of the bus gobbled and squawked intermittently, but long ago had ceased to struggle for freedom. Leaving Argos, we had begun the long winding climb that eventually brought us to a mountain-top view of the blue Gulf of Argos and of the small port city of Nauplion across the way beneath a fortress-topped summit. As always in Greece, the shifting light gave a magic cast to the hills whose eroded sides revealed a rainbow of color, to the brown cultivated fields below, and to the brilliant iridescent water. Such landscapes, ethereal in quality, are the paths into another world, where the legendary universe of Homer seems to have flowed into the pastoral existence of Greek shepherd families today. Suddenly, that life teemed about us.

The sheep were rounding the same curve as we were, but in the opposite direction — hundreds of them pushing and shoving and terrified at the sight of a noisy, shiny automobile. We quickly pulled to the side and parked. The shepherds whistled and called, brandishing their long crooks until they finally got the huge flock of sheep and goats past us. Having encountered and met this emergency, the shepherds were ready for a cigarette and a short chat. They were from the village of Valtetsi, a few miles beyond Tripolis, up in the mountains, and were headed with their flocks and families for Kranidi, approximately twenty-five miles below Nauplion. We learned that they were following the practice geographers call *transhumance*,[5] or the moving of the herds, as the seasons change, from a summer to a winter pasture, particularly from mountain to lowland grazing. These were not nomads in an endless round of movement on schedule from one good grassland to another. These people from Valtetsi had left their village of solid stone houses, where they spend approximately half of the year, for a definite location along a coastal plain where they were to spend the other half of the year.[6]

The shepherds to whom we talked represented five families traveling together. Each family had from one hundred to one hundred fifty sheep, its major source of sustenance and income; women and children accompanied the men and animals as a whole family. The trip from Valtetsi to Kranidi took eight days of slow travel. On this trek and at its lowland site each family managed its own affairs, with the father in charge.[7] There was no cooperative arrangement of a chief shepherd which I was to find later on in a journey to Northern Greece — simply a movement of parents and children, pots and pans, donkeys, and a few articles of clothing left them after destruction of their village by the Communist guerrillas several years earlier.

A later April day found us again in Tripolis. On the road we had once more been encountering flocks from Valtetsi, but this time they were headed up toward home. Fortunately, Stephanos Agriopoulos, our favorite waiter in the Reed Restaurant, had relatives in Valtetsi and was eager to take us there. We left the main highway at the new tuberculosis hospital, turning toward the mountains on our right. The road was barely passable, evidently the mere widening of a sheep track winding in and out but always up, along the edges of dry, bone dry, ravines. Now and then one of us had to get out to shove a rock from the road. En route Stephanos told us much about the people and the hard economic struggle they were facing. The road became less rocky as we neared the village. There were small fields, brilliant green, with trees along the edges. The trees stood tall around the school and church, the center of the village, where their spring freshness and sturdiness cast a sort of tender protection over the ruined stone houses that were Valtetsi. It was only after we let the people unburden themselves of their more immediate troubles, such as rebuilding their houses, that we could turn to a description of their customary semiannual migration with their flocks.

Valtetsi, with its one hundred eighty families, had not suffered under the German occupation as had so many other Greek villages. Completely off any reasonable facsimile of a road, it was not visited by the invaders; but for this very reason it was frequented by the Communist guerrillas in the 1940s as they struggled for control of Greece. The Communist leaders repeatedly tried to persuade the people to join their side, but the Valtetsi residents refused. In anger at this refusal and with the words, "if you are not for us, you are against us," the Communists descended upon the village one day and killed about one hundred people, mostly men. They burned most of the houses and took the women and children off with them. Each man to whom we talked had some personal tragedy to relate and could show us the name of some close relative or friend on the marble monument by the church erected in honor of these victims of the Communist guerrillas. As a constant reminder of that terrible day, the houses still stood in ruins — six years later. We went from house to house and found that through lack of lumber the second stories had not been built back, nor had there been tile available for the roofs. Many of the families were holed in, as it were, on the first floor, pretty much exposed to the elements during the six months of their sojourn "at home." Yet the people were friendly, glad to see us. Their mobile faces were alive. They smiled easily, were full of curiosity, and bubbled with wit. The state of dilapidation was even more noticeable when the village secretary and president, in order to give us a drink of ouzo "for the road," had to ferret out a bottle and a few chipped glasses from the dark basement of a roofless building which was serving as the office of the village council.

Around the Valtetsi school that morning were children curious about the strange adults, the car, and the ten-year-old American boy and the twelve-year-old English-speaking Greek boy in our party, who quickly established contact and were soon surrounded. Questions and answers about the children came naturally. When we talked to the two teachers, we began to see what migration meant to these shepherd children. The school year starts in September with everyone enrolled, but by December 1 the youngsters have all set off with their families on the seven- to ten-day tramp below. St. Demetrios' Day (October 28) is the traditional date for departure, and St. George's Day (April 23) is the date for the return. Nevertheless, school opens again on March 1. This year (1953) four pupils had been present then; a week later ten showed up; at the time of our visit business was picking up even more and before long would reach the expected 104 enrollment. Classes would continue to August 15, with only a small break before the September registration occurred.

During the winter pasturing, the children attend no school but help with the flocks as much as they can. We had often during the winter months seen these solitary shepherd children as we drove along a lowland road. As they stood motionless when our car approached, with the sheep and the goats climbing around them, their faded shapeless clothing melting into the barren hillside, they looked neither frightened nor submissive and were quick to respond to a wave or a greeting. Later on, I asked the men with whom I was talking where most of the children were born, in Valtetsi or down below. One of them replied, much to the merriment of his fellows, "They are usually born here, for it's here that the heat wave starts." One man, the proud father of nine, said that all of his had been born in Valtetsi, although each knew of occasions when a child had arrived on the roadside without the ministrations of even a midwife. We asked young and old alike in Valtetsi and elsewhere what the children thought of this semiannual change. All agreed that such a life was hard on children and that many of them dreaded the long march, but that there was no other livelihood open to their parents.

Since Valtetsi is at an altitude of 3360 feet, its hillsides are too exposed to make the pasturing of many sheep possible; in the winter months, removal to the plains below is therefore the only course of action open to the livestock owner. The families owning goats leave first, since the goats cannot stand the cold and they bear young earlier than do the sheep. Here in Valtetsi, the men pointed out, most of the pastures were communally owned and cost the people nothing; but down below each family had to contract with some peasant proprietor or commune for sufficient pasture for his flock, which now averages about 100 sheep in contrast to the 400 to 500 before the war. Rent is usually paid in milk, in an amount equaling the grain needed to seed the field pastured. If it takes normally 500 okas of seed (23.5 bushels) to put in the crop on the area rented, then the shepherd will pay 500 okas (1410 pounds, or 169 gallons) of milk. The land available has usually been in a crop the year or two before, but is allowed to lie fallow this one year and is thus free for pasturage. Only three or four Valtetsi families have been able to buy their own land down below, but they too bring their flocks back to Valtetsi in the spring.

As very little farming can be done on the steep and rocky hillsides around Valtetsi, many of its people, like those from Parthenon, go to the plains below in June to help harvest the grain. In the late fall and winter, while pasturing below, some of them help with the gathering of the olives. They are usually paid in kind for such work, an important way of eking out their annual food supply. Other income, of course, is derived from the sale of milk, cheese, wool, and an occasional live animal. Most of the shepherds are in debt to two outside "grocers" (whom they also call "outsiders" or "foreigners"), who advance the equivalent of about $33 to a shepherd against the following season's milk products and agree to the retirement of the debt at a fixed price per oka of milk or cheese. The price is said to be put so low that the grocer seldom loses, but if there is a rise in price he absorbs all of the profit, further disgruntling the shepherds indebted to him. Some of the conversation went like this:

"We had a bad winter this year. The pastures were not good because it didn't rain. We had to buy fodder to carry our flocks through and thus became heavily indebted to the grocer."

"Yes," added another, "the government shouldn't let these grocers exploit us so."

"But," we asked, "why don't you form a dairy cooperative like some other villages and market your own milk products yourselves?"

"Oh, we could never get together on anything like that," said one, and all the others shook their heads affirmatively. And they then smiled half-ashamedly and yet amused at themselves when a city Greek pointed out to them, "Why are you then blaming the government when you have just admitted that the fault lies in your own individualism and your failure to cooperate?"

As a flock passed through the village on its way to be milked after a morning in the fields, I began to ask about the bells, whose assorted sizes made a peculiar and not unpleasing harmony as the animals hurriedly moved homewards. Then the Valtetsi shepherds confirmed what I had been told before — that the selection of bells is one of the tasks the shepherd takes most seriously. He goes to one of the metalworking shops in the market town and picks out a very deep bell with a pleasing tone. This he will buy to put on his lead ram. Then he will pick another deep bell for his eldest ewe, but will always test it against the deepest bell for what seems to be harmony to his ear. As he buys the smaller bells with the higher sounds, he always compares each with the deepest bell. In a flock of about 200, he may have as many as 60 to 70 carefully tested bells. The sound of a flock grazing or in movement is always pleasing even to the casual passerby. But to the shepherd it is the sweetest music of all, for it is as though his own private orchestra were playing for him, telling him by each little sound much about the behavior of his flock. If one note is missing for very long, he becomes aware of it and investigates to see what is wrong. When all are ringing together, he feels his little universe is safe.

As I walked through the village, I tried to picture it in the cold and empty winter. Obviously, the people from Valtetsi scatter out quite widely once they get below. What kind of community can they maintain with such a migration pattern? The shepherd's answers to queries about organizational life gave a rough sketch of the Valtetsi community.

Like other villages, they have the village council. The president of the council, who happens to run a coffeehouse, must stay in the village throughout the year. He can, on occasion, get a two-week leave from the prefect in Tripolis.

"Suppose he owned livestock," I asked, "and had to take them to winter pastures below. What would he do?"

"Other members of his family would have to take care of the animals for him and he would remain here."

Local elections are postponed from winter until the return of most of the people in the spring. But for national elections the men leave the flocks with their womenfolk and older children and walk all the way back up to the village to cast their ballots.

Valtetsi also has its school board, church board, and a livestock cooperative that helps its members get some credit from the Agricultural Bank, with their flocks as collateral (it serves no marketing function). Yet the migration pattern affects even these organizations, for at the time of my visit the cooperative president had not yet returned from his winter's sojourn on the plain nor had all of the board members for the church or the school.

In spite of the periodic absence of its inhabitants, the loyalty to Valtetsi is strong. Not the least of village distinctions was the Battle of Valtetsi, in which local people claim that in 1821 the first victorious army of Greeks under Kolokotrones rose up against the Turks. Since the soldiers believed that the Virgin had aided that victory, taking part just as Hera and Athena did with their forces deployed in the Trojan War, a special church to the Virgin was built in the village in 1837. One of the most heinous crimes of the Communist guerrillas in the late 1940s, according to the people, was their willful mutilation by bullets of some of the church's prized icons of the Virgin and saints.

Even when their houses are repaired and a new school is built as a result of a gift by former Valtetsi residents now in the United States, the problems of the people will not be solved. Every year they find it more difficult to locate grazing land for their flocks on the plains below, and they cannot get back to their prewar standard of living unless they can double or treble the number of their sheep. One complained: "The different owners down below are putting in crops on the land that used to lie fallow. They ask more money if we increase the size of our flocks. Since I had trouble with the man from whom I have been renting in the past near Kranidi, this year I went to Messenia instead. I made arrangements with a farmer to bring my flock there, paid him in advance, but when I got there with my sheep he had plowed the land promised to me and had planted potatoes. He had even plowed beneath the olive trees so that there was no grass for my sheep. I could only pasture one month there, lost the money I had paid in advance, and had to come back to Valtetsi ahead of schedule to get pasture for my flock."

Other shepherds in the Peloponnesos are saying the same thing. Some, with whom we talked on the road from Kalamata to Megalopolis, were anxious to get to their home villages in the mountains. They were carrying their milk- and cheese-making equipment with them, but their women and children had gone on ahead to get the houses ready for summer occupancy. One man complained: "I haven't been able to make ends meet although I have two hundred sheep and have sold four thousand okas of milk. The pasture didn't grow because of the dry weather and I had to buy fodder for my animals."

We found some of the men working with others in partnerships termed *sebries*. One variety of sebria calls for a shepherd to look after and maintain the flock of another for three years. The losses and profits are equally shared. After the three-year time limit is up, each sebros (partner) takes by lot half of the common flock. If the cooperation comes to an end before the expected time limit, the division is made differently; that is, if it lasted for two years, the flock is divided into three parts and each partner takes one part; the third part is divided, two thirds to the man who owned the flock originally and one third to the shepherd. If it lasted one year, the owner receives five sixth and the shepherd one sixth of this third part. Another variation of the sebria was the pooling of animals by the owners into a flock which they jointly managed as a common flock and whose products they distributed in a proportion equal to the number of sheep contributed to the flock. This arrangement is made if the pasture land is too large for one man to manage. But even such cooperative arrangements do not go far toward meeting the basic economic issues faced by the shepherd today.

As we talked with these shepherds, all of them dressed shabbily in patched trousers and coats and none of them in the traditional white kilt (*foustanella*), I realized again the inexorable push of social change. Americans by the hundreds in Greece were diligently and intelligently teaching Greek farmers how to improve their agricultural methods, how to make use of fallow land without losing its fertility, and even encouraging the plains farmers to keep more sheep or cows of their own for milk production. But to the degree that these sensible, reasoned programs succeed, to that extent the shepherds of the mountain villages face what we call in impersonal terms "occupational displacement."

These were my thoughts as I reflected on the experience of my acquaintances in Valtetsi and the shepherds from other Peloponnesian villages with whom I talked at many roadside stops. As background for their hesitant but sincere discussion of their problems is the recollection of the natural setting for our conversations: the brilliant bloom of wild flowers, the blue flax blossoms, the tender new green of the mulberry trees, the leaves pushing out from the gray fig trees standing in terraces on the mountainside, and the vineyards and olive groves stretching out far below, with the shimmering indigo sea off in the distance. Close at hand the earth looked stony and inhospitable to growing things, but always at a little distance the springtime colors caught the eye and made one glad to be in Greece. Now and then I found the shepherds themselves appreciatively viewing the scene around them while keeping a careful watch over their dusty, weary sheep which still had many miles ahead before reaching the succulent summer pastures. I had a feeling that these men on the move would be the first to agree that transhumance in the Peloponnesos, though beset with many problems and facing a clouded future, still had its compensations in the serene beauty of the land through which they walked.

The "Nomads" of Epirus

I had no idea when I left the Peloponnesos and its sheep-filled roads that a month later I would be encountering the same kind of migration in Epirus, the rugged and legendary northwestern province of Greece.

There was one important difference between the shepherds whom I met in Epirus and those in the Peloponnesos. The latter, such as the people of Valtetsi, had been bona fide Greek rancher-peasants who just happened to live in mountain villages where transhumance was their basic adaptation to their environment. In Epirus the shepherds were "nomads," who from time immemorial have made their circuits through Albania, what is now Yugoslavia, southern Bulgaria, and Northern Greece.[8] They dress differently from the Greeks; their dwellings are very different; and some of them differ linguistically. Part of the lure of this Epirus trip was learning more about these people and their way of life.

I had already seen their rounded branch and reed huts, surrounded by wattled sheepfolds, put up either in some isolated, sheltered spot or at the edge of some village I was visiting. Although in Greece they do not number more than ten to twelve thousand families, they stand out picturesquely wherever they are. The men are dressed in tight-fitting black felt trousers and a black waistcoat and usually carry a black hip-length cape slung over their shoulder. They wear a round brimless lambskin cap (*kalpaki*). Many of the nomad women, in contrast to most of the Greek peasant women who now wear variations of Western dress, still keep to their heavy pleated homespun skirts, thick wool stockings, and wide leather belt.

Even such generalizations on dwelling and clothing are dangerous, for there are different nomadic groups. From many conversations with the nomads themselves as well as with others familiar with them, I was able to draw up tentative distinctions. On the basis of language, one can easily divide them into three groups. There are Koutso-Vlachs (the Lame Vlachs) who speak a Latin tongue in the home, although most of them, particularly the men, know Greek; the Arvanito-Vlachs (also called Karagouni because of the black cape they wear) who speak Albanian among themselves, although they still understand the Latin language of the Koutso-Vlachs from whom they derive; and the Sarakatsani, said not to be Vlach at all, who speak Greek as their only language. Many informants told me that the Sarakatsani were among the "purest Greeks" because they had practiced endogamy.

Another way of dividing the nomads is on the basis of type of settlement. The Karagouni and the Sarakatsani are called Skenites (literally, "tent dwellers"), for they do not usually have permanent homes either at their summer or their winter encampment. They build their reed huts anew each year or patch up those that remain usable from the previous year. The Koutso-Vlachs as well as the Greek peasants who practice transhumance (like those of Valtetsi) usually have a permanent village which they call home. In some interviews I found that the Koutso-Vlachs considered their winter home as the permanent settlement and the summer pastures the encampment; but most evidence seemed to indicate the reverse to be true.

The origin of these Koutso-Vlachs is one of the great ethnic puzzles of the Balkans, for their Latin tongue, although greatly corrupted by words from other Balkan languages, follows the four conjugations of ancient Latin. As in most riddles of this sort, nationalistic interests have led to several extravagant claims. Some of the modern Rumanians, chiefly in the old provinces of Moldavia and Wallachia, looked to the south across Bulgaria and what is now Yugoslavia to claim these Romance-language shepherds as long lost brothers to be reunited with the "homeland." They advanced these views during the last century and the early part of this century, when the struggle for independence was reverberating through Epirus, Macedonia, and other areas frequented by these nomads.

A detached assessment of the situation, and yet one without much tangible evidence to support it, would place these Wallachians as descended from Balkanites of Roman times, who were Latinized by colonists, army garrisons, or some other continued type of association. When the Slavs came pushing into the Balkans during the sixth century, the Wallachians retreated to the mountain areas and continued (or took up) sheep raising and remained relatively unmolested. Since they could not wrest an adequate living from their barren surroundings, many of the men found it necessary to migrate elsewhere for work. Some were gone many years, and some would go away for only part of the year, but almost all of them learned some trade, becoming important as builders and artisans all over the Balkans. Of even greater importance was their role as caravan owners and drivers. They raised not only sheep but many horses which they concentrated at certain points such as Thessalonike, loaded them with merchandise, and conveyed the goods through well-defined routes to Vienna or down to the Adriatic. Considerable wealth was amassed in this way. Some of their settlements two hundred years ago — for example, Moschopolis in present-day Albania — were centers of culture and wealth. With the coming of railroads, their caravans were no longer so necessary; and with the growing unrest in the Balkans during the past hundred years, free passage from one country to another was increasingly difficult. Although the various treaties following the Balkan wars and World War I provided for the free movement of these nomads from one country to another, particularly with their flocks, the borders had in effect been closed to them even before the start of World War II.

This, in a brief and general way, is the background of these Vlach nomads. In the days under the Turks, early in the century, when Bulgaria, Serbia, and Greece were claiming large chunks of Macedonia, each tried to make a case for large groupings of its own people. The Vlachs, chiefly Greek Orthodox in religion and with a knowledge of Greek as well as their own Romance language, were claimed by the Greeks as their own. Many Vlachs agreed with this, despite the appeals made by Rumanians to the contrary.

My chief contacts with the Koutso-Vlachs during 1953 were in Metsovo, one of their most celebrated villages, and along the roads of Greece. On the road between Arta and Ioannina, for example, one bold young shepherd girl named Maria, seeing women (my wife and the interpreter) in the car with me, asked for a ride. She was Koutso-Vlach and was on a nine-day trip back to the summer village in the mountains which she considered her permanent home. We passed some of her companions leading horses on which very small children were perched somewhat precariously on wooly blanket-rugs stacked up on the saddles. On one horse we saw several hens tied to a saddle and I wondered what the horse thought of being turned into a mobile poultry yard; cows, heifers, and goats were also a part of the procession under the care of the women. The women were carrying their share of the load, some with babies, others with water kegs strapped to their backs. The lowly donkeys were carrying the tent poles. As we passed the long straggling march of people and animals, we blew our horn and enjoyed the open-mouthed astonishment of the other Vlachs as they saw one of their number riding in such state.

She explained to us how they stopped before midday and rested, and then after milking the sheep traveled during the night. When we wondered whether or not the children enjoyed the six-month shift, she said, "They learn to make the move for it is a necessity." "How many times have you moved like this?" we asked. "As many times as I have years — twenty-three." She was amused at our ignorance. Her family also was having trouble over the rental of winter pasture, for the farmer from whom they had been renting wanted to put the land into crops. With an air of assurance, she added, "But we are holding it under the rent law." Before the last war legislation had been passed forbidding a farmer to put into cultivation pasture that had been rented for three consecutive years to a shepherd, unless he proved to the representative of the Ministry of Agriculture that he absolutely needed it. This action had to be taken a year in advance and the shepherd had to be notified.

After a while, our lively passenger told us that she wanted to get out at the next turn, for that was the rendezvous point at which the women would stop to unload the pack animals, set up camp, and wait for the men with the flocks to catch up with them before noon. Our conversations with other members of this group dealt more with the problems they were facing as a shepherd people than with the customs and beliefs which set them off from their fellow nomads. In Metsovo, to be described later in connection with a funeral I witnessed, we saw other aspects of Koutso-Vlach character which need not concern us here. Of the three nomadic groups they have been most fully described and documented in the literature, notably in the memorable book by Wace and Thompson, *Nomads of the Balkans* (1914), which was based on extended acquaintance with the people of Samarina, another well-known Koutso-Vlach village.[9]

Four of the effects of this migratory life which Wace and Thompson list seem to hold true for all of the nomadic groups even in 1953, and they deserve brief mention. Such a migration, for instance, presents a wider outlook on life in general in contrast to the utter stagnation normal in remote villages. At the same time, it is a serious financial drain, for two houses must be kept up; nevertheless, what is lost in cash is perhaps gained in health. A third effect is that agriculture is almost impossible and is in consequence despised. Finally, home comforts must be portable. That is why an abundance of rugs, blankets, carpets, and cushions seen in these migrations is a sign of wealth.

But what of the Sarakatsani, the Greek-speaking group? [10] Already on a recent drive between Thebes, Lamia, and Volos, cities in Boeotia and Thessaly, I had looked down from the winding mountain roads into their small winter settlements of conical reed huts and circular reed sheepfolds. As we had passed we found the men and boys with their flocks not far from the road. We stopped to pass the time of day.

"How is the pasture this year?"

"Not very good" was the cautious reply.

"Are you Koutso-Vlachs or Sarakatsani?"

"We are Sarakatsani, but we also are Greeks."

Nearer Volos we found that the Sarakatsani, who originally had their huts just on the outskirts of the village, had settled down, building permanent homes. It was a striking contrast to see the reed hut a few feet away from the square mud-brick and mud-plaster house and to know that in case the family got too large some of the members would retire to the old hut and get along very well.

It was in Kalpaki, however, a settlement beyond Ioannina toward the Albanian border, at the edge of the Iron Curtain, that we enjoyed true Sarakatsani hospitality. Actually a Greek peasant village, its members had been increased by the forty Sarakatsani families settling there since the war, primarily to take advantage of the land left untilled by people moving away from disturbed frontier conditions. These forty families really had another village, Kato-Pethini, one-and-a-half-hours walking distance farther up the mountains, where they had their stone houses — something exceptional for those supposed to be Skenites (tent dwellers). Since they were working the fields around Kalpaki, it was here they now lived all the year around, apparently content with their reed houses, most of which followed a rectangular pattern rather than the more common circular shape. The women handled most of the agricultural tasks, but the men went back to the old Kato-Pethini with the flocks and returned to Kalpaki every ten or fifteen days for a change of clothing and a bath. Konstantin, a twenty-two-year-old youth whom we found grazing his sheep around the edges of the cultivated Kalpaki fields, had come down below with his flock for that purpose.

He invited us into the hut to meet his mother and sisters. We first entered the anteroom of the simple reed structure, from which chickens flew out as we came in. There we saw the woolly puppies that would grow up to be the menacing sheep dogs so necessary for the shepherd when alone with his flock. There also was the inevitable water barrel and near the cooking hearth the *ghastra,* the dome-shaped cover that is like a dutch oven. We saw the framework of poles, supporting the walls and roof of reeds, black-ened from the smoke since there was neither chimney nor smoke hole in the roof.

The partition separating the entrance room from the main room was smoothed with clay stucco over the reeds. The total movable earthly pos-sessions of these people were either in these two small rooms or in the form of the sheep pasturing outside. We noted the mattresses on the pounded earth floor, a pile of dowry blankets in one corner, another hearth, a small kerosene lamp hanging on a post over the single bed, two windows about a foot square covered with chicken wire, a hanging shelf from which Konstan-tin's gentle twenty-year-old sister got a sweet liqueur (*mastica*), *loukoumi* (Turkish delight), and ouzo to serve to us. The flour was kept in a sack in a corner. The family living in this hut consisted of the widowed mother, two unmarried daughters, and two unmarried sons. There were three more married daughters, who were of course no longer in their parental home.

"The poorer the family, the more children you find; the richer the family, the fewer the children," said the mother. In an aside to me, Konstantin added, "For producing children is the only recreation of the poor." "But I understood," I said, "that shepherd families like to have lots of children to help with their flocks." Western influence was already making itself felt, for the mother said, "No, every child is just another mouth to feed." The look of fatigue on the faces of these people — the look of age on the pale twenty-year-old — showed that they had gone through more than their share of unrest and tribulation. Even their bodily movements, slower and listless compared to, say, the Valtetsi shepherds', reflected the strain of being in a border or frontier area where part of the enemy strategy seems to be to make the inhabitants feel so insecure that they will abandon their fields, just as the previous owners had done.

But these worn and weary frontier Sarakatsani have a saving sense of humor. When I was asking about the differences in the shapes of the huts used as dwellings and those used for animals, one of the unmarried daugh-ters who was serving us refreshments said with a smile of pure fun lighting up her pallid face, "Oh, we only use different kinds of tile to distinguish where we live and where the animals live." Everybody laughed at this ri-diculous reference to nonexistent tile roofs.

Here again I tried to learn how the Sarakatsani viewed themselves in relationship to the other nomadic groups. They assured us that they never married with the Karagouni or the Albanian-speaking Greek Vlachs. "Why not?" we asked. "Isn't the work of their women the same as yours?" "Most definitely not," affirmed the mother. "The Karagouni women don't know anything except pasturing the sheep and twisting their spindle. But we Sara-katsani women can work on the loom, work in the fields, and also if neces-sary care for the flocks."

This was the cue for us to go outside and watch one of the girls weave on a loom set in a hole about two feet deep and covered with reeds at a height enabling the girl to crawl in for protection from the sun and weather. There in her little foxhole she shuttled away merrily, eagerly and proudly displaying her technique on the narrow brightly figured belt she was weaving. The knowledge that she must get together a big dowry of woven goods before she marries keeps her constantly working. She seemed to experience a certain sense of creativity, both in the pattern she evolved and in the finished product. At least, she had a skill that in the minds of the Sarakatsani set her off from the Karagouni.

Before we left, we talked to Konstantin again. "What is it like up in Kato-Pethini?" we wondered. He told us that a few families still stayed there the year around. Often in the case of a large family the mother and children might stay below near the fields while the shepherd would take his eldest daughter up above to do his cooking and help with the sheep. Konstantin was a hired shepherd of the president of the village council up above, but he hoped some day to have a flock of his own.

This tendency of the Sarakatsani to turn to agriculture when land becomes available was evident in several places. An added incentive to settling may be the emphasis they have long placed upon education for their children. Earlier I had read accounts of large family groups of Sarakatsani of their own accord employing teachers to accompany them on their summer migrations so that the children would not be disadvantaged. When I was in the Lake Prespa area, where Greece, Albania, and Yugoslavia come together, I learned from one of the junior Greek officers there that the Sarakatsani from St. Germanos, who practice transhumance, hire a teacher with their own funds to tutor their children while the regular school is not in session. For such people any visitor who looks even a little beneath the surface of their lives must feel a sense of amazement and respect. Down to what urban Westerners would term the barest level of existence — tiny dirt-floored reed huts, incessant work, and unceasing vigilance — like our early settlers on the edge of Indian territory, they show wit, intelligence, adaptability, and the desire for education, as well as a half-humorous detachment about the difficulties of their life. Fatigue, and a wish for better things are apparent; but bitterness and complaining are not.

One of the most enlightening and entertaining sessions on shepherd life in general took place in the office of George Sakellopoulos, the agricultural director for Epirus. This was in Ioannina, the picturesque provincial capital city. When the director learned of my interest in the nomads, he called together Nicos Mitrocostas, the president of the local shepherd's union, Leander Xenos, an agricultural-extension worker, and Christos Berates, a chief shepherd whose flocks were then passing through Ioannina on their way north.

We started off by trying to identify different groupings among the nomads. Christos Berates was himself of the Karagouni (Arvanito-Vlachs), and even he found it difficult to draw the distinctions in dress between his people and the Sarakatsani and Koutso-Vlachs. The women of the Sarakatsani usually wore sandals with large pompoms attached; the Koutso-Vlach women usually wore an embroidered bolero, although the small hats they once wore have now disappeared in favor of a simple head kerchief. He recognized, of course, the linguistic differences and pointed out that the Koutso-Vlachs do not know Albanian the way his people do. When Berates spoke Greek, he did so with a liquid or French *r,* a fact which the Greeks present attributed to his Albanian linguistic background. Other Karagouni spoke Greek with the same peculiarity.

When the discussion turned to other customs, Berates indicated that the Sarakatsani (the Greek-speaking group) have their noses up in the air, thinking themselves better than the other nomads. As we have already noted, they have unwritten laws not to marry outside their group. They, like the Karagouni, will betroth their sons or daughters without the young persons having seen the proposed mate, while the Koutso-Vlachs allow the young man to see whom he is to marry quite a while before the wedding wreath is put on her head.

Conversation became animated when I asked the men to tell me what the income would be from a "fairly good-sized" flock. They assumed that such a flock numbered 700 sheep, 400 of these producing milk. Each of the 400 can be expected to give 25 okas (an oka equals one and a third quarts) of milk during the winter season and 10 okas in the summer, making a total of 14,000 okas per year. The whole fleece from each of the 700 sheep will average three fourths of an oka of wool, or 525 okas per year for the flock. In addition, about 150 male lambs will be sold for meat. Thus, the income over a year would be, with 30 drachmas equaling one dollar, 74,600 drachmas.

The animation came about when the agricultural-extension worker tried to raise some of the shepherds' estimates of income to what he considered a fair amount. They kept insisting that they received very little but finally reached agreement on the above figures. They were only too ready, however, to list with enthusiasm all of the expenses they had. In drachmas, these items included:

Winter and summer pasture	49,000
Hire of shepherds (6 for flock, each at 5,000 per year)	30,000
Food (chiefly bread for hired shepherds)	6,000
Salt (so sheep will drink more water and give more milk)	1,000
Travel expense of head shepherd	7,000
	93,000

On the credit side, one must reckon 5 to 7 okas of milk each year from the producing animals for family consumption, with some of this being worked into cheese. The family also has a supply of meat from the flock. But the greatest gain is a 15 percent annual increase in the flock that the owner can expect even if he sells the lambs listed in the table of income; this means that a year later the flock of 700 should number 805, barring serious diseases or natural disasters.

Some of the discussions revealed further interesting facts: winter pasture costs 50 drachmas per animal in winter and 20 in summer; a sheep needs more than one oka of salt each year; the chief shepherd, when he goes on business trips to arrange for the sale of his milk or lambs or to hire shepherds, travels by bus, sleeps in a hotel, eats in restaurants, and thinks of himself as a businessman; there is a small tax per oka of milk which is paid to the winter community by the "grocer," who buys the milk.

What was to have been a short conference beginning at five in the late afternoon extended to nine o'clock without a moment's let-up. There was much loud talking, which would lead a stranger to expect a fight the next minute; but then someone would make a humorous remark at which everyone would laugh. Use of pantomine, modulated voice control, appeal to the neutral listener to agree to the case one was presenting, humor, and willingness to follow an argument to its logical conclusion — all made one think of the agora of classic Athens transferred to a dimly lit, modestly furnished upstairs office of a gentle, well-informed government bureaucrat. And just at the crescendo of what seemed to be the verbal prelude to physical violence, the words "symphonia, symphonia" would ring out, thus showing that agreement had been reached. Voices and feelings would calm down for a while, before some new dramatic moment would build up again. Berates, the Karagoun, sat more quietly than the rest but seemed to enjoy the session just as much.

As we parted in the dark streets of Ioannina, where Turkish architecture with its balconies and minarets in the moonlight makes one suddenly feel very much a part of the East, Christos Berates agreed to visit us late on the next day in Konitsa and take us out to his night encampment.

In the time intervening, through the courtesy of the director of agriculture, I had an opportunity to read the classic Greek work on the nomads, published in 1925 as a bulletin of the Greek Agricultural Society under the title of *Nomadic, Permanent and Agricultural Livestock Production in Greece*.[11] It was most encouraging to find that the observations I had made corresponded as far as they went to those of the author, Demosthenes Sirakes. Needless to say, he provided many more details than I could have collected in the time at my disposal.

For one thing, he estimated the nomad livestock owners in 1925 at 13,700 families, divided as follows:

Sarakatsani	5,956
Arvanito-Vlachs (Karagouni)	786
Koutso-Vlachs	3,409
Greek peasants (like Valtetsi people)	3,549

He also gave the following distribution, by families, of the Sarakatsani, the type of people we had visited at Kalpaki:

Western Thrace	699
Macedonia	1,499
Thessaly	794
Roumele	1,112
Epirus	492
Peloponnesos	1,390
	5,986

This book also indicated that there in Epirus I was in the center of the Karagouni group, since relatively few of their 786 families were geographically much farther eastward or southward.

The next afternoon, with Christos Berates, we headed into the countryside and saw within a mile of town his camp of four tents up on the left. Since his flocks had not yet arrived, he was somewhat disturbed and asked if we could drive back toward Kalpaki to meet them. We passed at least eight other flocks whose shepherds Berates knew and with whom he talked briefly. These shepherds were very happy to accept the cigarettes we offered, but they were both awed and mystified — to Berates' delight — at seeing him riding in an American car. They kept telling him that his flocks must be quite far behind. Even when a flock came into view at some distance, Berates could tell it was not his by the sound of the bells. His anxiety grew as dusk came on and we saw no more flocks on the road. Then suddenly he asked us to stop. He said, "they are over there!" and pointed far to the left. Sure enough, we heard the faint tinkle of bells and then about two hundred yards away saw the sheep coming. His flock, taking a short cut, had left the main route. He called to the shepherd and found that everything was in good order. Reassured, Berates was ready to go back to the camp to wait for his sheep.

We had to leave the car along the main highway and scramble up the high bank before finding the path that led us up the hill. There in a row, about ten feet apart, stood the four tents of brown homespun waterproof mohair, each stretched on a frame consisting of three poles tied at the top. The first tent was that of Christos and his son and daughter. A small fire of *pournari* (the evergreen oak with hollylike leaves) was replenished with fuel cut by a small, sharp ax. In that tent alone were seven big woven duffel bags, stuffed full of household goods or clothes. The floor of the tent was covered with homemade blankets. The necessary water cask was also there. As we sat in front of the tent, we saw a scene of unusual beauty. The sun, setting in a red splash behind the Albanian mountains, was reflected in the Aoos River flowing in a small stream through its broad gravel bed; off to our right, the town of Konitsa spread like a jeweled fan up the hill. When we stood to warm ourselves at the fire, we saw a three-quarter moon rising behind the black mountain which towered just behind the tents, the moonlight on its patches of snow. The smoke of the campfire, the dogs barking, the puppies and lambs romping in the tent, the occasional neighing of the hobbled horses, made a scene that was distinct from the usual Greek evening landscape. It was incredibly different in time, too, from the atomic age, although in space only a score of miles from the Iron Curtain and twenty-eight flying hours from New York.

Berates' daughter, Vasilike, had been engaged for two years to a boy whom she had never seen but who was picked out for her by her father. As the father phrased it, "the word is given." At this point in the conversation, flustered and greatly embarrassed, Vasilike went into the neighboring tent to make some sirupy coffee. When we asked our host if his people had a dowry system, he grunted and said: "Ten years ago women took only their household equipment as a dowry; now they've started giving flocks as dowries. This accursed custom of the dowry has come up to us from the cities." Later, while we were sipping the coffee Vasilike brought, one of the shepherd boys came to play his flute for us. Because this was Saturday, the women two tents down the line had all washed their hair, with the exception of one little girl who was even then doing so in a small, shallow oven pan. The others had gotten to the stage of having their hair plaited. We could hear them at it, laughing and talking. But as the time dragged on, as darkness came down, and the sheep had not arrived, a nervousness became apparent in the camp. Everyone was marking time, waiting for the sheep.

At long last, the tension broke as we heard the flocks come nearer. They arrived at 9:30, and the available men, six in all, began the milking. A barricade of saddles, firewood, and thistles had already been made in which there was a small opening. The men seated themselves, three on a side, at the opening. The sheep were driven slowly up to the opening, and as a ewe came through one of the men would grab her by the hind leg and then proceed to milk her. Here, as elsewhere in Greece, the women never milked the sheep, nor the men the goats, although extra hands would have shortened considerably the tedious job that extended far into the night.

After the milking was well under way, Vasilike put a frying pan full of strained milk on the fire to boil. She then brought us a bowl of this warm, rich liquid to eat with bread and cheese. The bread had been purchased along the way and was paid for by cash from the milk sold en route. While we ate, we watched the milking going on nearby. There was a rhythmic pit-ter-patter as the milk was squirted into the big receptacles. Each animal was named according to some physical characteristic, corresponding to "Brownie," "Dotty," "Blackie," or after some person whom the shepherd thought the sheep resembled. As the men sat there we asked them how they milked when it rained. They told us that they simply put on their heavy waterproof capes and kept right on milking.

Some of the sheep were sheared. We learned that the shearing was done below (on the plains) and sold unwashed for "it weighs more with the oil in it." The unsheared animals were simply carrying up to the summer camp the supply of wool that the women would need to use in making their blankets and heavy garments. Some of the animals were sheared in various symmetrical patterns, a style of decoration which pleases the children, so the older people said. These fancy designs are not nearly so common now as formerly, according to Berates.

Despite the magnificent mountain setting and the fascinating activities going on in the fire-lit darkness, the conversation itself — focusing on the present problems facing nomadic peoples — stands out most vividly as I look back upon this evening. Since my central interest was social change, I welcomed the turning of the talk into such a channel.

Without any doubt, the life of the nomad is getting more difficult every year. A major problem had already been brought out in many conversations along the roads of Greece as well as with the people of Valtetsi: land on the plains below is no longer so available as it used to be. Scientific agriculture is winning the day and pastoralism is on the way out. But Berates and his men were most bitter about the difficulties they faced on the road between summer and winter pastures. We had noticed the many signs represented by a pile of stones perhaps a foot high or by tufts of straw twisted onto a branch, warning the nomad not to trespass. These signs were numerous even as one approached and entered the mountain areas. That was why the men had had to drive in one day the sheep all the way from Kalpaki to Konitsa, using routes shorter than the main road but nevertheless arriving late at night. Tired from this experience, they felt such a long march to be most unfair. One man said, "Here in the mountains a peasant will sow only one oka of seed in a field so he will have an excuse to keep us out." The field policeman, who serves a commune although under the authority of the central government, patrols his beat most vigorously during these days of migration. He not only sees that the animals keep out of the forbidden fields, but also enforces the custom that no nomad family camp in one place longer than twenty-four hours. But most field policemen are quite ready to show the nomads where they can find a camp site in the event some old one is no longer available, for these guards expect a tip — a box of cigarettes or "whatever one has the pleasure to give," as Berates put it.

These nomads apparently feel that many of the keep-off signs are put up out of spite, thus bringing to light the distrust between the peasant and the nomad. I had read a most unfavorable characterization of the Vlach, which discussed the peasant's hostility to the nomad, in *Home Life in Hellas* by Z. Duckett Ferriman. Writing in 1910, he said:

The Vlach ignores the law and defies it. His presence in the vicinity of civilization is marked by rapine. He will steal the flocks of the peasant when he can, and will pasture his own flocks on their growing crops. He is a nuisance to the neighborhood he visits, and the peasantry are heartily glad when he takes his departure in spring to share the mountain with the wild boar and the eagle. Devastation marks his progress. . . .[12]

In 1953 I gained no such picture of the nomad, nor did any of the Greek officials or peasants with whom I talked try to give the nomad such a bad reputation. Their major concern in the border area was more with the political reliability of the nomad, particularly the Karagouni. Perhaps it was some of the age-old distrust coming to the fore, but seldom did the Greek soldiers in World War II place much confidence in these wandering shepherds. Because of this, I was not surprised to learn from Berates and his men that they felt that the government was bent on destroying their way of life and forcing them into other occupations. At least three rather high officials in Northern Greece confirmed this point of view, but insisted that the policies were ultimately in the nomads' interest.

The whole problem was neatly summarized by Michael Adler, a field representative of the American Mission to Greece, who has had a long and distinguished period of service both in Epirus and Macedonia. He pointed out that what we were witnessing was an attempt to bring conditions of four hundred years ago up to date. Since under Turkish rule large areas of land were rented to these wandering shepherds, the tax collector knew where to find them as they came and went on their migrations. Upon liberation in the nineteenth century, the Greeks settled on the land and started developing their own flocks; competition became very keen and the nomads began to get the worst of it. With the coming of the flood of refugees from Asia Minor in the twenties, much land formerly used for grazing was turned into cropland. More recently the border areas, particularly those in Macedonia, which formerly supported thousands of animals, have been closed, with the result that the nomadic people are more and more being forced into a pocket toward the plain, where they are naturally not particularly welcome. Adler had found the nomadic peoples intelligent and fully aware of the situation, and he felt that most of them, particularly the young men, were seeking permanent settlement as fast as this could be arranged. In any event, the gaining of citizens' rights means for the erstwhile nomads that they can no longer be misused by those who don't want them. In other words, while their problems are growing, they are now gaining the constitutional means of handling them. They may feel oppressed economically, but they are not politically oppressed.

When I asked Berates if he wanted to settle down, he said that it was all right for the small livestock owners, but that it was impossible for a large owner like himself with eight hundred sheep. He would keep on trying to make a go of it as he had done in the past. When asked how he would feel if he did not have to move up to the mountains, his immediate reply was, "I would get sick," and all of the other men nodded their heads affirmatively. "I even have to go to the same spot, not just anywhere up the mountains. And the sheep need the change, too. They got sick during the war when they were not able to make the change."

THE DISAPPEARING TSELINGATA

One of the interesting types of cooperative organization which I hoped to find in Epirus was that of the *tselingata*. I had heard that, just as the agricultural peasants have their village community, so the shepherds in the past grouped themselves under a chief shepherd who directed their activities and also represented the whole group before the outside world. I had also been told that this form of association was found among the nomadic groups but that it was not necessarily identified solely with them.

A clear account of this primitive but practical shepherds' cooperative is contained in a helpful book by K. Koukkides entitled *The Spirit of Cooperation of Modern Greece and of Ambelakia, the First Cooperative of the World*.[13] In this arrangement each sheep and goat owner contributes his flock as capital and his labor. This union is usually governed by the eldest shepherd, who is called *architselingas* (chief shepherd), and who looks after the organization of the union, rents the pasture land, allots land to each according to the quality of land and to the different categories of animals to be grazed, specifies the work that each member will do, and makes payment for all of the necessary common expenses. In addition, he obtains credit to cover the living expenses of each member and the member's family, regulates the amount paid to each shepherd, pays taxes and any field damage done, and acts as the banker and the "grocer" of the union. At the end of each period he subtracts all these expenses from the general income or fund which has accumulated from the sale of the milk, wool, sheep, and cheese, gives back to his colleagues whatever is due each according to the flock he has brought into the union and according to the personal work he has done, such as pasturing, transporting milk to the cheese plant, milking, making cheese and other dairy products, and taking the goods to the market.

The quantity of milk is estimated according to the number of animals each shepherd has, so that if animal diseases occur in the merged flock the loss will be shared by everybody. An important part of the net profit is used for public works, especially for the operation of schools. All these accounts are regulated by the general assembly of the members of the union.

In my conversations with Berates, the visit to whom has just been described, I learned that he considered himself an architselingas. True enough, he owned most of the sheep, but he did allow the six men who worked for him to have flocks of their own, say fifty to sixty head, if they could get a start. One of his shepherds was assigned the task of keeping the records of milk production so that each one could have a share prorated on the basis of the number of animals in the common flock. Every six months Berates draws up a contract with those associated with him; he supervises the cheese production up in the highland pastures and even helps process the milk for some of the smaller owners who are not in position to set up their own plant.

Those who knew Epirus a generation or so ago tell of the great authority these chief shepherds had, each ruling in autocratic fashion his people and the area in which they were established. Should one of the shepherds associated with any of these chieftains become dissatisfied and want to move away, he found it impossible to attach himself to any other chief shepherd, for these men of position stuck together. In the days of turmoil and disorder early in this century, it was almost necessary for a small owner to be connected in some way with a leading figure who could protect him and represent him to outside authorities.[14]

The tselingata, from many accounts, were not necessarily based on kinship, though there were interesting examples of the group of relatives being so large that they formed a union by themselves. In such a case, age and generation would usually determine who had the authority and his word would carry great weight among the others.

Even today there are powerful chief shepherds. The mayor of the city of Egoumenitsa, along the Ionian Sea, was the head of the Petoules family which is run on the principles of the traditional tselingata. There are eighty members in the family and all of them obey him. In 1953 I was told that the Petoules family collectively owned from 12,000 to 14,000 sheep, in spite of the fact that on one day in 1948 the Communist guerrillas took 4,200 sheep from them. Although they owned sufficient land to graze at least 14,000 sheep, they were improving the pastures by sowing wild clover. The summer area alone added up to about 3,450 acres and the winter area was additional.

One official in describing this family said that in 1952 some of the governmental representatives in Ioannina were ordered by the central government to go to the head of the Petoules family and take some of the pasture land for the settlement of refugees who needed land. They expected trouble but were pleasantly surprised when the architselingas agreed to give the land and also went with them to select it. Two villages were constructed, but these did not hamper the family's activities at all — "Just like a flea on an elephant," as one of my informants put it.

Originally, late in the nineteenth century, when the family began to rise to prominence, there were four brothers. The second brother became the head, "because he had the most brains," it was said. Upon his death the eldest became head. When the eldest died, the third in line took over until he was killed by the Italians in 1940. Since that time the fourth brother has been chief. Now the family is said to be so numerous that it has run out of names and so has called the most recent arrival "Petoules Petoules." The chief's consent is necessary for the marriage arrangements for everyone in the family and also for all of the hired shepherds employed by it. The family still sticks solely to livestock production but is building huge refrigerators for the cheese awaiting sale and delivery.

The Petoules family is now the exception rather than the rule. For many years to come the tselingata will exist in modified form, but more and more the central government will become a substitute for the arbitrary rule of the chief shepherd.[15] Where some old patriarch still holds sway, his grandsons coming back from a tour of duty in the army will plague him with their new ideas, and many will, as many are already doing, refuse to go off on lonely vigils with their flocks. Today hired shepherds are hard to find and the army experience is mentioned over and over again as the cause of the shift to other occupations. Young men with vision, seeing that the future lies elsewhere, are planning accordingly.

STRESS AND STRAIN

The changing life of the shepherd is seen not only in the movement of his flocks from one pasture to another and in his adjustment to the solitude of days away from home; many facets of his life also are revealed in the study of his village, as our visit to Valtetsi showed. The real stress and strain between two coexistent ways of life — pastoralism and agriculture — are felt in personal community relationships even more than in the impersonal contacts between peasants and shepherds on the highway.

Greek villages, of course, run the gamut from those where every family is primarily pastoral to those where the only sheep or goats kept are the two or three around the house for a small family milk supply. In between are those with a mixed economy.[16] Two villages of this type, both of which happen to be in Roumele, illustrate the kind of conflict that springs up between farmers and livestock owners, a conflict reminiscent of our earlier American West with the hostility between the open-range cattlemen and the sodbusters who put up barbed-wire fences.

In the first village, near Mesolongi, the farmers complain that they have no security in their fields because the livestock owners have the major power and influence and they follow the old tradition of allowing the flocks to graze all over the community area as soon as the harvest is in. If the farmers leave any grain in the fields after harvesting, the sheep seem to think it part of their daily ration and tackle it with delight. The farmers have little recourse, since the sheep owners are elected as community councilmen and officers of the cooperative and are always in a position to defend their interests.

Much the same situation prevails in a village near Agrinion where over seven thousand sheep and over one thousand goats are kept. Recently, some of what was formerly pasture land has been distributed to those without land, through a cooperative association newly formed for that purpose, thus restricting the amount of grazing area. These new owners, as well as others without livestock, resent the invasion of their fields by the flocks immediately after harvest. Little control can be exercised unless shepherds so desire, for none of the parcels are fenced off and it is customary to let the animals roam at will when crops are in.

The nomarch of Serrai stated that in his area of Macedonia it was very common for the whole community to rise up in protest against the pasturing of the flocks by shepherds on land belonging to the community. The shepherds insist that they will continue to use these lands; so the villagers come to the nomarch and ask whether or not they must let those so-and-sos graze sheep on their land. The nomarch assures them that they are within their rights to keep the shepherds off, and they leave the office with a determined look, as though no number of shepherds could budge them from their resolve. When these local leaders get back home, some shepherd comes up to them and says: "My sheep will die, my family will die if you don't let me use that land." The people then change their minds and give the shepherd permission to graze his flocks there. Later on, when they see the nomarch and he asks them what happened, they say: "Poor man, we couldn't let him starve, so we let the sheep graze there." But such disputes do not always end so amicably.

Another source of conflict is the lowly goat. The parties to the conflict are not peasants arguing it out with one another, but rather the forest service trying to forbid the peasants from keeping goats. During the dictatorship of General Metaxas (1936–1941), a law was passed and enforced which forbade the peasants from keeping goats. The justification for this measure is that goats, a browsing animal, do much more damage to the forests than do sheep, a grazing animal. In the case of a pastoral village in Western Macedonia, not far from Kastoria, the prewar number of eight thousand sheep and goats shrank during the conflict because of requisition by the guerrillas, army of occupation, and such, to seven hundred and fifty. In order to rebuild livestock numbers quickly as a means of eking out a living, the people got together flocks of goats. The Agricultural Office has supported them in this, while the Forestry Office opposes the idea. The peasants argued to the foresters: "Ten communities in this area formerly made their living from goats and prospered; we know of no village which has made its living solely off forest products. We prefer the goats."

Then, as though to clinch their arguments, they pointed out that they must stable their goats for only forty days during a year, but their sheep, which cannot browse, need to be stabled and fed at home for one hundred and fifty days a year. To the peasants this is obviously an advantage; to the forestry program it is just as obviously a menace. The result: impasse.

The same question is being raised all over the country in villages as far apart as some on the Bulgarian border in Central Macedonia and others around Amphissa in Roumele. From the standpoint of these villagers the goat is the answer, but the central government seems to be backing the Forestry Office. Some commentators on the issue point out that the peasant's practice of setting fires to burn over land or accidentally starting fires through carelessness is perhaps as big an enemy to trees as the goat. It will be interesting a generation from now to see who has won out in these isolated mountainous outposts of Greece. (My bet is on the goat.)

A final contrast will reveal the complexity of small-livestock production in a country as regionally diverse as Greece. Many villages could be cited which twenty-five years ago possessed twenty thousand sheep or more. With the passing of the years, the numbers declined because of the gradual shrinkage of available pasture area. While sheep are still raised in these communities today, they are being further reduced and turned into "home flocks" fed in or near the village throughout the year. But a reverse process has also been in motion since 1950. In tobacco villages around Xanthe, in Thrace, sheep raising is being pushed by the agricultural authorities and loans are being extended by the Agricultural Bank — all to serve the double purpose of giving the depressed tobacco farmer some supplementary income and also to take advantage of unutilized pasture land in that part of the country.

This illustrates the fact that sheep (and goats) still are the best and at times the only sound economic adjustment to some of the terrain areas of Greece; almost everywhere they are good supplementary means of adjustment. There will probably be a stepped-up trend toward pasture improvement, which means that pastures — particularly those on the plains — can be made to carry more animals per acre. The day may come when the sheep will be driven in large trucks up to their summer pastures, thus avoiding the days of grazing along the roads of migration, or in many of the agricultural areas dairy cattle may replace sheep as producers of milk. But these developments are still in the future.

Symbolic of what seems to be in store for many shepherds was the quiet, middle-aged man we met in front of a coffeehouse in the refugee village of Menidi, between Agrinion and Arta in Roumele. There along the sea he seemed sadly out of place in his mountain dweller's lambskin kalpaki (brimless hat) and his shepherd's staff, sitting under a tree and looking out at the fishing boats.

"Do you have sheep?" we wanted to know, both curious and surprised to see him there.

"No."

"Then why are you wearing the kalpaki and carrying the shepherd's crook?"

"I've lost so much that I like to carry my crook just to have the illusion that I still have my sheep."

Some of the younger men in the group, separated by war from their mountains and their sheep, were full of talk and plans of farming. When we asked them if they had thought of fishing here by the sea, both young and old looked incredulous, even contemptuous. "We are shepherds," they said proudly. "We do not know the sea." Having lost the mountains, the younger men were willing to try the plain, but the older ones could not. The concept of occupational displacement took visible form in this fifty-year-old shepherd sitting idly and hopelessly under a tree, looking at the sea which he did not know and the plain which he could not understand, his big brown hands clasping the symbol of his lost world, the shepherd's crook.

·•◦❂[Part Three]❂◦•·

Family

··❧[VII]❧··

Woman's Work Is Never Done

In traveling in Greece from south to far north, one finds numerous variations in family life. Among the Greeks of Slavic descent, who more and more are being assimilated into Greek national life, a man feels a strong sense of responsibility for his brother's family. Among the Vlachs described in the last chapter there is persisting prejudice against the dowry system common in Greece. The Turks of Thrace follow Islam unhampered and continue to keep their women in relative seclusion.[1] Furthermore, the Greek refugees who left their ancestral homes in Asia Minor in the 1920s brought many family patterns new to those whose forefathers had lived in Greece itself. The women in refugee villages of Macedonia, for example, have more independence of decision than do those of nonrefugee villages, according to those government specialists trying to promote programs of child care and home economics.

There are variations, too, in the extent to which the larger kinship group participates in (or interferes with) the activities of a particular family. In general, one can say that the kin will take over the orphaned children, but the aged are supposed to be taken care of by their own children and not by their other relatives. Furthermore, a man who has a favored position which carries a handsome salary is not required to distribute portions of his salary to less fortunate kin, but he is apt to give quicker service to relatives who approach him than he would to others. A Greek who has gone to the United States will send money first to his own parents for their use or for the use of his younger brothers and sisters; then, if he has enough, he may give some to his poorer relatives — who are usually not backward about making their needs known. In some villages the rich men who give generously to their relatives are said to do so in the hope that more people will light candles for them. Kinship and matters related to it are discussed a great deal by village folk, a testimony to its interest and importance in their lives. What varies most of all throughout the country is the extent to which Western and urban ideas have penetrated to the point that individuals think primarily of their own immediate family and only secondarily — and perhaps only a little — about the larger family connection of which they are a part. Nevertheless, throughout the country, among all types of villagers, the family is still the basic unit; the father is supposedly "the head of the house"; and children "know their place."

One of the most straightforward characterizations of Greek family life I heard came not from a social worker, a home economist, or a political leader who knew the villagers well; it came from a bright but uneducated peasant girl who was asked to tell about the family life in her village in the northern Peloponnesos:

The immediate family consists of the father and mother, and the children and parents of the family heads. There are usually no other relatives living in the house.

The duties of the man: his highest duty is to provide a dowry for his daughters; send sons to school; enlarge the house; add to the fields.

The duties of the wife: to have children and look after them; to look after her husband (have him clean, feed him, be obedient to him); clean the house; do all the work and see that the boys are good workers; start weaving and embroidery for the daughters' dowry; work in the field; respect older people; see that religious ceremonies are observed in the home. The duties of the mother are severe, for the father is out all the time — during the day he works and in the evening he is in the coffeehouse.

The duties of children: to be good at school; at home obedient (although they seldom are); respect older people; work during part of leisure time, not because their work is needed but because they should get used to working.

The duties of old people: to look after the little children, take them away to give the wife some quiet; tell stories to the children; and otherwise do what they like. When sons and daughters marry, the old people expect the young folks to take over and let them rest.

This thumbnail sketch of Greek family life provides a general outline into which hundreds of colorful details can be fitted. Many of these revolve about the role of the woman in the home and her relationship with her husband and children.

Woman's work in Greece, as elsewhere, does not lend itself to neat, logical treatment. It does not have a beginning or any definable end. As a result, discussion of it moves from one topic to another with no necessary connection between them except the fact of the woman's involvement. As a wife, she is a partner to her husband; she bears and mothers the children; she prepares the food and still makes much of the clothing at home; she helps with the farm tasks; she has the responsibility for keeping the family well, or at least seeing an ailing member through an illness. To follow the women through the variety of these experiences is to move to the center of family life in rural Greece.

GETTING ALONG WITH THE LORD AND MASTER

The world of the Greek woman revolves around the man. When young, her first concern — and the concern of her family — is to find a man and, through a dowry, "buy" him. After marriage she moves unobtrusively in his orbit and keeps their children, when they begin to arrive, in their proper course. Tradition still influences the way the woman gets along with the man.

In any social relationship, including that between husband and wife, a pattern of dominance and subordination develops. The Greeks assume that the man has the higher position. One village woman, when commenting on this, said with genuine earnestness: "My husband is a superior being; I must keep my distance." This sentiment is reflected in the relative social status of men and women, as well as in legal, moral, political, and economic rights. But even in delineating the differences in status between husband and wife one must bear in mind that broad social changes are under way throughout all of Greece which are leading to a rise in woman's position.

Some indication of woman's place is given by the preference for boys over girls. In some parts of Greece, a man when asked how many children he has will reply: "Two sons and, begging your pardon, one daughter." Or he might say: "Two children, one girl." In some villages of Thrace, however, the father might use a poetic touch in answering "two sons, one guest," implying that the daughter's permanent home is that of her husband. Since, true to the patriarchal, agrarian tradition, the line is continued in the son, one of the tests of a father's manliness is his ability to procreate sons. Preference for a son is reinforced by the need to collect a dowry for a daughter, who thus represents an economic drain. Indeed, the interest in the sex of the unborn child is so great that many ways have been developed for predicting the birth of a boy or a girl. Such practices, although taken jokingly or at best semiseriously by many, do figure prominently in women's conversations.

In Aetolia a relatively simple method may be used. One need only take a piece of wood from the loom, put it in a public road, and see who passes over it. If a man does, a boy is on the way; if a woman, a girl. In Gortynia, you put an orange seed in the fire and name a pregnant woman. If the seed jumps high, it will be a boy; if low, a girl. Much is made of the size and shape of the child in the womb. If the expectant mother "has a small belly," she will have a boy. Another method is to wrap a knife in a handkerchief and put it in a chair. If a pregnant woman sits in the chair, feels the object, and identifies it as a knife, then she will bear a boy. The same will hold true if by chance she uses her right foot every time she steps into a house. Or one can take the half-moon bone from the head of a fish, throw it on the head of an expectant mother without her knowledge. If she starts looking down, she will deliver a girl; if she feels in her hair to see what hit her, she will have a boy. Thus, from his earliest days, a son is given a sense of importance, a feeling which tends to be accentuated as he grows older.

Women, by observing the formal proprieties, show their deference to men and seemingly manifest to all about them their status as inferior beings. Foreigners in Greece are deceived, however, if they mistake this *form* for the *essence* of family life, since the Greek mother is a key figure in the home, even though she stands up when her husband comes into the room or walks if there is only one donkey. Village men, when asked about this last practice, often reply, "Why, my wife would be ashamed to be seen riding if I were walking. The other women would laugh her out of the village." Younger men, whose ideas on these matters differ from those of the previous generation, proudly assert that they make their wives ride if tired. Yet the women who may be walking behind their mounted husbands do not feel inferior, for they are observing an accepted custom. According to some observers, a woman who lets her husband enter first or have the best chair feels no more inferior than would a man in the West who holds the door open for a woman or gives her his seat on a crowded subway.

It is hard to know what goes on in a woman's mind when she is at the fountain filling two five-gallon tins to carry back home and suddenly is joined by her husband who has just returned from town by bus with a small twine bag of groceries. He offers the bag to her and says that he will carry the heavy tins, but she refuses. Does she say to herself: "He has his work and I have my work"; "I don't want the other men to laugh at him carrying water, which is woman's work"; "I don't want the women laughing at me for letting my husband do my work when I'm capable of doing it"; "He probably offers to do this for me so he can ask me to do something else much more disagreeable"? Nevertheless, the upshot is that she carries the tins. To be sure, the women refuse to smile when they hear the men in the home joking about the way some husband in Northern Greece, at the end of the Communist guerrilla war, supposedly made his wife walk in front in order to protect him from any undetected land mines left over from the war.

If the wife has worries, she discusses them with other women and only occasionally with her husband. In the presence of guests she defers to him, even when questions are asked about the house, unless he suggests that she give the answers. But this does not mean that she is lacking in self-respect or forthrightness. If King Paul should make a surprise visit to her village, she would greet him in her homespun clothes without any indication of subservience; if she should attend a school reception held for a graduating class including one of her children, she would be very much at ease and would talk to those who spoke to her.

Further insight into the husband-wife relationship may be derived from the type of letter Greek village men write to their wives when they are in military service. There are, of course, many personal and even local differences: the Cretan soldier writes much more lovingly than the one from Macedonia, for instance. In the many I have seen, however, there is a single, almost universal, formula:

Dear wife, I salute you. If you ask about my health, I am fine. I hope the same goes for you. If you ask about me I am high up in the mountains somewhere in Greece. (I'm not allowed to tell where.) Longing for my home and all of you, I pray to God that soon I may be near you. [Now come all the problems of his farm.] Tell my brother John to look after the cow. Don't sell any property until I come. [If he has a couple of children, he will always express longing for the younger. If he has an unmarried sister who is engaged, he will say that he hopes, when he comes back, to arrange for her dowry. He is quite willing to surrender authority to his wife who is on the scene, which is quite the reverse of what he may do when he is at home. He will also boast in the letter about how good things are and how quickly they will lick the enemy. He may talk about his captain, if he is good, and say:] We have a fine captain and he promises to give me some leave as soon as things get easier. [He may also ask about the animals, mentioning them by name, especially the "home" animals. He will end the letter by naming all of his relatives and friends, perhaps eight or nine in number.] I kiss you, [wife's name], your husband, [his name].

To understand how the wife gets along with her "lord and master," one must also see the relationship the parents have with the children of the home. One person I spoke with who was very familiar with Greek rural life commented in the first place that the man is the nominal head of the home but that few people realize to how great an extent the woman is the administrator in the house. Although she has no acknowledged position, she is nevertheless very important. In many families she holds the purse. One of her sons earning money outside the home might give it to her to use in buying clothing or school books for the younger children. Her husband will consult with her if he is thinking of buying an ox, or if he wants to build a poultry house. He would talk over any improvements with her.

If he is thinking of buying land, he is apt to follow his own inclinations. The wife's own little private purse consists of money she gets from chickens and milk. She uses this money to meet "gaps in her budget."

Secondly, my informant pointed out, the wife is very influential with her husband when he is selecting a mate for the children. The father must give the official approval and the village looks to him, but the mother is the one who influences him. Rarely will the mother betray a naughty child to the man of the house, for she thinks the man might beat him too hard. She might refer discipline to the father if the child is fourteen or over or if he gets out of hand. In other words, children are threatened with the father. If the mother is the pillar of the house and the father considered weak, then the children protect the mother. If the mother is "no good," then everything is referred to and channeled to the father. In fact, a wife is called "no good" or "an animal" if she does not darn properly, sew all the clothes of the family, be economical with food, have meals ready when the others return from the field, or keep the house tidy.

Two home economists who had worked extensively in the villages of Northern and Central Greece reaffirmed that "the man is really the boss, not just in appearance but in practice": "When we want the girls to come to take lessons in home economics the girls say, 'My father won't let me.' But woman is the unknown heroine. Besides carrying all of the load she is also involved in major decisions. If the man tells his wife to go to the field to work and she refuses, they may quarrel, but if she has a reason he won't insist. Eggs and poultry are her responsibility and she can have her own money to get what she wants — such as shoes. In the everyday life of the children, the woman has the upper hand, but in decisions such as sending a son to the university the man will decide."

These two home economists made the further observation that the "married couple will quarrel if the man drinks too much, but the woman is inclined to keep her problems to herself and will not go home to her parents if she feels imposed upon. In general, romance in the Western sense does not exist, but there is a feeling of attachment and understanding. A good analogy is that between a senior and junior partner in some major undertaking."

One villager from Central Greece, a secretary of his local community council, summed up the status of woman by saying, "in the home the woman has the veto power."

There are several interpretations that might be placed on the seeming dominance of the man in Greek society. I could always arouse spirited discussion in any coffeehouse when I suggested that women were really the dominant force, that they had learned that their security lay in letting the men feel very important while the women went through the motions of showing respect to them. Actually, so this argument runs, women have made the men more and more dependent upon them so that a woman has to be relied upon for almost everything that occurs around the farm and in the home. Since the man is much more dependent upon the woman than she on him, the woman is actually dominant. She may refuse or accede to her husband's sexual advances. Proof of man's dependence and of woman's contentment with the status quo is shown, one might argue, in the fact that many of the village women, as much as, if not more than men, have resisted any effort to shift their present status. Most men maintained, however, that this argument, though clever, was not really true and that they had the responsibility for giving orders around the house. Some also pointed out that the new farm machinery was making the man less dependent upon the women in the fields.

Many Greeks look upon the subordinate position of women as archaic, behind the times, and ill adapted to the Western country that is the cradle of democratic traditions. A cotton merchant from Athens, who traveled all over Greece, noted that the conventions are changing and that "women are much more free nowadays and not so much put aside. Formerly they would serve the men and not be allowed to sit with them." He attributes this betterment of woman's lot "to education and to the war which has allowed contact with other nations. In the old days the woman was not allowed to work outside her home and was considered 'fast' if she did; nowadays there are thousands of women working in industry. That gives them a financial independence, which is why the women in the small towns are much better dressed than they used to be."

A further conditioning factor in the shifting status of women is the influence of the Asia Minor refugees of the 1920s, which has already been mentioned. Many of these refugees brought with them a family pattern where the wife had much more initiative and participated more fully in family decisions. This contrasts with many of the families native to Greece, where the women are more restricted and are reluctant to express an opinion if the husband is present.

The nomarch of Thessalonike emphasized the differences in the two population groups, pointing out the greater freedom of the refugee woman. He also characterized her as warmer and more sensual. He brought out the fact, reinforced by home economists from Northern Greece as well as from Attica, that the home-economics programs succeed better among the refugee villages where the woman is able to dispose of her time as she likes, without permission from her husband. He even characterized the refugee village as a gynecocracy, since those men will consult their wives before selling anything, whereas the autocratic men of the nonrefugee village might consider that beneath their dignity. Such men in Chalkidike (Macedonia) even go so far as to send their wives to make a request of the nomarch, particularly when they do not expect the nomarch to act favorably, for it does not hurt the dignity of the wife to be turned down, whereas it would make the man lose face.

Those familiar with village family life point out that wife beating is almost a thing of the past because women are learning that this is not the general rule and need not be endured. When I asked groups of young men whom I interviewed whether they thought they would ever beat their wives, one man said, "I probably will if I get drunk." Several said that they would beat her if she was not good, but they had a hard time defining what they meant by being "good." Another young man pointed out, "If my wife does not behave, I will make suggestions. If she doesn't change her ways, then I'll beat her." Beating, then, is no pastime but a last resort for keeping a wife in line. From time to time, a village woman may threaten to sue for divorce, but this is generally interpreted in the village as a desire on her part "to be fashionable" rather than as a way out of a bad bargain. Divorces are still under the jurisdiction of ecclesiastical courts and are very difficult to obtain. The growing legal rights of women as well as the social changes under way are making the woman, as well as her husband, think of herself as a human being and not as property to be owned and ordered about. This holds true in the villages as well as in the cities.

In 1952 the women were first given the right to vote in national elections, but they are rarely elected to an office and seldom make their way into governmental positions traditionally held by men. Village men generally agree that it is proper for women to have the vote but maintain that their women are not sufficiently educated to use the ballot wisely. In Attica a villager said that the women of his village were not yet "ripe" enough to be members of the local council, but then he added: "But we men just don't like the idea — that's nearer the truth." This lack of "ripeness" was interesting in view of the fact that in 1930 women won the right to vote in municipal elections if they could read and write and were over thirty years of age. In 1949 this was changed to allow any woman twenty-one years of age to vote, even if illiterate, in municipal elections.[2]

Nevertheless, any peasant woman who wants to get along with her husband had best concern herself with her household duties and assist in the farm tasks as best she can. Very much preoccupation with "women's rights" would tend to make her a spectacle in the village, thereby subjecting her husband to much teasing by the other men. If there is a public meeting, she is not supposed to attend, although she may stand with other women on the edge of the square to see the notables arrive and to watch proceedings from a distance. Americans connected with the United States Mission to Greece have adopted the tactic of trying to draw the women into more active participation in these public meetings and have been fairly successful in some of the villages where they have worked most intensively.

The patterns of deference required of women and their so-called rights reveal only some of the traits of the husband-wife relationship in rural Greece. It is equally important to see how this partnership operates day by day, season by season, year by year, for it is in the sharing of a common life, with its hardships and flashing joys, that this companionship based on mutual respect is fashioned. Great is the wife's satisfaction if her husband is considered a good provider. If he is, people say: "Tes dinei tou pouliou to gala" (He brings the bird's milk to her), or "Kai tou pouliou to gala echei" (She even has the milk of the bird). Such phrases go back to the practice of serving eggs beaten in milk to the sick, thereby showing that good care is being taken.

The wife, in addition to watching her own behavior toward her husband, is also responsible for seeing that the children are respectful. The lessons learned in the younger years tends to persist through adolescence into adulthood. Once while sitting at a meal in a Greek home I noticed the young man leave the table. Curious about his exit, I asked: "Where is Petros going?" The father, with a pleased look on his face, said: "He is going out to smoke a cigarette. He does not smoke in front of me." And wherever I went I asked young men singly or in groups whether or not they smoked in the presence of their fathers and found only a small fraction that broke this taboo. To be sure, in some villages and in some homes the young man no longer takes a trek outside if he wants a smoke, but he knows he is going against an old established custom. In one group of nineteen young men, for instance, only three said they would smoke in front of their fathers; in another group of twenty-eight, again only three said they would do so.

The son also shows respect for his father by not going to the same coffeehouse where his father is or is apt to go, but there are regional variations. In villages of the Pelion (near Volos, Thessaly) a man may take his son or even his wife to the coffeehouse, but in the words of the commandant of gendarmerie there "they may act this way near Volos but in my village in Boeotia it would be a great shame if the father and his son were in the same coffeehouse, and no woman would think of entering." As a general rule, even fewer of the young men would accompany their fathers to a coffeehouse than would smoke in their presence. In some of the smaller villages the people say that they do not have enough cafés and so the possibility of the two generations staying apart is not very great.

But on every hand there are signs that the formal etiquette governing respect is breaking down. One well-informed official near Salonica said, "The basic Greek tradition of showing respect for elders is weakening. Now you see boys teaching their fathers how to play backgammon and cards. In the United States you would think this fine but over here our system is patriarchal, and the young American starts life outside the home at an earlier age." A folklorist pointed out that in the past the reverence for Greek customs was looked on as necessary for national survival, especially under the Turks and where people were isolated. Where urban civilization has reached, the young people laugh at the old customs. In the Peloponnesos I heard that "the people are more intelligent today and are not as respectful of each other and their elders. They know the answers to questions themselves and do not have to ask." A man from near Thebes expressed the matter in a way typical of comments in many parts of Greece: "In my youth the father's opinion and word was law; nowadays a rebellious breeze is blowing among the boys. The old patriarchal atmosphere does not exist; the father still is the boss but not as much as formerly. The patriarchal idea was strong in the past because the old man had had experience and knew better than the rest how to meet emergencies. Today with education the young man can argue and reason. Nowadays, with the development of civilization, the youth has the possibility of getting knowledge." Military service with its travel outside the immediate region and the contact it affords with young men from all over the country instills a certain new independence in the sons.

Much mention has been made of sons and the young men. Daughters, too, have their problems with their parents. One man whose daughter had gone with him and the rest of the family to live in the city during the Communist guerrilla war did not want to return to her native village. She was fourteen when she had made the move.

We asked: "How will she get used to village life after being in the city for so long?"

Her father replied: "Where was she born?"

"Here, I suppose."

"Well, her roots are here and she should get used to living here again."

It was not the words so much as his tone and mien which communicated the thought that he was not going to allow his daughter to entertain any ideas that she was too good for village life.

Most daughters, however, do leave home as brides. There are beautiful customs which symbolize this separation. It is customary throughout Greece at such a time to break a pomegranate. Some say this is done so that the bride will have many children, for the seeds of the pomegranate signify fertility. Others says that it means a broken heart and expresses the sadness of parting from the childhood home. But parents, especially the mother, give much advice on how to adjust to the new home and urge the daughter to accept the new household as her own family. A particularly touching scene is the giving of the last glass of water by the mother to the daughter on departure.

The Wife and Her In-Laws

Part of getting along with one's husband is getting along with the members of his immediate family, particularly if they are living in the same household. In many cases, a newly married couple will live in the bride's home; in more cases, it will be in the husband's home. When the residence is patrilocal, a daughter-in-law is welcomed by the other women of a household since her presence means another pair of hands to help with the many daily tasks; but she may also be viewed as a potential source of conflict. But today so many young couples establish a home of their own that the in-law problem is not one of working together throughout the day but one of observing the proprieties when the couple goes to visit or receives the husband's parents. If the in-laws live in the neighborhood, the contact is more frequent and the daughter-in-law has to be on her best behavior to avoid offending the mother-in-law.

In those cases where the two women are in the same house, the mother-in-law is supposed to tell the daughter-in-law in a kindly way what is expected of her. This is of special importance if the younger woman comes from another village. Even during the brief engagement period, when the fiancée makes her visits to the young man's home, the mother-in-law will start the orientation. She shows the young woman how the bread is prepared and baked as well as how other household tasks are conducted. In Greece the relationship between the mother-in-law and daughter-in-law is said to be warmer and more cordial, involving less conflict, than that found in the neighboring Slavic countries. The young wife also must respect her father-in-law.

In reply to the question, "if there were a quarrel between a man's wife and his parents, with whom would he side?" the customary answer was that he would side with his wife. Many a husband said that he would refrain from scolding his wife in front of his mother even if he thought the wife were wrong. This generalization, though it may have some exceptions, shows that the wife is given a place of importance and not treated like a servant when she comes into the new home.

Many conversations revealed the sense of responsibility that women have toward their parents-in-law, even after their husbands die. Their remarriage is not greatly encouraged. One day at the Tripolis (Peloponnesos) market, a widow, whose husband had died seventeen years before, mentioned that she had an older son in Indiana who wanted her to come with her other son to the United States and settle with him: "I would like to go but my in-laws are too old to be left. If I went, who would look after them?" Such behavior, not at all uncommon, shows the continuing strength of family ties among the older generation.

CHILDBIRTH AND CHILD CARE

In Greece to be a mother is to be honored. Furthermore, childbirth is a joyous occasion. In the past, most children were delivered at home — it was a family affair and not a medical one, unless the birth was unusually difficult. More and more, expectant mothers are going to the provincial hospitals, but even there a family atmosphere seems to reign because family members are welcome in the patient's room. In rural Greece, as elsewhere, there are many measures which can be taken supposedly to ease the agony of childbirth. They vary from the practice in the village of Derikovo in Central Greece, where some of the women advise the one in labor to drink a glass of water into which the tail of her eldest brother's coat has been dipped, to the practice in Southern Greece of drinking water from a glass where a budding flower was placed to the accompaniment of the reading of gospel passages. When the flower has opened, the water will supposedly ease the labor pains.

The Greeks have a special word for the mother of a newborn infant — *lecho* — and give her solicitous treatment. The husband may insist that she observe the traditional eight days of staying in bed, although if there is much work to be done around the farm, she may in turn insist upon resuming various tasks as soon as she feels able. The other women of the household, or the neighbors, see to it that she observes many of the customs surrounding her activities and the care of the newborn infant. At night the child's clothes cannot be left outside, for it is believed that evil spirits will soil them. Throughout most of Greece the child's nails and hair are not cut before it is forty days old, when the clippings must be put in an envelope and preserved. In Aetolia anyone coming into the house must not go directly to see the lecho. He must sit for some time in another room and then enter her room; otherwise he brings her bad luck. Some families also insist that before a visitor enters the house, a burning charcoal be thrown on the doorstep for the newcomer to step over. In Artotina one is not supposed to enter the room of the mother in the afternoon or evening, although this taboo covers only the time after sunset in many other parts of Greece. Everywhere in rural Greece one encounters these customs surrounding the mother in the postnatal period and prohibitions which seek to forestall the visitation of any misfortune upon the infant.

In some parts of Central Greece as soon as a woman has given birth, she must "take the blessing." Someone from the house takes a jug of fresh water to the priest, who "reads" to the water, which is then taken back to the lecho. She takes the blessing (water) and washes herself, after which all the people who were present in the house at the time of the birth also take the blessing.

As long as the child remains unbaptized, it is thought to grow more quickly and is not subject to the Evil Eye because it still belongs to the bad spirits. However, as one informant stated, "The parents are afraid and want to baptize the child as quickly as possible so that they can put it on the path of God. As long as it is unbaptized, it is not allowed to wear the cross or have a little icon." [3]

In Greece today one finds an interesting mixture of traditional child-care practices and those based on Western medical knowledge. For one thing, swaddling is almost universally followed for at least three months. The peasants tell you that the baby must be swaddled if it is to grow straight, tall, and strong. This was the answer of a mother of a three-month-old infant in Leptochoria, a village near Kilkis, Macedonia. Although she had spent four years in urban Thessalonike during the guerrilla war, her ideas of child care had undergone little change. She never dreamed that there was any other way to take care of a baby than to swaddle it. She saw no need to point out the obvious advantages of being able to hang the tight little bundle under a shady limb near the field where she worked, or of being sure that the baby would not wriggle itself into a fall while the mother temporarily left the room where it was propped up.[4]

But when we talked about the field the mother said, "I took the baby with me to the field twice but each time it got sick. So the next time I go I shall leave it with a neighbor."

"Suppose you were working in the field and your husband were at home, would he take care of it?"

"Oh, he would look after it but he wouldn't change it." And then she summed up the different approaches of the two parents: "The woman will nurse the child when it cries; the man will slap it."

According to anthropologist Dorothy Lee, the child-care manuals published in Athens recommend nursing by the mother until the fourteenth month or even up to two years and deplore the use of a wet nurse; they urge against the handing of crusts or bones to the infants since fragments might lodge in the throat. Apparently, the rigid schedule of feeding which they urge is little observed in the villages, nor is the use of the crib or bassinet as substitute for the swing cradle which is in common use.

In pursuing the subject of child care, one confronts a cultural trait in Greek life — namely, an abhorrence of the naked body. One would think that the descendants of those who honored Phidias and Praxiteles would have a different conception of the body. Few, if any, Greek mothers enjoy the baby's bath as a part of the day's proceedings, for the infant's nakedness is covered as quickly as possible and no joy is taken in seeing its body in motion. This attitude of avoiding nudity persists everywhere, even in the husband-wife relationship, and contrasts strongly with the mixed bathing in the nude which one finds in many cultures or the stress upon the human form in many segments of Western society. Greeks, with whom this trait was discussed, tie it in with the Greek feeling of individualism which demands that some portions of one's personality and even the over-all view of one's body be kept to oneself — not through prudery of false modesty but because some things are never completely shared with another.

The disciplining of children in the Greek villages varies from harshness

to extreme leniency. All with whom I talked agreed that children were supposed to be obedient and respectful toward their parents, although now
and then someone would point out that the world was "going to the dogs"
because the youngsters were not as obedient as they used or ought to be. Fifteen teen-aged village boys from Northern Greece who were attending the
American Farm School in Thessalonike were asked who had punished them
when they misbehaved at home, and ten claimed that their mothers had
disciplined them. When asked up to what age the mother exercised this control, they said up until fifteen or sixteen years of age. One boy from Epirus
pointed out that he had a brother, now a teacher, who was still beaten by
his mother when she thought it necessary. The mother is in a position to
administer this punishment because the children in general feel much closer
to her than to the father. These schoolboys agreed that if they wanted something in the house, they would go directly to the mother for permission; if
they wanted something (such as a pair of shoes) which their father would
have to grant, they would go first to the mother with the request that she
intercede for them.

Children, though disciplined, are also enjoyed. A child soon learns when
he can rush into a family group and receive attention and when he is supposed to stay away because the adults are intent upon something else. But
he can stay around and listen to what is said, perhaps comprehending little,
yet not feeling shut out from the intimacy of the group.

Several people pointed out the close connection between child care and
the division of labor in the family. In some parts of Southern Greece, where
the women help only with the harvesting of the olives and grain, children
receive better care because the mother is around the house. In Central and
Northern Greece, where the mother is in the field much more of the time,
the child undergoes more hardship. However, one informant pointed out
that in the colder regions of the country the father was apt to be closer to
his children, for he would sit with his family around the fireplace in the
evening instead of going off to the coffeehouse. Even where the work of
the women differed, the approach to child discipline seemed to be about
the same, a fact which was reiterated time and again and borne out by personal observation. Furthermore, those who knew well both the so-called
refugee villages and the other villages said that the homes in each were
about the same as far as love and tenderness toward the child was concerned, even though the relative status of the woman differed. In matters
of discipline, the native villagers are perhaps a little rougher in that they
will use a stick whereas the refugee parents will be more apt to spank. When
the child approaches eight years of age, the punishment will become more
severe. Discipline is stricter with boys "since they are more disobe-
dient."

The child is often a real economic asset. In some areas, such as the tobacco-growing parts of Thrace, a child of six may be expected to help to the extent of his ability. In general, by the time he is five or six, he is asked to watch a younger brother or sister or to watch the sheep or turkeys; when not doing this, he can join children's play groups. By the age of fourteen a boy is already a competent field hand. A girl between eight and ten years of age is given little jobs, but between ten and fourteen she assumes much heavier burdens.

Yet life is not all work. Children in Greece also have their periods of play, frequently under the watchful eye of some woman in whose yard the children's play groups may be found. Some of the children, however, prefer to play away from home — along the street, around a fountain, or at the school yard — so as not to be called upon to do the chores which would be assigned if they were at hand. It is remarkable how many games can be played without toys. Much can be done with stones and little pieces of broken glass (where no marbles are available), and what dolls can be made by little girls from a few nondescript rags! Occasionally I would find two or three barefooted children damming up a stream near some pigs lying in the mud; or boys would roll iron hoops on the highway while their family worked in a field close by. So intent would the children be on their play that they would seem oblivious to approaching buses or autos.

One of the children's games played throughout much of Greece is a form of jacks. In the village of Laimos, near Lake Prespa, the children playing it called it *vroche* (rain) although elsewhere in Greece it is usually referred to as *pentovola*. Instead of using a ball, on whose bounce the jacks must be picked up and the ball caught, the girls threw a stone in the air and picked up other stones in time to catch the one that had been tossed. Pebbles figure also in the game called "forty stones." Eight stones are put in a straight line, with forty on each side of the center. At a signal all must run to a set place and return before the girl called "the gatherer" picks up all of the stones into a pile. If the gatherer wins, she sits on the pile and pretends to be a setting hen.

There are the familiar games of hide-and-seek (only the Greek children spit on the tree serving as home base rather than touch it), drop-the-handkerchief, cat-and-mouse. Many of the games require special songs which the girls especially seem to enjoy. Boys at play seem much less organized and more apt to argue over the fine points of the game.

Quite often we came upon children simply sitting still. "What are you doing?" we asked. "Oh, we are telling riddles." Not all of these we heard would have much meaning to an outsider, but some of them had almost a universal touch:

My lamb, my little curly lamb, climbs, eats, and gets fed on grass, drinks water, and dies. (A fire on the mountain.)

Around, around it's round and in the middle it is long. (A well.)

My master bought me, undressed me, cut off my head, and then as he was chopping me he felt sorry and started crying. (An onion.)

FOOD AND CLOTHING

Since fuel is so scarce throughout most of the country, fire is used for cooking only when absolutely necessary. Many families still do their cooking in the open fireplace, but many more use small sheet-metal stoves. The husband, when he has caught up on his other jobs, brings the fuel to the house by donkey from the village forest or from some mountainside where the holm-oak shrubs grow, but the wife may also help in this task from time to time.

If she can, the wife persuades her husband to build a brick and mud stove, which raises the cooking surface high enough to avoid stooping. In fact, a good indication of progress in a Greek village home is the height of the stove. Only a few kettles or pans exist where the fireplace is used for cooking, but metal casseroles are required for modern stoves with ovens. Even in those homes where cooking arrangements border on the primitive, a meal is served on clean, white tablecloths, with napkins and whatever dishes and cutlery the family can afford.

The food varies considerably by geographical region and by season. But everywhere one finds, in the words of Dorothy Lee, that "traditionally, food is not nutrition. Food is good, not good for you." [5] Therefore, when we describe the Greek diet as consisting of 2477 calories per day as compared with the United States figure of 3129, we are talking nutrition, not food. Or when we break these calories down according to their sources, as in Table 3, we are following a Western, not a Greek villager's, approach. No-

TABLE 3. SOURCES OF CALORIC INTAKE, GREECE AND UNITED STATES, 1948–49

	Percentage of calories	
Food group	Greece	United States
Cereals	61	25
Potatoes	2	3
Sugar and honey	4	15
Pulses and nuts	6	3
Vegetables and fruits	5	6
Meat, fish, and eggs	3	19
Dairy products	4	14
Oils and fats	15	15
	100	100

Source: Adapted from Leland G. Allbaugh, *Crete: A Case Study of an Underdeveloped Area* (Princeton, 1953), p. 132.

tice in particular the heavy concentration on cereals in the Greek diet in comparison with the more even distribution among other food groups in the American diet. The small proportion obtained from dairy products brings to mind a conversation with an official from Northern Greece, who noted that in a village near Kozane the cows were "about the size of goats," so small and unproductive were they. He told his secretary to arrange to have a good bull sent to the village to improve the stock and to announce to the people what he was about to do. But the women asked why.

"To give you bigger animals to work and to give you more milk."

"What will we do with the milk?"

"Drink it."

"Whoever heard of drinking cow's milk?"

There was no objection, of course, to drinking goat's or sheep's milk. This official went back to the director of agriculture for his region and said, "You hang a stone around your neck, and I'll hang one around mine. We've been here this long and haven't yet taught the people that they can drink cow's milk."

Thus food is more than a statistical table. We learn what is locally important when we hear a Greek village girl tell about the kind of food she has at home:

Throughout the year we eat bread, which is coarse, a little darker, and tastes much better than the bread in Athens. It is made of wheat flour from the grain grown by each family and milled in one of the seven watermills near the village. As a milling charge the miller will keep about one sixth. The flour is stored in a wooden box at home. When we make bread we mix the dough in a pottery bowl. At first, we may need to borrow or buy yeast from another family but then keep a little yeast for next time. We bake once a week in an outdoor oven; in the winter, if the weather is very bad, we use a little oven in the house. The outdoor oven is made of brick and is round. After we have built a fire from branches and gotten the oven very hot, we push the coals to the side and put the round loaves in between so that they will absorb the heat from the oven and the coals. We may also cook cakes or sweets in the oven.

Our people want bread all of the time when they are eating. We eat cornbread only in case of emergency. We eat potatoes more than rice, usually serving the potatoes in a stew of meat and red sauce.

We eat much [notice her definition of "much"] meat, especially pork because we feed a pig until it reaches a hundred okas; we kill it, cut it up, and put the meat in receptacles after salting it. The pig is butchered around March and its meat lasts us for about a year, if we use some of it about twice a week. We eat more chicken than lamb; we don't use beef.

We eat a bean stew about three times a week except in the summer, at which time we eat green beans. We eat many vegetables and fruits in season. We dry figs for use during the year.

The daughter-in-law does most of the cooking and is apt to favor her father-in-law's appetite. Our people don't spend much money on food, preferring to grow their own. If a person buys food at the market the others will become envious of him because he has money "to spend on food."

Meal times are as follows when we are doing field work: breakfast, 6 to 7 A.M. at which time we eat bread, cheese, olives, and sometimes eggs; at 10 A.M. there is a break for a snack; lunch is at 1 P.M. and supper about 8:30 P.M.

We drink tea every day, this being what we call "mountain tea" [*tsai tou vounou*], made from a wild flower which we gather.

Most of the oils and fats the Greeks use, come from olives rather than from animal products. Indeed, of the proteins eaten by Greeks, including the city as well as the rural Greek, only 19 percent is animal protein in comparison with 66 percent in the United States. As one study observed:

The majority of families in the villages have from 4 to 8 hens, each of which lays about 60 eggs per year. Eggs are used for feeding children up to the age of 4. Adults get few eggs except at Easter and on feast days. . . . A majority of the people have very little cheese. This is particularly serious since consumption of meat is so low.[6]

In traveling over Greece, a foreign observer is struck by a number of interesting and useful practices connected with food. The widespread use of one-dish meals, most of them vegetable stews, economizes fuel and cooking equipment and frees the women for other household and farm tasks. Bread can be dipped into the stew sauce, serving a purpose quite apart from its food value. Many families cook only one hot meal a day, starting off with a cold breakfast except in the winter when they have a warm porridge. Even though the climate during much of the year is warm, there is no home refrigeration, very little canning of vegetables or fruits, but considerable drying, brining, and pickling in order to conserve food for use when it is out of season. Eggs, however, can be stored for several months in water glass.

Various holidays have their traditional dishes, providing a festive occasion at which the Greek villager really gets enough to eat; at other times, he leaves the table hungry. A daily average of about 2500 calories per person for the whole country is no fattening diet, although more healthful than one in which individuals consistently overeat.

Regional variations in food habits throughout Greece depend upon the local products available. Where the olive is not grown, but is obtained only through purchase or barter, the peasant usually has milk products such as cheese or yoghurt. Where citrus fruit is lacking, more red peppers in the bean stews provide vitamins. Within a community there are also differences in diet based on differences in income.

Villages differ also in the day customarily set aside for baking bread in the outdoor ovens. In a village such as Malakassa in Attica the women bake on

Saturday; in other villages it may be on Thursday evening or Friday. Now and then one may come upon a group of women making use of a neighborhood oven where combined efforts mean greater economy of fuel. More and more, village bakers are relieving housewives of the baking chores, although the women must prepare the loaves and other food for the oven. Throughout rural Greece the bread is usually dark, since only about 2.5 percent of the bran is extracted.

It is hard to think of Greek food, however, without thinking of the resinated wine that is served to guests with the meal. Foreign travelers never fail to react quite strongly to the taste and properties of this unusual drink. Z. D. Ferriman in his *Home Life in Hellas* (1910) describes it as

a beverage whose odour has been compared to various things — furniture polish and melted sealing-wax among others. A high dignitary of the Church from Constantinople said of it many centuries ago, that it resembled the juice of the pine tree rather than that of the grape, an observation that is strictly true. To the novice it is extremely nauseous, and some people never acquire the taste. To the Greek it is nectar. He lauds its flavour of turpentine on account of its alleged peptic qualities.[7]

On holidays and special occasions the men, as already noted, may drink ouzo.

In addition to her preoccupation with food, although it is served simply and in limited variety, the housewife also has to spend much time preparing clothes for her family. This holds true even though the villagers throughout Greece no longer wear the highly embroidered costumes of two or three generations ago and have adopted the Western style of dress. Some villages, such as Megara near Athens, with an eye on the tourist dollar, are exceptions to this rule, for their streets become resplendent on Sundays and holidays as some of the residents stroll in traditional dress. There are, however, little touches of costume which vary from one region to another. The nomadic peoples, described earlier, can always be identified by their black garb; the Turkish men of Thrace by their baggy trousers and fezzes and their women by veils and ballooning Turkish trousers.

But the Greek peasant styles are becoming more uniform. In the northern Peloponnesos the women wear as a standard work garment a skirt and a blouse, along with heelless pigskin moccasins, pointed at the toe. In many other parts of Greece a chemise, with or without sleeves, is common. These garments and their underwear are woven and sewn at home; the "woolies" which are worn in cold weather are knitted by the women. On Sunday the women wear a "best" dress, which they may have bought in town or at least modeled on a dress someone else obtained there. Underneath is the customary slip. Regular Western shoes with heels are a part of the dress-up outfit. When the women are working outside they wear headscarfs, with the older women wearing dark brown and the girls white. Black scarfs are for mourning only.

In the Peloponnesos the men buy their trousers and coats but wear home-made underwear and shirts. They have a good suit for Sunday which, when it becomes threadbare, they wear every day. The socks are woolen and are made at home. Sandals are often worn in the fields while regular shoes are reserved for occasions when the men dress up in their best. The cap is such a favorite headgear in the Peloponnesos that if a villager sees a man with a hat he will assume that he is an outsider. The children dress like the adults, although the boys wear short trousers.

Behind the garments lie many long patient hours of painstaking work. The women make their own woolen thread but buy the cotton thread. They spin when otherwise unoccupied, for they feel that they must be busy with some handiwork except on Sunday, a day on which they do not even touch a needle or spindle. In many villages one still finds that practically every house has its own loom, stored during the summer but busy in the winter as each woman tries to supply her family's needs and as the unmarried girls work on their dowries. These looms eat up so much thread that spinning never seems to be completed.

Younger women, seeking some release from this onerous task of making so much cloth at home, use their meager funds for the purchase of store-bought goods. They even exchange with the town merchants some of the priceless costumes, which have been handed down through many years, for factory-made cloth that gives them a more fashionable feel.

In the Pelion district around Volos the only examples of popular art being produced today are the blankets and household linen which the women continue to make on their crude looms. According to Kitsos A. Makres, who has written extensively on this subject,[8] they continue this weaving because of a romantic, unconscious desire to give the same decorative color to the house that they have known all of their lives. He points out that buy-ing the industrial materials is more economical but that the aesthetic urge keeps the women's handicrafts alive.

The most detailed study of national costumes and the art of weaving and embroidering in Greece has been made by Angelike Chatzemichale.[9] She and others associated with her have tried to stimulate the increase in such handicrafts, for which there is a ready sale in Greece and abroad. She finds that the main variations in materials used are between the mainland and the islands. On the mainland the goods are handwoven from wool to stand hard wear, an exception being in Epirus where cotton and linen materials are made for household use. In the cities, such as Salonica and Volos, silk has long been popular. On the islands, however, few woolen materials are used since the preference is for cotton, silk, and felt.[10] The villages of the main-land, particularly in the mountains, have had to be much more self-sufficient and were therefore limited to the wool, which was available and which the women could work, even for underwear and sheets. Cotton, much more difficult to spin and weave, became known in the eighteenth century to the plains villages visited by outside traders, but it was considered a luxury.

In Macedonia the women use the looms chiefly for making heavy blankets and for the dowry items, but not for clothing. According to the home economists there, the families now buy underclothes, stockings, shoes, extra sheets, pillow cases, and towels. A woman will still knit undershirts for the men and pullovers for children out of the woolen thread she has spun for herself. She will buy material and make garments for children who go to school. At about sixteen years of age a girl will buy material and take it to the village seamstress to be sewn up into special garments for her dowry. But new garments are not the only problem. The woman is kept busy darning everybody's clothing, and few are the work clothes without two or more patches.

In many villages Friday is washday, demanding heavy work for which machinery is not yet a substitute. For the woolen garments the women follow the centuries-old method of beating out the dirt with sticks or paddles around the fountain or along a running stream. Most women prefer to carry the clothes to the water, often at some distance from the house. Warm water may or may not be used, depending upon the fuel supply. Women are especially interested in improvements in the water supply, and the forms these take seem to follow a set sequence. First, the women start going to a spring or a stream for the water, carrying one large jar on their heads and another in their hands or else loading casks full of water onto a donkey. Then someone, either the municipality or a prosperous Greek-American from that village, arranges to have the water piped from the spring or stream to a central fountain. To this spot, much nearer than the former one, all of the women come once or twice a day as occasion demands.[11] The third stage is that of piping the water by the municipality to different sections of the village so that there are neighborhood spigots instead of a central fountain. The fourth stage, that of piping water to individual homes, is not yet even talked about in most villages, although here and there one finds a native son returned from abroad who has enough capital to drill a well or otherwise arrange for his own private water supply. This is the exception rather than the common expectation. The villages of Greece, like those of other countries, demonstrate the close relationship between the extent of woman's toil and the presence of a convenient source of water.

FARM TASKS

The yard of a Greek village home is never a spic and span showplace; it looks lived in twenty-four hours a day. The geraniums in flower pots on the window sill and the basil growing next to it give a touch of color. Before

Easter the wife whitewashes the house, the wall around the yard, and the oven, even pressing her husband into service should this be necessary. She strings tobacco leaves in late summer; she also strings peppers and onions to hang under the eastern eaves or on the door post. After the shearing is done in the spring, she is anxious to get the wool washed and hung up to dry in festoons around the yard; she dries beans on a blanket out in the yard or, if she lives in Southern Greece or the islands, uses the cement cover of the cistern for the beans as well as for drying figs and almonds.

The so-called home or house animals — one or two sheep or goats, which are often petted, and the donkey — are under her supervision much of the time, although the man on his way to the fields may take the smaller animals with him and stake them out to graze. The women also have full responsibility for poultry except around Attica, where commercialized poultry raising also absorbs the attention of the men. Caring for the swine and a family cow, should there be one, is a woman's job. But the men will assume responsibility for a herd of cows, a flock of sheep, the oxen, or any horses. When new homes are built, special stables for these animals are provided in the yard. The women are busy, as would be rural women anywhere, when a pig is slaughtered. As a matter of fact, every member of the family usually participates in some stage of the proceedings, looking upon it as a gala occasion, more fun than work.

Although gardening is looked upon as woman's work, the man usually prepares the soil and leaves the planting and cultivation up to the woman. Nor is he apt to help when his daughter goes out with a neighbor woman to gather acorns for the pigs, even though it means that one of the women has to spend most of the afternoon up in the trees shaking down the acorns to the woman below.

Woman's participation in field work is gradually changing throughout much of Greece. In Polygyros, the chief city in the Chalkidike Peninsula, the men proudly point out — as they do in Crete — that women do not work in the fields. More and more the men are taking over the field work and the cutting of wood, in which they formerly expected the women to help. One still will see many women out in the fields chopping cotton or planting rice, with a man — apparently directing them — sitting down in the shade. As the Bishop of Messenia pointed out, many of the women working in the field are widows, or their husbands are away at work, at the market, or perhaps sick. He thought that the Greek women working their own land were better off than American women employed in factories, although the Bishop did not know that one third of the Greek labor force insured under sickness and pension plans (which means paid employees covered by government regulation) was made up of women.[12] At harvest time, too, the women wield their sickles day in and day out in areas where the mechanical harvesters have not reached. They also help in the gathering of olives, grapes, and many other products requiring patient labor.

The woman is increasingly being viewed today as a supplementary source of labor in the fields, to be employed only when the need is urgent, although regional variations are still important. When she does go to the field, she may take the baby and the small children along and care for them as she works. Various explanations are offered for this lightening of field labor by women. Today, more of the village women have seen how the city women live and have resolved to put city ways into practice in their homes and villages. Furthermore, men seem to be showing more interest in their farms due to the help the government is giving in providing fruit trees, opening up of farm-to-market roads, and helping the peasant participate more actively in the national economy. Agricultural and home-economics extension workers, who now visit the majority of villages, not only tell the men that it is their job to do the field work, but they also show the men better methods for reducing the work load. Where tractors exist, the woman is relieved of much field work and can occupy herself with other tasks. She works more on her loom, takes care of her children, and cleans her house. She also has more time for gardening on a plot fairly close to the house. One recognizes the need for this in a place such as Ioannina (Epirus) where peasants in the outlying villages, with plenty of land near their house, buy at the city market vegetables which they could have grown at home if the women had had sufficient time.

KEEPING THE FAMILY WELL

Work, however, is not the only responsibility of a Greek housewife. Any ailing person becomes the immediate concern of the mother or the mother-in-law, with the older woman usually considered wiser in the mysteries of folk medicine. The patient also becomes the concern of the neighbors for, as one man put it, "when somebody gets sick, everybody goes to visit him and to look after him." For quite understandable reasons, the living standards of rural Greece are far below those found in Athens or in most countries of the West. Consequently, health practices, many of them surrounded with superstitions, are the outgrowth of the experience of people who for centuries have faced pain, illness, and death without the benefits of the accumulated medical discoveries of the modern world.

Indeed, for much illness the peasant has a supernatural rather than a scientific explanation. As one writer has put it:

The whole of popular medicine is based upon the knowledge of charms and incantations. Many simples and drugs are of course known and employed; but it is still generally believed, as it was in the old time, that "there would be no good in the herb without the incantation." For the most ordinary diseases are

credited to supernatural causes, and there is no ill to which flesh is heir, —
from a headache to the plague, — without some demon responsible for it. A
nightmare and the sense of physical oppression which often accompanies it are
not traced to so vulgar a cause as a heavy supper, but are dignified as the work
of a malicious being named *Vrachnas,* who in the dead of night delights to
seat himself on the chest of some sleeper, and by his weight produces an unpleasant feeling of congestion. . . .[13]

For cures, then, one turns not only to the doctor but at times to the priest,
who will come and read from "the holy books," or even more frequently to
the village wise women, who understand what herbs to use and the particular charms appropriate to every occasion. These wise women usually keep
their activities secret from the priest. Many remedies which seem fantastic,
such as curing boils by putting pus from them on a piece of bread and giving
it to a dog to eat, make sense to the peasant. One symbolically and supernat-
urally transfers the illness from the patient to some other host, susceptible
or immune as the case may be.

A mother will pass on her knowledge of folk medicine to her daughters,
although they will often seek the help of some wise woman particularly
skilled in caring for the sick. In order to learn more about the ordinary
folk remedies, we compared a list drawn up by D. Loukopoulos for Aetolia,
a district in Central Greece, with those cures believed in by Chrysoula, a
wise woman on the island of Spetsai, just off the Peloponnesos.[14] As was
expected, the prescriptions did not tally on all points, but their general purpose and approach were much the same.

To cure malaria:
Wash a cup out, give patient holy water on an empty stomach without letting
the patient know what he is drinking. After he drinks this once or twice at
dawn he'll feel much better. (Aetolia)

To cure stomach ache:
Boil powdered acorn caps in one hundred drams of water, add clove and
four pieces or *rigane* (wild origan). When it has been boiled down to size of
an ouzo (brandy) cup, strain it and add some rum. When the sick man drinks
it, all pains will ease. (Aetolia)
Boil the stem of the poppy plant and give the brew to patient to drink.
(Spetsai)

To cure insanity:
Insanity cannot be cured with medicines. The priest reads to the insane person out of the Four Gospels, then may take him to a monastery. If he does not
get better, he is tied (often chained) to the ring in the tiling of the church
floor. (Aetolia)
The priest exorcises the demon by using the ritual of St. Basil the Great, or
some sacred relic may be taken to the insane person in the hope of driving
away the demon. The patient is not taken to the monastery. (Spetsai)

To cure terrific abdominal pains, or "twisting the navel":

The constant pains and vomiting are said to be due to the untwisting of the navel. If the patient is to recover, his navel must be retwisted. Only a few people know how to do this. The one effecting the cure presses the navel with the index finger of his right hand, holds it firmly and starts walking around the patient. As he turns around he halts — at the head, at the feet, and at each side. He goes around like this seven or eight times and the patient recovers. (Aetolia and Arcadia)

Only special women can do this. The one who helps puts a rag around her finger, twists the navel several times until she feels it catch. Then she withdraws her finger and puts a compress on the navel. This compress is composed of blue paper into which some incense melted in *mastica* has been placed. (Spetsai)

Even though some of these practices are restricted to particular regions of Greece, and are carried out by only a few people in a given village, they do constitute a folk approach to healing. But there is one important belief, general throughout Greece, which is associated with illness: the Evil Eye. In one family, in a village near the town of Thebes, some of the members wore amulets which the priest had blessed and into which communion bread had been sewed. Elsewhere in Greece I saw amulets containing splinters of holy wood or earth from Jerusalem, worn around the neck. The women in explaining the Evil Eye said that one cannot always tell who casts the Evil Eye, but that there are some people in the village suspected of doing this and that they are to be avoided or else watched carefully.

If a child is believed to be under the spell (that is, shivers and does not feel well), the person suspected can be brought before the child and asked to spit three times to get rid of the curse, or the child can be taken to the priest who reads a blessing. Perhaps the cure thought most efficacious is a secret formula which an older woman passes on to a younger one with the instructions that it is never to be improperly revealed. Not all village women know the formula but only those who have been particularly selected by the wise women, or an older relative, for this purpose. In this village home, the women after much whispered discussion, decided details of the formula would do no harm since we were outsiders and would be leaving soon. Here are the basic elements:

> Christ and the Virgin Mary
> Passed through a crossroad;
> They spread their golden apron
> And ate. Crumbs fell on the apron.
> They took those crumbs
> And tossed them into the sea.
> The sea waters were stirred up
> And man was cured.

But again we asked, "How can you be sure that the Evil Eye is the cause of the trouble?" "One can be sure," we were told, "if you take a pan of cold water to a high place, break an egg into it, and notice whether the egg cakes or not. If it does, the child has the Evil Eye but will get well. Or one can drop the coals from the wood of a thorn tree into the pan and, if the coals turn over, one knows that the evil will turn over and the boy will get well. We then sprinkle the water from this pan onto the child." This is one time when the incantation is surely used.

Chrysoula, a wise woman of Spetsai, gave me further information about the Evil Eye that was similar in essentials but differed in details. She said that when her young granddaughter comes back from a walk and is restless and nervous, it is clear that an Evil Eye has been cast, in which case one must test to be sure. To do this, Chrysoula takes the *kanteli* (little oil lamp) from the household shrine and gets a glass of water. She picks up the child, makes the sign of the cross over her three times and then crosses the water three times. After that she dips her fingers into the kanteli and lets one, two, or three drops of oil fall into the glass of water. If the oil spreads or mixes with the water, the child has the Evil Eye; if the drops remain as oil drops and do not mix, then the child is not suffering from the spell. Should it be the Evil Eye, one crosses the child with the water on the lips or forehead and whispers words from the gospel or gives special prayers. But unlike our informants in the village near Thebes, Chrysoula refused to tell us the text of the special prayer because she said she would lose her power; she did say, however, that if she were away from her village she could repeat it. Yet she was ready to fill in many other details.

To find out who cast the Evil Eye in a particular case, according to Chrysoula, one gives cloves to three suspected persons with the request that each in turn toss them into the fire. The one whose cloves pop is the one who cast the Evil Eye. There is another way: one can drop three pieces of charcoal into a glass of water, and if any piece floats then the person represented by that piece of charcoal, whether present or not, is said to have cast the Evil Eye. The same procedure was commonly used in Aetolia.

There are also other ways of knowing. People whose eyebrows meet together or those with green eyes can cast an Evil Eye. Even a mother, if she does not take proper precautions, can cast the spell on her own child. Chrysoula told about a relation of hers who looked at her sleeping baby and said, "my, what a nice baby you are!" and failed to spit on it as a guard against the Evil Eye. Four hours later the child spit up some froth and died. A person who learns that he has cast the Evil Eye, and this is often done quite unintentionally, can undo the spell by spitting three times on the neck of the person suffering if he spits without the sick person's knowledge.

The children of the home, whether supposed victims or not, cannot help feeling the mystery and fear that surrounds the whole discussion of the cause and cure of an illness attributed to the Evil Eye. As they grow older, they understand why the parent of a child or the owner of an animal will say in reply to any words of admiration: *Phtyse* (Spit) or *Phtys' to* (Spit it), at which you must pretend to spit.

It is into such an atmosphere of half-truth, and even harmful customs, that those interested in scientific medicine must practice their profession. They quickly find that patients are often brought to them after the priest and the wise women have done their best and failed. They also know that merely giving a prescription is no guarantee that it will be followed as directed, but may even be blended with folk medicine that makes it ineffective. In Greece today there is one physician for every thousand people, a proportion usually considered adequate in the United States. The difficulty comes with their maldistribution, for over 50 percent of all doctors are concentrated in the Athens-Piraeus area. Consequently, many villagers have to travel long distances to obtain medical treatment, but the improved roads are making such trips less time-consuming.[15]

Once in a while some member of the family has to be hospitalized. An American, thinking only in terms of scientific sanitation concepts, is often amazed at what he observes if he chances into a small Greek provincial private hospital, one of which has been well described by Dr. Ernestine Friedl:

One knocks on a door and enters a small room about twelve feet square. There are three ordinary iron bedsteads along three of the walls of the room. On each of the beds, fitted with her own bed linens in the typically varied colors of the Greek village, lies a woman patient. Two are older women wearing their brown kerchiefs and dressed in their own pink flannel nightgowns. The third is a young woman without a kerchief, lying on the bed fully dressed. It is not possible to move beyond the door because the entire center floor space is covered with a blanket, around the edges of which five relatives of one of the patients are sitting, just finishing a meal which they have been eating picnic-style. The remnants of bread, wine, and cheese are quickly gathered up as the relatives make way for the new visitors and apologize for taking up so much space. The husband of the young woman is warming some macaroni over a small kerosene burner on a tiny table near her bed. When the food is warm enough he serves it to his wife. The daughter and the husband of the third patient are standing near her bed watching the goings-on. The daughter coughs violently. It is midwinter and she has a cold aggravated by sleeping on a pallet on the floor of her mother's hospital room. A nurse comes in to leave an ice-bag. The daughter helps her mother to adjust it.[16]

Before one condemns too quickly such medical practices, it is well to try to understand some of the cultural factors which explain them. These have been pointed out by Dr. Friedl. The bedclothes from home give the patient a chance not only to show a part of her dowry but they, being familiar, lessen the unfamiliarity of the hospital. Human companionship is considered an absolute good. To be left alone by one's family, especially when one is sick, is dreaded.

The family has especially important social and psychological functions in Greece. Therefore, the presence day and night of family members in the hospital fulfills the latent function of emotional support. Such support is essential for Greek patients, because they feel useless and unwanted whenever an illness prevents them from fulfilling their customary roles in the household. When the family members can also care for a patient in the hospitals much as they can at home (e.g., bring and cook food for him and, if necessary, even feed him) his sense of isolation and strangeness is further lessened.[17]

Then, too, the presence of relatives overcomes any doubt the patient may have about the doctor, for they can keep a check on him and discuss in constant family conferences the kind of treatment he is giving.

These are only some of the cultural influences surrounding hospital care. They have their advantages and their disadvantages, as Dr. Friedl points out, but they do show the pervasiveness of the family system and the fact that woman's role in medical care, even when a relative is in the hospital, is indispensable.

Women in rural Greece today are conscious of their hard lot; they long for an easier physical existence, for their contacts with the cities have been frequent enough to show them the advantages of the conveniences there. At the same time, they are not discontented in their social relations. They observe that a man honors his mother and is solicitous over his sister's welfare; in the beginning, however, he behaves differently toward his young wife who is less experienced in the world than he and whom he must command if he is to retain the respect of his fellow villagers. Later on, his wife — though still observing the proprieties of deference and obedience — becomes almost his equal in many matters most essential to her. He consults her about the children or about any important shift in agricultural activity, although reserving for himself the final decision.

Rural Greeks would probably not see the intended humor in the sign once posted in an Alabama restaurant — "Keep your wife for a pet, and eat with us" — since the Greek peasant wife still maintains an indispensable economic role in addition to that of sexual companion and the bearer of children. Her chief security in a male-oriented society is her very indispensability, and the more dependent her husband is upon her, the greater her sense of satisfaction. To be merely a pet, even though this carried with it a lightening of physical toil, would threaten the very foundations of her existence. In the Greek cities also, both the sophisticated and unsophisticated men and women agree that a woman's place in life is to cater to the man's desires, to build up his ego, to be "a good wife." As long as there is mutual agreement in this regard, marriages remain stable. Instability begins when there is disagreement over what the roles of husbands and wives should really be.

Courtship and Marriage

A young woman, who had grown up in the traditionally sheltered way in a Greek village, after spending several months in an American university, made these comments:

> The father here in America is like a brother instead of a father.
> I like the way the American mother reasons with the children and doesn't order them around.
> In Greece you never tell anybody about your boy friend — not even your parents. Over here people talk about private matters. If you should do so in Greece, your parents would throw you out of the house.
> In Greece we marry for love; in America you love without marrying.

One may question the last statement as far as the Greek villager's marrying for love is concerned; but there is no question about the Greeks' stress upon keeping the boys and girls apart until they are married. The honor, or chastity, of the bride is a value of great importance, and any breach of the sex mores may have dire social consequences. To be sure, there are violations of this taboo and in many areas a gradual erosion of the rigid enforcement, but in rural Greece one can count upon parents and brothers actively to try to safeguard a young woman's honor. This is even institutionalized in what is called *e time tou adelphou* (the honor of the brother), for the brother is supposed either to avenge any violator of his sister's honor or, if she is to blame, to punish her. Whereas formerly he was supposed to act swiftly, today he tries to get the man to marry his sister; if the man does not, then the brother, "if he wants to rinse the honor of the family," beats or kills the man. He may kill his sister if she is thought responsible. Nowadays matters seldom come to such an extreme point, but the tradition of protection is still very strong. The folksongs reinforce it, as shown by these summaries of two from the island of Euboea.[1]

The Betrayal

A bad young girl dressed herself in European clothes, got her lover and went to the coffeehouse. She ordered the proprietor to bring coffee and the hubble-bubble (narghile, or pipe whose smoke passes through water). Two friends of her brother betrayed her. They said to the brother: "Why do you sit there, Vangeles, and do not go to the coffeehouse to see your sister who 'drinks' the hubble-bubble?"

Vangeles got up and went to the coffeehouse and found the bad sister who was "drinking" the narghile. "Get up, Eurydice, to see your shame. You, who have put me and all our family to shame."

He thrust his knife in her twice in the right side, striking the liver and half of the heart. Two words the poor thing was able to say before she dropped and was dead: "The friends of my brother were my death because I had the courage to have a boy friend." The friends of the brother took her up, carried her home, and handed her over to her mother.

Soussa

Soussa, the willowy, the pride of Kyme, loved Saribeys, the handsomest boy of the village. He loved her and she loved him for fifteen years. She had a brother who was away with the consuls; every morning she would sit on her bed, take her little handkerchief and fill it with tears. Her master [lover] asks her, "What is wrong with our Soussaki? Why does she sit and cry?" and her mother tells her, "Hush, my Soussa, don't cry and don't torment yourself. For your sake your brother is roaming in foreign countries."

At night, at midnight, they heard bang after bang on the door. Her mother shouted to her and her master told her, "Get up, my Soussa, open and see who is outside." Soussa got up, opened, and saw her brother. Immediately she thought and she became faint [her eyesight became shorter]. Her brother said, "You turned the house into a brothel. I cannot stand it." He pulled his little knife out of the golden sheath, thrust it in her heart like a worthy *pallekari* [handsome young man, brave fighter for freedom].

"Soussa, mine, who killed you? May he be cursed. May he wear my curse forever as an amulet."

There are conflicting stories about what actually occurs in villages throughout Greece. From the Peloponnesos I received the reply: "In our village there is very strict control between unmarried boys and girls. Not

even 'good morning' is exchanged." From near Arta: "In this village there
are no premarital relations among the young people, and very few cases of
illicit relations even among the adults." From a Macedonian village: "There
are illicit relations among the young people but they are kept secret." There
are cases of young people living together after engagement, for three stated
reasons: (1) to save the cost of wedding at the present time; (2) to wait
until the girl has her dowry completed; and (3) to avoid the boy's entry
into the army. As long as he remains single, he can be exempted on the
grounds of being the financial support of his family, but if he married he
would not be exempt, unless he is the son of a widow. In a village near
Grammos Mountain any illegal relations are legalized by force, whereas
in a village near Serrai the young people are said to lead very restricted lives
and to engage in no premarital relations. At the same time, a double standard does exist, with the men not feeling bound to the restricted code imposed upon the women.[2]

The age of marriage has some connection with the emphasis upon the
girl's chastity. One informant half-seriously said the girls are married off
between twelve and eighteen years of age before they have gotten "into
trouble." Over fifty years ago, William Miller reported that the church did
not permit men to marry before the age of fourteen or women before that
of twelve. Ordinarily, a peasant father would begin to look for a husband
for his daughter when she was fifteen, although in some parts of the country eighteen or nineteen was considered the usual age.[3] But in Greece today
the age at which girls marry has risen, probably due to the difficulty many
face in acquiring a dowry. National statistics for 1957 show that 13 percent
of brides marry before 20, 41 percent between 20–24, and 30 percent
between 25–29. This means that 84 percent of all brides marry before 30
years of age. For the grooms, the marriage-age is somewhat higher: 2.5
percent before 20; 17.5 percent, 20–24 years; 39 percent, 25–29; 21 percent, 30–34. These figures account for 80 percent of all grooms. Further
detailed information about the rural population comes from ten village
studies as shown in Table 4.

In the villages of Attica, such as Malakassa or Pentele, the girls marry
at eighteen or over and the boys at about twenty-five after they have completed their military service — a practice which Table 4 shows to be quite
general throughout Greece.[4]

SELECTING A MATE

In such a society as rural Greece, how do the boys and girls become
acquainted? One method, common but by no means universal, is the
"bride's walk," as people often refer to the Sunday afternoon promenade.[5]
Boys stroll together and eye the girls who pass them in groups of three or
four. Even in those villages where there is no such promenade, the young

TABLE 4. AGE OF MARRIAGE IN TEN GREEK VILLAGES
(about 1951)

Village location	Age for men	Age for women
Near Veroia	From 18 and over; median age, 22.	From 17 and over; median age, 20.
Near Lamia	Age differences play a minor role due to heavy emphasis upon financial arrangements. Women should be 18 before marriage.	
In Macedonia	Between 20–25, even before completing military service.	From 18–22. At 25 girl is an old maid.
In Macedonia	Usually after 23. Men wait until they finish military service. Shortage of women here so men marry girls from two nearby villages.	From 18–25. In some cases girls under 18 elope. After 26, girl is an old maid.
Near Serrai	No information.	From 17–25, but usually around 20. After 25, girl is an old maid.
In Grammos	Serve in army first and marry older.	18 and above; at 25 girl considered old.
In Central Greece	After 25 when completing military service.	Can marry at 16, but usually do so at 20.
Near Agrinion	Complete army service and marry about 30.	From 21–25, seldom before 20. Old maids after 30.
Near Mesolongi	Cannot marry if they have unmarried sisters near their own age.	No strong restrictions about age.
Near Mesolongi	Generally complete military service. In 43 families studied, 30 unmarried men were 20–37.	Average age, 23. In 43 families studies, 14 unmarried women were 20–50.

Source: Village studies conducted by Near East Foundation, Greek Ministry of Agriculture, and United States Mission to Greece.

people get a chance to see each other at a fountain, on the street, or at some festival dance, although any conversation may still have to be surreptitious. Other social events where boys and girls meet occur at the beginning of the wheat harvest, the gathering of grapes, and the harvesting of olives. But once a few more daring young people have successfully flaunted the

local customs in this regard — and they are asserting themselves throughout the land — then others will follow as the old people shake their heads
and lecture those in their own home with varying success.

In following up the inquiry about mate selection we stopped one day
near Marathon. There in the hot summer sun three unmarried girls were
harvesting wheat. With great dexterity they held the stalks in one hand
and cut them with a slicing motion of the sickle held in the other. Two of
the girls were sisters and the third was a first cousin, and this was their
uncle's field. They expected to be paid a little over a dollar a day.

"What will happen to the money?"

"It will go into our dowry. We'll give it to our mother who takes care of
it and knows what to buy. Of course, when she's short of money for coffee
and sugar she will go nibble from the dowry money. We do our own dowries
on the loom. We weave, sell the cloth, and then buy underclothes from
the city."

"If you are working outside, how can you do your weaving for the
dowry?"

"Our mothers may do it. An older sister may weave for herself and a
younger sister working outside."

But we were interested in the girls' marriage plans. In their village they
make use of the *proxenetra,* or marriage broker, when this is necessary.[6]
But often the girls become known in other villages where their former
friends or cousins are married and now live. One of these married cousins
will say to an eligible bachelor: "I know just the girl for you back in my
home village." She will then describe the girl, perhaps show pictures of her,
and seek to interest him in her. One of the girls said, "I don't have much
dowry but the boy came and asked for me anyway." We asked her what
dowry she had. She will get fields and, since her sister and she are the only
children in the family, whoever marries her is sure of at least half of her
father's holdings. "So the groom will get a lot," we observed. "Oh, yes, and
her name is already over the whole village" was the reply of the first cousin.
One of the girls had been engaged for eighteen months and would marry
in the fall. She would go to live with her husband's people.

A generation or so ago, parents had a decisive voice in the choice of
mates, but times have changed greatly (though not completely). Answers
to a question, put to young men in a group interview, as to how they would
choose their wives ranged as follows:

Epirus: I will suggest to my parents the name of the girl I wish to marry. They
will get information about her; if she has a good reputation and they agree, I
will marry her. If they do not agree, I won't marry her.

Thasos (island off Thracian coast): If parents have any objection to the girl
I pick and can give good reasons, then I won't marry her. If they don't have
good reasons, I will marry her anyway.

Syros (island): I will not marry if my parents object.

Central Peloponnesos: In my village the young people pick their own mates. Twenty years ago the parents picked the mates but we still have to get parental consent as a matter of courtesy. We have no matchmaker in our village. You find these near the cities where people make money in such matters.

Macedonia: I would marry whom I picked out for I am going to have to live with her. I don't see why my parents will object, for I am going to pick out someone who is respectable. [Second speaker:] I have loved a girl from an early age and, if my father objects, I will marry her anyway since I am the one who has to live with my wife and my father can live with his old woman. "But what if your father disinherits you?" I will marry and do without his fields.

Northern Peloponnesos: If I see a girl whom I want to marry I will go directly to the girl's parents. If the girl accepts me, then my parents will go to arrange for the marriage. "What do you say when you talk to her parents?" I have seen your daughter and would like her for a wife. Could you find out if she likes me and if so would you accept me? By doing it this way, the rest of the village does not know that a boy has been turned down. But boys are always accepted unless they have done something very bad.

These comments from the young men themselves illustrate that one could divide the villages of Greece, and the families within the villages, according to the way mate selection is carried out. First, there are still villages where the young people have almost nothing to say about whom they are to marry and leave the matter up to the parents entirely. For example, in another group interview of nineteen young men, five said that they would expect their fathers to select their wives. One young man said, "I'll follow my father's selection since no father would want bad for his son." Villages where such views predominate are becoming fewer all of the time and tend to be found where the economy is based upon livestock production, including the nomadic shepherd tribes. Second, there are villages where parental consent is essential but where the young men are expected to take the initiative, suggest to their parents the names of the prospective bride, and let them carry on the negotiations from there. Almost nowhere does the girl have the right of initiative, although in some villages she would not be forced to marry anyone to whom she had strong objection, unless there were overriding family or economic considerations. Third, there are villages where the young people make the decision almost entirely on their own but expect their parents to agree, nevertheless being ready to strike out on their own should the parents prove "unreasonable" and try to prevent the marriage.

The peasants look at the changing marriage scene in terms of "marriage for love" and "arranged marriages." What they really mean by the first term is active participation of the young people in mate selection, but they do not mean that the young people subscribe to the romance of the Hollywood movies where love is glorified as an end unto itself. By "arranged marriages" is meant the lack of initiative on the part of the young and the willingness on the part of the boy or girl to give up a preferred mate if the parents strongly object.

It is safe to say that the pendulum is swinging from the arranged to the marriage for love. But in most Greek villages the parents still play an active role in negotiating with each other on behalf of their children and in trying to forestall what they would consider an unfortunate selection. Where parents and children disagree in such cases the situation becomes known to the village at large, and public opinion sometimes supports the young people. The father may be told at the coffeehouse, "Why don't you let your daughter marry Theodore? He is not such a bad boy after all." And the neighboring women take the mother to task, reminding her that her husband was not such a wonderful catch when they first married but that he had worked hard, had done well, and had earned everybody's respect.

THE DOWRY

What are the criteria of a fortunate and an unfortunate selection? Young people were very explicit about this, although by no means unanimous in their answers. Looming large throughout most of Greece is the dowry, or economic resources which the girl brings to the new union.[7] One father from a village near Thebes summarized the situation as follows: "If you have gold sovereigns, you marry off your daughter; if not, you don't." In the villages the surplus of girls, existing since World War I, has been increasing. This came to light when we asked where the men sought their mates — in the home village or elsewhere. Often the reply would be: "Wherever the men can get the best *proika* [dowry]." But there were those who disagreed with this emphasis on money: "If you marry just for money, all day long the wife will hold the purse strings and then where will you be?" In the case of the girl, honor or chastity ranks high as does good health, without which the wife cannot be a good worker. Beauty and good looks are also most welcome, although now and then one would say that "beauty is not too important if the girl has a good heart." As for the man, wealth, education, and position make him a proper risk as a husband if he has a good reputation as well.

These traits which prospective mates should possess have much meaning because in Greece marriage unites two families, and dowry arrangements are contracts between families and not just between two individuals. One keen observer of village life pointed out that "in a village one always hears people speak of families as 'good family' or 'not a good family.'" The standard of *good* is largely in terms of money. The individual from a good family has a big head start in life in a country where financial resources are so limited. In the village of Laina, near Thessalonike, people said of a girl: "Every boy in the village wants to marry her; she is from a good family and has five hundred golden sovereigns as a dowry."

Another informant, describing the village from which she came, also cited the importance of family background. In her village "the boy wants a mate who will be a good tidy housewife, attractive, strong enough for field work; money comes in but is last. The family background is very important. If there are two girls, equally attractive, and one brings a bigger dowry and the other comes from a better family, the boy will choose the latter. The girl, on the other hand, wants a fast worker and does not mind too much about his family's reputation or even his own if she thinks him kind and considerate enough not to make her go out and work; he shouldn't gamble or drink (too much); his looks don't matter, but he should be loyal and not more than five or six years older. If a woman marries a man younger than herself, there is a lot of gossip at first but it then quiets down. The girl knows about a man from hearsay."

There are undoubtedly regional differences in the emphases placed upon the traits most sought after in one's prospective mate, as was borne out when I asked sixteen soldiers stationed near the Albanian border what they would rank first in choosing a wife. Those from around Kavalla and in other parts of Northern Greece placed honor first, being a good housekeeper second, and beauty third. Those from the Peloponnesos and the island of Chios stated beauty, honor, and money in that order, while a man from Thessaly said that in his village the dowry or money would be first. A Cretan listed beauty at the top. But the danger of an easy generalization from such comments as these should be avoided, even though they do correspond fairly well to those made by well-informed Greek home economists for two of the areas mentioned above: "Around Kavalla, for instance, if a girl's father offers a big dowry, she will first want someone from outside the village and does not care too much about his looks. He doesn't have to be an Apollo. If she is considering someone from her own village she asks about his family, his looks, and his reputation.[8] The village man pays more attention to looks and wants to be sure that his wife will be a good worker. In the bigger towns he is more concerned with the dowry. Around Larissa (Thessaly) questions of love are secondary, for the man there is more interested in the dowry. If the girl has a 'fortune,' or large dowry, she is apt to choose someone from the town and may expect the husband to come and live in her village. But it is not uncommon for a man and wife to sell her land to build a house in the city."

Some of these regional differences in emphasis take on new light when one sees that the dowry consists of different property in various parts of Greece.

Usually, the eldest sister is supposed to marry first, followed by the next eldest. Nor is a young man supposed to undertake marriage on his own account until those sisters near his own age have all been provided with a suitable husband, which means with a dowry. Sometimes this may take a man until his fortieth year, after which he begins to contemplate matrimony or forego it altogether. A reverse twist, somewhat in evidence today, is for a man to marry a woman with a good dowry and then turn around and use that dowry for the marriage of his sister. But, in reality, this defeats the main purpose of the dowry which is to enable the young couple to have the necessary wherewithal to start a home of their own. There is no install-ment-buying procedure on which they can rely; the husband's income will only be enough to meet daily expenses and not large enough to cover furni-ture or payment on a house. These should be provided when one marries or the family will never have any economic security.

It should be pointed out that among some of the shepherd groups there is no dowry requirement at all. The same holds true for some villages in the Grammos Mountain area and in villages around Kozane, on the Mace-donian-Thessalian border. In fact, near Kozane money may even be given to the girl's father because he is losing part of his labor supply (his daugh-ter) which he had produced "with the sweat of his brow." In other villages such as Litohoron, near Katerine in the shadow of Mount Olympus, few young men demand a dowry, but people there recognize that they are ex-ceptional in this regard. Around Arta, dowries are given but are not con-sidered important in some of the villages.

Throughout most of Northern Greece, certainly in Macedonia and Thrace, a girl's dowry consists only of the necessary household furniture, mattresses, linens, blankets, and clothing. In some places, such as Kavalla, the girl upon marriage may be given the share of her father's estate (land), which would normally be hers at his death; but throughout other parts of Macedonia, such a division may not be made until long after her marriage upon her father's disablement or death. She may have some money, but that is not stressed as a part of her dowry unless she is angling for someone from a large town or city. The demand for cash is beginning to infiltrate into the villages around Serrai (where a small holding or a pair of oxen has usually been considered sufficient), as it will eventually throughout many of the areas where it is not now customary.

As one moves southward, the importance of land as an element in the dowry increases. In Thessaly, for instance, land and perhaps some livestock are sought in addition to the household and linen contributions. Where there is no land, the girl may offer from fifty to one hundred and fifty sovereigns, depending upon the value of the land in the village from which she comes.

But, more and more, gold sovereigns are considered the basic element in the dowry, with the understanding that household goods and linens are provided in addition. In some of the poorer villages fifty sovereigns are the going price, but much more often one hundred or one hundred and fifty are mentioned. Localities as widely scattered as Agrinion and Mesolongi on the west coast, Ioannina in Epirus, villages near Thebes, those in Attica, and some in the Peloponnesos report such demands, but often add that an equivalent amount in land (thirty to forty stremmata) would be accepted.

Some villages, however, particularly those in the Peloponnesos and Central Greece where the lure of the city is strong, set as the chief goal of the dowry a house in Athens to be provided by the bride. To be sure, this house consists of only two rooms and a kitchen, but it means that the new family can either take root in Athens itself or else rent out the property at a high rate of return. In place of the house, three hundred gold sovereigns are considered acceptable and land is much less important than formerly.

There are doubtless other types of dowry arrangements, but these suffice to show the regional variations and the growing emphasis upon money as the chief resource a young couple will use to get a start in life. In some cases the dowry is paid directly to the husband to use as he sees fit and may be subject to return if he fails to live up to his part of the marriage bargain. But in many cases the wife maintains considerable control over the disposition of her dowry. One thing is attested to on every hand: the wife who brings a big dowry, particularly in cash, is not sent to the field by her husband except in most unusual circumstances. Thus, privileged status both in her own home and in the community is assured her. If a girl brings no dowry, around Lamia at least, she has to work very hard and may even be subject to chastisement.

A clearer picture of what is meant by household goods and linen can be gained from a simple list of what a girl from the village of Spathari, in the Peloponnesos, is supposed to provide: This list, though not the same throughout all of Greece, is indicative of the long hours of labor and financial drain represented:

45–50 blankets	3 small pans
6 sheets	1 big frying pan
12 pairs pillow cases	1 medium frying pan
15–16 towels	2 round cake pans
2 big rugs	2 big and 1 medium spoons
6 rag rugs	6 of each piece of cutlery
6 big sauce pans	Fireplace equipment (big kettle,
3 medium pans	2 andirons, hanging arm, scuttle)

A dowry is a cumulative matter, often reflecting the savings of previous generations. That is why the devastation of war works far more hardship than is at first apparent. It is still a strong tradition among Greek families to make as many of the objects at home as possible and buy only those articles of clothing, such as undergarments, which the rude looms cannot suitably fashion. Women have been urged since early childhood to get up at break of day and work on these trousseaus for themselves or for their daughters long before it was time to go out to the fields.

Most families have a common fund from which expenditures are to be made for dowry items. From time to time, husbands and wives quarrel over the use of further funds for the dowry, since the man will claim that the daughter already has enough household items and linens or sufficient sovereigns, but the wife will not agree. As the girl approaches marriageable age, most people in the village have a shrewd way of sizing up just what dowry she will bring, and the local girls are even roughly ranked along this line. Nevertheless, in discussing the desirability of some young woman, people are quick to mention her family background, what a good worker she is, and other personal qualities which may favor her. A girl will start accumulating her dowry as a serious pursuit from her tenth year on, but no final decision will be made as to the exact amount of land or money she will bring to her husband until some young man seeks her out, or the family begins in earnest to try to marry her off. Family fortunes can vary too much to permit a decision of this sort very far in advance. At times, the exact amount is the subject of bargaining, for the young man may ask for whatever sum he wants and the young woman's parents will tell what they can give. If a mutually satisfactory sum is reached, then the engagement is announced.

In those villages where there are active contacts with some city, the family may find it necessary to send a daughter there to help earn her dowry (for instance, if there are three daughters in a family). As early as eight years of age, she may be sent to some relatives and gradually accumulate a sufficient sum from her meager wages. Some parents may borrow money for the dowry from some richer relative without interest, but seldom from outsiders. If necessary, too, they may sell some land to get the required amount. Now and then a well-to-do man may arrange to marry a girl without demanding a dowry and this gives the village something to talk about for quite a while. Or some young men were encountered, particularly in the Peloponnesos, who fall in love with a girl and then try to find out a way to get a house built even though the girl has no dowry. Such variations illustrate that, even in a society with patriarchal overtones, one finds in rural Greece the belief that "love will find a way," whether it means persuading recalcitrant parents to give their permission or accumulating the wherewithal to buy a house so one can marry. And although there are mercenary overtones to any dowry agreement, it is the general rule that parents are trying to look out for their daughter's welfare to the best of their ability, that they are anticipating the in-law relationships — very important in Greece — with the parents and relatives of their daughter's husband.

THE ENGAGEMENT

Once dowry arrangements have been completed, the couple becomes engaged. This is invariably a festive occasion at the home of the girl, which calls not only for the hiring of musicians but frequently the preparation of special dishes, such as fried octopus, and the serving of great quantities of brandy and special liqueurs. The significance of the engagement is stressed by the fact that it often involves the village and not just the families concerned. One day while riding muleback in the mountains of Epirus we heard the sound of music from a distance. As we approached a small hamlet, small because most people were afraid to live in that politically unsettled area, we recognized the music as that of the *daouli* (big drum) and bagpipe. As we passed through, the president of the community came out and invited us to stop and join in the festivities. Here, as elsewhere, I learned that there were ceremonial ways in which the couple plight their troth: exchange of glasses of sweet liqueur from which they each drink and, more importantly, the exchange of heavy rings. If both sets of parents are alive, it is the custom in the Peloponnesos for the bride's mother to be the first to hand the rings over to the couple, the groom's father then repeats this, and the bride's does so for the third time. The priest is not involved nor is the *koumbaros* (sponsor at the wedding to follow and godparent at the baptism) called upon at this time.

The engagement period is not viewed as a time of exploration and reaching a decision by the young people as to whether they are actually suited to each other; in Greece, once engaged, the couple is expected to marry, and there is almost no breaking off of an engagement. This step is regarded as serious as the wedding itself, for it is a public recognition that two families are to be related. But customs during the engagement period vary considerably in Greece. For example, the customary length of engagement may vary from one week or less in a few villages to less than a year in other places, although most generally the engagement period would be at least a year. This is a feverish period of activity on the part of the family to ensure the collection of all necessary dowry items. In some parts of Greece the young man may go to live in the home of his future in-laws if he is needed there. He may be working in the village where he found his bride-to-be and, rather than maintain separate bachelor's quarters or board with some other family, he may move into his future home. Or, if he has no fields of his own and goes to work on his in-laws' estate, he will probably move into the in-laws' home. In Aetolia, if the boy is from a different village, he can come from time to time to the bride's house for a visit of a few days; if he is from the same village, he also can visit the home but seldom spends a night there.

The casual way in which young people occasionally talked about their engagement stressed the social rather than personal aspects of this experience. On the island of Salamis, not far from Athens, while visiting in a village home we asked a young woman to tell us about her engagement. This is her account, which highlights some of the points previously made:

A matchmaker arranged our marriage. When my mother finally decided that it was time to have a man in the house, we discussed with which family we wanted to affiliate. We had heard my father say before his death that he wanted his daughter to marry one of the sons of a retired chief petty officer in the village. My mother and sisters named one of the sons who was still single and I said, "All right. Whatever you decide," even though I didn't know the boy. So my brother-in-law (my oldest sister's husband), as head of the family, arranged the contact through a third person. I had said that I would take anything but a bald-headed man. [At this point everyone laughed for the one selected was prematurely bald.] On a Tuesday both families had said *Entaxei* [all right], and on Saturday the groom-to-be was supposed to visit me. He didn't try to see me in advance, for he had faith in his parents and, besides, we all live in the same village. But he sent word that he couldn't come on Saturday, for as a petty officer he was on duty. Instead he came on Thursday with a friend. He sent his friend in first to announce that he was here and to ask if he could come in. I said certainly but spoke in the plural form; he said not to do this for it annoyed him. We looked at each other for the first time. He asked, "Do you like me?" I said, "Of course." What else could I say? I shrieked when I saw his bald head, shrieked with disappointment. He came and sat near me. My mother said, "You see, he has already become very bald." [The fiancé, who was present during the interview, was asked what had been his thoughts when the match was made. He replied, "Since her father and my father had known each other, I said what is the use of pretending."]
On the Saturday following his visit to me I went to pay my first visit to my in-laws. I took candied almonds and flowers to my mother-in-law and we all ate, drank, and were merry. Then he and I started visiting each other. But the people began to say, "How does such traffic go on since they don't have an engagement ring?" So we decided to have the formal engagement. We were going to do it on his name day, but he got sick and we postponed it to Easter. The groom bought the ring and gave me a silk dress, shoes and stockings, and his relatives gave me some earrings and beads. I gave him slippers, pajamas, shirts, and handkerchiefs. On the day of the engagement, I sent his mother a large bread ring with thirty-one red Easter eggs on top and she sent a cake containing five eggs to my home. At the engagement ceremony the fathers of the couple usually place the rings on the fingers, but since my father was dead his father put the rings on both of our fingers.

Engagements in this Salamis village last two years or more unless the families are rich and can hurry the matter along. The length of time is based on the dowry that the girl must accumulate. Not only must she bring the house but must furnish it with a bureau (or chiffonier), a buffet, six dining-room chairs, four kitchen chairs, and a mattress. The groom provides the dining-room table, a cupboard, and a bed.

MARRIAGE

Even before an engagement is agreed upon, relatives check the kinship of the boy and girl to be sure that they are not too closely related to marry. In Mesolongi, for instance, a few years ago those related up to the fourth degree could not marry, but this is beginning to break down somewhat. Around Arta second cousins may marry, but in many parts of Macedonia there are restrictions up to third cousins. Generally throughout Greece, young people with the same godparent are considered "spiritual brethren" and cannot marry. It does not take long for some knowledgeable relative to review the kinship lines and decide whether the engagement would violate local customs, which are as important as the official church position on this matter.

Panos D. Bardis, in writing on the main features of the Greek family during the twentieth century, summarizes the teachings of the Greek Orthodox Church regarding the goals of marriage as follows: 1. increase of the human race; 2. promotion of mutual helpfulness among the members of the family; 3. restraint of passions; 4. Christian training of the young. He points out that some of these goals have been only partially achieved because of the patriarchal and authoritarian nature of the Greek family, but they remain those set forth by the church. Bardis also makes a useful summary of the essential elements of the engagement and wedding ceremonies:

1. Rings: the man's ring is of gold and symbolizes the sun, whereas the woman's ring is of silver and symbolizes the moon.
2. Crowns: these denote the marital bond and the glory of the sacrament. In Greece, these crowns are made of flowers, or evergreen, while the Russian Orthodox Church in earlier days preferred replicas of the Royal Crown.
3. Wine: this is offered to the couple in remembrance of the marriage in Cana, and symbolizes their mutual sharing of unhappiness in life.
4. Public confession of consent by both parties.
5. Blessing of the priest, which is considered very essential and is repeatedly stressed in the writings of the early church fathers.[9]

If one bears these five points in mind, the description of a peasant wedding takes on more meaning and makes greater sense to one not brought up in the Orthodox faith. Furthermore, it is apparent that the church ceremony itself is only one part of the unfolding drama in which the whole village takes a keen interest. Here, in free translation, is a day-by-day account of what happened in the village of Artotina in Aetolia, just prior to the outbreak of World War II.[10]

When the bride is ready with her dowry and the amount of money has been given to the groom's family, the date of the marriage is fixed, always on a Sunday unless one of the two people has been married before, in which case the second marriage is set for a Saturday evening. (This custom brings to mind a common Greek proverb: "Everything was wrong, and even the wedding was on Monday.")

On the Wednesday before the date of the marriage, both homes "start the leaven." In the evening the relatives of each home are present at the baking done from freshly milled flour and "untouched water." The kneading trough is placed in the middle of the room, and over this a girl and a boy hold a sieve through which the flour is sifted. Everybody is silent until, all at once, people start throwing coins into the sieve saying "Kalorizika" (Good luck). Three shots are fired to announce to the village that this has been done. The baking starts when enough flour has been sifted. Some of the people take dough which they smear onto the bride's or groom's face. After a late dinner, toward midnight, the people in the groom's home suggest going to the bride's home. When the two parties meet, there is dancing and singing and the firing of pistols. Later on, the groom's party goes back to his home to continue celebrations until daybreak.

On Friday the display of the dowry starts. Women from all over the village come in to look at it and bring with them basil, rice, and cotton "just for good luck." When the women have seen the dowry, the "filling of the sacks" starts after the mother has put a copper container into a large homespun sack. While the bride stows away her household equipment and her own clothes into these sacks, those present throw in coins. Once the sacks have been filled, the mattresses, covers, and cushions are placed in piles and the friends sprinkle everything with rice and pin sweet-smelling herbs in between the clothes. Then the women, and especially the young girls, start dancing in the bride's courtyard. On the same day the groom sends two boys around the village, one of whom carries a jug full of wine and the other a written invitation for relatives and friends to a dinner on the wedding day. The bride's father does the same. From Friday on, the special dishes are prepared: loaves of bread with symbolic patterns across the top, pies, meat, and wine. If a person is in mourning and is invited to the wedding dinner, he is obliged to take some food on Saturday evening.

On Saturday morning the bride calls the young girls "to help her get married." Some of her friends take Turkish delight, bonbons, and other sweets and go with these offerings to invite the rest of the young girls to the wedding.

On Sunday after the regular morning church service, people begin to gather in the homes of the bride and the groom. The girls go to the bride's home to form an honorary escort and dance in her yard, while the boys dance in the groom's yard. During this time, while the bride is getting dressed, a party goes from the groom's home to fetch the sponsor (koumbaros) who either rides or goes on foot to the groom's home. There a white flag, adorned with apples and sweet herbs, is hoisted. The koumbaros is always the groom's godfather or one of his sons if the godfather has died. If for some reason the godfather cannot be present, he gives his blessing and permits the groom to choose another "best man" or sponsor. When the koumbaros has arrived at the groom's home, the procession is ready to start for the bride's home.

First comes a young man carrying the flag, followed by the priest and the groom's relations. There is gay music and much shooting, which continues once the party has reached the bride's home. There the flag bearer puts the flag on the bride's roof and receives a ring biscuit from the bride in return. The groom gets off his horse and goes up the steps. As he reaches the top step, the bride's mother offers him wine and a boutonniere of basil, marjoram, or other plants, wrapped in a white handkerchief. The groom kisses her hand and she kisses him on both cheeks. She offers him wine, which he drinks, asking for her blessing. He returns the glass and puts the boutonniere in his lapel. The groom now enters the bride's home whereupon all relatives join him and, if they follow the old custom, give a small sum of money to the bride, who now turns toward the east and bows, then west, north, and south, so as to form the sign of the cross.

As soon as the relatives have received some sweet, the bride, usually leaning on the arm of a cousin, starts for the church. The others, including the groom's relatives, follow on foot. Then comes the church ceremony. When the couple have arrived at the altar, the priest begins to read the liturgy and then takes from a box the two wreaths of artificial blossoms, tied together by a ribbon, which the koumbaros has brought; the priest puts them together and says, starting with the man, "the Lord's servant [name] engages the Lord's servant [name]." He touches the foreheads of each as he says his or her name. He then holds the wreaths between the couple and makes the sign of the cross, "in the name of the Father, Son, and Holy Ghost," three times for the groom and three times for the bride. The koumbaros, who is standing between the couple, receives the wreaths from the priest and, as the priest starts a chant, holds the wreaths over the heads of the couple and starts crossing them back and forth. When this is done, he puts the proper wreath on the proper person though the ribbon still connects the two wreaths. The same thing happens with the rings. After the koumbaros puts the rings on the correct fingers, the priest reads from the Bible, "what God hath joined together let no man put asunder" and separates the couple, who have been holding hands by the little fingers, by moving his hand between them. He next administers the communion — a sip of wine to the groom, the bride, and the koumbaros.

Perhaps the liveliest part of the whole proceeding is the "dance of Isaiah" which follows next. With the priest holding the Bible in one hand and the hand of the groom in the other, with the groom holding the bride, and the bride the koumbaros, the principals go around the table where the wreaths were laid before the ceremony started. They make the circuit three times, stopping four times in each circuit. During the course of this procession everybody is throwing bonbons and rice at the principals, sometimes with such telling force that the priest stops to warn the people not to be so energetic. The circuits completed, the couple and koumbaros resume their earlier position before the altar and listen to the priest read the final Scripture and receive his blessing.

In Artotina, the procession goes from the church to the bride's home. She is led by the groom and the koumbaros. The dowry is then loaded onto the pack animals to the accompaniment of traditional songs. The bride climbs upon the best animal and the groom, when mounted, takes a stand on her right. He takes a golden coin out of his pocket and hands it to her after making the sign of the cross three times on her forehead. The procession then goes to the groom's house, and the young couple are the only ones who ride. The musicians have already arrived at the groom's house and start the music as the procession approaches. There is more shooting and the flag is now put on the groom's house. The bride, before she gets off the horse, throws an old piece of iron on the roof as a symbol of strength in her new home. The mother-in-law gives a ring biscuit cut crosswise. The bride holds it over her head and squeezes it into four pieces: one she eats, two she puts on her breast, and one she hands to her mother-in-law who offers her a glass of wine. She makes the sign of the cross with wine and returns the glass. After this a boy, both of whose parents are alive, is given her to hold. She kisses the child and gives him sweets and hangs a ring biscuit around his neck. Now the bride can dismount from her horse.

Her brother-in-law, or some other close relative of her husband, will take the bride into his arms, turn around three times, and then let her down. The dowry is unloaded and displayed. The tables are set. The wives of the relations have already brought baskets of food which are set on the table, and each small family gathers around its basket. Any stranger present is allowed to sit at one of the tables. There is drinking, dancing, eating, singing. Later on, the other villagers who were not related to the groom or bride, and were therefore not invited to the wedding feast, will join the party in the courtyard or at a nearby threshing floor for a continuation of the festivities.

At night, after the supper, the mother-in-law guides the couple to their room. On Monday morning she inspects the bride's nightgown to make sure that she was a virgin. Before lunchtime the bride takes a boy and goes to the fountain where she throws a coin into the water, fills a jug, and then returns. The boy retrieves the coin which belongs to him.

On Wednesday the couple gets up early and goes to the field. On the return the bride will carry on her back a bundle of wood or branches and follow her husband who leads the way back home. The first Sunday after the wedding the bride will receive the female relations; the following Sunday the couple will go to church and after the service the bride returns the visits of these female kinfolk. At each home the housewife will call "cotton" to the bride, which means that she will give her a piece of cotton and will wish her "may you live and get old enough to see grandchildren." Then the marriage period is finished.

Anyone even casually familiar with Greek life will realize that this authentic account differs in many respects from the wedding customs found in other parts of the country. For instance, in many villages the groom and the bride go separately to the church, for it is considered bad luck for the groom to see the bride on the wedding day before meeting her at the altar. Then, too, it is quite common to have both a male and female sponsor, one representing the bride's family and the other the groom's family. There are other details which are fairly common throughout the country. Supposing that the wedding is to be at six o'clock in the evening, the bride will start her bath about three o'clock in the afternoon. After this, she is perfumed. Her friends and a "wise woman" do the dressing, although in some parts of Macedonia the bride's brother is supposed to help with the dressing. Proximity to the city changes many of the traditional patterns. The bride, for instance, may have her bridal dress made by a dressmaker and the dressmaker may be present at the time the bride dresses to be sure that the veil is in proper place. Also, the bride may have gone to a beauty parlor to get a permanent wave. The frizzier her hair, the more beautiful she is thought to be. If she cannot get to a beauty parlor, her friends will put her hair into curlers or will wet her hair and make waves. The bride's hair is combed before she puts on her dress, and it is quite a trick to get the dress on without mussing the hair. The wise woman or dressmaker will help her with her makeup: rouge, lipstick, much powder. The veil is pinned with two little bunches of orange blossoms and, of course, the richer the bride, the fuller the gown and the longer the veil. White gloves are becoming more common, as is a small bouquet. The bride's best friend must give her something old (perhaps a garter) to wear and the wise woman busies herself doing knots of various kinds to control the fates in behalf of the bride.

The duties of the koumbaros vary from place to place. If there are two sponsors (normally, a married couple), the koumbara, or woman sponsor, may be expected to buy two big white candles, quite expensive, and enough silk material for the dress of the bride and for tying the candles with a bouquet of orange blossoms. One of the diversions in the ceremony in the church is to watch the two small children holding these heavy candles and to notice how frequently their inattention seems on the point of starting a general conflagration.

There is also a ritual connected with the dance held at the bride's house after the ceremony at the church. One of the fathers of the young couple will throw some money into the musician's box so that he can lead the dance in honor of the bride and can choose any dance that he likes. This dance may last from six to ten minutes. Then the bride's nearest male relative will pay the musicians and lead a dance in honor of the groom first and then the bride. Then it is the turn of the koumbaros. This continues until each one who wants to honor the couple will do the same; after this, the dance turns into an ordinary one, and anybody who wants to lead can do so by paying the musicians, thereby gaining the right to name the dance and therefore the music that is to be played.

There are wide variations, also, in the greeting given by the mother-in-law to the bride when she first arrives. Sometimes, the mother-in-law puts a dish in front of the daughter-in-law who breaks it; sometimes she gives an ax which the bride is to use in showing all present how well she can chop wood. Then, too, instead of taking up the small boy, as the bride does in Artotina, the boy may come and sit on her knee and receive a round piece of bread for supposedly bringing her good luck. In Kilkis, Macedonia, the brother of the bride has a big round pie which he breaks on her head upon the return from the church and then distributes the pieces to the guests. In the same place, an open lock is placed in the groom's pocket before he goes to the church, and it is shut tight during the ceremony to signify that the union will not be broken.

Another widespread custom is the attempt on the part of the bride to try to step on the groom's foot during the ceremony when she has to promise to obey; being forewarned, the groom tries to step on her foot, for this is supposed to show who will be the boss of the new home. Couples who want to appear modern agree in advance not to compete in this respect, although in ceremonies around Larissa it is not unusual for the groom's friends to call out to him to be sure the bride does not step on his foot. Another touch of modernity is the honeymoon to Athens, which some of the couples in the more prosperous villages of Thessaly think an important part of getting married.

As would be expected, each couple wishes to move into a house of its own. In some parts of Thrace, where there is still communal land, a plot may be given to a young man on which to build a house; or he may find room for a new dwelling not far from the parental home, providing the house is his responsibility and not the girl's. The determining factor, however, is the cost of building a new home. Elsewhere in Greece, if the bride brings enough gold sovereigns, they may be used to help pay for the cost of a home; or if the bride brings a new house, as she does in the islands, then the couple is set up for separate housekeeping.

In the Peloponnesos, where there is no longer much communal land, it is not unusual for the bride's parents to provide a strip of land on which a new home is to be built. In the dowry discussions they agree to give money to the future son-in-law in two stages: first, an amount sufficient for the construction of the house which he builds according to the girl's wishes and after much discussion with her. This sum must be spent on the house. The second installment is in land or money to cover the cost of furnishing the new home. The young man has the responsibility for seeing that the house is built, but the house belongs to the bride.

Where there is no new home available, it is most common for patrilocal residence to follow, and the girl must learn to adjust to the family circle of her husband. But the Greek peasant is practical enough to decide each case on its merits. If the girl's family has greater need of a man, then the couple will go to her home to live. For example, if the girl has no brother and she is to inherit her parents' house, then the couple go to live there. Only in a few parts of Northern Greece, where Slavic influence is found, do two or more married brothers live as a joint family with their elderly parents. In most Greek villages one of the brothers, often the eldest, inherits the ancestral home, and it is expected that the other brothers will manage to set up separate establishments.

As a final note on courtship and marriage, it is proper to ask what happens if a marriage does not turn out successfully for either or both parties. Until about twenty years ago a divorce was never thought of as a possibility by peasants; indeed, they considered even the thought of it a disgrace to a family. Even today, when so many changes are present in Greek life, village divorces are still relatively rare. When they do occur, the divorcée has a hard time getting another husband, for the relatives of any prospective mate are afraid that she might start to lead a bad life and bring shame on them. In some villages where there is considerable urban influence, the idea of getting a divorce is tied in with the newer conception of women's rights, and in this connection it is not viewed as a matter of shame but as a matter of fashion. A woman who wishes to stand on her legal rights begins to talk in terms of divorce in case she thinks her husband is abusing her.

As in the case of the divorcée, the fate of the widow is much more difficult than that of the widower. The widow, if she is dutiful, observes a long period of mourning which keeps her out of circulation in the marital market; also, she is in competition with a surplus number of unmarried women who are apt to be preferred. In any event, she must have a dowry to contribute to her new husband. Under some circumstances, such as having children who are the pride and joy of their paternal grandparents, she may stay on in her deceased husband's home. If she does not meet a functional need there, but is an extra mouth to feed, she will try to arrange for her own relatives to take her back.

··◦[IX]◦··

Ceremonies and Holy Days

Greek family life also has its serious overtones. In such a closely knit unit the illness or death of a member may be more keenly felt than in a family system where one's own security is not so closely tied in with the fate of the others. In a society such as rural Greece, where there is so little room for the unmarried woman, the task of finding a suitable husband for a daughter or sister can become an overriding consideration coloring all of life's relationships. Where the family is the economic and producing unit, economic ups and downs are intimately geared with the ups and downs of the family. Should the bond between husband and wife become strained, the home increasingly becomes the center of tension with fewer outlets than exist in an urban setting. In such cases, the man stays around the house as little as possible and the wife seeks the company of the neighboring women or of some relatives.

Fortunately for all, just when home life has become a bit ruffled, some ceremony or holiday appears to make the family forget for a while their differences in order to carry off the ceremony with the proper flair. The housewife can immerse herself with good conscience in the time-consuming preparations; the father knows that certain duties are exclusively in his domain; and the children wait expectantly for their cues from the adults so that they, too, may participate.

A VILLAGE BAPTISM

One ceremony which has deep meaning for the family members is the baptism of a recently arrived infant. First of all comes the selection of god-parents, although this is usually determined by the custom of having those who were sponsors at the wedding also be godparents of the children which issue from that marriage. But if many children have come subsequently it is only fitting that the honor be given to someone else. The father is free to invite some notable, say a political figure from the area, to serve as god-father, an opportunity which few politicians pass up. On the other hand, if the couple is dissatisfied with the godparent who would normally be invited, it may follow traditional procedures to select another. An inquiry into these takes one deeply into folklore and belief in magic. When childlessness, still-birth, or infant mortality is blamed upon the godparent, villagers assume that a new godparent might lead to better success. According to Chrysoula, the wise woman of Spetsai, her sister bore a child who died within twenty-four hours after birth, and later on she had a pseudo-pregnancy. In her desperation she prayed to the Virgin: "Please give me a child of either sex. If it is a girl I'll give her your name; if it is a boy I'll dedicate it to you but will have to give it the name of its paternal grandparent." This was on the morning of March 25 (Evangelismos Day); that afternoon she had inter-course with her husband and on Christmas Day a little girl was born. As soon as she was able, the mother picked up the baby, put the baby on the porch of the church dedicated to the Virgin, and waited to see who would discover the baby and, by so doing, be designated godparent. People stand-ing around consider it lucky to be a godparent on such an occasion, and several may be inclined to volunteer. An especially eager person may throw a handkerchief ahead of a rival and thus stake out a claim. The mother watches from a distance. When the child has been taken into the church for the ceremony, she goes home to prepare sweets and other food for the baptismal feast.

The same procedure for gaining a new godparent as a replacement for the one who sponsored the wedding of the couple is followed in most parts of Greece but occurs only infrequently, since people reluctantly change their godparent ties. Once the godparents have been selected, the guests have to be invited — relatives and very close friends or, as was fortunate in my case, an interested foreigner who happens to be in the vicinity. The women of the household allow themselves a few days in advance to plan and pre-pare for the festive occasion. The church ceremony is a lively affair. If the child is baptized within forty days of birth, as it usually is, the mother does not attend, for she is still unclean. The principals in the ceremony are the priest, the infant, and the godparent, with the latter's responsibility suppos-edly extending to the spiritual oversight of the godchild, today a matter of little importance. (A pregnant woman is not supposed to serve as a koum-bara, for people say that something bad will happen either to her or the child being baptized. A person is also supposed to baptize only children of the same sex, for if he serves as a koumbaros of both boys and girls, two of these with the same godparent might fall in love, which would be considered incest since spiritual bonds count as much as biological kinship in determining marriage prohibitions.)

After the small group of friends and relatives has gathered, the priest comes out from behind the altar. He usually displays great skill in handling the infant, even if the baby starts to howl his displeasure at the proceedings. The priest first turns the baby toward the east, blows into its face three times to chase away the evil spirits, seals it with the sign of the cross, and utters four exorcisms against temptation. Then the godparent renounces for the child "the devil and all his works" in answer to a thrice-repeated question from the priest, after which he recites the Apostles' Creed.[1]

The tepid water standing in a large copper basin is next blessed by the priest, who pours consecrated oil on it. Then the godparent, who has rubbed the baby all over with oil, hands it to the priest who three times plunges it into the font while he recites the appropriate formula. Once the immersion has been completed, the priest anoints the baby in different parts of its body and holds it up to the altar three times if it is a boy. The baby is next dressed and carried around the font three times by the godparent who holds a candle in one hand; the priest also joins in this procession. The ceremony concludes with additional words from the New Testament and a few words of admonition to the child, whereupon those present congratulate the god-parent with the wish, "may it live." Then everyone goes to the home of the parents for a tremendous dinner, usually featuring roast lamb, which is just as important a part of the affair as the church ceremony. The god-parent is given a place of high honor. (He also has had the responsibility of choosing the name for the child, usually that of a grandparent.[2])

Although I have attended many social functions in Greece, the joy and fun which characterize the baptismal feasts stand out in my memory. Not only is the food delicious and plentiful, but there is invariably plenty of wine and good-natured bantering. Most of the time, too, there is dancing, spirited and informal. Children of the guests as well as the brothers and sisters of the newly baptized infant are often present, and manage to end up in the dance or very much in its way, thereby adding to the general merriment. Weddings, such as the one described in the previous chapter, are occasions for merriment because they give promise of providing children, especially boys, to continue the family line; the baptism is merry because this promise has been fulfilled.

THE ANNUAL VILLAGE FESTIVAL

The annual village festival, held on the name day of the saint for whom the local church is named, although a community event, serves also as an occasion for absent family members to return for a visit.[3] On such days literally hundreds and sometimes more than a thousand outsiders visit the village to join in the local excitement. Many families have so many guests that they hardly know where to put them all; food and drink are plentiful, and dancing is the order of the day. The local shopkeepers count heavily on this occasion to bring them out of the red, even though traveling merchants also make their appearance to take care of the swollen number of clients. The local government sees to it that these outsiders or their transactions are taxed. A relatively few attend the masses being held in the church since the festival is more secular than religious. One is impressed in talking with villagers about these festivals how frequently they stress the fact that they all "put on the best clothes and new clothes if possible" in order to make a good impression upon the visitors and other villagers as well.

Throughout Greece one can see many well-known national dances on these festival days. Most of them are round dances, with the dancers holding on to hands or wrists of those next to them. The musicians stand in the center of the circle and strike up the tune. A slow "dragging-trailing" dance is called the *syrtos;* one calling for jumping or leaping steps is a *pidictos;* and others are mixed. Many of these dances have much in common with ancient dances depicted on friezes or described in the writings of classical times.

An example of the syrtos type is the *kalamatianos,* named for the town of Kalamata in the southern Peloponnesos. Here the dancers hold each other by the wrist. The leader of the dance may break away from the circle and go through gyrations which would do credit to a professional acrobat; throughout this performance he flutters his handkerchief (the symbol of leadership), and when ready he may throw the handkerchief to his neighbor or someone else who wishes to lead the dance. The *geranos,* another syrtos dance, is supposed to have been danced by Theseus and the youths and maidens with him on Delos when he returned there after slaying the Minotaur on Crete. The movements of the dance are said to imitate the twists and turns of the labyrinth which was the lair of the mythological monster.[4]

Another syrtos dance is the *zalongos,* which commemorates the dance of the Souliote women in Epirus who, upon the defeat of their men folk in December 1803 by Ali Pasha of Ioannina, took refuge on a high and inaccessible rock situated above the river Acheron, where they began to dance and, still dancing, threw themselves over the precipice into the gaping abyss below, with their children clasped in their arms. "Farewell ye springs, ye forests, ye mountain-ridges" begins the folksong which accompanies this dance.[5] Thus the dance keeps alive in the memory of the people what their forebears suffered under the alien Turks. The *zervos,* another syrtos dance, is "left-handed" in that the dancers move from left to right rather than in the customary direction from right to left.

Perhaps the most picturesque leaping dance is the *tsamikos* of Epirus, the region where the Souliote women lived. In dancing this even today the men sometimes wear their small arms as they used to many years ago, reminiscent of the ancient Pyrrhic armed dances. This dance and the zalongos, mentioned above, have done much to re-emphasize the stereotyped image common throughout Greece that Epirus is a place of violence, heroic men and women, and a fortress of the independent spirit. Other leaping dances derive from the *klephts,* or guerrillas who fought against the Turks before Northern Greece gained her independence in this century. The chief dance in Thessaly is the *karagouna,* probably Wallachian in origin; the *yerakina,* which is a Thracian dance, has also become popular throughout Greece.

The most common example of the mixed type is the *hasapikos,* or butchers' dance, which comes down from Byzantine times when the butchers' guild used this dance on its feast days. Whereas many of the other dances are stately or heroic, this one provides an outlet for considerable comic activity by dancers so inclined. In other words, there are dances to suit everyone's taste and it is up to the leader, who pays the musicians, to call for the dance he wants and at which he is most adept. Certain dances are prescribed for certain occasions but, once the formalities have been observed, other dances can be chosen. It is disconcerting to a visitor, who has been held entranced by the color, intricacies, and ancient lineage of the folk dances, to hear the orchestra strike up some American popular music of twenty or twenty-five years ago and then see the young people shift from the round dances to dancing in couples. Young men who have displayed great agility in their leaps in a klephtic dance now have to be led like sheep by the girls who have taken the trouble to learn a few of the new steps; or if the girls do not know the steps either, the boy, usually a beat or two behind the music, tries to imitate the movements of some good dancer.

Thus festival days bring everything one could ask to a village: dances old and new, visitors of every description, wares not often sold locally, and an occasion to eat and drink to one's full capacity without fear of criticism. Most of all, it gives the community a chance to have its day in the sun, to be the cynosure of the surrounding territory, and to store up incidents which family members and neighbors can talk about in the days ahead.

RELIGIOUS HOLIDAYS AND NAMEDAYS

Family members, however, do not have to wait for the coming of an annual festival or fair to find an occasion for dancing or taking things easy. There are many other religious holidays calling for special observances in addition to Easter, the most important, and the Twelve Days surrounding Christmas. For example, Greek civil servants observe, with pay, approximately twenty-five holidays throughout the year, and industrial workers honor about half this number, some of them with pay. The villager, closer to the traditions for which the holidays stand, will celebrate the full twenty-five and others added for good measure.

To trace all of these holidays would call for a detailed Calendar of Customs, a list far too lengthy to be incorporated here even if one had mastered through the years the many regional variations throughout Greece.[6] What is more important is the realization that holidays do play an important part in adding rhythm and color to family and community life, as well as indicating to the farmer, whose agricultural work cycle is closely meshed with the regularly recurring holidays, that it is time for him to take up or finish some important activity.

I tend to associate each of the major Greek holidays with the particular village or city I happened to be in at the time of its observance. On one May Day, for example, I was in the heart of the Peloponnesos where groups of school children with their teachers were taking walks through the fields, an excursion-picnic. And, then, in the early afternoon to be invited to participate in the festivities at the school proved pleasant indeed. An important part of the activities was the hanging of the wreath over the door of the school, a pagan custom supposed to drive away evil.

Near Phlorina, in 1953 and again in Athens in 1955, I observed the commemoration of the holiday in honor of St. John the Baptist on June 24. This pagan midsummer festival has survived on into the present so much so that even in Athens, to say nothing of the villages, on St. John's Eve small boys light fires in the yards or streets and jump over them. One is supposed to burn all worthless things as a symbol of purification of the house and, as token of personal purification, one jumps over the fire while shouting "I leave my sins and my fleas behind me." [7] Into the same fire the peasants throw the withered May Day wreaths. This too is the evening when the girls of the village seek to learn their fortunes from the "dumb" or speechless water which a maiden or, in some places a young boy, brings from the fountain while remaining absolutely quiet despite the efforts of the bystanders to make the bearer talk. Later, each girl drops some easily identified possession into the jar which is "locked" until the next evening, thereby giving the name of *kledona* (from *kledi,* key) to this particular custom. When it is unlocked, the girls sing songs which foretell

whom they will marry. This is done by associating the verse being sung
with the girl whose forfeit is drawn from the pitcher or jar at that particular time.

To call attention, however, to the major holy days is to overlook the importance of the minor holy days in regulating much of the life of the older
villager who is still apt to be tradition-bound. For example, on July 2, the
Day of the Virgin the Sheafbearer, many peasants will not harvest for fear
that any sheaves they would gather would be destroyed by fire; or on
July 7, the Day of St. Kyriaki, peasant women in many parts of Greece
will not bake bread for fear that it will be eaten by snakes; or on July 17,
the Day of St. Marina, the people go to the vineyards to collect grapes. On
this same day they may make a public sacrifice of a calf, letting the animal's
blood run in a special ditch; they follow this sacrifice with a common meal.
On July 20, the Day of the Prophet Elijah (Elias), there are also festivals
and sacrifices, chiefly because so many churches are named in his honor.
Some people go to worship on the mountaintops; others try to foretell the
weather since Elijah is associated with rain and thunder; and still others
light fires on the mountainsides or in the villages.

Thus one could run through each month. There are dates when livestock
owners can begin to let their animals pasture freely in fields and vineyards
(September 14), when master and servants are supposed to draw up the
contract between them (October 26), when the wine cask is to be opened
(November 3 or 11), when agricultural work is to be finished for the year
(November 14), when the fountain is to be fed with seeds (November 21),
when the icons are to be dipped into the sea (December 6).[8] Each of
these dates in and of itself is perhaps not very significant, for the taboos
and customs are of a relatively simple sort; but they do illustrate the rich
heritage of folklore which surrounds every village, day in and day out,
and which adds to the color and vividness of rural life in Greece.

These saints' days also afford the basis for the custom of observing
namedays. In Greece, a person and his family pay little attention to his
birthday but make much of the day of the saint whose name he bears. In
Amphypolis, for instance, on a boy's nameday his parents will sacrifice a
lamb. They will sing and dance and afterwards feast on the lamb because,
as one village girl expressed it, "each boy belongs to a certain saint and the
lamb is for the saint." Throughout Greece one visits a friend on his nameday, enjoys the good food that is served, and wishes the individual long life
and happiness. In a village where there are many people named Constantine
or George, people go from one party to another until they have had more
than enough food and drink.

The greatest holidays of the year are Christmas and Easter, with the
latter being the more important. As a matter of fact, Christmas is only one
part of the so-called Twelve Days (*Dodekaemeron*) between Christmas

Eve and Epiphany (December 24–January 6). It is preceded by a week's fast, which formerly lasted forty days, ending on Christmas Eve. Throughout much of Greece it is traditional to kill a pig for Christmas, although in many villages of Thessaly people are satisfied with fowl. Indispensable is the *Christopsoma* (Bread of Christ), a large round loaf, with a cross formed of dough in the middle and with four chestnuts on each side and a fifth in the center. This is a leavened loaf but without any sugar, although in the cities it is so highly decorated with candied fruits that it resembles a sweet loaf. Special Christmas cakes as well as a number of other dishes are also prepared for the occasion.

Christmas Eve is a time for caroling, or the *kalenda*. The carols are about the birth of Christ, the joy that is spread all over the world, "so good master give us something so that we can enjoy with ease Christmas Day." In some parts of Greece adults as well as children go caroling. In addition to triangles which they play while singing, the children may carry little paper ships or houses and lighted lanterns. The carolers in the cities receive coins or sweets, but in the villages they are content with currants and nuts. They avoid homes that are in mourning, although earlier in the day many people have probably visited the cemeteries with offerings of food for the dead.

On Christmas Day itself the more devout go to the early communion service and then on to the home of the eldest relative (if he is very poor, then to the home of the richest relative). Here, in Thessaly at least, they drink *kokorozoumo,* a boullion made from boiled chicken, lamb, and beef, to which a lemon flavoring has been added. In Macedonia, a traditional dish is *dolmades,* or stuffed pickled cabbage leaves prepared on Christmas Eve and allowed to simmer in a sauce pan on a low fire all night. The men in particular drink a great deal of liquor throughout the day and generally end up inebriated, partly because they have been to call on those named Christos or Christina and been duly treated. Christmas Day, though not a time for exchanging gifts, is a special occasion to be celebrated.

Yet throughout this whole twelve-day period many of the peasants reveal an unusual anxiety, for they believe that the Evil Eye is unusually active at this time. Windows and doors must be kept shut so that bad spirits will not bring in illnesses of any kind; furthermore, these spirits — called *kallikantzari* — are usually mischievous as well. They are supposed to be little men with goats' feet, enormous heads, and big ears; they are black, for they come down the chimney which must be kept closed. To be on the safe side, it is well to put a little sugar and a glass of water by the fireplace for them to eat and drink and thus be less inclined to do harm. Every village literally teems with stories about the kallikantzari at this time of year and details differ greatly as to their appearance and pranks. Their presence is considered so real that many villagers going outdoors after dark take both a light and a cross for protection. Nor should one do any washing of clothes during the Twelve Days, go to the fields to work, borrow from a neighbor, or believe in the efficacy of dreams since they will not come true at this time.[9]

After the Emmanuels have had their nameday on the twenty-sixth and the Stephens theirs on the twenty-seventh, the women start preparing the traditional New Year's Eve dishes. On the thirtieth special attention is given to the baking of the *vasilopita,* a special cake named in honor of Saint Basil (Hagios Vasilis), a very important figure. A coin has been placed in the cake, on the top of which the date of the year is written. Chestnuts and almonds are used for decorations.

On New Year's Eve, throughout the day, the children go around caroling again much as they did on Christmas Eve, but on this occasion it is St. Basil's kalenda. The children carry a highly decorated branch of the sorb-tree or sometimes the olive with which they tap people on the shoulder in order to wish them good luck during the year. In return they expect a gift such as dried fruit. The youngsters add a festive air to the day and help build up the emotional crescendo that becomes quite evident as evening approaches — everyone is anxious to find out what their luck will be for the coming year. Excitement is particularly keen around midnight with the cutting of the vasilopita; first, the head of the house cuts a piece of this cake for the Virgin, then one for the house, then one for the job that the head of the house does, then his own piece to be followed by one for his wife and each child in turn. Everyone is curious to find out in what piece the lucky coin will turn up. Should it be in the Virgin's piece, it will be placed on the household shrine, but if any member of the family finds it in his piece he feels fortunate indeed.

If the family members exchange any gifts, it is done at this special event on New Year's Eve and not at Christmas. In Northern Greece especially the villagers play cards to test their luck. If anyone loses he is apt to say, "If I lose at cards, I'll win during the year." Those who win say, "I'll be lucky."

The devout go to the New Year's Day church service at which the liturgy of St. Basil is employed, and when they come home they are careful to step into the house with their right foot; if they have brought a new icon from the church, the one carrying it will step into the house first. During the day the men pay calls on such village notables as the community president, the priest, the doctor, or the schoolteacher and are served wine with a sort of canape. The women, dressed in their very best, serve the guests. Students, soldiers, and others away from home try to get back to their village for at least a two- or three-day visit. On New Year's Day the card games are taken up again.

The second, third, and fourth of January are ordinary working days, but on January 5 people expect a half-day off since it is Epiphany Eve, at which time children also sing the kalenda about the baptism of "the child of God." There is a five o'clock service in the morning at which occurs the first blessing of the waters. Those in attendance have brought jugs or cups for the blessed water which they take home to use in curing the sick or preventing the Evil Eye during the year. But on Epiphany itself occurs the most spectacular second blessing of the water, done in front of everybody at the church or near some body of water into which the cross is thrown. Swimmers are ready to dive in after it and struggle for its possession. The one who succeeds in gaining it is not only assured of good luck during the year but he can pass throughout the crowd and even the community to collect money from those solicited.

On Epiphany the priest visits the homes of the parish to bless each room by sprinkling holy water there, thus guaranteeing that all kallikantzari have been exorcised and chased back to their lairs beneath the earth until the next Twelve Days comes around.

Easter brings with it a wealth of customs, a blend of the pagan and the Christian, which are lightened by the coming of spring and the renewal of nature. Although they are "all of a piece" in the peasant mind, they can be best understood by the outsider in terms of Carnival, Lent, and Holy Week.

Carnival begins nine weeks before Easter and runs for three weeks. The second week is climaxed by Meat Sunday and the third week by Cheese Sunday. This is the time for weddings which otherwise could not take place until after Easter; this is the time for masquerades, although these are less pronounced in the villages than in the cities; this is also the time when family groups get together for little feasts before the Great Fast starts forty days before Easter. The last two Saturdays of Carnival and the first Saturday of Lent are *psychosabbata,* or memorial days for the dead. On the Thursday of the middle week of Carnival, members of the family, bringing their own food with them, gather in the home of the eldest relative to have a special meal, and on this occasion they allow some dish to scorch on the stove and smell up the house in the belief that this will bring good luck. This day is called *tsichnopempti,* since *tsichna* stands for the odor of burning flesh.

Meat Sunday is the eighth one before Easter (the villagers count Easter as one of the Sundays). On this day the people are supposed to start doing without meat products for the Lenten period. On the following Sunday, called Cheese Sunday, the forbidden foods are broadened to include milk products as well. This latter holiday is especially colorful in many parts of Greece, for on this day the village boys prepare piles of wood on various heights to be lit after dark. This is also the day for visiting older relatives and godparents in order to beg their forgiveness. Before the evening meal begins the younger members of the family kneel before their parents to ask their pardon for a wrongdoing and to receive a blessing. Carnival is definitely at an end.

Over and over again I asked local informants how many of the people kept the Great Fast before Easter. In the villages the replies were often as high as 80 percent of the older people, but more and more it seems that the younger generation keeps the fast for the one week immediately following Cheese Sunday and then takes it lightly until the Holy Week just prior to Easter. The villagers do not find it hard to give up meat because they actually have little available, but they do find that doing without eggs and cheese is restrictive. The pious manage to live on vegetables, bread, olives, and fruit.

Lent gets off to a frantic start with Clean Monday (*Kathara Deftera*), which is supposedly a period of purification of body and soul. Kitchen utensils are polished until they shine, walls whitewashed to make them look like new, floors scrubbed, and everything made ready for the big holiday which is in store. Townspeople in particular spend this day with their families on a picnic, with many localities having favorite spots that may originally have had a sacred meaning.

Eight days before Easter is the Day of St. Lazarus. On its eve the young girls sing what are called Lazarus songs, and on the day itself they go visiting. They are decorated with flowers and hold palm or laurel branches in their hands. They represent the death and resurrection of Lazarus and receive presents in return for their performance. On this day, too, there are frequently dances in the village squares.

On Palm Sunday the palm or laurel branches are woven into the form of a cross, around which several folk beliefs center. For example, some villagers believe they can tell the future from the cross; and others say this palm cross can be used against the Evil Eye.

Holy Week finds the emotional build-up for Easter increasing day by day. On Monday the housewives put everything in order, particularly if bad weather previously has kept them from getting all the cleaning done. The devout go to church, usually in the evening, although a liturgy is held in the morning as well. In some villages the residents may tie rags in their front door to keep away insects. On Tuesday the people do very little regular work because, as the housewives put it, "we are getting ready for Easter." On Wednesday those attending the morning service are anointed with oil on the forehead, chin, and cheeks (sign of the cross) and, in rural areas, new yeast is prepared in the church and distributed to families for use throughout the year. On Holy Thursday everybody takes the afternoon off, "for it was on this afternoon that Christ was seized." To commemorate the crucifixion in the evening service, the priests read twelve passages from the Gospel and the cross is brought out to the center of the church where people can kiss it, place flowers before it, and show their sorrow over the crucifixion which has been called to their mind. Eggs are dyed red on this day, which is sometimes called Red Thursday, thus symbolizing the blood of Christ.

Good Friday is a holy day on which no one works. The women pick flowers with which to decorate the holy shroud (*Epitaphios*) or sacred icon. All day long the coffeehouses are closed and the people abstain from alcoholic drinks, olives, fish roe, or leavened bread. The evening church service lasts from eight to midnight. One of its features is the carrying of the flower-bedecked Epitaphios in a sacred funeral procession through the streets of the village. The priests in their rich robes, the altar boys, and the congregation walk solemnly as though they were actually burying their Lord. The procession goes around the church before the simulated bier is brought to rest before the church door at such a height that the worshippers can pass under it into the church, crossing themselves as they do so.

On Saturday members of the household prepare the Paschal lamb. A few attend the services from 10 A.M. to 1 P.M., but almost everybody attends the evening service. The bells summon the people at 11 P.M. and by 11:30 the congregation has gathered. At midnight, when the sacred fire supposedly descends from heaven and the glorious Easter hymn *Christos Aneste* bursts forth in joy, people hurry to light their candles, shoot off the firecrackers they have brought for the purpose, and greet each other with *Christos aneste* (Christ is risen) and expect the answer *Alethos aneste* (Risen indeed). The service may continue to daybreak, but many of the people go home much earlier, each carrying his lighted taper with him. Upon arriving at the house, the worshipper uses the taper to smudge a black cross on the lintel. In some villages it is customary earlier in the day to make a cross on the door from the blood of the Paschal lamb. Once back home, the family ends the long Lenten fast by eating the red-dyed Easter eggs and *mageirites,* a highly seasoned stew made of the lamb's visceral organs. The lamb, which has not been sufficiently roasted on the spit, is eaten later in the day, not only by the members of the family but by the many guests and relatives who have come back to the village from their homes in the city.

All of Monday and the afternoon of Tuesday following Easter are considered national holidays. By Wednesday people can get back to their regular tasks. Religious ceremonies and festivals have added a meaningful dimension to their lives and have reminded them of the long continuity which links them with their ancestors who, as they see it, became the guardians and proponents of pristine Christianity, which lives on in their own Orthodox Church.

❦ Part Four ❦

Community

⸱⸱◦[X]◦⸱⸱

Mutual Aid and Cooperatives
in Rural Greece

The Greek village provides many evidences of mutual aid, although the Greeks are not renowned for their cooperative tendencies. Indeed, those commenting on Greek national character usually state that the Greeks cooperate only in a crisis. If there is no crisis at hand, they have to make one in order to get the job done. This view is partially correct, since some examples of mutual aid respond directly to a sense of urgency, while others follow traditional patterns at a leisurely pace. For instance, a group of potato diggers near Neochori were brought together to meet a sudden need.

A POTATO-DIGGING GROUP NEAR THEBES

It was March 28, 1953. We had turned off the main highway between Thebes and Athens and were headed eastward along a secondary road in search of some villagers whose relatives in California had insisted that we carry their greetings in person. Before we had found the right village, we noticed more than forty people busily harvesting potatoes in a nearby field. We stopped the car, walked into the field, and were greeted by Yannes P. Katseles, the owner, who lives in Neochori, the village just up the way. The men were digging the potatoes; the women were picking them up and cleaning them; and a commission merchant standing on his truck was directing his four helpers in sorting and sacking them. We were much less interested in what happened to the potatoes than in the means whereby forty people were gathered together at one time to help with the task at hand. We asked Yannes a number of questions:

"What do you call this kind of group?"

"We speak of it as *daneike ergassia* [borrowed work]. I received word that the commission merchant from Thebes would buy my potatoes if I had them ready by tonight. I have about an acre which I had not yet harvested, but this was too much to handle with just my immediate family. So I had to get others to help me. Last night my wife went around to the women and said, 'Tomorrow I'm going to pull potatoes. Will you come and help me?' I asked some of my relatives who live near me and a few close friends."

"What do you have to pay these people?"

"Usually we repay the others by working for them when they need help. One of us — my wife, daughter, or myself — will go help them with their potatoes when they have to harvest them. We keep a pretty good record of what we owe to others and what they owe to us. Five or six of the men working here do not have any potato fields so I agreed to pay them wages. They are particularly good at helping the commission merchant sort and sack the potatoes."

Such a crowd gathered around us while we asked these questions that we saw we were interrupting proceedings. So we strolled around to see how the men did the digging and learned that they worked under the close supervision of the owner. This fact reminded me of the Greek proverb, "The owner's eye is manure to the field." In fact, as the men dug, they moved in a long row across the field with the result that any laggard would soon be noticeably behind the rest. The villagers joked a great deal as we took pictures and asked about the length of the work day. The workers had come to the field about eight in the morning and would remain until the job was done, with the "estimated time of departure" set by the owner at about four or five o'clock.

The highlight of a day spent in such a work group is the food that is served to the workers about ten o'clock. Since the people were supposedly observing the Lenten fast, Yannes served a bean stew, candylike halvas, olives, fish, and wine. If they had not been fasting, they might have had cheese and eggs. Yannes insisted that they would only on rare occasions serve meat since they do not even eat that at home more than twice a month. But the workers, when asked about the food, said that it had been good and plentiful. "In fact," one man volunteered, "when Yannes invites us, we all say that we'll eat well today." Further inquiry showed that nobody ever turned down an invitation to a work group simply because he expected the food to be poor, but he would do so on other grounds, such as being busily involved in some work project of his own. At two o'clock Yannes planned to serve olives, onions, and bread with plenty of red resinated wine.

We could not stay much longer with the potato diggers, for we still had to carry our greetings to the village farther on. But a few days later I did return to Neochori and went to Yannes' home to find out who had been invited and why. In some ways this visit proved even more interesting than the sojourn in the potato field. The men were all away from the house; so Yannes' wife invited us into the square room which served as the center of family life. We sat around a table and began to list the twenty-five men and the eighteen women who had been a part of the mutual-aid group. Soon we saw neighboring women peering at us through the open window; then they moved on around to the door where they could hear better what we were talking about. News of our arrival must have spread like magic, for before we completed our list the room was full of women — some sitting on the beds along the wall, but several standing in order to observe more minutely everything that was going on. It was out of the question to interview the wife confidentially about why she invited some women and not others. As a matter of fact, two or three women had already taken it upon themselves to answer every question put to Yannes' wife, so that she was simply nodding in assent to what they said.

In no time at all, with the help of the most vocal members of the group, we had listed the relationship of each potato worker to Yannes and his wife. A later count of this information showed that, after we excluded Yannes, the commission merchant, and his one helper from outside, only six of the twenty-two remaining men were unrelated to Yannes. Each of these six persons was a neighbor. Of the seventeen women invited (excluding Yannes' wife), all but four were related to Yannes, but four were neighbors. Thus it was evident that family considerations and neighboring played a significant part, even to the point that some relatives who were not good workers were invited "because they were relatives." In other words, family values rather than economic values, such as efficiency, came into play.

We had noted that many of the women in the potato field were in their late teens or early twenties and found that they were preferred to the middle-aged women who are, of course, not excluded. Perhaps the younger ones have stronger backs and have no grounds for refusing if their father or husband tells them to go and help. Although a man is preferred for this kind of work, there would be no ill feeling if Yannes repaid some man who helped him by sending one of the women in his household. "We don't keep such close count that such a substitution bothers us " was the way one woman reacted.

In the course of our crowded group interview we learned that women issuing invitations usually avoid other women with whom they have had a recent quarrel, although they do not hesitate to invite two women on good terms with the hostess but not on good terms with each other. These women can usually stay far enough apart in such a large group that they do not have to associate with each other or air their differences. Men are said to be less inclined to let previous disagreements affect their invitations, even inviting those with whom they may have sharp differences. Their main concern is to get the job done. Just the same, they rely chiefly upon relatives and neighbors. The women in Yannes' living room all agreed that there was no one in the village who had the reputation for not paying back the work that others had contributed, which shows the seriousness with which this obligation is assumed and discharged.

But no interview in a Greek village is a one-sided affair. The visitor has to answer questions if he has asked them. Never have I heard questions fly quicker and faster than on this visit to Neochori when the women sensed that I had finished my inquiry about potato diggers. My interpreter was quizzed about her life in Athens, where she got her clothes, how she had learned to drive a car, and about members of her family. I was asked about my income in America, what kind of kitchen my wife had, and about many details which she could have answered much better than I if she had been able to accompany us up from Athens on that particular afternoon. This occasion showed that when the Greek villagers began to express themselves on their home ground, in a familiar setting, they stood out as inquisitive, interesting personalities who shared many of the same concerns as fellow human beings in other countries despite their noticeable differences of dress, speech, and other cultural manifestations.

In driving back to Athens we had to pass the same potato field which had been the cause of this excursion. I thought at the time that a study, at a later date, of changes in the mutual-aid groups would tell much about changes in Greek life in general. Will mechanization eliminate the necessity of group harvesting? Will economic considerations so rule a later day that Yannes will invite only efficient workers from throughout the village, or will he continue to use relatives and neighbors because of his close social bonds with them?

TRADITIONAL PATTERNS OF MUTUAL AID

Throughout rural Greece one finds many examples of mutual aid. Even proverbs attest to the value of cooperation: "bean by bean the bag is filled"; "many streams make up the river"; "many stones knock down the walnut." Union in strength is stressed as well: "where there are many, God's blessing"; "where there are many, many riches"; "the many are the ones who will take Constantinople."

It is understood, too, that each party will live up to his end of the bargain, for the proverbs say: "agreement is law"; "one ties the oxen by the horns, the man by his word." But the rugged individualists can also quote proverbs to show the dangers of depending upon others: "better a threshing floor small but your own"; "the donkey owned in common is eaten by the dogs"; "the wolf has a thick neck because he has to work alone."

Perhaps the simplest form of mutual aid is found in the case of two farmers, each of whom possesses but a single animal. They take turns using both animals to pull a plow or to do some other task where a team is needed. These partners are often called *smichtes* or *sebroi*. The Yannes described in an earlier chapter, who was disconsolately waiting for his partner to finish with his horse so that he could take the team to his own fields, was engaged in this kind of mutual aid. In Epirus, for instance, those with a single animal are called *monovodoi* (or single-oxen farmers), and each tries to join up with someone else in order to have a team available when needed. Similarly, someone with a donkey or two lends his animals to another farmer who needs to haul his cereal or hay from the fields or to market, in the expectation that he will have the use of the borrower's animals when in similar need.

Somewhat more complex in detail but similar in type are the arrangements that shepherds make concerning the care of their flocks and the distribution of the produce, which was mentioned earlier in the description of the changing life of the shepherd.

Mutual aid also extends to the exchange of agricultural labor, as in the case of the potato diggers. It can also occur between two families who throughout the work season combine their labor resources, culminating in tremendous output at harvest time. Or labor can be repaid by some other kind of service, as was the case in Malakassa (Attica), where the president of the commune went to the coffeehouse and said that he needed some help in harvesting a crop. Sixteen men from the coffeehouse went along to aid. When we asked the coffeehouse proprietor what these men would receive in return we were told, "The president has a cart and will help each of these men haul in stuff from their fields when they need him."

But there are times when much help is needed for some special event which does not recur frequently in the life of an individual family. Here the traditional "working bee" is assembled. For example, a family decides to plant a new vineyard or to put up some kind of a building. It calls upon its neighbors and relatives for help, feeds them well, and eventually pays back the labor provided when called upon by those who contributed. We found mutual-aid groups also busy making cheese for their own use and for sale or digging clay which they worked into home-made brick.

Women, however, seem to be more fully involved in a wide variety of mutual-aid arrangements. They may help each other with certain household chores — carding wool, baking bread, carrying fuel (*pournari* branches) from the hillsides to the house. But the most frequently described and the most romantic arrangements are the *nychteria,* or the groups of women who work together in the evening:

In the nychteria women help each other finish lighter types of work such as carding, the breaking and cleaning of almonds, cornhusking, kneading of ring biscuits, and the like. In these nocturnal pursuits in certain places customs are strict and men are strictly forbidden to participate. Because this type of work is housework and is carried out in the late hours of the day, it usually takes the form of a social gathering. Drinks and roasted chickpeas are offered, jokes are told, games are played, stories and anecdotes are told, and there is singing and dancing.[1]

Once in a while this dancing may last until dawn. In the summertime, especially, the women gather in the village lanes and spin by the light of the moon or a torch of resinous wood.

When a woman, whose husband is dead or off in the army, needs help which no kinship group can provide, she will go to the head of some other family and say: "My son has gone into the army. I have only daughters. If you will help me in man's work my daughters will help you." They then become *kollegoi* (colleagues or partners) and carry out the agreed-upon obligations.

These examples are not intended to cover the wide range of mutual-aid activities, but they serve to highlight their main features. Fishermen have numerous arrangements for helping one another; farmers may rent a field and work it jointly, or even own olive or nut trees in common. In general, these mutual-aid arrangements are viewed as quite different from land-lord-tenant contracts which occurred in many forms before the land re-distribution in the 1920s. Those tied together in mutual-aid agreements think of themselves as coequal and not as superior and subordinate part-ners. Nor do these mutual-aid traditions ordinarily apply to cases where money alone is given as full payment for services received. Instead, they make it possible for villagers to meet many of their important needs with-out having to pay money for services rendered. The mutual-aid practices discussed here differ also from what might be called philanthropy or deeds done for "the good of the soul" which will be looked at more closely in connection with the villager's religion.

Beyond any question, there is a strong strain of cooperation even among the individualistic Greeks. Although somewhat overidealized, the follow-ing comment by T. K. Papaspyropoulos about his Peloponnesian village portrays the essence of mutual aid there:

When somebody gets sick everybody goes to visit him and look after him. When a young girl gets married all the village goes and helps. When they sow, plow, winnow, or do any other village tasks one person helps the other.

Even when death is there, there is help. Who can bury the dead by himself? The village all cry together, they all suffer together, and the whole village buries him. He too is not far away from them. His soul roams around them and, as they say themselves, he watches them.[2]

THE AGRICULTURAL COOPERATIVE MOVEMENT IN GREECE

One could logically argue that a people with as many kinds of mutual aid as the Greek villagers should take readily to the cooperative organization designed to assist cooperators, through organized efforts, to achieve goals which they could not hope to satisfy individually. But the transition from informal mutual aid to an organized cooperative proves much more difficult than one would at first imagine. In the first place, since the village mutual-aid patterns are a "here and now" undertaking, those participating can see the immediate results of their labor and can hold the person helped accountable to return assistance to them when needed. The formal cooperative organizations, on the other hand, have to set goals which are removed both in time and place from the average peasant. Not only are the centers of financial control and the markets distant, but the member has to wait for benefits to accrue in the case of a marketing cooperative. In a credit cooperative, the loan received is more tangible, but its attainment has probably seemed to the peasant a long, laborious procedure.

The transition from village mutual aid to the formal cooperative organization is difficult, in the second place, because the *formal* organization itself is an urban rather than a village development. To participate in and guide an organization takes as much "know-how" as repairing a tractor or managing a flock. But it is a different kind of skill from any which the peasant has been trained to use, and he is therefore either ill at ease or grossly inefficient when he tries to work with such a new social mechanism. Parliamentary procedure, the keeping of books and membership lists, and the preparation of reports go on around him all of the time, but he is seldom called upon to participate in such activity. This means that, as a member, he is apt to be passive and apathetic; he is also apt not to understand much of what is done in the cooperative organization and is therefore chronically critical of management, the government, and perhaps the whole idea of formal cooperatives in general. Once he has learned to deal with the social mechanism of the organization, he is much more self-assured and agreeable, but getting to this point takes a great deal of time for most villagers.

But perhaps a third difficulty in the transition from local mutual aid to membership in the cooperative society is most crucial. Basically the mutual-aid groups consist of family members and neighbors; only occasionally do they even call upon others in the village. The cooperative association makes an immediate leap beyond family and neighborhood to encompass men from the whole village — men who know each other but who have not been accustomed to working together. Even more, the cooperative becomes closely identified with the central government, which immediately introduces not only nonfamilial but even nonlocal considerations. This is a psychological gap which many peasants cannot quickly cross. Promoters of cooperatives from outside may see in them a strong support of family and village values; but the peasant sees in them the impersonality of the political authority, the introduction of money rather than exchange of labor as the unit of measurement, and, at times, even questions the motives of those "who are running around trying to get us to join something we don't know anything about." Throughout Greece I found villages at all degrees of opposition or readiness for cooperatives, but where there was resistance these three difficulties were present along with a dozen other reasons the people gave to explain why they did not want to join.

The cooperative movement, like so much in Greece, has an interesting past. One important landmark noted by students of cooperatives in Greece was the rise of Ambelakia, a city on the Peneios River in Northern Greece, which became such an important manufacturing center of cotton and silk goods in the seventeenth century that it had trade connections throughout Europe. Its dyed thread was particularly well known then, although its wine is its only product renowned today. Ambelakia rose to economic greatness because of the well-run association which administered the community's affairs. Although this may have been more in the tradition of the guild than a modern cooperative, it nevertheless showed what a single community could do if it organized its efforts in a systematic fashion.[3] The association of Ambelakia, as well as the modern cooperative movement, is thought by some to have its roots deep in the traditions of local self-government, as the later discussion of this topic will show. Not only would one community organize itself as a viable political and economic unit, but several communities in an area would band together to deal with the Turkish masters. But, significant as these unions were, they were quite different in scope and intent from the agricultural-cooperative movement in Greece today which goes back to 1900. At that time a schoolteacher in the village of Almyros in Thessaly, aroused over the fact that local usurers were charging peasants interest rates as high as 100 percent, organized a local credit or loan society which he called a mutual treasury. This type of organization spread to many communities throughout the country.

In 1915 a new law provided for the establishment of cooperatives, with at least seven persons required to form a society. Such a cooperative could be of unlimited liability, with each member having one vote, or it could be of limited liability, with those having more shares being allowed up to five votes but no more. The Cooperative Act provided certain privileges: exemption from import duties on agricultural implements and machinery, seeds, spray materials, and other essential agricultural materials for the exclusive use of the members of the society; and protection by law from interference by outside interests. In return for these privileges, the state reserved the right to approve the by-laws of the cooperatives and to inspect and audit their books.[4]

Between the two world wars some of the cooperatives took on a compulsory character. For instance, many refugees who were settled on land in the 1920s were formed into cooperatives which could not be dissolved or from which individuals could not withdraw until complete payment was made. In some districts citrus and grape producers were compelled to deliver their products to the cooperatives. Also, compulsory cooperatives, organized by a majority vote of the farmers in a region, could take over the common utilization of land, forests, and pastures, or the task of grafting of barren and wild trees. Quite aside from these compulsory cooperatives and the widespread credit cooperatives, there were many voluntary cooperatives for marketing, production, and insurance against fire, hail, and frost.

In Greece, as in all other Balkan countries, the agricultural cooperatives through the years have been under the supervision of the Agricultural Bank, from which the government channeled credit to the rural sector of the economy. The local societies were grouped into regional cooperative unions. Instead of having to deal individually with each peasant who wanted a loan on his livestock or against the next crop, the government officials could leave the initial screening of applications to local cooperative officials, then to those at the regional level, while reserving for themselves final approval. Under Metaxas, who ruled as a dictator just prior to World War II, the cooperative section of the Agricultural Bank received no support and, in all probability, cooperatives would have found continuation difficult if Metaxas had been in power for a long period.[5]

Then came the war years, which were difficult for cooperatives as well as for everything else in Greece. The situation at the end of the war was described in 1946 when the newly created Food and Agriculture Organization, a specialized agency of the United Nations, sent its very first Mission team to Greece to survey the situation and make recommendations. This team, headed by Franklin S. Harris, President of the Utah State College of Agriculture, found that the "machinery" of cooperative activities had developed to such a point before World War II that it could provide an important facility for postwar rural rehabilitation.[6] Most of the FAO Mission's recommendations dealt with ways in which this facility could best be used. However, at least two points were brought out which have a direct bearing upon the peasant himself. The first suggests that greater responsibility be given the local village cooperative, thereby placing more control over making individual production loans, receiving repayments, and keeping the individual loan accounts in the hands of the peasants themselves. The general tendency in most cooperative systems is for the center of gravity to shift away from the village to the national capital, where the Agricultural Bank is located, or to the provincial cities, where the bank has branches to which the individual peasants are supposed to go to "process" their loans.

A second important question touched upon in the FAO report was whether the producers' cooperative ought to be compulsory in one or both of two ways: first, requiring all of those who produce a given commodity (such as tobacco) and who live in a given village to belong to a cooperative and, second, forcing all cooperative members to market their produce and buy their supplies only through the cooperative. The FAO Mission counseled against making the cooperatives compulsory, and the same point of view has been held by most of the American advisers who have worked with the American Aid Mission in Greece. Greek government officials, however, sometimes think that legal sanctions would strengthen cooperatives and thereby tighten the economic machinery through which 10–12 percent of the Greek tobacco crop and about 80 percent of olive oil, to mention but two crops, reach the market.[7]

The cooperative leaders, however, face a problem of social as well as legal sanctions: they would like to guide the cooperative movement from the stage where each cooperative member is a law unto himself to the point where any farmer who fails to sell his produce through his cooperative has to reckon with the disapproval of his fellow farmers. This can only be done through a long-term program of education which stresses not cooperation as an abstract ideal but the fact that a cooperative organization depends upon the support of every member and is not much stronger than its weakest link. It is in this matter of interpretation, of teaching the villager the meaning of cooperation, that the cooperative movement is not very successful. Cooperative officials are so busy being administrators that they do not take time to be interpreters, to be sure their communication strikes a responsive chord in the peasant. Then, too, they tend to feel that they have so much authority (such as fiscal control) in their hands that they do not have to depend upon the subtler forms of authority — namely, pressure by loyal members upon those who would deviate from what is considered good cooperative practice. This is tied in with the psychological problem of making the members feel that the cooperative is theirs rather than the instrumentality of cooperative and governmental officials who live outside the community.

One report by A. W. Willis, an American marketing specialist, goes so far as to say: "The Greek cooperative law makes cooperatives an arm of the Government and actually prohibits member control as well as any profit acquiring to members. The entire agricultural economy of this state could profit through true Cooperatives but not through those now in existence under the present law."[8]

How strong are cooperatives in Greece today? In 1957, they numbered 7,127 and had a membership of 718,000.[9] They therefore constitute the principal farm organization in Greece. Those who lead the cooperative movement are quick to point out what they hope to achieve: to narrow the ratio between prices received by the farmers and prices paid by the farmers; to market members' products and purchase for them equipment and supplies; to process farm commodities, produce pesticides, farm machinery; and to provide special services for members such as plowing, cultivating, and harvesting.[10] Since many of the Greek farmers are too impoverished to raise sufficient capital on their own to finance a local cooperative, they are therefore dependent upon those cooperatives for which the government, through the Agricultural Bank, provides all the funds and over which it insists on centralized control.

How the Villagers View Cooperatives

What the FAO study team, the American missioners, and even the Greek government officials think about agricultural cooperatives is secondary to what the Greek peasants themselves think. Their opinions ranged all the way from those of open resentment and hostility to those of great pride in local cooperative achievements. To be told, as was mentioned in Chapter 5, that some villagers whom we wanted to see had hid upon our arrival, for they thought that we were either cooperative officials or connected with the Agricultural Bank, was an object lesson in itself. We asked one of them why he had run away. He replied: "I still owe the Bank a great deal. We have to pay 9 percent interest on what we borrow, 1 percent to the cooperative and 8 percent to the Bank. Last year I hadn't paid off my loan ($70.), so I couldn't get a new loan. I borrowed what I needed from a private individual at 20 percent and paid off this loan to the bank so that I could obtain potato seed on a new loan. Now I have sold my potatoes and the Bank will be after me to pay them what I owe."

When we asked what happened to people who did not repay their loans, we were told that in such cases the collector came out, wrangled with the people, and if he received no repayment took them to court. To such villagers, cooperatives were chiefly credit agencies and in no sense stood for a local association of farmers pooling their energies and resources to achieve joint goals.

Now and then we found peasants who were anxious to start a cooperative but considered the initiation difficult. In a village near Megalopolis in the Peloponnesos, the people were well aware of the difference between prices received in the village for watermelons and what such products cost in Athens. Like farmers everywhere, they thought the price differences unjust. They blamed bureaucratic red tape for holding up the establishment of a cooperative. Some of the more dubious went on to say: "Even if we do get a cooperative, we will have to wait a year to get a loan approved, and by that time we will have no need for the money." They thought that from 12 to 14 percent would be the customary interest charges set by the cooperative and the Bank and also assumed that security requirements would be very high.

Peasants in the tobacco-growing areas in Northern Greece appreciated the fact that cooperatives there tried to introduce mechanization and also, from time to time, did some lobbying in their behalf. When in 1953 we asked the commandant of gendarmerie for Volos, who was in close touch with the villagers, about their views toward cooperatives he replied: "With the occupation and the war the cooperative conscience more or less disappeared. Now it is reviving and if things go normally there will be quick improvement. One reason for the difficulty is the effort by the government to mix politics in with the cooperative movement. Now the cooperatives undertake no teaching function. They did this before the war, which partially explained what success they achieved. Before the war, if a person wanted to be on the council of the cooperative, he had to go through special training. The authorities say that they will do this again, but the Ministry of Agriculture is centering its teaching approach in the newly formed Agro Clubs."

He thought that in his area about 60 percent of the cooperatives were working and that 40 percent were either anemic or altogether defunct. Around Volos the producers' and marketing cooperatives organized on a commodity basis — vegetables, dairy, fruit, olives — worked better than the general-purpose or purely credit type. Very often, he pointed out, the relationship between the local cooperative and the representatives of the Agricultural Bank is strained, for the local council will give inaccurate information to the Bank, saying that a would-be borrower has twelve acres of land when he really has only five.

One of the most interesting examples of the blending of traditional and modern mutual-aid practices was found in Kalivi, a village of about 2500 in Attica. This village owned some pasture land. In 1914 it formed a committee which took charge of the management of this community land, deriving revenues for the community. In 1920 there was talk of organizing a cooperative, but it did not really get under way until 1926, at which time the village pasture land was turned over to the cooperative which superseded the former committee. Thus, the transition from the older social form to the cooperative went smoothly. The Agricultural Bank had helped the local people decide what was the best kind of cooperative organization for their purposes. They decided that membership should be compulsory for all family heads. In 1928 the cooperative acquired a threshing machine with the funds obtained from the pasture land. This machine as well as newer ones were in use when I visited the village near the middle of June 1953. Organized pandemonium seemed to reign as new loads of wheat sheaves were fed to the threshing machine by the girls, who were wearing goggles and what seemed to be gas masks to protect them from the dust. The women also were wiring the bales of straw which were taken away to be stacked. The president of the community told me:

Anyone who wants to work signs up. Every fifteen days we put on a new crew so that quite a few people are employed and paid. We do have to keep a small permanent crew on the job throughout the threshing season, which lasts about sixty days, but almost every family has a chance to get some benefit. We only do the wheat belonging to the people of our community. We determine by lot the order in which a family's wheat is to be threshed. All the people bring their grain here, for we can thresh it much more cheaply than they could do it with animals.

We then went into the large olive-pressing plant, built in 1948, with a loan of about $30,000 from the Agricultural Bank, and learned how this part of the cooperative's business was conducted. We learned that each family's batch of olives, like its wheat, was processed separately and that it gave 8 percent of the oil to the cooperative, which is a standard amount taken by presses over Greece, plus an extra 3 percent contribution until the machinery is paid for. After that, it will have to pay only 4 instead of the customary 8 percent. When I noticed an icon in the pressing plant, the manager said that they asked the priest in to bless their work at the beginning of the season. Another man in the company remarked, "we like our religion, but we don't like our priests," a comment with which the others seemed to agree.

The more I learned about this cooperative in Kalivi, the more I realized what a shrewd investment the pasture land had been. The cooperative accumulates no money for itself but reinvests all profits into public works or special funds as determined by the directors of the cooperative. For example, a doctor is paid out of a cooperative philanthropic fund in return for looking after the poor of the community free of charge.

In addition to this general cooperative, to which all family heads belong, there are in Kalivi five other cooperatives. First, there is the credit cooperative explained to me as follows: "Since many people here have to depend upon the Agricultural Bank for loans, the credit cooperative gets the money for them and they do not have to make the contact themselves. If a local peasant wants sulphur or insecticides, the cooperative gets all that is needed. The individual then owes the cost to the cooperative. He pays no membership dues. Both men and women belong." It so happened that the president and the secretary of the community, plus three other people, made up the five-man executive committee of this credit cooperative.

Second, there is a livestock cooperative which the owners of the five thousand sheep in the community support. The members number forty, the executive committee five, and the supervising board three. This cooperative helps bring in fodder, sell milk, arrange loans. If a member has taken a loan, he must give milk to the cooperative as payment on the loan. In some types of loan the shepherd can be responsible directly to the Agricultural Bank. There are three other cooperatives of lesser importance. Everybody belongs to the vineyard cooperative, for all grow grapes, but this cooperative has not been very active of late due to a number of economic changes taking place in the village. Fifteen people belong to an apiary cooperative; and fifteen others belong to a poultry cooperative, since this is a growing source of income for the local people.

These reactions to cooperatives document some of the general observations made earlier about the movement. There is a tendency for the foreigner to side with those peasants who are most critical of the way cooperatives are now being run, but any such critic must be prepared to explain how one can expect much local control unless the local villagers put up some of the working capital, as did the villagers of Kalivi with their pasture land. For the most part, members of the Greek cooperatives make no contributions, buy no shares, pay only nominal membership fees, for the reason that they do not have sufficient economic margin. Those officials who lend public funds have to concentrate on control and collection, since it is an accepted practice in Greece, as in many parts of the world, for the farmer to borrow as much as he can and pay back as little as he can. The educational task, then, is the difficult one of teaching the necessity of honoring one's contracts to the cooperative as truly as the peasant honors his informal agreements to pay back labor in a traditional mutual-aid activity. It also calls for the community-wide recognition that peasants who are defaulting on their payments are hurting fellow members in the cooperative and should in time be made to feel the censure of those who are keeping agreements. But, most important of all, the cooperatives could be interpreted as social mechanisms through which the peasants can do more than merely borrow money or get fertilizer on credit — as avenues through which they can effectively increase their general economic well-being.

In the final analysis, however, mutual aid in a Greek village consists of more than the informal patterns, such as the potato-digging group of Neochori; it is more than the cooperative organizations in all of their variations. It also includes the philanthropic assistance, to be discussed in connection with religion, and the "voluntary labor" required of the community members by their community council, an interesing form of mutual effort to be discussed under local government.

···⊰[XI]⊱···

The Village Coffeehouse

Eventually the coffeehouse, instead of being merely the setting for many lively conversations about village life, became an object of interest in its own right. It, too, is a village institution which takes its rank along with the school and the church. The coffeehouse, or *kapheneion,* is more than just a structure. Like the English pub, it is a place of assembly, a communication center, a place to transact business, satisfy one's thirst, or find out about the health of one's friend.

Most coffeehouses are located near the main square or at some crossroads where things are apt to happen. They find their fullest development in the cities. In the early evening, the time of day when Washington "rolls up its sidewalks" and becomes quieter and quieter, the squares of Athens, the Greek capital, literally burst into life. Constitution Square, for instance, after hundreds of chairs, which have been stacked during the day, are set up around small tables, the waiters begin their hazardous dashes back and forth across the busy street to the food shops which line the square. Their frenetic activity contrasts with the leisurely attack by the patrons upon the small cup of sweet, sirupy coffee and glass of water before them, although a conversation at some table may reach such proportions that one becomes oblivious to the automobile horns, the radio blaring out some popular tune, or the clink of spoons on a glass as people try to attract the attention of a waiter.

Transposed to a rural setting, the coffeehouse seems rude by comparison, its patrons less well dressed, but it meets the same needs. In the village it has a variety of forms.

COFFEEHOUSE TYPES

The coffeehouse, as used in this description, comes in at least three assorted forms. One form is the shop or small variety store which sells some merchandise and serves drinks as well. A second form concentrates on drinks alone, alcoholic and nonalcoholic. A third specializes in coffee and sweets and usually serves little if any alcoholic beverages. As one would expect, the larger the village, the greater the likelihood of finding the second and third types. To understand the social utility of the first type one must travel to a small village, such as Psathotopi on the Arta Plains.[1]

Psathotopi, with less than four hundred people, has three coffeehouses which are the only business establishments in the community. Each sells a few articles in addition to the coffee and ouzo. Women who want needles or marcaroni either go or send their children to the shops' windows to make the purchases, for they are not allowed to enter the shops, which are man's domain. The least prepossessing of the shops, interestingly enough, is the meeting place of the community officers. It is a branch-covered hut, four by five yards in size, which has no chairs or tables inside but only benches along the walls. Coffee, ouzo, and a few articles are sold here by the proprietor, who is also the church sexton. A second shop, of mud and reed construction, is larger (four by twelve yards) and contains four tables and six chairs, plus benches around the walls. Again, the merchandise consists of coffee, ouzo, and a few articles. The third shop, considered the best, is rented from the church. It is six by nine yards in size, of mud brick and stone construction. Its stock of merchandise is a little larger and it serves Turkish delight as a special attraction. This shop has five tables, twelve chairs, and more benches than the other two. In other words, these three shops represent the local commerce of Psathotopi.

In the Peloponnesos, when there was a lull in the conversation at a shop of three by five yards in a village of about six hundred, I noted what this emporium contained. On hand were cigarettes, Turkish delight, flints, ouzo, brandy, horseshoe nails, macaroni, kerosene lamp wicks, bobby pins, needles, thread, candy, sugar, and coffee. There was the customary counter, two tables and five benches around the walls. The kerosene lamp cast a kindly glow about the place, contrasting with the dark unlit village streets of a winter night. A wood stove, fed charily, provided warmth. When I passed this same shop in the daytime, I realized what an ideal spot its front courtyard provided for basking when the sun shone in the winter and for shade during the summer when patrons could sit under the plane tree and watch the women come to the fountain for water. All that was needed was a supporting Greek version of "Standing on the Corner, Watching All the Girls Go By."

Or, in Northern Greece and the Grammos Mountains, one would find in the village of Kotili, with about six hundred people, that there were two shops which sold cigarettes and coffee.[2] A score of the men, in addition to being farmers and shepherds, were woodworkers; another score were masons, and one was a cobbler. That represented the specialization of that village, since all the other men were farmers-shepherds-laborers. But it is at coffeehouses such as those in Kotili, close by the border, that one gains an insight into the real meaning of Balkan politics. For here the older villagers will tell the visitor of the days back in the first decade of the century when Bulgarian *komitadjis,* while the area was still under Turkey, came to try to persuade the people to join the Bulgarian cause. But the people remained loyal to the orders of their church authorities and resisted the efforts of the Bulgarians to enroll their local children in special schools or to enlist the adults in a premature revolt against the Turks. As one listens to the stories of violence and national struggle, the surrounding mountains which at first seemed peaceful begin to assume a brooding look. And one learns that national traditions are preserved and passed on in the coffeehouse, with the old men telling the eager young men of the price that was paid to keep them Greek.

Vamvakia, on the Serrai plains, provides a final illustration of the combined variety shop–coffeehouse.[3] This village, too, numbers about six hundred people and has as its only business a cheese-making establishment and three coffeehouses. There is also one carriage maker who farms as well. The merchandise for the shops is brought from Serrai by the bus driver, who takes in the orders and brings back the supplies for a small fee. These coffeehouses are of brick and clay-mud construction and have the usual equipment of small tables and chairs. Two of them have battery radios for the entertainment of the customers. Coffee is the usual beverage, while ouzo and soda drinks (in summer) are also popular. Spoon sweets, such as vanilla or fruit preserves, are often sold.

We may conclude, therefore, that in most villagers of less than a thousand people one will generally find coffeehouses of the combined variety-shop type. Although the women may now and then view them as shops, the men almost invariably think of them as coffeehouses. This social function outweighs any economic function they might possess.

As size increases, say to more than a thousand people, the variety shops and grocery stores become separate establishments and the coffeehouse devotes itself almost exclusively to serving beverages. This is what most Greeks would consider the typical village coffeehouse, although the relative numbers of each kind are not known.

The specialized coffeehouses can frequently accommodate fifty to seventy people without any great difficulty. Many of the buildings are rented by the proprietors either from some owner who built them as an investment or from the community, which derives income from the structure. In a Macedonian village of Kimine, twenty-four miles from Salonica, there are three coffeehouses:

All have adequate furniture, little tables and chairs being the standard coffeehouse equipment. All are fortunate to have battery radios also. . . . The largest coffeehouse is a community building and is rented from the community. Most of the village's middle-aged men frequent here. . . . The second coffeehouse is also rented, this time from a private owner. This coffeehouse is smaller and much neater than the previous one. Here we usually find the old men of the village, sitting around and quietly drinking and talking. The third coffeehouse is the meeting place of all the younger men in the village. This is a new building, pleasant and big.[4]

The third type of coffeehouse, found much more frequently where urban influences are strong, seldom sells ouzo and other alcoholic drinks, not because of any temperance drives, but because it caters to those who prefer coffee and an occasional sweet. This type is much more apt to be patronized by women, often in the company of a husband or father. Elsewhere in the village or town will be found *tavernas,* where wine — often that produced by the owner for his own clientele — is served in an outside courtyard with food. Many travelers to Greece have commented on the moderate use of alcoholic beverages in that country and have often pointed out that they never saw more than one or two drunk people during their whole sojourn.

But all three types of coffeehouses — the combined variety shop, the drink emporium, where liquor is served as well as coffee, and the urban type where only coffee is served — are important for reasons other than what is consumed. That is secondary, for many villagers visit a coffeehouse without buying a single drink or sweet.

COFFEEHOUSE ATTRACTIONS

As I sat in scores of Greek coffeehouses I wondered, in looking around me, why these particular men were present at this time and what the rest of the village men were doing. I also tried to find out why certain men, perhaps five or six, were talking to each other around one table while another five or six were in earnest conversation around another table. And here and there I would find a smaller group of two or three seriously intent upon some point of discussion. What formed the nucleus of each group? Did the same people tend to cluster together each time they came to the coffeehouse? This was more than idle curiosity on my part, for I knew that the answer to such questions would reveal a great deal about how public opinion was formed in the village, opinion which in turn would be directly related to Greek national policy and even to Greek-American relations. In the Greek coffeehouses we find the equivalent of what Chester Bowles has referred to as the "tea house jury":

> One evening in Taipeh I asked a world-wise old Chinese diplomat what he thought would happen on the mainland. "Have you ever been to China?" he asked. When I said that I had not, he said, "In every one of China's one million villages is a tea house. Every day at the tea hour the people, especially the wise people of the village, gather to talk.
>
> "Chiang lost," the old man continued, "because this great 'tea house jury' decided that he had failed. The villagers came to believe that the Communists could do no worse, and they might be better.
>
> "Someday perhaps the 'tea house jury' will bring a verdict against Mao. Then China will be ready for a change." [5]

Although my study of the Greek coffeehouse never got beyond the introductory stage, I felt fortunate indeed to find that the investigation by John Photiadis of Stavroupolis in Macedonia had addressed itself to many of the specific questions in which I had been interested.[6] No one would claim that all of his findings for one village in Northern Greece would automatically apply to the whole country, but they do possess enough generality to provide some penetrating insight. For example, his discussion * of the coffeehouse attractions are most helpful.

The primary appeal is *kouvenda*, or conversation, explained as follows:

> *Kouvenda* means conversation without any particular purpose, a recognized form of "passing the time." It is rarely desultory, or the mere exchange of ideas or description of events, or delving into the past in a quiet manner. But sometimes it is contrapuntal virtuosity, incisive, combative, loud, a statement or a question is countered by a challenging question, tact and gentleness have no part, insults are hurled, but within appropriate limits. A discussion is a battle of personal opinions, and its end is neither to reach truth nor to reach a conclusion; its end is sheer enjoyment of vigorous speech. But whatever impression this occupation of passing the time makes on someone who is a stranger to this custom, to these people it is their enjoyment. It constitutes one of the attractions that makes the coffeehouse a necessity for the villager.

Photiadis points out that during the kouvenda the participant is involved emotionally, is not only trying to prove his point but is also enjoying this oratory. The irresponsible statements are not to be taken seriously, although they sometimes are, with unfortunate consequences. In this connection, I was always interested in what the men argued about most in the village coffeehouses and found that they did not discuss politics to the same extent as the denizens of the urban coffeehouses. They preferred to talk about community affairs, crops, and personalities, although the announcement about some

* Relying on some of Dorothy Lee's analysis.

earth-shaking political event would call forth a variety of opinions force-fully expressed.

A second attraction is drinking with one's friends. According to Pho-tiadis:

The alcoholic or non-alcoholic beverages tend to contribute to a considerable degree to the attraction of the coffeehouse, even though the men can drink all they want in their own homes. *Ouzo,* the alcoholic drink, is drunk only in the coffeehouse. When asked why they don't drink it at home and save money, they will answer that *"ouzo* is drunk only with good company."

It is interesting to remember what has already been pointed out: that a son is customarily supposed to visit a coffeehouse in which his father is not likely to be found. Although "times are changing," a breach of this custom throughout much of rural Greece would still be considered disrespectful. It may have some connection with the fact that a father, who is supposed to set a good example before his son, might find his storytelling or his con-vivial drinking dampened if a son were present. This is why, in village after village, where there are almost always three coffeehouses, one is favored by the old men, another by the middle-aged, and the third by the young peo-ple. Informants will say that the young people will go to their coffeeshop because one can listen to phonograph records, watch the girls pass by, or play noisy games that the older men might not tolerate. The real reason for differentiation may lie in the older traditions which originated in the men's desire to drink with their friends and equals. Photiadis in his study points out how the Greek peasant during his hours at work looks forward eagerly to the time of day when he can go "to the coffeehouse to meet his friends, have a few drinks, and continue this cycle again and again."

A third source of pleasure in the coffeehouse is the games. Playing for drinks is common with the loser paying for them. Very rarely do they play for money since it is prohibited by law. Sometimes they become involved in a game quite emotionally and when the game is over they eagerly look forward to the next meeting. A good card player is well-known and therefore is always surrounded by others watching him. Quarrels sometimes go along with the game. Char-acteristic is the sarcasm of the winner, or perhaps the participants, which tends to raise their emotions.

In addition to various kinds of card games, backgammon is commonly played. Once in a while one sees a chess game in progress.

A fourth and very important attraction of the coffeehouse is the availa-bility of the recent newspaper and a radio. As Photiadis says:

Non-farmers or part-time farmers stop to listen to the early news before they go to their work. During the day the older men sit for many hours in the coffee-house listening to the radio. In the busy coffeehouse the early part of the evening or the very late hours are the times when the people pay most attention to the radio. During the busy evening hours it is very difficult to listen to or enjoy the radio because of the noise the participants make.

The different outsiders who stop by the coffeehouse, particularly the most central and attractive one, bring news and diversion. The bus driver, a government official en route to some other village, a commission merchant after agricultural products or livestock, a stray American tourist, are links with the larger society. Frequently, some offhand remark by one such stranger, because it has the ring of authority, influences the opinions of those present and thereby the opinions of others in the village who receive the information secondhand. Not to be overlooked, of course, is the eye-witness report some fellow villager brings back from the city or a provincial town where he has gone to arrange a business or legal matter. More often than not he can hardly wait to get to the coffeehouse so that he can hold the spotlight as long as he can stretch out the account of what he saw.

These attractions do not begin to exhaust all the possibilities. Anyone with business to transact arranges to meet the other party or parties at a coffeehouse. One may also go to the same place for a haircut. In Kimine, all three of the coffeehouses have what passes for a barber shop in one corner. Since there is no partitioning, the barber chair, mirror, and all tonsorial activities are in full view of the coffeehouse patrons. The barber is particularly in his glory on Saturday and Sunday nights, when the coffeehouses are at their busiest. Likewise, in Anthili, in Central Greece, the three barbers there ply their trade in the coffeehouses, and so it is throughout most of rural Greece. Now and then one even comes across a singing barber who entertains when business is slack. Most coffeehouse proprietors consider him a prize asset.

THE COFFEEHOUSE CLIENTELE

But knowing what attracts the villagers to the coffeehouse does not tell us who is attracted and to what coffeehouses. Nor does it give us sufficient insight into the way community decisions are reached in the coffeehouse setting. For such information we need to take a closer look at the findings for Stavroupolis:

Ninety percent of the adult males of the village visit at least one of the seven coffeehouses from time to time. Almost all of these go at least 1–2 days a month throughout the year, with about four fifths going an average of at least 1–2 days a week.

More people go during the summer, but those who go during the winter go more often. Most people vary their frequency from winter to summer and those who change least are obviously those who go every day.

Most people spend at least an hour whenever they go to the coffeehouse, but they spend more than twice as much time during the non-busy period than during the busy period.

Apparently Stavroupolis also follows the pattern generally encountered throughout Greece in which the peasants spend much more time during the day in the coffeehouse in the winter months but more time during the evening hours in the summer. This of course follows the cycle of farm work.

When asked to give the reasons why they go to the coffeehouse, those with high yearly participation in Stavroupolis coffeehouses replied as follows: have nothing else to do (76 percent); to play a game (74 percent); to have a drink (64 percent); to see friends (63 percent); to hear what is new (56 percent); to talk with someone (51 percent); to go to a place where men go (25 percent). On the other hand, when all the men — not just the "high participants" — were asked to check which three of the seven reasons above were most likely to apply in their case, and the checks for each reason were computed as a percentage of all checks, the following distribution was obtained: to hear what is new (32 percent); to meet friends (26 percent); to have a drink (14 percent); to talk with someone (13 percent); to play a game (8 percent); nothing else to do (4 percent); it is the place where men go (3 percent).

These differences in response deserve a word of explanation. Apparently the high participators have gotten to the point where going to the coffeehouse is an end in itself, a habit which requires no justification other than to say that there is nothing else to do. Most men, however, try to give a more logical explanation, since they are aware that there are supposedly serious alternatives to going to the coffeehouse and that there are other things they might be doing. So more than half of all the reasons checked included the two most socially acceptable: to hear what is new and to meet friends.

But what are characteristics of those who are the "high participants"? In Stavroupolis, at least, the following facts hold true:

The higher a man's education, and particularly the higher his wife's education, the less time he spends at the coffeehouse.

Older people participate more than younger people.

People of higher economic efficiency participate more than those of low economic efficiency.

Nonfarmers participate more than part-time farmers, and part-time farmers more than farmers.

The most frequent participants are also apt to be leaders in the village organizations.

Furthermore, more high participants look unfavorably upon farming and living in the village than do low participants.

The native-born participate much less than do the settlers from eastern Thrace or Asia Minor who moved into the village in the 1920s, thus showing that participation may have something to do with cultural traditions.

These factors associated with participation may themselves be related to others which have not been spelled out. Then, too, the fact that participation increases with age would also be tied in with the leadership in organizations, since young people seldom attain official positions. Although findings such as these have to be tested in many ways before they become accepted generalizations, they do at least suggest some fruitful leads for further research.

Of equal interest is the reason the peasants give for going to one coffeehouse instead of another. Other accounts of village life had listed cleanliness, reputation, honesty, services provided, and the credit extended as the determining factors in the choice of coffeehouses.

One village study reports as follows:

Determining factors in the choice of a coffeehouse are the reputation of the owner, his cleanliness, honesty, and the extent of credit given to customers. Social class of an individual does not determine choice of a coffeehouse. An outsider coming to the village for the first time may visit any coffeehouse, but gradually as he becomes acquainted with the village people he will be drawn to a certain shop according to his interests, age, associates, etc.[7]

In this same village one coffeehouse is preferred by aged people. Youngsters, noisy people, and those who play technical games such as cards, chess, and checkers are not found there. A second coffeehouse is preferred by adult and old people, while all the younger people of the village gather in the third coffeehouse, which is popular because of the different games available there and because of its dance floor. This latter innovation means that girls, in the company of their parents or relatives, may visit this particular coffeehouse on Sunday afternoons or holidays in order to dance both the traditional folk dances and what passes in rural areas for modern dances.

One additional study is worth mentioning because it summarizes the type of patronage a village's seven coffeehouses enjoy:

A. Frequented by out-of-towners and employees
B. Employees, strangers, workers in village
C. Dance floor, so attracts mostly young men
D. Adult and old men of village
E. Village residents — not young men
F. Card-playing, so frequented mostly by young men
G. Outdoor coffeehouse — frequented by young men in summer.[8]

A villager will usually patronize the coffeehouse of which a relative is in charge so that he can get credit more easily, or simply give his trade to the relative upon whom he might need to call at a later date. Many men are careful to visit two or more shops from time to time "so as not to offend any of the proprietors." Also, as one informant put it, "The peasant comes from the field, washes up, goes for a drink to a coffeehouse where he might be tied by blood, but in order to do business he goes to other coffeehouses to find people with whom to arrange use of animals for plowing, etc., and will stop for a drink with these people."

Anyone trying to understand the sociology of Greek village life needs to pay special attention to these coffeehouse groups. First of all, the regular patrons of each coffeehouse can be viewed as a group whose members possess certain bonds in common. They have heard many of the same stories; they have learned to react in almost the same way to the buffoon, the over-important person, and the fellow villager constantly seeking sympathy. Although they may frequent a second coffeehouse, they are apt to feel a primary loyalty to their first choice and will find any number of reasons to justify their opinion that it is the best coffeehouse in the village.

This general group, however, most of the time is broken down into cliques, varying in size from two during the day to as many as seven persons by evening. Each group has its own informal leader. According to Photiadis: "The informal leader in the coffeehouse gives the other members of his clique group his advice and the satisfaction that they are associating with a person of higher status, while he has the satisfaction of performing his role, the dynamic aspect of his status, which is his reward." Therefore, when some outsider, such as an agricultural agent, approaches the farmers at a particular table, the informal leader considers him a rival. "The agent is a person of higher status who can talk about things the others cannot. This exclusive selling of ideas makes the informal leader feel that his authority is lowered in the eyes of his subordinates, and as a result, he fears that he will lose the satisfaction he has had." No wonder, then, that he is very likely to oppose the ideas which the agricultural agent is trying to advance.

Of special interest is the way news spreads from one clique to the next as part of the community-wide decision on some proposal new to the village. Photiadis takes as an illustration the use of a new insecticide which had been demonstrated by the agriculural agent to a number of farmers earlier in the day:

The cliques which have members who have seen the demonstration will start discussing the matter and, after a series of objections and agreements, they will probably reach a decision or have split decisions. The opinion of the informal leader during this discussion has a considerable influence on certain members.

Around the table of each clique there are usually one or more persons belonging to other cliques, or there are isolates sitting with the clique. These "isolates" . . . often move from table to table exchanging ideas or presenting the decision of the previous group as their own. The store owner and the waiter, who know everyone's business, present the opinion of the group on the matter while they are serving them. In this way the uninformed cliques are informed of the matter and the others have a new aspect of the topic for discussion if it differs from their own. Through this process, each clique's opinion diffuses through the coffeehouse. The rate of this diffusion varies according to the importance of the topic. If the subject is more important than usual, the leaders will find some means of discussing it among themselves, or a number of people may ask the opinion of informal leaders belonging to other cliques.

But the matter does not rest there. Many people move from one coffeehouse to another and introduce as their own the general consensus prevailing in the coffeehouse from which they have come. Thus, the men of the community tend to form a "public opinion" on a matter, frequently basing their decisions on either flimsy or inaccurate evidence. They prefer to be psychologically related to what others in their clique or coffeehouse think rather than to be individualistic and out of step with the rest. Truly, there is in Greece a "coffeehouse jury."

THE COFFEEHOUSE AS A MIXED BLESSING

The coffeehouse has its critics throughout Greece. Those responsible for improving the economic situation cite the economic disadvantages resulting from the unproductive expenditures at the coffeehouse as well as the many hours wasted there. This is recognized as a regional matter, for in many villages, such as those on Mount Pelion near Volos, one seldom sees people at the coffeehouse during the day. But in many of the mountain villages elsewhere, where economic opportunities are particularly lacking, more time is spent in such places.

Some oppose the coffeehouse on moral grounds. From time to time wives berate their husbands — not for economic inefficiency — but for drinking too much ouzo or for gambling away money that the family desperately needs. It also is said to corrupt youth. The nomarch of Thessalonike, Kostis Koukourides, pointed out: "The coffeehouses are our misfortune. I have two objections to them: the lost time and the bad habits of drinking and gambling. They also corrupt the youth, for in earlier times a boy had to be twenty-five years of age to go into the coffeehouse and would then never sit with the elders. Now he does so, which shows that he is losing respect for his elders."

Schoolteachers and agricultural-extension workers, although admitting that the coffeehouse can at times serve as a useful forum, generally think of it as a place where much misinformation spreads. It irritates an agricultural worker to think that he has persuaded a peasant to adopt some new farm practice only to learn the next day that the peasant has decided against it because of a conversation the previous evening with his cronies at the coffee-house. One villager got to the crux of the matter: "In the coffeehouse we get into arguments over our political leaders and don't attend to our fields. We do this because we are uneducated and people do little to help us, and so we spend our time on foolish things. The government doesn't send people here to instruct us; we are farming the way our fathers did."

With the spread of the program of agricultural extension, perhaps this peasant can no longer legitimately make the same complaint, but the chances are that the men of his village are still arguing about many matters and, perhaps in his opinion, spending their time on "foolish things."

Even the critics admit that there are still many conditions which encourage the men to patronize the coffeehouse quite apart from the attractions already described. For most village men, home is a most unattractive place in the evening. Dimly lit, poorly heated in cold weather, dominated by women and their silly prattle, the home cannot begin to compete with the masculine company found at the coffeehouse. Furthermore, most men can think up perfectly valid reasons (in their opinion, at least) for going to the coffee-house: they have a business matter to talk over; they want to know how some world crisis is shaping up; they need some advice on a farming decision.

Should they be found at the coffeehouse during the daytime, when conscientious farmers might be finding something worthwhile to do, they do not experience many twinges of conscience. They are not pricked by any Puritan ethic that teaches them constantly to be busy; instead, they save their energies for the time and place where it is unquestionably in their interest to work hard and long. When no such occasion presents itself, what more could a man ask than to enjoy his leisure, unplanned and unsought though it be? Nor does he think that it is up to him to seek out productive uses of his time. If people have good employment opportunities, they will seek him out, and he will respond. If he is from the tobacco-growing districts, the chances are that he has put his only resources (wife and children) to work for him and can take his ease until he must return to see how the work has progressed. He has no idle capital to invest but does his best with the human labor at his command. When heavy work is required, he will do his part, but when that is done others can harvest, string, and manipulate the tobacco. He provides the entrepreneurial skill.

Perhaps the coffeehouse and the attitudes of its habitués clash more strongly with American value orientations than do any other aspects of village life. To the Greek peasant, to be idle is no sin; to converse in the kouvenda can be as satisfying as to be a spectator sportsman; to seek to learn "what's new" if you live in a village is just as worthy as the search for novelty which motivates many in the United States. To get away from the women, the Greek peasant does not have to go on a long hunting trip to

Maine or a fishing shack on the river; he simply goes to his coffeehouse. To feel important, he needs only to provide some morsel of news which others may not have heard or to give words of wisdom to those younger men who seek his counsel. He has a club — something which the middle-class American male does not possess and for which he constantly seeks substitutes.

··›[XII]‹··

Local Government

If the Greek villager did not have a government to curse, he would be in a bad way indeed. Somewhere he has to find a scapegoat for the hard life that he leads. He could berate his wife or beat his children, but that would give only limited relief, since he knows they are not responsible for his difficulties; he could raise his clenched fist to the heavens and curse the Almighty, and he does this in some of the most colorful language known to man, but that too has its possible dangers, since the Almighty in a less genial mood might give him his comeuppance. What better object for his scorn could he find than the government, which is always wanting taxes, takes him off to military service, asks him innumerable questions every time he seeks a loan, and stages a periodic election prior to which "lying" politicians come to seek his vote.

At the same time, the peasant is shrewd enough to distinguish between Greece as a nation, to which he can be tremendously loyal should anyone cast aspersions upon it, and whatever national government is in power. He also draws a distinction between the local government of his village and the central government in Athens, with his views of the former going up and down, but his regard for the latter seldom going up. There is no mercurial quality, therefore, to peasant politics. If the peasant does shift his vote, it is in sullen protest and not because of any wildly enthusiastic support for some new leaders seeking the reins of government. He does not think of government in abstract terms; he feels more comfortable talking about specific persons and events. He will know, for instance, that his country is a monarchy and that King Paul and Queen Frederika visited his village last year and drank coffee with the community president and that the queen went into one of his neighbor's homes to see how the housewife was weaving a particular pattern; he will know that there is such a thing as a national parliament, for his wife's second cousin, a representative there, regales them on occasional visits with all the smart things he does when he is in Athens.

Or, as happened in Phokia, a coastal village between Athens and Sounion, the community president interrupted our conversation on a cool September evening (in 1959) to show us pictures taken of himself with the shipping magnate, Onassis, and the Greek premier, Konstandinos Karamanlis. The former had anchored his luxury yacht off the shore near Phokia a few months previously and had invited the premier to come to Phokia, from which a small launch would take him out to the yacht for dinner. True to tradition, these personages received the greetings of the community president, posed for their photographs with him in a village taverna, and listened to his requests for funds to extend the village dock out to deeper water.

I often wondered whether the Greek villager was as interested in politics as the Athenian thought that he was, for I found many villagers almost totally ignorant of governmental affairs, a fact which could be duplicated among the least educated in almost every country. Indeed, many people who knew village life well said that the peasants were much more interested in talking about agriculture than national politics.

GREEK TRADITIONS OF LOCAL GOVERNMENT

The strongest governmental tradition in rural Greece is that of government by elders, who represent the accumulated wisdom and authority of the village. One would expect this in a family-centered society, but, in the case of Greece, it has been further reinforced by historical developments.

These influences are primarily Byzantine in character. True enough, one can go back to the city-state, or *polis,* of the ancient Greeks and show how even the settlements outside the fortified town, which were a part of the polis, had their representatives on its central council and played their part in raising military and financial levies in case of war; or one can trace the decline of the polis under Macedonian and Roman rule between 350 B.C. and 330 A.D. and assume that many of its earlier functions must have persisted. But it is not until the flowering of Byzantium that a transformation of local government took place. As Harold F. Alderfer has stated:

Instead of being organized on the basis of individuals living in a geographic area, which was the classical mode, the community became a body of believers united by a common purpose. . . . Within this framework, new concepts of local government grew. One was the council as a vehicle for the consensus of the community as a whole. Another was the assembly of all members of the Christian community to give assent. Still another was the leadership of clerical authorities in local government and community activity. These ideas are indigenous to Byzantine culture and they are a part, even if not immediately visible, of present-day local government in Greece.[1]

With the fall of Byzantium in 1453, the Greeks came under Turkish rule. But the Muslim masters worked through already existing institutions, and Mohammed II went so far as to recognize the Patriarch of Constantinople as the political leader of the Greek nation. In the provinces, the metropolitan bishops, and priests exercised the rights given to the Patriarch, and his executors, through the *euphoria* (supervising committee) or the *demogerontia* (group of village elders). These village elders collected taxes from their compatriots, rendered justice when differences arose between Orthodox Christians, and settled any disputes which contesting parties referred to them. Basic to this self-government was the idea of the autonomous community, which centered around the elders selected by popular vote. These elders (*demogerontes*), in turn, selected "first elders" (*protogeri*), who administered the provinces and conferred with the monarch's counsellor in the provincial capital about the amount of taxes to be collected for that province, while each demogerontia tried to specify the share of each larger village, as well as the personal contribution of each individual taxpayer within a village.[2]

In addition to tax assessment and collection, the elders had many other important functions: they divided the uncultivated land or fields or any other land remaining without heirs, regulated the flow of waters, determined the rights of inheritance, handled the community's funds, and supervised the payments made by Christians to be relieved of military duty and the serving of court papers. Since the tax function remained paramount, the local authorities brought pressure to bear upon their compatriots, by advice or scolding, to pay what was due and to avoid any mishaps with the Turks. These leaders, because they supervised the tax collection, also had local funds to use at their discretion for the community. As Koukkidi says: "The great strength of the Greeks was the continuity of communal life. The community to them was a small democracy which organized its life and shaped itself." [3]

With the liberation of Southern and Central Greece, and the ascent to the throne of King Otho, the governmental patterns of Western Europe were imposed upon the traditional councils of elders. But this came at a time when, with the exception of the loyalty to the Patriarch, there was no governmental structure which tied together these separated local governments into any larger whole. Thus, as Greece moved toward modern nationhood, the type of local government which had existed under the Ottoman Empire began to wither.

One Athenian professor said to me that after ten years of revolution (1821–1830) the people wanted a king who could end anarchy and bring order. They had to accept a centralized government and put up with laws not natural to the country but which were necessary if Greece were to appear "civilized" enough to get loans from abroad. "We still need a legal system agreeing better with our country," he concluded. This is one reason, he thinks, why the peasant tries to get around the laws; he does not look upon them as his laws, as Greek laws.

During the first forty years of this century, the greatest changes in community life occurred under Venizelos in 1912 and under Metaxas in 1935. Venizelos, for instance, refashioned the old demes, or local units consisting of several villages, and made each village a unit responsible for supporting many local services under a community council and president. The deme still had the taxing, police, and judicial powers. The central government attempted to supply teachers for communities, a step which meant much less local autonomy but which was essential if Greece were to have a uniform system of education. Many other activities which local governmental bodies had handled up to this time had to be approved by the nomarch (administrator of the nomos) and ministry. Even the Constitution of 1927, though leaving to local government matters managed directly by the citizens, left the definition of "local matters" so vague that the demes and communes were at the mercy of the legislators and ministries who, by law and decree, could "outline their powers, procedures, and revenues." [4]

Metaxas, after abrogating the Constitution of 1927, imposed on the total Greek population "modern" methods of hygiene, childrearing, and education. He even attempted to introduce early weaning and the use of bottles. In community affairs, local elections were abolished and local officials could be dismissed and replaced by the Minister of the Interior.

Today, according to one authority:

The local government units in Greece are demes and communes. There are 217 demes and 5,746 communes. Demes, under the 1912 law, were those units with 10,000 or more population; but recent amendments allowed so many exceptions that there are now 144 below this minimum standard. Communes are supposed to have 300 or more people and an elementary school; but this standard was also relaxed so that now there are many below this figure. As a matter of fact, half of the communes today have less than five hundred inhabitants. [5]

Since such small population centers cannot support all of the expected services, some kind of amalgamation of units is thought desirable. But how this is to be worked out puzzles Greek politicians as much as it does American politicians interested in United States counties, laid out in horse-and-buggy days and ill adapted to today's rapid-transit world. In any combination, one center will gain and the other lose, a fact which has local political repercussions in a democratic system. Some of these become apparent as one views the work of the community council and its president.

THE COMMUNITY COUNCIL

In Phrangista, a mountain village of Central Greece, I was shaken out of pleasant contemplation as two loudspeakers on the village square suddenly began to inform one and all of the latest news of the day.

This was in the spring of 1953, and we were on a coffeeshop verandah newly made of concrete. Across the dusty thoroughfare, some hens had discovered wheat sheaves drying in front of the house of the carpenter; next door, potted geraniums were blooming in the window of a handsome stone house. We were shut in from the outside world by hazy mountains. The proprietor's wife and daughter had just brought us preserved walnut sweets in a spoon with the traditional glass of water. One spooned the sweets, gulped the water, and commented on the good flavor of the walnuts preserved before they had fully ripened. And then came the radio. These loudspeakers, sounding forth noon and evening, featured the broadcasts from Ioannina, Patras, and Athens. The radio, obviously much more powerful than the battery sets frequently encountered in the ordinary coffeehouse, aroused my curiosity. I turned to the president of the community council, who was sitting nearby. He told me that the radio was community-owned, that it had been placed there by the American Mission, and that it had "brought civilization" to that place. But the more I talked with him, the more I realized that bringing in civilization through this medium created some local administrative problems.

The American Mission, preferring to distribute the radio directly to the local authorities rather than through a regular government ministry, stipulated that the community would have to provide the gasoline for the motor which furnished the energy for the radio. So the first problem was to find the money to buy the gasoline, which cost a great deal by the time it was transported over the mountains from Lamia. A second problem was locating someone (in this case, two teen-aged boys) who could operate the complicated machine and tune in the radio. The president proudly reported that on the previous day a screw had worked loose and the program was temporarily interrupted — but only temporarily — for these competent youngsters quickly found the trouble and replaced the screw.

Before I left Phrangista, the president wanted me to see the church which the villagers had recently rebuilt. It had been completely and deliberately destroyed by the Nazis. The archbishop had given some funds for its restoration, but most of the job had been done by "personal work" (*prosopike ergassia*). This is an old, old practice whereby the community council assigns the families or adults of the village so many days of "voluntary" labor on a task that needs to be carried out in the community interest. In general, a community may call for ten days of work (or pay in lieu thereof) from each able-bodied villager, although it need not do this if there are no projects requiring this much labor.

"Everybody who could," according to the president, "went to the quarries and cut limestone; others cut wood. We paid laborers to construct the lime kiln and then produced our own lime at a saving of twenty million drachmas [over $1300 then]. While the construction crews were building the new road through here, we brought the stones they unearthed to the church site and, with the help of good masons, put up the structure." Here again local government was getting something done.

On another trip in 1955, returning from a visit to Mount Athos, the Holy Mountain on a peninsula in Northern Greece, I saw a notice nailed to a plane tree near the main fountain of the village. It looked official, so we went up to have a look. It announced the auctioning off of the right to collect a certain kind of tax:

Announcement of Bidding for the Lease of Farming of Animal Sale Tax for Fiscal Year 1955–56

The President of the community of Neochori declares that . . . a bidding is announced for Sunday 17 June between 10–12 A.M. in the Community Building for the highest offer to lease the farming of taxes on animal sales during fiscal year 1955–56.

The amount of 3000 drachmas [$100] has been determined as the first offer and the amount of 300 drachmas as a guarantee to be deposited by any participant. The tax has been determined at two percent on any sale of animals. Citizens having debts in the community are not accepted. The amount of lease shall be paid in four equal installments, the last to be paid on 31 March 1956. All expenses will be charged to the lessor.

Here the local authorities were following the ancient practice of "farming" out the taxes to the highest bidder who, in turn, was expected to derive from rigorous collection much more than he paid for the right. Every time a bleating goat or an ox changed masters, the successful bidder would collect his 2 percent of the sale price.

The community council has other duties in addition to managing a community-owned radio, rebuilding churches, and collecting taxes. It conducts local elections as well.[6] By 1951 the political situation had stabilized to the point that local elections could be held throughout the country. Of the registered voters, a greater proportion of women than men voted, thereby showing their appreciation of the right of suffrage. From nine to thirty-one councilmen could be elected in demes and from five to fifteen in communes, on the basis of population.

An account of local officialdom taken from almost any commune in Greece closely resembles that from other communes, although the number of council members may vary. Here are the facts for Gourie, near Mesolongi on the western coast of Greece.

The village has the following officers: a president and a deputy president, who replaces the former in his absence. The president is the paid governmental representative in the village. The secretary is a salaried, permanent employee of the community, whose duty is to keep all community records, conduct all correspondence, and do all other clerical work. The village council: it is the duty of this council to help the president solve the various community problems, to attend regular meetings and take the necessary resolutions. The councilmen are unpaid officers; the president is paid a yearly allowance of one thousand drachmas for his extra expenses. The council and the president were elected during the last national municipal elections. Later the president was elected by the councilmen.

The old school building is now used for the community office. This has two rooms; one is used for the president's office and the other for the secretary's; its furniture is very poor; it has six chairs, a divan, and a bookcase used for filing.[7]

Of course, villages differ in the facilities provided for the community-council officers. In Tsepelovo, an Epirus village, the office of the council was well furnished. Cushioned benches lined the walls. Other furniture included a long table at which the secretary worked; a storage chest; a glassed, built-in cabinet containing shelves for filing; four straight-back wicker chairs; and another cabinet built into the wall which contained a store of medical supplies. The room was decorated with an *Ohi* sign, commemorating the refusal by Metaxas to capitulate to the Italians early in World War II, pictures of the royal family, portraits of local dignitaries, and two pictures of Eisenhower. Some American Mission material lay on the long table. This council, too, had the responsibility of taking care of the high-powered American Mission radio, similar to the one in Phrangista.

As I talked with the village officials here and throughout Greece, I tried to understand their conceptions of their jobs. I knew what the law stated to be their functions but wondered how closely their own ideas corresponded with the legal description. In an Attica village (1953) I found a council consisting of eight members and the president. The secretary there, as elsewhere, had no vote at council meetings, but introduced the topics on the agenda. I asked this secretary whether he considered himself an employee of the community council or of the central government. In Communist countries to the north I had known that the secretary of local government was usually a trusted Communist imposed on the community and therefore the guiding hand in local affairs. But in Greece I found no such use of the secretary's role. He generally considered himself a servant of both the state and the local people. In this Attica village the secretary said: "I do all the difficult work. I am kept so busy that I even work at night. Recruiting for the army, for instance, is done through me. I was awakened at five this morning by a man who wanted a certificate. I am also head of post and telegraph here. This is an unusual job for a secretary but the local government couldn't afford such an official and asked me to take on the job. I reckon I must work eighty hours some weeks." But he seemed to be thriving on his job.

When I inquired more carefully into what the council does, I learned that, in addition to collecting the taxes, it has the problem of determining what families are poor enough to qualify for welfare assistance. The president and two other citizens comprise a committee on social welfare and classify families according to need. The two citizens had been selected by the Ministry of Welfare from a list of nine local people nominated by the president, and they serve two years. The poor people are officially listed according to categories A, B, and C, which are based on family income and size of family. The poorest (A category) will get free medical care, free hospitalization, free maternity service, and free drugs at the expense of the Ministry of Welfare. Those in category B are entitled to the same advantages, but have lower priority in the event sufficient facilities are not available to all. Those in C category must pay for their drugs, but at reduced prices, with the price difference being made up by the Ministry of Welfare. Of the 560 families in this village, one half were in one of the above categories. Since everybody in a village knows everyone else's business, there is much discussion of the fairness of the list. A person in need comes personally to ask for help, but he may be removed from the list at the end of three months when the names must be reviewed.

Around Volos, in the villages on Mount Pelion, I found emergency welfare needs handled on a much less bureaucratic basis. The commandant of gendarmerie for the Volos area learned in March 1953 that many families in the villages on the eastern part of Pelion lacked food. Unlike those in the Attica village, these people had made no complaints. They ordinarily live on returns from olives, apples, chestnuts, and some potatoes, but storms had destroyed their chestnut and apple crop to the extent that they had received little income the previous autumn. By March, they were without funds to buy bread. Part of their poverty could also be traced to the number of times their villages had been pillaged by the guerrilla bands which had earlier operated in that area. Their clothes were a pattern of patches. They kept little livestock because pastures were lacking and because any lambs produced did not mature early enough to be sold at Easter.

The commandant, in view of these circumstances, asked help from the representative of the International Red Cross, who arranged with the organizational officials in Athens for an immediate distribution of rice, sugar, and molasses (for children). Momentarily, the representative also secured money for bread, telephoning from Athens to the commandant to buy the bread locally. The Red Cross representative had expected the commandant to buy about eight hundred one-oka loaves of bread, but he had different ideas: "Why not give the people flour and cut down the expense of the salt, water, and manipulation that goes into the baked bread?" So he bought nine hundred and eighty okas of flour and persuaded the flour mills at Volos to contribute another two tons. He also handled the problem of transportation with originality. Since these eight villages are remote, the trucking costs to them are high. The commandant, suggesting that the distribution be at four points, appealed to the local transportation cooperatives to supply the trucks after the Union of Trucks had voted to help. Then the drivers agreed to donate a day's free labor, with the "day" totaling sixteen hours for many of them before the distribution was completed and the trucks were safely back in Volos.

But the role of the village notables should not be minimized. Although the commandant had made a trip through the district to look personally into the condition of many families, he depended upon the president, the priest, the teacher, and the gendarme to prepare the list of the needy in each village. The role of the president came to the fore at the distribution points, to which he brought some men and pack animals. The commandant explained in great detail to each president the basis on which the distribution was being made, who had made the contributions, and what families were to receive how much. The supplies for each village, when weighed out from the trucks, were turned over to the community president. He then supervised the loading of the pack animals and headed the animal train back toward his village. Once arrived, he was to see that the distribution was carried out according to instructions.

Such an experience leaves many impressions: the deep personal interest which the commandant of gendarmerie showed in the welfare of the people in his area; the dignity of the village presidents who asked very intelligent questions to be sure that they properly understood the instructions about distribution; the tattered clothing worn by these quiet, almost impassive villagers. And here, as always in Greece, one sensed deeply the beauty of the natural surroundings: the mountains where patches of snow still lingered, the dark glades through which the road sometimes wound, the occasional olive groves and chestnut forests, with lively pedestrian traffic ready to greet one every few hundred yards. Down on the plain, on a sunny afternoon, the meadows were full of a profusion of wild flowers so delicate in color and stamina that they die soon after they are plucked or after the hot sun of late April and May beats down on the unprotected plain. On our way back to Athens the next day as evening began to fall, we saw Mount Parnassus, snow-topped, off to the west, and knew that beyond it lay Delphi and its sacred shrine. In an ancient land, peasants of today were still wrestling with the problem of hunger; and generous people — Greek officials, millers, truck owners and truck drivers, and supporters of the International Red Cross — were expressing a common humanity. Village presidents, or local government in action, were the final link between the outside world and those in need.

Other trips, however, left one in a different mood. In the Peloponnesos, as in many parts of Greece, I found villagers who did not feel very kindly toward their community president, even though they had elected him. In one place a peasant, not without a trace of prejudice, remarked: "My brother-in-law was president of the council when the village road was built. He and the council decided how many days men of the family had to contribute and we got the job done. But our president now is a poor type of political leader. He plays favorites. He does not promise anything for the village as a whole; he has no concern for a much-needed bridge at the place where your car almost got stuck crossing the stream."

In another village, an old man who had spent five years as a young man in the United States complained: "In community affairs we have to elect a president who is 'in keeping' with the government in power, or else we get left out. But many of our village presidents take revenge on those villagers who disagree with them. In the States, if you are a Democrat nobody cares." When I asked in what ways the president could take revenge, he said that the president could make unfair work assignments to a community voluntary-labor project, make unequal distribution of welfare goods, and create difficulties for a man trying to get a loan through the cooperative.

But in many ways the community council has some control over the president because it can outvote him on crucial issues. In fact, a council will frequently have real discussions since each member feels well informed on village matters, which is all they are supposed to discuss, and can reflect the ideas of his friends, followers, or his coffeehouse clique. As one Greek official said, "The community council is a lively element in village life. The only point to remember is that council members are not educated enough to measure up to their tasks."

Some brief insight into how this process works is found in the case of Stavroupolis, a village whose coffeehouses were treated at some length in the preceding chapter. According to John Photiadis:

Stavroupolis and the three other villages which form the Stavroupolis community are incorporated, with their government located in Stavroupolis. This government consists of an unpaid nine-member council elected by vote every four years, and a salaried mayor. For specific projects and activities, special committees are appointed from the council members and sometimes non-council members who are in some way connected with the project or activity. The mayor usually introduces topics for the approval of the council, but no action can be taken before the prefect of the area gives his final approval.

In Stavroupolis, people respond quite emotionally to each method applied by the village government. Problems are discussed by the council before decisions are made and are discussed again by the male population in the coffeehouse with interest and emotion. . . . The village government's business is their business and these informally-made decisions are important since no project can operate normally or smoothly if their informal decisions are opposed.[8]

But no picture of local government is complete without some sketch of the tax and financial picture. According to the 1950–51 legislation, local governments gain their revenues from the following sources.[9]

Property Revenues
— For the use of slaughterhouses
— Grazing rights on communal-owned land

Dues and Excises
— Building dues, ½ to 1 percent of the amount of cost
— For the use of sidewalks, streets, and public squares
— Dues on hotels, beds, and bills
— Weight and measure excises; advertisement excises
— For the use of municipal and communal property, works and services including garbage and cleanliness, electricity and gas

Direct Taxes
— Tax on agricultural and forestry products: 2 percent mandatory, 4 percent optional
— Tax on cattle; tax on poultry and fish up to 3 percent of price
— Tax on vacant plots within town plan areas in demes over 20,000 and those in the capital area and Thessalonike area
— Tax on property which has gained value owing to deme or communal public works

Indirect Taxes
— Tax on sale and purchase of cattle
— Tax on olive oil dregs

Contributions
— Contributions determined by council not over 30 million drachmas per head in Athens, Piraeus, and Salonika; 15 million on other demes; 5 million in communes

Personal Work
— In demes and communes under 10,000 population, men over eighteen work ten days a year. Also includes their animals and motor equipment

Loans, Donations and Legacies

Sale of Real Estate and Movable Property

Although not all of these taxes apply directly to villages, some of them do. Mention has already been made of the personal work on community projects, as well as the tax on sale and purchase of cattle as evidence by the Neochori notice of bids for farming these out. In addition, there is a "head" tax ranging from twenty to fifty cents annually on each animal. A list of animals over two years of age is drawn up in March, or three months before the commune budget is due. Perhaps the most important of these revenues from the peasant point of view is the tax of 2 to 4 percent on his agricultural products, which the local government keeps. He pays this in lieu of a property tax on the land that he owns. When I explained to some of my Greek friends that property taxes were the chief source of revenue for many local governments in America, they asked if I meant agricultural land. When I answered in the affirmative, they were nonplussed and pointed out that it was much fairer to tax the products of the land than the land itself, since the products showed best of all the value of the land.

THE VILLAGE AND THE CENTRAL GOVERNMENT

To understand the community council, one must see its relationship with the central government.[10] It does not, for instance, undertake to maintain law and order, since the local police are not under its jurisdiction, nor does it have much to say about its local school, except through an elected school board of limited powers. Even in those affairs where it is supposed to have jurisdiction, such as drawing up its own budget or arranging for the collection of taxes, it has to gain the approval of the nomarch, who is appointed by the Minister of Interior.

Only as I got to know some of the nomarchs did I begin to appreciate the relationship of the central to the local governments. One nomarch, Yannes Gotsis, was in charge of the nomos of Serrai in Macedonia in 1953. He seemed dedicated to his task and epitomized several of the qualities I have come to admire in many Greeks. We discussed the specifics of local government and the part that the nomarch plays, but he soon went beyond the technicalities of administration to something of its philosophy:

In the majority of the Greeks there is a submerged desire to make a better future for as many people as possible. The Greek really wants a better community life, although he at times gives the impression that conflict is his basic urge. But along with his sense of community he has an appreciation for human personality, which means that if another person disagrees with him he does not try by force to get his own opinion accepted; he tries persuasion and explanation. If others continue to disagree, it is not because they fail to appreciate him but because they each have their own personality to put to the use of the community.

This led into a discussion of some of the kinds of conflict which occur in the community and the part the nomarch has to play in resolving them. The location of a new village church sometimes becomes an issue. Many arguments are not based on any vested interest in a particular spot but on the individuals' assessment of what would in actuality be the best spot. In order to get proof that his idea is better than other ideas, a person will leave his farm work or close up his shop and go to the city where he can get the advice of some authority whom he can quote to support him. Or several villagers in disagreement will decide to go to the nomarch to get his opinion.

On another occasion I went with the nomarch of Kozane to visit a village for which he had responsibility. The agriculturist for this nomos, who had come with us, introduced many of the peasants to the nomarch before the meeting began at the schoolhouse. Eventually the meeting got started. The nomarch, flanked on one side by the council president and on the other by the council secretary, got down to business in a most direct way. One man got up and described the condition of his home, in which he said he was ashamed to live. This village had been destroyed by the guerrillas and the need for help had been great. Because he had a special file for each village in his nomos, the nomarch knew that when he took office 75 percent of all the houses needed rebuilding but that now that figure had dropped to 29 percent. He reminded them that in his nomos there were four thousand families without housing or even an elementary roof over their heads, but said he would see what could be done. He then found out what they expected to do with the self-help program based on voluntary contributions of labor. He reminded them that on two occasions the state had given them about $1700 to help in the construction of a road to the village and that, in view of their present need, he would see if he could get another grant. This time he would pay wages so that they might have some much-needed income.

When we emerged from the crowded schoolhouse, I noticed that about twenty men had stood outside trying to overhear what was going on. The nomarch stopped to talk to some of them. When we had climbed into a truck which was to take us across a muddy patch to our cars half-a-mile away, the black-robed priest came running up, an unkempt, unattractive fellow, to make a last-minute complaint to the nomarch. "Sir," he shouted, "did you know that the coffeehouse proprietor is now opening up on Sundays before the church service is over, which is contrary to the law?" The crowd looked amazed and eagerly waited to see how the nomarch would handle this troublesome complaint. He replied: "My good fellow, you go on and give them good enough sermons, and then the men won't want to go to the coffeehouse during church time."

Reference to one other nomarch will be enough to show the type of men who were filling that post in 1953. Mr. Aronis was the nomarch of Kalamata, at the southern part of the Peloponnesos. When we discussed the attitude of the peasants toward Athens and the central government, he commented: "Life in the village is difficult; Athens has had special privileges. The villages are 100 percent right in their complaints. In my nomos many of them have no roads, no irrigation or drainage. Their education is so far behind that it is pitiful; their homes are in awful condition. How can a peasant under such circumstances feel gratitude! Paying for the priest and the teacher should be the job of the central government in the same way that a father supports a child. The recent decision to turn back to the communes a share of the tobacco tax is encouraging the villagers very much. Here it will amount to about one dollar yearly per capita."

When I asked him more about the actual workings of the communes in his nomos, he repeated much that others had said:

The president of the community represents in a small way the national government. So the community council is both an arm of the central government and also a representative of the local village. All decisions of the council have to be communicated to the nomarch; this is compulsory. If the council and president decide to spend any of the local funds the nomarch has the right to say "yes" or "no." If they wish to add a paid employee, the nomarch will check to see whether it is legal or not. If the nomarch does not answer in two weeks' time, then the local council has the right to go ahead without further permission. But the villagers for the most part are not conscious of their rights after the expiration of the two-week period and are capable of waiting fifteen years. The chief reason for delays in such matters is the lack of sufficient personnel in the nomarchy.

During 1952–53, the possibility seemed strong of developing a capable, well-trained group of nomarchs, all of whom were supposed to have security of tenure and not be subject to dismissal except for carefully defined "cause." These nomarchs were being sent to England, the United States, and elsewhere to study how local governments functioned, and to see what ideas might be adaptable to Greece. The community presidents, over and over again, expressed appreciative comments on the work of many of these nomarchs. To be sure, in some villages I found that the nomarch had not yet made himself known, but I had the general impression that a much better relationship was building up between the peasantry and the national government because of the changed attitudes of friendliness and understanding on the part of these key officials. When I revisited Greece in 1955 for another study period, I found that the Minister of Interior in early March 1954 had rescinded the career-nomarch legislation and had immediately dismissed one third of the nomarchs. According to one observer:

The odd characteristic about these dismissals was that they were not necessarily based on political opinions nor on efficiency. Several strongly-pro-government nomarchs were dismissed despite known efficiency. Apparently this arose through internal dissensions with the government group, which came to light a week or two later on the replacement of the Minister of Interior among others and the secession of the Markezines group. It was a question of removal of antipatronage elements. The dismissals were legally contested, and subsequently several of the career nomarchs were restored to office. In late 1955 the re-organized government partly introduced legislation again re-establishing the career nomarchs.[11]

Whenever I found peasants complaining about their government, I asked them to list for me what services they received from outside the village. One of the men who had been complaining most vociferously in a Theban village was somewhat startled at this request, especially after he had delivered himself of such eloquent sentiments as: "People in Athens live in paradise; here in our village they live in hell. The Athenians consider us slaves to work so they can eat." But he put his mind to the problem and said:

What do we receive from outside? Well, our priest is paid by the government although we contribute something to the archbishop's funds; our teacher is paid by the government and they gave us a little for our school building, but we gave the materials and the labor. As for our roads, the villagers give their labor, break the rocks and put them in place, and then beg the government to help complete the road with machinery. The government engineer will come and supervise.

Our field policeman, who watches to see that animals do not get into the growing crops, is paid from an independent treasury; our gendarmes are paid by the central government.

The government does not provide us with medical care, for we have an arrangement [*kondota*] whereby any family agrees to give forty-four okas of wheat to the doctor, and he comes when called during the year. This does not include the cost of medicine. If you are not in this system, you pay for each visit. We have had this system a long time; it is deeply rooted. We used to pay our priest the same way, giving him twenty-two okas of wheat per family before the government took over his pay.

In this village, as elsewhere, we got conflicting opinions about the quality and usefulness of service rendered by the government, but there was a growing awareness that such services were available through the national government.

Once, on a return trip from Northern Greece to Athens, while we were having coffee in Levadeia in Central Greece, the commandant of gendarmes for that area asked if his wife and he might ride with us to Thebes. During the drive of less than an hour, we had a lively conversation on many points. I asked him about the young policemen or gendarmes whom we found in every village and town. He said that most of them were fulfilling their military service, although as gendarmes they have to do a three-year rather than a two-year stint. But they do get higher pay than those in the army. They must apply for this service, are carefully investigated before they are accepted, and then are carefully trained. Some stay on after their three-year tour of duty is up and are given, at the end of twelve years, a lump sum as severance pay. With this, many of them open up some business of their own.

The field guards, also under the Ministry of Interior, are under a different administration but work closely with the gendarmerie, since many cases, such as theft from a field, involve both services. The gendarmes, because they are responsible for public security, also make their own investigations. In the village of Kyparissia (Peloponnesos) at the time of our visit, the people were temporarily without the services of field policemen, although they still received gendarme service from Tripolis. They were then working out an arrangement to pay a field policeman in products, although they would hold him responsible if he did not find the animals which had damaged crops. They expected him to work only during the day, for there was little danger at night. Far to the north in Epirus, near the Albanian border, we came across field policemen who also assumed security functions not only against animals but also against infiltrators from across the Iron Curtain.

The larger villages and towns serving as centers for governmental services enjoy many advantages that the smaller, more isolated villages do not have. In Dimitsana, in the Gortynia section of the Peloponnesos, the local people say that their economy is kept going only because of the state employees located there. It is the seat of a gymnasium (secondary school), a lower court, the gendarmerie command, a field-guard office, a tax office, and a postal and telegraph office. In Northern Greece the governmental facilities in Stavroupolis include:

1. The court house which serves the area of thirty villages.
2. A police station which also serves a neighboring commune.
3. Farm-security service (field policemen) which operates under the auspices of the government but is supported by a separate local tax on the area.
4. Tobacco board which operates on an area level and is responsible for the taxation and standardization of tobacco.
5. Extension service which serves the whole area. There is a home club which operates under a home agent who belongs to a different institution but is supervised by the extension service. The rural club located in the village operates under the supervision of the extension agent.
6. Forestry-conservation service which controls lumbering and protects the forest sections of the area from erosion.[12]

Perhaps the least appreciated service which the central government carries out for the commune is the collection of those taxes used in the support of church, school, police, and a number of advisory services. Many tax specialists think it undesirable to have over 90 percent of all taxes collected by the national government, as is done in Greece, even though much of it is channeled back through various services to the local communities. At the same time, they admit that there is great reluctance on the part of local authorities to take on the tax-collection function and that in those instances where they do collect local funds they do so inefficiently. Obviously, the golden mean has not yet been found in this delicate area of the relationship between local and central government.[13]

When the topic of conversation turns from the services to the officials who carry them out, local informants respond fast and furiously, much of the comment in disapproving tones. I have yet to find a description of Greek life, past or present, that deals very kindly with Greek officialdom. This might be said of many countries, but in Greece the lowly and even high-placed official is beset with so many difficulties that it is a wonder he functions at all. His first problem is the low standards traditionally expected of the civil servant. Most Greeks think that it is perfectly proper procedure for them to bestow a favor upon some official so that he will give their case preference, either in considering it before other cases or in recognizing certain extenuating circumstances in their favor. The law may or may not be abrogated and regular channels set aside, but the irregularities deal quite often with rearrangements and interpretations within the scope of the limits set by the law so that one person gets preferential treatment over others. When one comes face to face with the great number of papers that have to be signed to do even a simple transaction involving governmental authority, one realizes how great is the temptation to bribe or bring to bear some other consideration (such as working through the good graces of a relative of the official) to shorten the red tape and wind up the matter more quickly than usual. Not all officials would condone such measures, but they are subjected to much temptation.

A second problem, tied in with the first, is the low compensation which officials receive in the face of increased living costs. Since many government workers cannot live even modestly on their salaries, they take on other commitments. These part-time jobs cause them to slight their full-time government employment, for which supervision is frequently lax.

Insecurity in the job is a third difficulty for many of the higher officials. The ministries, which in countries like France are run by highly skilled civil servants no matter how many cabinet ministers come and go, are staffed in Greece by people, many quite capable, who are apt to be swept out of office when a new minister comes in. Many, because of sheer competence and skillful legerdemain, manage to survive from one change of ministers to the next, but are never sure that they will weather the next changeover. In some ministries there have been as many as forty different ministers in six years.

A final difficulty lies in inadequate personnel and equipment to do many of the highly technical governmental tasks as they should be done. Engineers who are responsible for numerous activities in many villages may not have transportation facilities sufficient to visit these villages as often as would be desirable. Those responsible for accounting and fiscal matters may not have sufficient clerical help to keep up with the work load, thereby delaying reports or requests from local governments.[14]

But despite these difficulties, I would place the crux of the problem of the relationship between local and central government in the attitudes which the officials assume toward villagers and even townspeople. There is something about being an official in Greece that tends to make one officious. The officeholder may not realize this but, as he takes on the roles that go with a new governmental position, he tries to carry an air of authority that does not quite ring true, or else he tries to bolster up his feeling of insecurity by lording it over those who are in some measure under his control. He preserves his own *philotimo,* or self-esteem, by clinging to all the symbols of prestige to the bitter end. I could want no better documentation of this state of affairs than a notice distributed in November 1952 by the Minister of Agriculture, which appeared on the walls of the director of agriculture in Kozane. It read:

Mr. Director:

1. Don't forget that we are the servants of the people.
2. Don't forget that your pay comes from the work and the sweat of the people.
3. Please be polite and just to the people and your employees.
4. Keep working hours; do not go away during working hours which are for the public.
5. Reply willingly and quickly to requests and petitions of the people. "Come by tomorrow" is not accepted.

People — Farmers:

1. Do not ask for illegal things but demand your rights.
2. If you do not get your rights or have complaints write to Complaints Office of the Ministry and you will get a quick reply.
3. Even then, if you don't get justice, write directly to me.

Minister of Agriculture, A. Apostolidis

In official Athens, over the past few years, there has been many a tug of war, sometimes silent and sometimes raucous, between those who would decentralize many functions of government to the local units and those who, for a variety of reasons, would maintain strong central control. It is safe to say that those who favor the former course are those who think of government chiefly as an administrative apparatus through which citizens' needs are met. Certainly, many members of the American Mission have sought to strengthen the hands of those favoring decentralization in the belief that this would accomplish more with American aid money. On the other hand, those who favor strong centralization tend to think of government primarily in political rather than administrative terms. They see government as an arena where personalities and parties struggle for the opportunity of directing the affairs of state. They realize that much political power is built on patronage or at least the promise of patronage; they also argue that the political process is built upon compromise and that many administrative practices are established in governmental bureaus to forestall any such compromises. Which group is prompted more by disinterested, public-spirited motives can best be determined by the observer on the spot as different personalities, representing these varying points of view, step onto the stage.

THE PEASANT AND POLITICS

Shortly after my arrival in Greece in the fall of 1952, I encountered an interesting case study of the peasant and politics. All over Greece, one September Sunday, the farmers demonstrated against their government. This affair was treated, as one would expect, quite differently by the various Athenian newspapers, but the general tone of argument never got down to the facts of the peasants' grievance but instead haggled over who was responsible for getting them all stirred up.

One newspaper, *Philelevtheros,* under the caption "The Farmers' Plight," wrote:

There is no Greek who does not admit the rights of the farmers, or the fact that they are, and always were, the most neglected class in this country. Everyone feels the farmers' plight as if it were his own, and they know that Greek society will never stand on its feet as long as the farmer's lot is a miserable one. Their present fate, however, is not the fault of the Government, but is due to a whole century of reactionary rule. The farmers' demonstrations would have been even stronger and more genuine if the Rally Party agents had not attempted to exploit them. However, they failed in this attempt.

Ethnos, a newspaper representing a rival party, reported under the caption "Farmers' Demonstrations":

Over the whole of Greece, in all those areas where men strive to get the maximum crop from our not very fertile soil, solid demonstrations were held last Sunday. The farmers were protesting with absolutely justified indignation against the indifference the Government is showing in handling their problems, and the way in which it has withdrawn its promises to them.

In the face of this Pan-Hellenic uprising, the Government, through its comic Minister of Coordination, and through its press, finds nothing better to give in answer than that the farmers were incited by the Rally Party. As if there were any need of incitement in their case. One does not need incitement when one is hungry and sentenced to despair.[15]

The year does not matter, the name of the party does not matter, for in Greece a political, if not a social, gulf between the village and the city remains. Since 1952, as a later chapter will show, much has been done through the Agricultural Extension Service and other programs to better the condition of the peasantry. The success of such programs inevitably depends upon the skills and attitudes of those trying to carry them out in the name of the central government, but even more depends on the stability and continuity of the central government so that measures which are under way are not canceled and other political adventures substituted instead.

A peasant or a village president has three ways of straightening out some grievance involving the national government. First, he and his fellows can resort to strikes, demonstrations, and — in the case of the guerrilla war — to the support of those who would change the situation by revolution. Second, he can work through the regular administrative or executive channels already described. Through his local president and through the nomarch, many affairs can be carried to those in a position to settle the grievance, or in some cases he may take the time and trouble himself to go to some responsible official in the appropriate ministry for help. In other words, he is trying to find his way through the administrative apparatus of government and to use it to accomplish some objective. A third approach is to work through the political or legislative rather than the administrative channel. This means going to the representative from his district who serves in the national unicameral legislature in an effort to persuade him to intercede with the proper administrative officials. It might also mean going to some political leader, a former minister perhaps, to see if he can use his good graces in the matter.

Enough has been said thus far about Greek officialdom to show some of the difficulties that a villager, as an individual or as a community president, would face in making use of the administrative channels. Are the political outlets any more promising?

I once asked a peasant about a solidly constructed bridge we were then crossing. He said that it was obtained because one of their local people had been a member of parliament and had arranged to have this built. I wondered how long it would be before they had another member of parliament and thereby received some other needed project. And a mayor of one of the Thracian towns confided that he preferred the politically appointed nomarch to the career nomarch because one could go to the members of parliament and have them get an inefficient politically appointed nomarch replaced. Indications such as these showed the importance of the legislature in keeping the administrative apparatus in check, but did not provide any guidelines as to how this might best be done.

But this approach has its negative overtones as well. Over and over again I was told that such-and-such a thing was impossible for the village because it had not voted in support of the party in power. This was one of the points cited by a prosperous Greek merchant, who travels much throughout the country, when he listed changes he considered necessary in the rural parts of the country:

1. Smaller interest rates so there will be greater ease in handling money.
2. Less red tape so that the peasant when he comes to borrow money for a drill doesn't spend more money waiting than he spends for the pump.
3. State employees must understand that they are in the service of the people, especially the peasants, and not expect to be bribed to get a job done.
4. Greater justice so that the gendarme and judge are not primarily interested in a person's party affiliation but will carry out justice.

In other words, party affiliation may influence the administration of justice. From another point of view, working through a member of parliament is really the peasant's way of trying to get around a law. To do this is considered a great accomplishment, for he thinks that rules are made to be broken and evaded. This is because the rules have been made by others whose criteria for developing them are different from his own. For him, individual criteria are more important than rules others have made.

I had an impression, gained from hundreds of conversations with peasants throughout Greece, that the peasant prefers the political to the administrative approach. At first, the explanation was hard to find because it was obvious everywhere that the government agencies, though inefficient at times, were helping him reconstruct his destroyed home, assisting him in the purchase of agricultural equipment, teaching his wife and daughters how to can tomatoes and cook fish, and bringing more water to his parched fields. The reason became apparent, however, when I remembered that the Greek peasant is more interested in personal relationships than he is in things or in concrete achievements. He complains if he does not have things, especially if those in other villages are getting them, but does not value them in their own right. They are a measure of how his personal relationships are working out. He honestly feels that he can deal with the politicians sent up from his district to parliament and continues to share this optimistic frame of mind no matter how many times he has been disappointed in the past. Of course, he is content to work through the government official if he can personalize that relationship, to his own advantage, and not be treated as an anonymous citizen who must be dealt with impartially in keeping with the rules. He would rather be dealt with as a person and receive fewer material rewards than to be dealt with impersonally and receive more material goods. Efficiency, then, whether in administration or in farm work, is something he does not initially value; he must be taught to value it if it is to assume any importance in his life.

As many observers have pointed out, the Greek — be he peasant or city dweller — is not loyal to an abstract political principle, nor is he loyal to a political organization as such.[16] He is loyal to a political leader but only so long as following that leader does not mean that he must become disloyal to himself and go against his own cherished opinions of what ought to be done. Therefore, he can switch from one political leader to another without any sense of betrayal and sees no inconsistency in contradictory political behavior because he does not behave by the principles by which contradictions are gauged. Each situation is a separate case to be judged by itself and precedents have little relevance.

The peasant, sitting in his smoke-filled coffeehouse, is interested in hearing what others say about politics in Athens, not because he feels very closely identified with one party or the other, but because he tries to figure out what the meaning of each event is for his own particular existence. Few villagers are truly partisan in their political allegiance, which explains why it is almost impossible to maintain even a semblance of a party organization in a village. The parties do not even try. When elections are coming up, the candidates know the names of local people who have been sympathetic in the past and, through their help, try to work up a little political rally at which they can state why they should be supported for office. Around election time I chanced to be in several villages when these candidates made their appearance. On the whole, they drew small crowds, and even those who had decided to vote for them did not bother to go take a look at their chosen man. If this office seeker is to be "used" later on, one would think that here would be an excellent opportunity for the villager to establish the personal contact he might later exploit. But the peasant does not think this far ahead and, furthermore, probably assumes that the need for the politician's help might not arise.

When I listened to the peasants criticize their politicians, even those for whom they had voted and still supported, I realized that a foreigner might be tempted to read too much disapproval in comments which were made primarily to build up the ego of the critic. For, when I turned to such a critic after he had devastatingly, in his opinion, torn some program or political position to shreds, and asked "what do you suggest that the political leaders do instead?", the only reply given was: "I don't know because I'm not a politician."

I was also interested to note that there was relatively little disruptive political factionalism in a Greek village. Forty percent of the people may tend to support one party or leader, and they are not apt to switch to back the rival party the other sixty percent support. However, should occasion seem opportune, a great number of them might switch to the support of a third party simply as a means of expressing disapproval of the performance of the ones they have been supporting. But let the men of a village find some common denominator, such as the erection of a school or a church building, and they will forget their political differences.

In conclusion, the best way to characterize "the peasant and politics" is in terms of indifference. This is especially true if one looks on politics as an organized way of bringing certain measures to pass through the election of officials committed to carrying them out. This has never worked for the Greek peasant in the past, and he is dubious about its merits in the future. If one means by politics the utilization of personal and family contacts with politicians and officials to get some gain for oneself, then the peasant can understand its significance and see its value. For, after all, politics and politicians are associated with the city and especially with Athens. Villagers are caught up in the backwash and, in their view of the world, have little importance as active agents. Political phenomena, like the weather, have to be endured, although now and then some useful protection from each might be sought in personal initiative, but not by group effort.

··⊰[XIII]⊱··

The Village School

What Will Happen to Us If We Can't Read?

"I was making a distribution of goods in the village of Tsarakina, near Trikkala, during the days of the guerrilla war," explained Elle Adossides, who is well known for her humanitarian activities during and after World War II. "Four field policemen were helping with the distribution. Suddenly a boy of about ten years appeared before me. His legs were like matches from undernourishment, his face was yellow, his arms were bare, and he was dressed in flour bags. With a determined look, such as only a child can assume at times, he spoke up and said: 'I too have something to ask.' 'Something to eat? Some chocolate perhaps?' I inquired, in what I thought was a kindly voice. 'No,' he said impatiently and then raised his head, giving me a piercing glance, 'what we need is a teacher, books, pencils, and paper. What will happen to us if we can't read and do our sums?' "

This incident highlights in a vivid way the Greek's thirst for education. On every hand, one reads and is told by Greek informants that "education is perhaps the most prized good in Greece." [1] Young people from Greece who come to America to study are told in letters from their village friends back home: "Don't sleep, learn all you can." The same theme is voiced in conversations in village squares throughout the country as local officials stress the point that their people value education very much, citing instances of parents who disposed of some of their precious livestock to get the necessary money to help a son finish a year in a secondary school in the nearby town.

This appreciation of education has many roots. For one thing, the old folks keep alive the stories of the secret schools which were held clandestinely during Turkish times in those areas where the Turks did not permit schools to operate. In such cases the priest, the only literate man in the village, would open a night school to which the boys would go to learn to read and write. Since the Greek villagers, like many peasants in other countries, dislike to be out after dark, the boys were always a little fearful as they went between their homes and the secret school. They longed for a full moon to light their way and sang the following song, which is still heard today in village schools as a tradition:

> My brilliant small moon,
> Give me light to walk and go to school,
> To learn the alphabet
> And to be educated into God's work.

In the old days, then, education was precious because it was hard to get and involved a risk.

But it also is one of man's best ways of expressing his own individuality. Education, though a socializing influence in the early stages, becomes individualistic in the upper reaches. There each student seeks to appropriate for himself from the lecture, the reading, or the discussion that which fits into his own evolving interests and plans. Though socially derived and acquired, education in its essence is highly individualistic. This the Greek can appreciate.

In addition, education in Greece, as elsewhere, is the ladder of opportunity which youngsters can climb to reach the city or to move into some coveted profession. For, along with valuing an education, there is the corollary honor paid to those who can boast an education and wear it well. Furthermore, an education and a well-paid white-collar job resulting from it eliminate the necessity of manual labor, which the Greek finds most uncongenial. The university professor, for instance, is not only a man of repute but is also a man of affairs. When the king needs a caretaker government to hold things together until a new government is formed after a forthcoming election, he more often than not asks a professor to serve as prime minister.

In spite of the high place given education, the village boys and girls have to earn theirs the hard way. For them there is truly no royal road to learning. In confirmation of this, we turn again to T. K. Papaspyropoulos and the account of his Peloponnesian village.[2]

The children in our village are tyrannized. Just as they sit down to study their mother says, "Get up. Break your bones, take your papers and the goat, and take her out to pasture." "Get up, get some water, get some wood, go and bring in the oxen. Don't you hear? In the evening you can study." The children go do their different tasks and in the evening come back broken with fatigue and drop off to sleep. In the morning they are cuffed by the teacher because they haven't written their lesson, and thus it goes. Black letters they learn! As if they had a lamp! Most of them read sitting on the floor; they drop on their stomachs near the fireplace and read in the light of the burning wood. From exhaustion they fall asleep and there is danger that they might get burned if the elders do not pull them away. In spring when the days are longer they read outside; they take the hog and the goat and go here or there and read while the animals pasture. What sort of reading can they do? As soon as they start, the hog escapes here and the goat there; they try to catch the hog, the goat escapes again. They start crying and lost is the reading. They also get beaten if the animals cause damage to the crops. Most of the children work also in the field; they also do some heavier tasks. What sort of letters can they learn? It's lucky they learn as much as they do.

When I discussed parental attitudes toward education with an experienced school man in Northern Greece, he said: "Less land and more knowledge is needed. A farmer can't see the need of educating a son who is to farm. He will keep the one to succeed him at home and send the others off for an education." The people of Vilia, a village in Central Greece, brag that the parents there see to it that the children go through eight grades but indicate that the other villages do not do this. "We do this," they say, "because an educated man commands more respect." But what about the children in the other villages?

From time to time an Athens newspaper comes out with some shocking statistics which cause a sensation and are then forgotten. Such accounts point out that the Article 16 of the Constitution states: "Elementary education is obligatory for all and is supplied gratis by the state." In 1951–52 it was estimated that two hundred thousand Greek children of school age were not in attendance. Conditions have improved considerably since then, but the effects of this nonattendance will be felt for many years to come. At that time it was also stated that at about the third grade the numbers of those who started are halved, a truly high drop-out rate, although other reports place this reduction at the end of the fourth grade.[3] One article comments:

Although the Constitution states that elementary schooling is supplied gratis, the various stamps and taxes, not to mention the prohibitive prices of schoolbooks, writing materials, and other paraphernalia, make this statement null and void.[4]

Incidentally, the illiteracy rate (in 1951) was 18 percent among urban Greeks (24 percent of the women, 8 percent of the men); and 30 percent among rural Greeks (45 percent of the women, 14 percent of the men). Many extenuating circumstances explain the high illiteracy rate among the women, for great numbers of them grew up in parts of Greece which were under Turkish rule during their childhood. Furthermore, education of women in rural areas has not had the practical significance to the villagers that schooling a boy would have. As for the younger age groups, they were deprived of schooling during the war years. Even during the guerrilla war many schoolteachers stayed away from the villages because as intellectuals they would have had to take sides either for or against the Communist-led forces, and they did not want to get involved. Thus children were deprived of educational opportunities. School buildings also were destroyed. No wonder the more ambitious among them were asking, "What will happen to us if we can't read?"

LOCAL SUPPORT FOR THE SCHOOL

Local school affairs are in the hands of the school board, which may consist of the teacher *ex officio* and of two others chosen by the village if it is small, or of five members if it is larger. The parents of the children in school are the ones usually involved in the election, but they know full well that the board can deal only with local matters such as finding money for current expenses including necessary books for the library, maintaining the building in reasonable repair, and determining various fees to be paid by the children. If the teacher, sent in by the central government, is not satisfactory, then the school board can complain to the inspector of schools but has no assurance that the next teacher will be any better suited to their needs should the present unsatisfactory one be replaced. Nor does the local school board have anything to say about what is taught in the school, since a uniform curriculum is followed throughout the country. In many parts of Greece, it is customary for the teacher to serve as cashier for the board, which handles fairly large sums contributed by the local people and the community council toward the education of their children.

One nomarch in Northern Greece said that out of the two hundred schools in his nomos (one hundred forty villages and sixty in urban suburbs), the patrons of sixty of them were willingly contributing money to pay for extra teachers as well as labor to pay for school enlargement. In spite of the comparatively large sums that are entrusted to the school board, the nomarch said that he had not known of a single case where money had been mishandled or misappropriated, a fact he attributed to the serious attitude the people take toward education. One problem, of course, is the uneconomic attempt by every little village to have its own school. Yet, because of transportation inadequacies, Greece is not ready to support consolidated elementary schools, even if the educational administrators should consider them desirable.

Most villagers show a pride in their school and try to locate it on one of the best sites in the village, quite often near the main square. These buildings come in all sorts of shapes and sizes. In the middle of the Peloponnesos we found a village school over a hundred years old, which had been privately endowed. The building was a one-room, poorly lighted structure which must have been truly grand by standards of a century ago. But today it seemed sadly inadequate for the many children crowded into its rows of benches. In Metsovo, the picturesque Wallachian village between Ioannina (Epirus) and Trikkala, we found an attractive, two-story stone structure of a type characterizing the more prosperous established mountain settlement which furnished pack horses for the caravan routes before the coming of the railroad. In Malakassa, in Attica, we saw a school being built of concrete blocks in 1955 by a joint effort of the American Save the Children Federation and the local village authorities.

An American senator once became interested in the welfare of a village near Mount Olympus, since some of his constituents of Greek descent told him that little was being done to remedy the deplorable conditions there. An American Mission official went to investigate. Part of his report gives a vivid postwar word picture:

The school was not completely ruined. The roof had collapsed, and the flooring, window-panes and furniture, all made of wood, had been used for firewood. The building remained and is being repaired. Unfortunately, the funds for school repairs are limited throughout Greece. The whole Nomos (Prefecture of Larissa, for instance, in which Kokkinopoulos is located), is comprised of 160 communities, most of the schools of which were damaged to some degree. The Nomos received $21,000 for this purpose, $2,371, of which went into the repair of the school at Kokkinopoulos. The roof has been replaced and the stairs finished, as have two of the four classrooms. In some villages, the State assistance was supplemented by the private initiative of the villagers, either in terms of materials or labor, and the schools were finished. In any case, the two classrooms are considered relatively adequate for the 158 children of school age in the village.[5]

The educational figures for 1956–57 throw some added light on the problem, since they show that there were in the whole country, including the cities, towns, and villages, a total of 8,527 elementary schools with about 940,000 pupils, or an average of 112 per school.[6] The chances are that in most village schools there are from 50 to 60 children per room, if the room happens to be large enough to accommodate that many, since approximately 60 percent of all elementary schools have one room and a single teacher.[7]

Therefore, the school board in many villages has its hands full trying to provide an adequate school building by seeking aid from the King's Institute, from the local community council, or from whatever other source can be tapped. The village is much more apt to procure and hold a teacher, since teachers are in such short supply, if it can provide him something approximating satisfactory living conditions. That is why some school boards, in constructing a new school, include a room in which the teacher can live, for such private accommodations are not available in many Greek villages. Providing necessary equipment and school supplies is another persistent problem for the school board, particularly since many of the parents cannot afford to buy for their children what the teacher thinks essential. Nor should it be supposed that the national government is indifferent to this state of affairs. Its funds for education are necessarily limited and these are first earmarked for teachers' salaries. What kind of person, one might ask, would care to teach under some of the difficulties encountered in the village schools?

THE VILLAGE TEACHER

For the almost 940,000 pupils in elementary school in 1956–57, there were 19,872 teachers. This means a national average of about 47 pupils per teacher, although as an average it indicates that a large number of teachers have more than this. In many of the smaller villages, the teachers have from four to six grades in one room, reminiscent of the rural one-room school in America of many years ago.

If we turn to accounts of village life, we gain a quick insight into, but certainly not a representative sampling of, the number of teachers one would meet, since each of these villages has at least three teachers:

In a fairly large Macedonian village we find five teachers, three with the rank of "instructors" who have finished a two-year normal school beyond secondary school. The two others are trained kindergarten or nursery-school teachers. They have 402 pupils, of whom 358 are in the regular six grades and 44 are in kindergarten and nursery. Most of these teachers have been in this village for at least five years. Nevertheless, because of their urban background, their thinking is urban and they find it difficult to take part in village activities.

In a village near Xanthe there are three teachers, all new to the community, who are paid by the central government. Two of these are from the Peloponnesos far to the south. All are graduates of the pedagogical academies. They have 156 pupils with an average daily attendance of 142.

Another village in Central Greece has three teachers: one man and two women. The man has resided in the village since 1947; one woman was appointed head of the school in 1942 but was away during the German occupation; the third was appointed in 1951. All are graduates of the normal school.

They teach 183 pupils, 78 percent of whom attend regularly during spring and early summer and 90 percent during the fall and winter.[8]

Early in my stay in Greece I had occasion to speak at considerable length with the director of one of the leading secondary schools in Athens. Later on, as I talked with village teachers, I found how accurately this educator had sized up the situation. He started off by giving some necessary background:

In my young days we had only four grades in the elementary school and, furthermore, not all villages had schools. Since 1929, the elementary school has been made six years and more villages have gotten schools. Since 1930, the number of pupils attending elementary schools has practically doubled. With the influx of the refugee population in the 1920s there was no possibility of increasing the buildings and staff in keeping with the population. For instance, the secondary-school enrollment has tripled, but unfortunately the revenue of the state has not tripled. Don't forget the four wars (1912–14; 1918; 1922; and 1940–45, with the guerrilla war following that). The northern provinces, especially, have suffered most because of the occupation by the Bulgarians.

He then pointed out that up to 1912 the role of the teacher was far greater than now. When I asked the reason, he said that then only the teacher and the priest were literate, but now the so-called educated people, originally from the village who have spent some time in the city, go back and say that what the priest and teacher advise is not important. This superficial education proves very harmful, he warns, because people who think themselves clever say to the villagers: "Here in the city we work six hours; in the village you work longer." The director then explained:

The teachers are far better educated now than before. The university studies are better than they used to be. The spelling is not much better due to the many differences resulting from the use of the popular language [*demotike*] and the "pure" language [*katharevousa*]. After a uniform language is established, the spelling will take care of itself.

About four fifths of the teachers come from rural areas. Although each teacher is better-trained now, he faces many more difficulties than before. Each teacher used to have thirty pupils; now he has sixty and these have to be crowded into the same old building. Every year the proportion of men in the university decreases as the numbers of women rise. Many more women are going into elementary teaching now than formerly because of the low salary. A man cannot support his family on that salary and women take teaching jobs because they have to add to the family income. Also there are many graduates of the pedagogic institutes, who are trained as teachers, but who find better jobs elsewhere and never do any teaching.

He felt it the teacher's duty to be deeply involved in the social life of the village, which required more knowledge about agriculture, cooperatives, and financial matters. "But a really pernicious element in the village, today," said the director, going back to an earlier theme, "is the half-educated person, who sits in the coffeehouse, reads the newspapers, and gives his half-baked ideas. He thereby undermines the influence of the teacher." Nevertheless, many dedicated teachers exert tremendous influence despite all the handicaps they face. He mentioned the case of the teacher in Phlorina (western Macedonia), a Greek refugee from Russia, who in the late 1920s planted with the children in the school garden the first apple trees, destined to become the basis of the extensive orchards now in that area. The teacher persuaded the villagers to take slips from these trees for planting. But not all teachers show this initiative. "We fail to teach the teachers how to teach the children how to behave and meet the various problems as they arise." The fault does not lie with the children, since they have an incredible thirst for learning: "To the child, the school is cherished," he concluded.

It was always easy to get people not only to compare education in the past with the present but also to get discussions of the regional differences in emphasis upon education. In a Macedonian village I once listened to a long discussion with a local official and an outsider, originally from Southern Greece, who had brought a truckload of beehives from Chalkidike to pasture on the special variety of blossoms there. The beekeeper asserted: "The standard of living in the Peloponnesos is higher than here in Northern Greece. In my village there has been for many years a gymnasium, and you won't find anyone who hasn't gone to school, while here you don't find people with the same interest. That is why the standard of living is higher in the Peloponnesos."

But the Macedonian would not accept such a comparison without a verbal challenge: "You forget that you got liberated almost one hundred years before we did. We had five hundred years of Turkish rule over our heads; it is not true that we don't want our children to get a better education. For instance, in my village of Balta we have a semigymnasium where there are 365 students. The state wants to close that school, and we said that if they did this we would be obliged to send our children to a distant gymnasium. We have eight teachers in that school; four are paid by the state, but we local people give them a supplement since their salary is not sufficient; the other four teachers are paid entirely by the parents. In the first three grades each pupil pays $3 per month and in the next three grades $4 per month. This shows we value education. Everything goes for Southern Greece; we are neglected here."

Here, at least, was one indication that the teacher was much appreciated. But throughout my village visits I also found those who were impatient with the teachers. One Greek official, who knows many parts of his country intimately, agreed with many of the points that the Athens gymnasium director had made, as the following summary of his comment shows:

About thirty or forty years ago the community was independent. It was something solid; it elected the best people to office. Why? They elected their own teacher, their own priest, and the field guards. Three main points of their life — education, religion, and security — were all in their own hands. The central government wanted to take into its own control all of these functions in order to put in its own appointees who would influence the people. The peasants lost their ability to manage their own affairs, and became hostile to the government and to the teacher. The teacher is no longer responsible to the farmer but to the government. Nowadays, because of this and because of the anti-government attitude brought in by the refugees from Turkey, the peasant has separated himself from his government and asks everything from it.

The teacher has no obligation toward the village, no sense of community relations. He stays in the coffeehouse and aims to move to a town or city. Formerly a village would give some bright boy a chance to go outside for an education and then he would come back and live in the village where he had his own home. He was one of the best teachers.

When one begins to sift from many conversations the findings about the village teacher and to read the village accounts which include him in their pages, a few matters stand out. First of all, it is true that the allegiance of the teacher is to the national government and to the bureaucracy upon which his advancement depends. He thinks of himself as a representative of the national ideal, which he is supposed to instill in every child studying under him. His loyalty is therefore to Greece, and one of his major purposes is to help the village child feel a close identification with the national state. Second, he tries, often like a drillmaster, to get the pupils to master the course content worked out in Athens. The brighter ones need encouragement to go on to the gymnasium and must receive the preparation that will serve them in good stead there. Third, the teacher must train children to participate through song, recitation, and national dance in the various holiday celebrations and festivals that come along and at which the school makes an appearance. This serves a village purpose in that it encourages local traditions and provides some diversion in what many would consider the humdrum life of the villager. But there are few teachers in the national school system, unless they are in one of the specialized schools set up for the purpose, who undertake any adult education or even try to make the younger scholars look around at their village environment for ways in which it can be improved. Very often I got the impression that many teachers were even trying to make the villagers forget the present and its problems by focusing their attention on the past and its glories as a substitute for action today.

But one must not be too hard on the teacher. The local people do not expect him to be an important agent of change. He is to teach their children so that some of them can go on to the gymnasium and eventually achieve glory outside the village. He is to be sure that the youngsters learn to read and write, which is becoming a modern necessity even in the out-of-way places in Greece. Along with this he must act the way an intellectual is supposed to act. He dresses in the urban styles; he talks of the plays and other activities going on in the city; he even reminds people occasionally how stupid they are to be doubly sure that they respect the knowledge that he has acquired. In many villages if he were to trouble the children about the flies that annoy them, suggest that the water they drank might be impure, or tell the farmers that they ought to be using more fertilizer, he would be branded as a meddler and told to stick to his teaching. It is all right to have a school garden, but this is often viewed as an aesthetic rather than as an educational undertaking. If the school is to make an impact leading toward village improvement, the teacher will need much broader support than he has received in the past from others in the Ministry of Education; his training will have to be modified, and he will have to be relieved from the heavy pupil load that he carries. To expect any teacher, responsible through the day for fifty to sixty children, even if they do come in morning and afternoon shifts, also to take on the task of trying to remake the peasant world is asking more than is reasonable. If the teacher is to prepare children more effectively for a changing world, according to many of those who have studied the Greek educational system, a beginning will have to be made with the curriculum and the textbooks.

THE SCHOOL CURRICULUM

Any discussion of what is taught in Greek schools must include not only the course of study for the first six grades (elementary) but embrace that for the gymnasium (high school) as well. To be sure, only in the largest villages does one find a gymnasium, of which there are 701 in Greece (1956–57), with an enrollment of 195,000 students and a staff of 4,775 teachers. As has already been suggested, children from the outlying villages who have completed the elementary grades may walk several miles back and forth to the gymnasium in the central town or large village; if they live too far away, several of them may live in a fairly simple dormitory during the week and go home for the weekend. But Saturday is a school day, so the weekends are abbreviated affairs, although now in some cases bus transportation is provided to save the long walks home.

In approaching the curriculum found in the Greek schools it is important to remember that "when Greece became independent in 1830 her primary concern was not to teach her childern how to transform their thinking and behavior from the mentality of an occupied power to that of a self-governing nation, but rather it was to study the ancient Greek culture as a basis for the new state and to establish the new Greek state as an extension of the old." [9] A general view of the curriculum, however, may be seen in two tables, the first of which (Table 5) is for the six-year grammar school.[10]

TABLE 5. CURRICULUM FOR SIX–YEAR GRAMMAR SCHOOL, WITH HOURS ALLOTTED PER SUBJECT

Subject	Class hours by grades per week						Total (per subject)
	1st	2nd	3rd	4th	5th	6th	
Religion	1	1	2	2	3	3	12
Greek language	8	9	9	9	9	9	53
History			1	2	2	2	7
Geography	3	3	2	2	2	2	14
Natural science			3	3	2	2	10
Physics, chemistry					2	2	4
Arithmetic	3	3	3	3	3	3	18
Geometry					1	1	2
Drawing	1½	1½	2	2⎫	2	2	17
Writing		2	2	2⎭			
Handicrafts	1½	1½	2	2	2	2	11
Singing	2	2	2	2	2	2	12
Physical education	2	2	2	2	2	2	12
Total class hours (per week)	22	25	30	31	32	32	172

In the first two grades the pupils study religion, begin the reading and writing of the popular language (*demotike*), study some local geography and start arithmetic, and spend time on drawing, handicrafts, singing, and physical education. In the third grade history and biology are added, while in the fifth grade physics and chemistry and geometry are taken up. At this level such subjects have to be rudimentary, but at any rate they are begun so that in high school the teachers have a foundation on which to build in intensive fashion. The history courses are so planned that by the time the child has completed the sixth grade, he will have some knowledge of European history up to the sixteenth century.

Turning now to the high school, we find a very full curriculum indeed. For an illustration we can look at the boys' high school (Table 6), since it is customary in a few of the cities to separate the boys and girls at the time of secondary school.[11] The only differences between the curriculum for the boys and the girls are that the latter has three hours less of ancient Greek, no Latin, three hours less of mathematics, but one more hour of hygiene and a six-hour home-economics course.

The official purpose of the various courses included in the high-school curriculum shows intent if not actual accomplishment:

Religion. To convey a clear understanding of the moral works of Christ and of the Orthodox Church; to instill a proper respect for these works and thus elevate the students' religious and moral spirit so that it will become the major factor in their individual and social life. (Twelve hours total over six years.)

TABLE 6. CURRICULUM FOR BOYS' HIGH SCHOOL, WITH HOURS ALLOTTED PER SUBJECT

Subject	Class hours by grades per week						Total (per subject)
	1st	2nd	3rd	4th	5th	6th	
Religion	2	2	2	2	2	2	12
Ancient Greek	8	8	8	9	9	9	51
Modern Greek	3	3	3	3	3	3	18
Latin			3	3	3	3	12
French	4	3	3	3	2	2	17
History	3	3	3	3	2	4	18
Mathematics	3	4	3	3	4	5	22
Science	3	3	3	3	3	4	19
Geography	2	2	2	1	1		8
Hygiene					1		1
Handicrafts	2	2	1	1	1		7
Singing	2	2	1	1			6
Philosophy					2	2	4
Physical education	3	3	3	3	3	3	18
Total class hours (per week)	35	35	35	35	36	37	213

Ancient Greek. To familiarize the students with the writings of the ancient Greeks; teach them a reading knowledge and understanding of ancient Greek, as well as the ability to write in the Attic dialect. Give them an appreciation of ancient life and its thoughts in order to better understand modern Greek. Better to appreciate good writing by reading selected texts of ancient Greek authors. Study of ancient civilizations so as to better understand our own age. (Fifty-one hours.)

Modern Greek (*katharevousa*). Spoken and written use of Greek language; improvement of the students' literary education; leads to a greater understanding of modern Greek civilization and enhances students' national awareness. (Eighteen hours.)

Latin. To learn the Latin language in order to understand the work and thought of ancient Latin writers; to understand and appreciate the Roman civilization. (Twelve hours.)

French. To learn to speak, write, and understand French; to understand and appreciate French literature and through it modern French civilization. (Seventeen hours.)

As a sidelight, it is interesting to note that out of the 213 hours covered in high school, 98 are in languages. Twenty-five percent of the time is devoted to ancient Greek.

History. To study the way of life and thought of peoples. Comparison of ancient with modern times so as to allow the formation of an opinion which will help the student understand the influences of one historical period on another. History should lead to understanding of the Greek nation and civilization and their influence on contemporary religions, economies, science, arts, and morality. Teaching of patriotism and performance of the duties of citizens. (Eighteen hours.)

Mathematics — Cosmography. To improve the ability of students in understanding arithmetic and geometry; in thinking clearly and precisely; to create the belief that mathematics is an important, independent science. Purpose of teaching cosmography: Learning about the celestial bodies, their relations, and the laws concerning their movements. (Twenty-two hours.)

Physical Sciences and Biology. Study of nature and importance of the physical sciences in life. Increase the students' love of nature. Application of science to industry and technology. Biology: Study of life and habitat of all living creatures in order to understand the uses of plants and animals in daily life. (Science: nineteen hours.)

Geography. Study of the surface of the earth, especially the area of Greece; influence of the land on human life; study of the people of Greece and the beauty of the land. (Eight hours.)

Hygiene. To improve the students' knowledge of hygienic conditions in life with relation to hygienic habits in personal and social life. For girls: Study of woman's body. Hygiene for babies and children. Hygiene of married and unmarried women; hygiene necessary for various ages of life. Nursing, elementary first aid. Use of drugs and medicine at home. (One hour for boys; two hours for girls.)

Philosophy is an introduction to psychology and logic, while handicrafts are taught not as manual training or shopwork but to further the "artistic education of students and to teach them to make small things with their hands."

And the curriculum guide correctly advises: "It is wise to create a musical life in the high school. The students will be better occupied during their recreational and relaxation time." Gymnastics consists of "physical exercises, games, swimming, dances, excursions, and several military (elementary) exercises for the boys and classic and folk dancing for the girls."

Such is the intellectual bill of fare for peasant boys attending the gymnasium in the nearest large village or town. There is, of course, no connection between this curriculum and the requirements of farming in the village. The peasants recognize this, for they do not send the eldest son, who is to take over the farm, to such a school. Some completing the gymnasium will go on to get a university diploma and will therefore find this curriculum directly related to their needs in many university courses. Others will go no further than the completion of high school, but this will be enough to open up certain government jobs to them.

But what of the eldest son who expects to farm? Is his education to stop at the sixth grade? In most cases it does, but there are about eight government agricultural high schools in Greece where boys can go to learn to be better farmers. Some of these government schools admit boys who have finished the fourth grade and others require the sixth grade, but all give those who complete the course through the eighth grade a certificate. Here, again, the graduates are not so much interested in going back to their family's small farm as in going on to government jobs in the Ministry of Agriculture as technicians. In the school in Phlorina one can study horticulture and viticulture; in Kozane winemaking has recently been added to horticulture and viticulture; in Ioannina the emphasis is upon dairying and in Larissa upon cheesemaking and horticulture. The others, in the Peloponnesos and Crete, also stress horticulture and viticulture. In addition to the government schools, there are four private agricultural schools: The American Farm School in Thessalonike,[12] and schools in Konitsa, Amaroussi, and the island of Chios. The two government Superior Schools of Agriculture are near Athens and Thessalonike and rank at the university level.

The lower agricultural schools as well as certain technical schools in carpentry, brickmaking, and the like, set up by the King's Institute, are viewed by Greeks as training schools rather than as paths to becoming an educated man. In other words, education in Greece is utilitarian in that its pursuit helps one achieve life goals in the government bureaucracy and the social structure of the country; it is not utilitarian in the sense of preparing one for practical or vocational matters while absorbing at the same time general education from courses in language, history, mathematics, and the like. Greece, in this respect, follows the traditional European pattern.

Many Greeks are acutely aware of their educational problems. One nomarch told of a move toward closing down some of the classical gymnasiums and putting young people into trade schools. "But this presents problems," he said, "because the boys who finish think they are carpenters or blacksmiths and don't want to go back to the village." He thought the attack upon the flight of the educated people to the cities must begin with the mothers, for it is they who say: "But, son, you have your education; you can't go work in the fields."

LANGUAGE: POPULAR OR PURE?

The Greek elementary school has been caught in the no-man's land of a controversy which makes the current educational debate between traditionalists and progressives in the United States seem pale by comparison. The epic struggle has involved the particular form of the Greek language to be used in this school. After the Greek savant has established the point that modern Greek is the same language as ancient Greek but that it has been modified over the past thirty centuries, he will then differentiate between the three representations of Greek.

First, of course, is the ancient Greek which was by no means a uniform language. There were four main classic dialects: the Ionic in which the *Iliad* and *Odyssey* were originally written and which came to be identified with epic poetry; the Aeolian which was thought of chiefly in connection with lyric poetry; the Attic which was used for tragic poetry, oratorical art, and philosophical debate; and the Doric, used mainly by Spartans who wrote very little, and which therefore had no significant literary development. With the spread of Greek culture under Alexander the Great, another type of Greek, the Helleniki Koine, was used by many people speaking other languages but united under the same political ruler. It used only the commonest Greek words found in all of the Greek dialects; it also incorporated non-Hellenic words. It was the language in which the four Christian Gospels first appeared. The Koine, however, was not classical Greek and is not studied as such.[13]

Today one finds a popular form of Greek, again in a rich variety of dialects, which is called *demotike,* or the people's language. Just as the educated people in the Hellenistic period continued to use the Attic Greek when all the uneducated people were speaking Koine, so today many of the educated people frown upon the demotike as a vulgar form which is to be avoided.

In its place they would substitute a third form of Greek, the *katharevousa,* or purist language.[14] This is an artificial language, based as much as possible upon classic syntax and vocabulary, which became in effect the official language of the Greek state after the war of independence in 1821. The contrasts between demotike and katharevousa have been clearly explained by Kimon Friar in his discussion of modern Greek poetry:

> The purist is the official language used on all formal occasions by those in government, business, and university, although the same people speak demotic or some modification of it. By the time of the eleventh century the demotic had closely approximated its present form, which in grammar today varies but slightly from that spoken during the downfall of the Byzantine Empire in the fifteenth century. The purist is condensed and synthetic; the demotic is periphrastic and analytic, rich in many concrete words and phrases but extremely

poor in those abstract words of the arts and sciences which were not the concern of the common people who kept it living. Today, this lack of abstract words is the despair of the modern poet who wishes to express a thought of any metaphysical nicety, and he is driven to paraphase or symbol.

Since the eighteenth century, when the demotic had crystallized in folk poetry, the battle between the use of purist and demotic in prose and poetry has raged, but the battle has finally been won by the demotic, Today the contemporary poet may hold his expression on a living language and borrow his vocabulary as he can from a rich tradition of three thousand years, from Ancient, Hellenistic, Byzantine, Medieval, and Modern Greek and its many dialects, and especially from the purist itself.[15]

Not just poets but almost any literate Greek can construct a private language of his own, within limits to be sure, and use a vocabulary which others may understand and appreciate but which they themselves would never use under the same circumstances. A person is always on safe ground in criticizing the sentence structure, vocabulary, and idiom of a Greek writer, since he is criticizing what is of necessity a personalized style. In other words, the Greek language is still evolving, which means that "the language question" has perennially plagued the school authorities.

Should, for example, the beginning pupils in the first grade start out learning to read and write the kind of Greek they speak at home (demotike), or should they start out studying a kind of Greek which they cannot understand but which they will have to learn to understand if they are to be considered educated? There seems to have been little disagreement over the matter of teaching the purist Greek in the secondary school. That is an accepted fact. But what about the elementary school?

In the beginning of the new state in 1830, the purist language was supposed to be used throughout the whole school system, even with the beginning pupils. By 1911 people were suggesting that maybe it would be best to use demotike in the elementary school but the Royalists, then a political opposition party, raised such a hue and cry that action was deferred. The Royalists were supported in their stand by some professional men "on the grounds of prestige, and from some teachers who only knew the grammar of the *katharevousa*." [16]

In 1917 Venizelos adopted the proposal, but when the Royalists came to power in 1920,

they forbade the use of *demotike* in schools and made a public bonfire of the new textbooks which had just been written in it. Chaos followed. Every change in government meant a change in the medium of primary education: in 1922 *demotike* was reintroduced by Plastiras; in 1925 Pangelos forbade its use; in 1928, it was restored by the Coalition government with the proviso that *katharevousa* should be taught four hours weekly in the two top forms; in 1932, *katharevousa* was to be taught in all forms; in 1933 the two top forms were to be taught exclusively in *katharevousa;* and in 1936, Metaxas, always using *demotike* himself, re-established teaching in the popular tongue throughout the primary schools and ordered the publication of an official grammar of the language.[17]

Since then, despite much outcry to the contrary, the demotike has remained the language of the elementary school.

I asked the Greeks on a number of occasions if the two languages about which they were arguing were really two different languages. They usually answered "yes" and "no": yes, because the demotike has a number of foreign words not found in the other and uses a different grammar; no, because there is considerable overlapping. In other words, to be educated is in a sense to become bilingual, an accomplishment which tends to create social distance between the upper and lower classes. But, interestingly enough, two members of the upper or educated class often speak to each other, not in the purist form, but in a demotike which has been transformed to a medium above the peasant level.

But what does all of this mean for the villager who has never studied katharevousa? He admits that when the teacher or the priest begins to use the latter he experiences, "a shiver of holy enthusiasm," [18] but he does not really follow fully what is said. Therefore, to reach the peasant, one must use demotike, which is a written as well as a spoken medium of communication. This is what the Communist press started doing, making use of what many consider a rather strange type of demotike but nevertheless one aimed at trying to get the Communist message across to the villagers and the lower classes in the cities. The non-Communist papers, although using demotike for news stories, continue to write their editorials in the learned, purist Greek, and official government documents continue to appear in the purist form. As a matter of fact, if one seems to prefer demotike as a writing medium over the katharevousa, many people consider one leftist and therefore somewhat suspect. This is why some of my Greek friends describe the language situation in Greece today as one of "anarchy and confusion." But there is some hope in Kimon Friar's words:

If in all this confusion, poverty and richness, the modern Greek poet [and he could mean any writer] sometimes despairs, he may remind himself that in periods of language formation great poets have arisen, a Chaucer, a Dante, and even a Shakespeare.[19]

···⫷[XIV]⫸···

Religion and the Greek Peasant

The Greek villager's religion, a special blend of classical Greek pagan-ism and Christianity, illustrates the capacity of Greek culture to absorb a new religious force, early Christianity, in such a way as to preserve un-broken continuity. The discussion of "Orthodoxy and Greekness" which follows bears upon this point. Yet, despite its antiquity and the accretions of past ages, Greek religion, while imposing a certain discipline through fasts and obligatory ceremonies, always managed to avoid becoming sim-ply a burdensome set of obligations. It did so by the typically Greek device of finding a light touch in the midst of solemnity. The village priest, whose role is described in some detail, has for many centuries furnished unwit-tingly the necessary comic relief, although often capable in times of ex-tremity of providing inspiring leadership.

At the same time, Greek religion is also humane, responding to need and affliction through individual action rather than through organized charitable institutions. The section on "The Bishop of Messenia and His Good Works" shows what one imaginative individual can do. Greek reli-gion also reveals its practical side in its confrontation of death and calamity. The somber shades of war, pestilence, and oppression are not strangers to sunny Greece, and the Greek religion teaches people how to face such mis-fortunes stoically and with dignity.

Although a rare Puritan strain appears now and then, Greek religion is also supposed to be fun, as any attendance at a religious festival will show. In fact, most religious occasions provide an excuse for merriment, even during the ceremonies. To the uninitiated such behavior borders on the irreverent, but the Greek might well argue that joy and even levity should prove as pleasing to God as assumed sorrow or feigned piety. Indeed, festivals are as old as Greek religion itself, with each carrying its own sacramental message to be expressed in dance as well as in formal liturgy. But religious expression is not confined to formal occasions; it permeates the daily life of the people, as we shall see.

ORTHODOXY AND GREEKNESS

To start any discussion of religion and the Greek peasant, it is necessary to state clearly and unequivocally that adherence to the official religion of Greece, the Greek Orthodox Church, is tantamount to being Greek. Only 2 to 3 percent of the population of the country are not members of the Orthodox Church. Though those comprising this small fraction may have political citizenship, may speak the Greek tongue, and may take pride in the legacy of ancient Greece, they are at best suspect Greeks if they do not nominally at least belong to the Orthodox Church.

But what is the syncretism that is called Orthodoxy? This question can be answered on at least two levels: first, that of the peasant and, second, that of the educated Greek. To the peasant, the coming of Christianity did not mean an important break with many of his previous practices, beliefs, and even deities. What were formerly deities became saints, with some of the more powerful deities becoming identified with the most powerful saints, such as the Holy Virgin. It seemed perfectly fitting and not at all surprising to find an old, old church dedicated to St. Theodore in the southern Peloponnesos, two of whose columns were from an ancient pre-Christian temple standing on their original pediments. Many scholars have described in considerable detail various aspects of this easy transition from pagan to Christian worship.[1] William Miller, a keen student of Greek life, has pointed out that the saints play a very important part in Greek life: their functions and names often prove that they are the legitimate descendants of the old Greek gods, the new religion having been grafted on to the old. He indicates that Helios, the sun god, has been succeeded by the Prophet Elias (Elijah), whose chapels crown almost every eminence in Greece; the Virgin has replaced Athena Parthenos, and the Parthenon in the Middle Ages was the Church of St. Mary, whether as a Greek Cathedral or as a Latin minster; St. Dionysios has dethroned Dionysis; St. George and the Dragon are the Christian version of Theseus and the Minotaur, so that the Theseum naturally became in Christian times the Church of St. George.[2]

Marcu Beza, who describes many pagan survivals with Christian names which are found throughout the Balkans, speaks of the rich texture of Christianity there, which came to the Balkan nations in the shape of Byzantine Orthodoxy and which meant a particular culture, comprising art, literature, and theology, in the service of the Church.[3]

One has only to review the brief description of the peasant and nature or the peasant approach to sickness and child care in earlier chapters to see how lively is the environment for any peasant who believes in the Evil Eye or the omens of spiders, birds in flight, or the hooting of an owl.[4] The peasant, instead of being made over into some sort of revolutionary Christian image, was able to take early Christianity and make it over into the even earlier Greek image. That is what survives in rural Greece today.

The educated Greek went through almost the same process, but on a much more sophisticated level. Instead of equating the sun god with St. Elijah, he equated Platonic teachings with the doctrines of St. Paul. Thanassis Aghnides sets forth this theme:

> As regards religious life, let us not forget that the New Testament was written in Greek, and most of the principles of Christianity are loans from Greek moral philosophy. Plato's ideas could find no better means of diffusion in the world than the New Testament.
>
> Thus a Greek never feels that the Christian religion is a Jewish gift to the world. When he reads the New Testament he is reminded of the highest precepts of the Greek classical period. Here again the modern Greek is not very conscious of the lines of demarcation between the high precepts of Christianity, and, let us say, those of Socrates. The latter's principles and those of the Galilean are derived from the same source. The modern Greek is confusedly aware of this. He may not say it in as many words but he feels the modern ethical standards of the Christian world as being part and parcel of his own heritage from his classical ancestors.[5]

In support of this point of view among the peasants, I can mention the consternation shown by some Greek village women when, for the first time, they learned that Christ was a Jew. They had always assumed that he was Greek and would not believe otherwise until they had gone to check with the priest.

Orthodoxy and Greekness are tied in together not only because of the continuity between ancient traditions and Christian doctrine; the Orthodox Church was also the vehicle through which Greekness was preserved under alien conquerors. Church and politics went hand in hand. The Greek Orthodox Church, which was the basic institution of the Byzantine Empire, continues as such within the modern Greek nation, and contemporary Greeks, like the Byzantines, find it hard to accept political ideas which do not assume the complete unification of church and state. Today the church is still an integral part of the Greek government, its affairs administered within the Ministry of Education and Religion, the salaries of the clergy paid by the state as civil servants, and religious belief a part of national patriotism. Nothing really fundamental can be done in the nation down to the smallest commune without clerical interest and participation. This is not written law, but deep-seated custom.[6]

Greeks view contemporary events in terms of their own adaptation of New Testament teachings and claim that the Greek nation, though it has suffered many "Golgothas," has recovered from these disasters to experience a "resurrection" each time.[7] Such comparisons with the life and sufferings of Christ are also intelligible to the Greek peasant, who has little difficulty in identifying them with the sufferings of Greece through which the rest of the world will be saved. Greeks give episodes in Greek history, such as their defeat of the Italians in World War II and their fighting back the spread of Communism in postwar years, a political-religious interpretation highly charged with emotion because these touch upon what is sacred in the Greek national tradition — the unique contribution Greece has over and over again made to the preservation of Western civilization through the frequent ordeals she has endured.

THE VILLAGE PRIEST AND HIS PARISH

An American walking down the street with a Greek friend is usually surprised when the Greek hits him on the shoulder and says, "I give you the priest." This act supposedly transfers to someone else the misfortune that might follow from meeting the *papas,* or priest, who passes dressed in his flowing black robes and his tall stovepipe brimless hat, and wearing a handsome black beard and his long hair neatly done up into a bun. Should he be accompanied by a woman, she is probably his wife, for in the Greek Orthodox Church there are both married and unmarried priests. The married priests can take the ordination vows after marriage, but no priest can marry after ordination. The married priests are usually the parish priests, and it is rare to find the village priest unmarried. On the other hand, the unmarried priest, recruited among the monks, can alone rise to high administrative positions in the church. He may, for instance, be a bishop over one of the sixty-seven dioceses or, if properly qualified, eventually be one of the twelve bishops comprising the Holy Synod which guides the church under the presidency of the Metropolitan of Athens, the actual head of the church. The Patriarch of Constantinople at Istanbul is the titular head, but this is more of a traditional and honorary office, since the Metropolitan is looked upon as the chief functionary. In Greece the king has no authority over the church.

In the village the parish priest, married as he is, settles down, digs his roots in deeply, so to speak. He knows that he has no opportunity for advancement in the church hierarchy; so there is no need for him to spend his time "politicking" for appointment to some choice position in the church courts. The village priest, therefore, acquires land and farms, in many cases just as diligently as the other villagers; he may even embark upon a few small-scale business enterprises on the side. His regular salary from the state gives him a steady income which the rest of the local people usually lack. This, combined with thrift and diligence, helps him acquire a little more property than the average farmer and enjoy a slightly higher standard of living. This is not guaranteed, of course, and one can call to mind many village priests who obviously were living on the barest minimum. At the same time, the priest is able to maintain what has been called a "comradely equality" with his people.[8]

The priest, however, is not necessarily a permanent fixture. The bishop appoints him to a post and the local congregation can refuse him, or it can raise objections to a bishop about a priest who conducts himself in ways the local people do not like. In most cases, the bishop tries to find the kind of priest that the local parishioners prefer. Since the priest often acquires land, as has been pointed out, he wants to pass that on to his children. He may try to persuade one son at least to follow him in the service of the church. In one Peloponnesian village I found that a priest's son now off at the seminary was coming back to succeed his father, thus making a fourth generation of priests from the same family serving that parish. When I mentioned this to bishops and others familiar with church matters, they pointed out that this was a common phenomenon, and even gave the names of villages where a fifth-generation member from the same family was ministering to the same parish.

Should a parish vacancy occur, the bishop, who is informed about it as a matter of course, announces in the local papers as well as in the church papers that there is a vacancy in such and such a village and that all qualified people may apply. He goes through the applications, selects the eligible candidates, and posts their names on the door of the cathedral, with the notice that anyone who knows any reason why these people should not serve as priests should inform the bishop. After due time has elapsed, he makes the choice, giving heavy weight, according to one bishop who discussed this, to educational qualifications and moral considerations.

In pursuing in greater detail the relationship between the parish priest and the state, I learned that it was under the leadership of Archbishop (Metropolitan) Damaskinos, who played such an important part in helping his country through the politically troubled waters from German occupation back to self-government, that the priests were put on a salary paid by the state. Before that, they had been paid from fees and also by products from the parishioners. *Kondota,* or the subscription by families of so much wheat, eggs, olive oil, and such, to the priest if he would serve them was widely practiced before the present salary arrangement was made. In round figures, the parishes now contribute about one fourth of the amount needed to pay the priests' salaries, with the difference coming from state revenue. Also, the local parishes have to pay an amount equal to 6 percent of their priest's salary to the bishop toward the retirement fund for the local priest.

For salary purposes, the priests are divided into four classes: those who have gone through the theological faculty of the university; those who have attended the seminary, perhaps one or two years beyond gymnasium; those who have no seminary but who have finished gymnasium; and those put in a miscellaneous category. There are apparently sufficient candidates for the priesthood now, and some effort is being made to fashion their curriculum to prepare them to serve village needs more effectively; even the older priests are encouraged to come back for periods of study. One member of the Holy Synod thought that the priests ought to know more about agriculture, economics, and first aid, so that they might play a more vital part in community life. His view of the priest's role was that "he is to help people with their problems of all kinds and settle any disputes among the villagers."

But what part does the village priest really play? As has already been indicated, the Greeks are ambivalent toward the priest.[9] "As an individual, he commands respect, and gives advice to those who seek it. However, he is also a figure of ridicule and of ill omen." [10] A great deal depends upon the personality of the priest himself. One informant told me that when he was a boy their village had had a wonderful priest who was very important. Today, even though the people are probably just as much attached to their religion, the present priest is not popular. In the course of an extended conversation with the people in a village near Volos, we asked what kind of priest they had. "Oh, our priest is from around Karpenesi. He has five children and is a good family man." He was not singled out for praise because of any priestly performance, but because of his conformity to basic village values. But children in that same village must have heard many, many times the local account of what happened to some monks who lived in a monastery not far from the village. This had been built in 1714 as an annex of a Mount Athos establishment, but in due course of time the monks became "naughty" in that they called to and teased the women who were on their way to work in the fields. Finally the villagers could stand this no longer, so the men took the monks to a rock overlooking the sea and told them to jump. The monks jumped and were never heard of again. The present priest, unlike the monks, is "a good family man."

Very persistent and widespread is the belief, already mentioned, that an encounter with the priest brings bad luck. If peasants starting on some new venture meet a priest, they will turn back home and not begin it on that day for fear of failure. Anyone who meets a priest, in addition to "giving" the bad luck to a companion by hitting him on the shoulder, can tie a knot in a handkerchief, thereby putting the priest under his control so he will do no harm. But, bad luck or not, the priest is indispensable. At numerous repasts celebrating a christening, a nameday, or some other important event, we had to wait what seemed an interminable length of time because the priest could not arrive any earlier. Without him, nothing could get under way. One serious student of Greek rural life said: "In Greece when a priest is missing, it is a great calamity, for the Greek is not used to praying by himself without a priest." [11] In earlier days when the belief in vampires was much more widespread than today, it was the priest, the minister of God, who alone had any power over them. He could calm the fears of the people.

The responsibility for the local parish does not fall entirely upon the priest, although the chief responsibility is his. There is a church board, consisting of three to five members, with the priest as president. The nominations for this board are submitted to the bishop by the priest, and the bishop designates them as official members of the board. One member of the board is the treasurer. When these local officials are asked just what their duties are, they usually include in their replies: to help the priest, to look after the finances, and to care for the church building. This board has as one of its chief duties the sale of the candles in the church vestibule and can use the proceeds of the sale for local church needs. In most communities it is considered a great honor to serve as a member of this board, although this position requires much work and frequently has more responsibility than the presidency of the local cooperative.

A recent development is the growth of the Sunday school, held after the regular morning service. Young boys, girls, and a few women are usually found in attendance, although young people up to the age of twenty are urged to attend. Throughout much of Greece the priest gives the instruction, although in Northern Greece we found many villages where the teacher had taken over this extra duty. Usually the same lesson is given to all age groups at the same time. It is customary in some places, such as the Attic villages we visited, for the school to be held on a weekday by the teacher, in which case it was not called Sunday school but "the preaching school."

The heart, however, of the Greek Orthodox Church — as of many other Christian bodies — is the Sunday-morning Mass. Anyone attending cannot help but notice the building itself, usually in the shape of a Greek cross, with the ends terminating in apses. Over the center there is a dome representing heaven. In front, the altar screen (*eikonostasion*), on which one finds the icons or pictures of various saints, separates the altar (*vema*), which no woman can enter, from the nave, where the worshippers congregate.[12] The priest moves back and forth between altar and nave in what seems a random manner to the uninitiated. As he turns to face the altar, the icon of Christ is on his right and that of St. John the Baptist next to it. To his left one sees on the altar the icon of the Virgin, and farther to the left the icon of the saint for whom the church was named.

The congregation stands during the service, except for a few infirm who can lean against supports along the wall; there is no instrumental music, as the priest and the chanter carry the service themselves in a language that much of the time is unintelligible to the worshippers. The gospels are read in Koine, or New Testament Greek, and the liturgy, written by St. John Chrysostom toward the end of the fourth century, is in the Greek of that period. When the priest delivers a sermon, he uses his version of katha-revousa, if he is sufficiently schooled; otherwise, he speaks in demotike. Apparently the worshippers are moved by the ceremony, the procession, the swinging censers, and the chanting even more than by the actual meaning of the words to which they listen. Now and then in the liturgy, however, come familiar passages which most can understand because of having learned their meaning in school or from some relative.

The worshippers, among whom small children may be running or tugging, include very few men. They come out for special festival services but show no interest in the regular Sunday-morning service, which is viewed as the woman's social hour. Even during the service women catch up on the latest happenings throughout the village.

The priest, however, is busy at other times, too. Dorothy Lee describes it this way:

Religion permeates Greek life, punctuating it with ritual. No Greek, urban or rural, would think of initiating anything important without a religious inaugura-tion. Schools open with the inaugurative *agiasmos*, "making holy"; the founda-tion stone of every house is laid with *agiasmos;* merchants begin new under-takings with the proper religious inauguration. On Epiphany, the sea is made holy for those who journey on it. In the country, blessed water is carried from the Epiphany Mass to sprinkle on the fields. The Virgin and the Saints are in-voked, but not mainly as correctives; their main function is to endow an under-taking with good and success, it is not primarily to prevent or correct. . . . Priests are called in, and Saints and the Virgin invoked, also, when difficulties arise. Vows are made for the recovery of a loved one; the priest is called when the family has had a run of misfortune, to "make holy" and exorcise the evil. Priests conduct a rain litany to break a drought.[13]

The parish as such consists of no such array of organized groups as comprise an American congregation; the priest is not trying to convert the unbeliever or change the daily life of his people. He is there to help them meet life's emergencies, to instill a love for their religion and their country, and to act as peacemaker when disputes threaten the harmony of the com-munity.[14]

THE BISHOP OF MESSENIA AND HIS GOOD WORKS

The contrast between an ordinary priest's home and the bishop's palace in Kalamata is quite marked, for the latter was once the ornate building housing the local branch of the Bank of Greece. But the bishop's interest in the people of his diocese, both the city dwellers in Kalamata and the farmers in the surrounding villages, equaled that of any priest for his parishioners. The bishop, when visited in 1953, proved a friendly, jovial person, with an iron-gray beard, a dignified though rotund figure, and a very forward-looking social philosophy. It was this latter quality in particular that had made me seek him out after hearing from friends in Athens of his unusual achievements in the welfare field.

He began to talk about what he had done and hoped to do for his people: "I became interested when I saw their great needs, for, as a church leader, I am responsible for the welfare of whatever people are under me." But before he started on any specific projects after his arrival in this diocese, he had thought it best, as he phrased it, "to put myself at the disposal of the people." He gradually gained the confidence of the members of his diocese by making available to them for local use all of the church's funds derived from festivals. The people began to realize that this bishop was interested in them. Later on, when he began asking them to support the various projects which he started, they gladly cooperated.

His first project was a day nursery, which takes care of one hundred and twenty children whose mothers are at work, started in 1947. Visiting this nursery in the afternoon when all of the children had gone home, we noted the cleanliness and the simple but adequate facilities. The success of this nursery prompted the bishop to start another one in Mycenae for one hundred children in 1948.

One perplexing problem was that of illegitimate children. In many cases the mother would kill such a child or leave it with people who exploited it unmercifully. So he started a home for these children in 1947. Since then, two hundred and fifty children have gone through the home, sixty of them have been adopted and fifty were there then. The equipment was simple and bare, but everything was spotless. When we entered, the children came up to the bishop with great pleasure, for he is a favorite with the young children. One of the nurses told us: "When we have a child that is lonesome, who won't eat, we ask the bishop to come feed the child. When he comes, the child always eats."

The bishop noticed, however, that many of the boy foundlings, but relatively few of the girl foundlings, would be adopted. The boys who were not taken by foster parents by their fifth or sixth year would go into the National Boys' Orphanage of Kalamata, largely supported by the state, which had one hundred and fifty boys in 1953. Something had to be done for the girls.

So the bishop arranged for nuns at a convent on the edge of town to teach some of the girls to spin and weave silk. For two hundred years the nuns of this convent have been leaders in the silk industry. In 1770, under the Turks, the nuns with their abbess were exiled to Constantinople, went to Broussa, and learned the manipulation of silk. Later, when they were able to come back to Kalamata, they brought with them the silkworm eggs and started the silk industry. Many local girls come to the convent to learn how to carry on silkworm production and weaving on a simple loom at home. So, the bishop thought, these same nuns would be able to teach these orphan girls the silk industry, and many other things as well. When we visited the convent, eighteen girls were living there, but buildings were nearing completion which would accommodate up to fifty girls. Queen Frederika had come to help dedicate the cornerstones. But the nuns were anxious to show us where they produced the fine silk cloth we had been admiring. It was a strange experience to go with the nuns into the big room full of textile machines and to see the dexterity with which these women clad in medieval garments managed the complex machinery, even to the point of making many mechanical repairs.

One institution which the bishop showed us with evident pride was a tuberculosis sanatorium. To reach it we had to ride from his palace through the town to a mountain a few miles distant. We could not help notice the people's affection for the bishop: men, upon seeing him, would take off their hats and women would cross themselves. Some of this, we knew, was done because he was a bishop and thus due a certain amount of reverence, but the expression of warmth on the faces of the people indicated their genuine appreciation of what the bishop was doing for them.

When we arrived at the sanatorium, the bishop explained: "Why should a few old monks have such a beautiful site to live in when tuberculosis was proving such a scourge to so many people? I told the monks they could go pray somewhere else and that we would make this into a sanatorium." Of course, the bishop admitted that he was oversimplifying the problem a bit, for even the Greek Orthodox Church has its red tape. In any event, he had succeeded in getting about twenty patients out into this healthful spot under proper care. One of the first things he did upon our arrival was to go check the menu posted in the kitchen, for he takes a personal interest in what is being served to the patients.

While at the sanatorium we noticed a number of donkeys tied outside and many peasant men and women sitting at the door of the little church dedicated to St. Elijah. We learned that many of these peasants had come quite far on this Sunday and had brought gifts of food and oil to the sanatorium as *psychiko,* a word which comes from Byzantine times and means property donated to monasteries or churches by pious pilgrims for the salvation of their souls. These peasants proved a lighthearted group, probably because the mere act of bringing whatever they had to contribute gave them an emotional uplift.

But still we had not seen the end of the bishop's good works. In 1949 he had organized a home for the aged where seventy elderly people live in relative comfort. The most ambitious project of all, however, was a polytechnic school started for the youth of the area. He had already spent about $37,000 on the first floor alone. The school had opened the previous November (1952) and already had two hundred pupils. Here was an institution that the Marshall Plan had helped. The school bore the name Papaflessa, in honor of one of the Greek patriots of the war of independence. While looking over this school we also learned about one more activity, a hospital of one hundred and fifty beds whose foundation had just recently been laid by the bishop and his coworkers.

The financing of even one of these undertakings, not to say the whole complement of institutions, would be a staggering task in any country, especially in one as poorly endowed as Greece. Although the bishop never confided the secret of his success, I heard from others that skillful diplomacy had stood him in good stead. He would start with a certain amount that he could take from his bishop's fund; he would then go to Athens and persuade the people in the Welfare Ministry that local people would match the funds of the central government if it would contribute; then, back home, he would call together the leading businessmen and say that he could get so much from the central government if they would put up such-and-such an amount. Since all parties did their share, he was able to get the necessary money for capital expenditures.

For the operation of these institutions, and their total number of inmates or patients is considerable, he draws upon other resources. Some of the people in his diocese upon death will to some specified institution their homes, olive groves, or money. Instead of having an expensive memorial service, with several priests, for a dead relative at the stated periods required by the church, the people are having simple memorial services and giving the difference in what they would pay to an institution; instead of buying expensive wreaths, they are giving the money to the foundling home, the sanatorium, or perhaps the old people's home. The bishop, too, has organized the rural parishes so that each parish turns over olive oil, meat, cheese, and eggs to a person who collects this produce and distributes it to the institution. Or, as already mentioned, some of the people want to bring their contributions in person. Many are asked to donate labor: one builds a door, another puts in windows, and everybody has a sense of participating.

Visiting the bishop raised many questions in my mind about all that I had learned in America about modern child-welfare practices, care of the aged, and the like. Social work as a profession is just getting a start in Greece; much humanitarian activity is carried on by upper-class women of the cities in the spirit of *noblesse oblige*. Under the circumstances in Greece today, nothing could seem more natural to the local people than to have the church, in the person of a gifted bishop, work out arrangements to meet their pressing welfare needs. How such a complicated network of institutions would be kept going should the energetic bishop not be around was a matter that gave one pause; but one must live in the present when human lives are at stake, and that is what the bishop was doing. He was following a well-established practice in making the church the channel for helping others.

The kind of help called *psychiko* is done for the soul, for the forgiveness of the souls of one's dead loved ones; it is customarily given in the form of helping the poor members of the community — the sick, the widows, and the orphans — out of purely Christian feeling. When some family is suffering misfortune in a village, the priest announces the fact in church and invites those who can help to do so. This is a form of aid in which those helping are not usually repaid, which makes it differ from the kinds of mutual aid discussed in an earlier chapter. In Koroni, in the western Peloponnesos, for instance, if a widow needs a crop harvested or threshed, grapes picked, or some field work done, the priest will announce that on such and such a day this widow has *xelassi,* as this arrangement is called, and those who wish can go to help. She feeds them, but they derive a spiritual rather than a material benefit from the work they contribute.

Or in Epirus, some important member of the community, not the priest, may send out the town crier or field guard to call from some height: "Listen, village, tomorrow we will carry from the mountain some wood for the home of Kyra Tassena, the widow of Tasso. All those who have mules must send them and those who haven't got any must come to help. Nobody must be missing." [15] He will then close with the proverb, *tona cheiri nivi talo kai ta dio to prosopo* (the one hand washes the other, and both of them the face).

Sundays and holidays, days on which peasants are not supposed to work in their own fields, are quite suitable for psychiko, or work done for the good of one's soul. D. A. Petropoulos, on whose article much of this discussion of psychiko is based, maintains that what characteristically distinguishes Christian philanthropy from ancient Greek philanthropy is that the first connects religion with the salvation of the soul, while in the ancient days help was given out of a purely logical understanding in order to have a normal social and communal system. [16]

The transition from this method of dealing with human need to the professional approach of contemporary social work is quite a leap. What progress is being made in training social workers in Greece is through the Young Women's Christian Association (but this again is a semireligious attachment), or through the Queen's Fund, providing scholarships at

Pierce College. It is hard for most Greeks, no matter how highly trained, to bring into the social worker–client relationship an objectivity modeled on the doctor–patient relationship. The Greek social worker finds it difficult to think of the client as a case and almost immediately empathizes or scolds in a way that would be considered quite unprofessional by American standards. Psychiko, hardly the twentieth-century rationale for social welfare, continues strong in Greece today, and the Bishop of Messenia is doing much to keep it alive in his diocese, which seems much the better for it.

The Peasant Confronts Death

The peasant assumes that there is an afterlife and talks about doing kind deeds "for the good of the soul." But these practical villagers do not talk much about death, although they do have some fixed beliefs and prescribed customs which stand them in good stead when confronting it. For example, there is the matter of Charon who, according to the beliefs of ancient Rome, was the boatman transporting the dead across the River Styx. I shall never forget the sensation of riding along in the northern Peloponnesos between Kleitoria and Kalavryta, enjoying the bright May afternoon, when my interpreter pointed out a small and pleasant stream said to be the waters of the Styx.[17] Greek peasants do not assign the same role to Charon as did the Romans, for they think of Charon as death itself, or as the angel of death whom God sends down to bring back the soul of someone whose time on earth has run its course. There are many songs and stories about Charon, who is personified as one who wrestles with individuals for their lives or who uses craft to draw the soul out of the body. From time to time he is supposed to have displayed something akin to human sympathy:

God and Death: Once upon a time God sent death to reap a soul but when death heard the lamentation of the relations and saw the beauty of the girl whose soul he was supposed to reap, he felt sorry and returned to heaven without accomplishing his mission. When God asked him why he didn't bring the soul, death replied that he couldn't stand the crying and despair that he had heard and seen. God got very angry and hit death so that he became deaf, blind, and lame. He made him deaf so that he couldn't hear the crying, blind so that he couldn't see whether the soul to be taken away belonged to an old person or a child, and lame so that he could not run away from the place where he was sent.[18]

Although church art, depicting the medieval Christian conception of heaven and hell, has had some effect upon the view peasants take of "the next world," the people very often reveal a more basic belief in Hades as "a common meeting-place of all whose lives are ended, without distinction of merit. Death is a deprivation of the joys of life, which, with all its troubles and cares, is sweet. The old uneasy feeling that after death it is not well is ever present; and the dying man laments that he must see the sun no more, nor the light of the moon, the mountains, the shade of plane-trees, and the cool fountain because in Hades there breaks no dawn, and sings no bird, and no fountains of water flow." [19]

This same theme is brought out in the tradition which the villagers call the "water of forgetfulness."

Each person upon dying goes to the underworld. There he starts crying and is in despair because he died and had to leave the world which still seems so sweet to him. The other dead laugh at him. This happens for just one day because the other dead feel sorry for the newcomer, take him to a spring and tell him to drink some water. After he has had some he in his turn forgets the upper world and laughs at the newcomers who come later on. This happens to all who die.[20]

When a person is believed to be dying, a candle is lit, probably so the soul will be sure to have some light as it moves into the other world. If any of this candle remains after a person dies, according to some village people, for three successive days you must put water in a little coffee cup and light the candle for ten minutes after sunset. You then take the water and throw it outside where nobody will be apt to walk on it. You also cut a narrow piece from the shroud and tie three knots in it, placing it in front of the icon. For three days you untie one of the knots and then sew the piece of cloth in the shirt of one of the male members of the family, who wears this piece until the shirt wears out. In the Naupaktos area, after a person dies all windows and doors are closed so death cannot get out. One person of the household shouts, "Death, leave the old man [or whoever is dead]." This is repeated many times in the hope that death can hear. It is done, the people say, to keep death from coming again to take someone else from that home.[21] Such shouting is not the custom in all parts of Greece, however.

What one does find quite generally in the rural areas, however, is the *myriologion,* or funeral dirge, which the women of the household and those from the neighborhood begin to sing as soon as death has come. Some of these have been conventionalized to the point that several women may all know the same dirge for a husband, child, or mother, and sing parts of it in turn rocking back and forth; in some parts of Greece the women improvise dirges in keeping with the prescribed musical form. These songs, sung in the house before burial, at the grave at stated intervals after death, or even as a woman is passing by the cemetery, may consist of questions put to the dead: "Why did you leave us?" "Why did you go so soon?" "How do you think the house can get on without you?" [22] Those myriologia that have traditional content passed on from generation to generation are the source of many of the popular beliefs about the afterlife, and they illustrate as well as any aspect of Greek rural life the persistence of pre-Christian

traits. From time to time, the men of the village may scoff at these myriologia as "women's business," and they certainly do not join in the singing,
but many of them would feel uncomfortable if these dirges were not sung
in their homes when occasion demanded. In the cities such customs as
these are dying out, but not among the rural people.

   The body is washed in wine and prepared for burial, with the interment
usually taking place within twenty-four hours. A most vividly recalled
procession was that of a seventeen-year-old boy in Metsovo (Epirus) who
had been killed the day before by a land mine left over from the guerrilla
war. This was a Wallachian (Koutso-Vlach) town, mentioned in my description of the life of the shepherd. We watched the procession form just
outside the church. First came a boy carrying the lid of the coffin, since it
is still customary to leave the coffin open as the procession moves through
the streets of the town; then the altar boys carrying the banners, followed
by three priests in their liturgical robes, then the coffin — all in white —
carried by six young men in black homespun. Next followed the boy's
father, supported by his relatives, a weeping fourteen-year-old brother,
then a score of other men. The children from the school playground went
up to watch the procession pass. Shortly afterwards, the mother, loudly
wailing, came out of the church, also supported by her relatives and about
forty or fifty women dressed in their traditional holiday costumes, brilliant
despite the absence of much of their finery and the heavy accent of black
trimmings. They formed a second procession which headed up a hill to the
family home because in Metsovo, unlike the villages which are ethnically
Greek, the women do not go to the cemetery. The grandmother, easily
identified, was striking herself on the head in a display of grief.

   As the two processions went their separate ways, the square remained
quiet and even the children seemed hushed in their play. At such moments
it is apparent that in a village the family is not alone in its grief, but feels
strongly the bonds that bind it to the rest of the community. Although death
does mean separation, the villagers deal with it in a way that reinforces the
social ties among the living. And grief has its rituals, too, which come down
from prehistoric times. Women are supposed to express themselves loudly
and in public, giving outlet to their pent-up emotions and freeing themselves
from the repressions that might otherwise build up. Men, too, can cry in
public, although they prefer to do it in the presence of other men rather
than before women.

   In watching the progress of a funeral procession in another village, I
noticed that, with its approach, the doors and windows of shops and houses
all shut down tightly, but only until the procession passed. Some said this
was done "so the evil could not get through" to the living, but people in
the village of Terpitsa claimed that they shut the doors so that only the door
of the other world would remain open to the dead person.[23]

1. The Acropolis, its profile held unobstructed by city ordinance, shades the Athenian in legacy from the Golden Age.

2. Kyparissia (Cypress Village) of Peloponnesos, amid its pattern of mountain, and field, and cypress trees that hide a cemetery.

3. The square of Metsovo, Epirus, village of the shepherd Koutso-Vlachs; the children quieted while a vivid funeral procession passed along this road.

4. The village of Valtetsi, near Tripolis, Peloponnesos, is abandoned for half the year as the shepherds follow pasturage. The walls remain broken, testimony of wartime guerrilla raiders.

5. A Peloponnesian home, walled from the road, hugs a rock slope near Megalopolis.

6. Plowing an olive grove near Lechonia, Thessaly. The olive harvest will draw a crowd of young people to the grove to rake or beat or gather as their foreman orders.

7. A wheat combine traces the plain of Thessaly, below Mount Parnassus.

8. On the tenth day after transplanting, Macedonia; his hoe is said to be short-handled so that he can watch the fragile tobacco leaves as he moves.

9. Our hosts in a **Peloponnesian** village: *Xenos* is the password for stranger and guest. Their hospitality was radiant; their posing was a serious project.

10. Mr. Papaspyropoulos and his wife. He wrote the account of Ano-Kleitoria, Peloponnesos.

11. At the oven for Sunday afternoon lamb and rice, Attica.

12. A widow at the loom, Salamis. For two years there must be no levity in her presence.

13. Lunchtime in Thessaly in a day of spring plowing.

14. A girl at work at the kneading trough in the village of Malakassa, Central Greece.

15. The schoolmaster and his pupils by their century-old school, Kyparissia, Peloponnesos. Originally the school was privately endowed.

16. A school building under construction in Malakassa village, new promise for two dozen children. The Save the Children Federation provides the materials; Malakassa, the labor.

17. A monk on the ageless journey to Salamis with casks from his monastery to be filled or to sell.

18. Godparents hold the child before the priest for a controlled moment in the exuberance of a baptism, Macedonia.

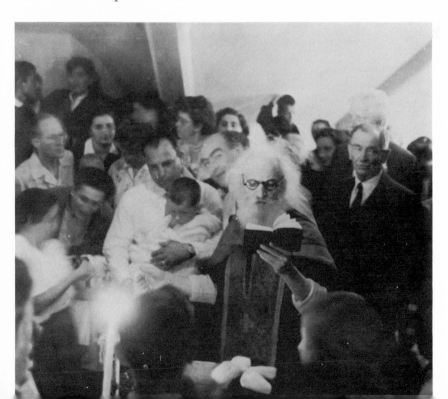

19. Porto Raphti, Attica, at the close of day.

Throughout Greece, even in the cities, people never go to their own home or a friend's home from a funeral without first stopping somewhere for a sweet. In many villages it is the custom to wash one's hands before entering the house.

The official period of mourning lasts for two years. Part of the complex of traits connected with mourning is the Feasts of the Dead held at fixed periods, such as the eighth and the fortieth day after burial. Similarly, on the anniversary of the death a feast of remembrance is held. On such occasions the grave is decorated with flowers, a mass is sung, and offerings of *kollyva* are made in the church. Kollyva is "parboiled wheat mixed with pounded walnuts, raisins and parsley, and covered over with a coating of sugar, with the sign of the cross, and sometimes the initials of the deceased worked on it in raisins. The wheat is interpreted as a symbol of the resurrection: as the grain is buried in the earth, rots, and rises again in the shape of a blooming plant, so will the soul rise from the tomb. . . ." [24]

In addition to these ceremonies for deceased individual members of a family, the Greek villagers also have collective feasts for the dead known as Souls' Sabbath (*psychosavvata*), which correspond roughly with spring and harvest, or the life and death cycle of the year. Relatives visit the graves where they leave sweetmeats, parboiled grain, and cakes, and where they kneel and cry beside the tombs as the priests read prayers over them. It is a memorable experience for a foreigner to come unexpectedly upon a graveyard where as many as one hundred and fifty people are wailing over different graves and to see the priests in their colorful robes and with their swinging censers move from one small group to the next.

Priests when they die are treated differently. With an ordinary person the bowl used when the dead are washed for burial is broken and thrown away; but with the priest (in Spetsai at least) it cannot be broken, but is thrown into the sea. The priest's body is not put in a shroud but is dressed by another priest in a *peritrachelion,* or stole which a priest wears when he hears confessions. Also, the first book from which the priest read after becoming a priest is put in the coffin with him. There is another difference, too. At the end of three years after burial, it is customary to dig up the bones of the deceased and wash them in wine and water, but the bones of a priest are washed with oil. When the bones are disinterred, they are put in a basket and taken home to be put under a table on which there is boiled wheat. The priest reads a prayer; the people kiss the skull, put it in the box with the other bones, and this is put in a vault in the cemetery.

Much is made of the condition of the bones. If they are yellowish-brown, this means that the person lived a good life; if they are black, he lived badly. It is also considered a bad omen if the body has not disintegrated.

An excellent summary of the way the peasant fits death into the general scheme of things comes from a study by V. T. Valassis:

Generally, in the old villages the church is in the outskirts. To the back of the church is the cemetery, which is walled to keep out both wild predatory animals and farm animals. For Greeks it is a sin to step on a grave. The church may have a belltower, or the bell may be hung from the branch of an old tree. There is always a well in the churchyard and the cemetery of the old village. It is used as drinking water and for the purification after a burial. The main church of the old village must be the tallest, the largest, and the best-constructed building of the village. This signifies respect for God; the past is not forgotten. This is very much after the pattern of the ancient Greeks who built their shrines as the best buildings while they themselves lived in huts. . . .

Both the church and the cemetery of the old village must be located in a landscape of natural beauty and scenery. Thus faith, worship, and death are in close relation with the natural scenery.[25]

But Valassis adds a discordant note. The new churches are now being constructed in the center of the village, while the cemeteries remain on the outskirts. No longer, therefore, do the peasants, after a Mass or ceremony, go to the graveyard to pay respect to their ancestors.

·∙◦[XVI]◦∙·

The Village Community

A Greek village has a much richer social texture than the casual visitor would imagine. As already indicated, it has its patterns of mutual aid, its church, school, local government, and coffeehouses — which often are the focal points for intense activity — but it also has its neighborhoods, kin-ship groups, and even a status system according to which people are sorted out by other villagers. Furthermore, if any villager "gets out of line," strong social sanctions can be brought to bear to make him conform. The village notables whom I met enjoyed telling how things got done in their communities and of the factions and cross-pressures at work. Many times, simply by watching them perform their official and unofficial roles in behalf of the community, I observed the community in action. A mother came to ask how she could get her son out of the army long enough to help with the spring plowing because her husband was disabled with a back injury; an official from the Ministry of Agriculture left some forms about crop production for the secretary to fill out; a man who had received a letter in English from a nephew in the United States wanted one of the notables — who had previously been in the States — to translate the contents. The variety of tasks seemed endless, but some village notable was usually able to rise to the occasion.

THE VILLAGE NOTABLES

Contrary to popular belief, one does not always find the village notables sitting around the coffeehouse. Most of them are usually busy people, working in their fields, around their houses, or in a shop. They do make at least brief appearances around the square some time during the day, most probably after supper. Loafers do not become notables in a Greek village. To learn who these notables were, I asked throughout mainland Greece: "Who are the most important people in your village? Why are they important?"

I was struck by the fact that in 1955 and 1959 more people seemed to stress the high prestige of the community president than they had done in 1953. This impression, if fully verified, would indicate a growing importance of and a re-emphasis upon local government in the Greek scheme of things. One priest in the Peloponnesos attributed this shift to the fact that "interest in religion is not as great as twenty years ago and church attendance has declined." A few typical replies, many contradicting each other in some details, will convey the villager's view of the notables in his community. From Central Greece:

The greatest honor in our village is to be president of the community. Those who are most respected are those with the most money. Anyone who has money receives a hearty "good morning"; without money he doesn't. This is because our people are not educated. In fact, the priest gets more respect than the teacher, which is not as it should be. The local doctor, too, is respected.

From another village in Central Greece we hear:

The most important people are the most educated, either the doctor or the teacher who, thanks to his education, can solve a problem in which the people are interested. We have some clever people who try to overshadow the teacher in order to influence other villagers, but if they are to do this they must be respected. If an extremely clever person is immoral, he has no great prestige. Two things influence other people: to be just in his judgment and honorable. We respect a man more if he is honorable than if he is rich. Even an uneducated man who is a good farmer and has good judgment and is honorable can have influence.

Party leaders in former times would have been included among the notables, according to a businessman from Thebes:

In my childhood days the party leader would have ranked as most important, particularly if he belonged to the strongest party and would be able to help local people solve their problems. Nowadays in the village the president of the community would play a great part. The doctor, if there is one, has high position, provided that he is respected by the others. In the old days the priest and teacher were more respected than today. In my childhood when the teacher or priest would pass through the village square people would stand up. The local merchants in the village have changed their status little, for their role in life is still to do commerce.

The extent to which the priest or the president of the local cooperative, where it exists, is considered important depends today very much upon the personalities of the individuals involved. One person said:

The role of the priest should be mentioned along with the teacher and doctor. He should lead because he represents the church and is more educated than the peasants. But there are some priests who play little part in community life. I know of one who drinks too much, shoots off his revolver, and is not respected.

The relative prestige of the village notables has been influenced by the practice of the central government in providing the teacher and the priest. Only the community president comes into office as the result of local initiative, but even his status, though gaining ground, is not what it used to be thirty or forty years ago:

The president of the village is usually a better man than the president of the cooperative because there is more tradition behind his office. But it does not always hold that the best man is picked as president. In Thessaly forty years ago when the president came into the coffeehouse all the men rose in deference to "their president."

A man from a mountain village in Central Greece who is active in the cooperative movement contrasted the various statuses in his community:

I find that the teacher enjoyed more prestige formerly than now. Earlier there was a higher percentage of illiterates, but today many village sons have gone away for a higher education and so people are not so dependent upon the teacher. Since officials do not wish to undermine the position of the teacher, the agronom and other representatives of the nomarchia always consult the teacher when arriving in the village.

This man thought the secretary of the village more important than the president.

When I put the question of relative prestige of the notables to a group of students at the American Farm School in Salonica, I found the anticipated difference of opinion. The majority of the boys, all from villages, said that the president of the community was most important, but others said that the priest would be "if he is from the village itself and has a good reputation." They pointed out that the president of the community becomes involved in politics and is therefore apt to antagonize those who may differ with him politically. Of the twenty villages represented, fourteen had doctors. Only six of these were considered community leaders. These village boys also thought, for the most part, that the wealthy peasants were not necessarily considered in the select group unless they held some other office such as community president. In Northern Greece, if a villager has achieved renown by fighting in one of the wars for the liberation of Macedonia, he will rank high. He becomes the personification of local history, and what he says about the war will be given more credence than what the textbooks say. He was there and saw things with his own eyes.

A generation or two ago one's age had much to do with the respect shown to him but this value is shifting:

Older people used to be the leaders. Now the tendency is toward the educated and wealthy, although the community president is chosen much on the same basis as before. He generally ranks first in importance. The teachers and priests are better-educated than they used to be so their influence is greater.

The above sentence seems to contradict the observation that as people become more educated they rely less on the teacher and priest. What actually happens is that the basis for respecting these two notables shifts. In villages where a progressive spirit is abroad, if they show an interest in doing things for the community and are not merely functionaries carrying out the narrow round of activities connected with their jobs, then they acquire prestige. But it is only the better-educated priests and teachers who show any genuine community orientation. This was reaffirmed by a nomarch in the Peloponnesos who, while listing the president of the community as actually and legally the most important man, also observed: "On the other hand, a teacher or priest may rank high due to outstanding personality characteristics."

I noticed in Central Greece and the Peloponnesos that from time to time some native son, who had spent several years in the United States, would be included with the notables. At first, I wondered whether he was trotted out because he could speak a few words of English, but then I noticed that others who also had been to the States were kept in the background. To receive prestige in many, though by no means all, villages, the returnee must show generosity that no other local inhabitant is expected to demonstrate.

Nor can one overstate the omnipresence of these village Greeks who have spent some time in America.[1] In one village of less than two thousand I found more than forty older men who had been to the United States. The net social effect of this reservoir of foreign experience was almost negligible. One returnee said: "Even if you come back with new ideas, you must conform to life about you, for those ideas are not applicable here. If you stay here you will be like a peasant in a year; if I went back to the States I would become a gentleman again."

SOCIAL CLASS IN THE VILLAGE

The notables just described constitute the village élite; they are at the top of the status system and represent the village's contact with the outside world. If they are originally from outside, they are supposed to possess the qualities that the peasants ascribe to the educated city person. Their reputation in turn is based largely on the traditional classical education which sets them apart from those less fortunate. As one commentator pointed out: "The civil servant or poor lawyer has little out of life other than his prestige. This takes the form of petty autocracy and the assumption of superiority over the nonprofessional classes." Such a person coming to live in the village feels it incumbent upon him to maintain something of a social gulf between him and the peasants, who also share this feeling. But this "assumption of superiority" is in itself not enough. It will wear thin after a while if the individual does not prove himself competent in his job or show an understanding of the problems that the villagers face. Even if he does it arrogantly, he nevertheless must produce some benefits for the villagers. There is a shrewd practicality in the Greek peasant with which any intellectual has to reckon.

Those notables who are from the village, whether educated or not, must also possess those qualities stressed locally. To some extent, they have to fit into the value systems of both the city and the village, not favoring one so much that they alienate those subscribing to the other.

Very few studies have been made of the status distinctions in Greek villages, with the result that we cannot prove or disprove the existence of regional differences in ascribing status. In a Greek community, as in an American one, people when asked about class differences will be apt to deny them, claiming, "everybody here is as good as everybody else. We have no class distinctions." But as the questioner probes, he learns that one part of the community is considered a very good residential area and another part very poor; some families are at the very top of the social scale for a variety of reasons, others are generally recognized to be at the bottom, and those in between can be sorted out in a loose way according to the criteria (or social values) prevailing in that place. John Photiadis lists the following as the factors for class distinction in the Macedonian village he studied: education; occupation; money; family name; approved achievement; community activities; origin (whether refugee or not); area of residence. On the basis of these he delineates three classes in a larger-than-average village:

The *upper class* consisting of professionals (doctors, lawyers, teachers), tobacco merchants, larger storekeepers, and office managers.

The *second class* consisting of small storekeepers, farm owners, and skilled workers.

The *third class* consisting of persons not quite acceptable by society.[2]

Although this scheme is not precise and is difficult to apply in its present form to other villages in Greece, it does tend to stress the economic and occupational factors which play an important part throughout the country. This is particularly borne out in the studies of the Near East Foundation, to which references have already been made in preceding chapters. In two of their villages there seemed to be no class differences, but in others these were recognized and explained as follows, with each paragraph applying to a different community:

The economic position of the person is all-important. Those who are well-to-do and willing to help another in time of need rank high. Family and education play little or no role.

There are no noticeable differences in the village, but the villager who is financially better off than his neighbor is accorded a somewhat higher place.

Although there are no obvious class distinctions, the farmers who are better off are honored if they are not too conservative, which most of them tend to be. The priest, community president, cooperative president and certain village councilmen form the highest social class due to their judgment, diplomacy, education and vision.

Wealth is the only determining factor in this village.

Economic factors are most significant. The richer have the higher position. Shopowners are higher than farmers. People value a person's ability to help others in time of need or to promote the interest of the village. Family background is minor.[3]

These statements show that in Greek villages it is possible for an individual who is honorable and good to gain recognition even though the reputation of his family might not be very high. Without any doubt, what is most important is the financial ability of a family to afford education for its children which, in turn, provides them with a means for occupational advancement. The status of the family with several highly educated people is almost invariably higher than that of the family where no one has gone beyond grade school.

One must not assume, however, that the status system in the Greek village is something rigid or exclusively hereditary. It is unusually mobile. This is borne out by Photiadis when he compares the pre- and postwar class structure of his village:

Social mobility became easier after the war except for the upper class. It became much more difficult to move to the upper class. The high prices of tobacco before the war gave a number of people the opportunity to be close to the economic level of doctors or large storekeepers. Now this factor has diminished considerably concerning tobacco producers and has also affected smaller storekeepers, allowing less chance for them to expand their enterprises.[4]

He concludes that the ends of the "social pyramid became closer and it is difficult to separate the second from the third class, while the upper class became smaller." Land ownership and money, two factors which were stressed before the war, are no longer very important, for a peasant can rent a field quite inexpensively. With the prices of tobacco as low as they are, land is not in as great demand.

VILLAGE ORGANIZATIONS

Almost every village today has one or more clubs or associations which have been promoted by governmental officials and people from the city in an effort to effect some change in the rural way of life. Most of these organizations appear to be well intentioned and are accepted as such by the local people, but this does not mean that the peasants become eager joiners or loyal members. Other village groups have much deeper local roots: mutual-aid groups and the cooperatives; the church board, the school board, and the community council. In many villages I inquired about the formally organized groups. Three widely scattered communities listed a variety of associations, some of which will be described more fully below:

Ano Kleitoria (Peloponnesos): community council, church board, school board, and Friends of the Forest.

Kalivi (Attica): the regular boards, five cooperatives, agro club, hunting club, home-economics club.

Polygyros (Chalkidike, Macedonia): the regular boards, two cooperatives (agricultural, apiary), boy scouts, lawyers' union, athletic club, professional union, medical union, olive-oil union, woman's philanthropic group.

One widespread and rapidly growing organization is the Rural Youth Club, which is modeled on the 4-H Club in the United States and promoted and supervised by the Extension Service of the Greek Ministry of Agriculture. Each member carries out an agricultural project, and together they operate a field owned by the club. In the Macedonian village referred to they also operate the village library located in the community building. They meet once a week to listen to a lecture, which is followed by recreational activities.

The women, too, have their own club. It is the home club or home-economics club similar to the Home Demonstration Club in the United States. It includes farm and nonfarm women, young and old. When field work is slack, the members attend classes in canning, sewing, and cooking, several times a month. The home agent helps them acquire knowledge and skill through lectures, demonstrations, and group participation. Often the club has its own workship and kitchen.

For men, the cooperatives are the chief associations, although meetings are relatively infrequent since these are primarily service organizations. They have not yet really taken on the educational role displayed by the youth or women's groups.

At best, these organizations which have been described exist to satisfy the interests of the members who affiliate. Unlike the institutionalized church board, school board, and community council, they do not exist to serve community-wide needs even though many of their stated purposes might contain grandiose aims. Most of these are not organizations which the villagers themselves have created, but have been formed in response to outside pressures and have been founded in the hope that they will do something to help the villagers have a better life. What makes the promotion of such organizations difficult is the utter lack on the part of the peasant of an abstract loyalty to an organization; he goes if he wants to or if he likes the agent from outside — not because he feels it his duty as a member to support the group of which he is a part.

Even if the numbers of organizations in rural Greece were doubled and the membership quadrupled, it is hardly likely that the Greek peasant would think of the "organizational approach" to problem solving. Where some Americans might get together and form a group to deal with a problem, the Greek peasants would either say "let the central government do it" or, if they are more sophisticated, relegate it to the community council to worry about. There is no tie-in between individual responsibility and membership-in-action groups, such as one finds in suburban America; the peasant is in the preorganization stage, which perhaps indicates why his life seems so untrammeled to those who get to know him well.

THE SENSE OF COMMUNITY

Greek village life has a unity in the sense that the peasants see their life as a whole and do not compartmentalize it in the way that it has been presented here. They make no distinction between religion and agriculture, family life and recreation, mutual aid and local government. Life flows on day by day, each day with its own tasks and joys, but marked by the variations which the seasons bring. Nor does the Greek villager distinguish in his mind among his village as a place or physical setting, his home, or the people who walk the streets. All these, to which we might also add the donkeys, goats, and other animals, possess a unity in that they fit together as a part of his accustomed world.

But Greek village life does not have a unity in the sense that there is perfect agreement within the community on every course of action or in the sense that people placidly sit by and concur in what a few self-appointed leaders might choose to do. Factions arise, and many of them persist. These can arise in time of war when rival armies visit the village in the search for enemy sympathizers, thus presenting a wonderful chance for the unscrupulous person to denounce a fellow villager with whom he wants to even an old score. In the choice of sides in the Communist-inspired guerrilla war, for example, definite factions came into existence and their lines have not been altogether obliterated today.

Despite factionalism and the lack of idyllic harmony, it is correct to say that most villagers feel a sense of community. It may seem entirely absent whenever people are trying to persuade the villagers to carry out community improvements from which they can see no immediate benefit, but it is there to be reckoned with whenever the reputation or the safety of the community is threatened. To try to explain the basis for this sense of community is to review much of what has already been said, but perhaps it can be understood in terms of four divergent strands: *philotimo,* or ultrasensitive self-esteem; a common living space; shared institutions; and an accepted system of social control.

Philotimo. Social phenomena in Greece must be seen first in terms of individuals, who in turn cannot be understood without recognizing the national trait of philotimo. Dorothy Lee has clearly explained this complex character trait:

Everyone has his *philotimo,* as an individual, as a member of a family, and, most of all, as a Greek. On this rests Greek individualism, since it is sheer being which is respected, not position in the world or achievement. On this rests Greek democracy and equality, since everyone, both as a person and as a Greek, is equal to everyone else, neither superior nor inferior. . . . This does not mean that there is lacking a balance of roles or interpersonal structuring; but these relationships of interdependence, of leader and followers, of division of areas of responsibility and work are not cast in the mold of superiority and inferiority. Inferiority comes only with the forfeiting of the *philotimo.* . . . The inner core of the Greek must never be exposed; and *entrope,* the Greek word for shame, modesty, decency, propriety, self-consciousness, embarrassment, means: "turning inward." This is a concept both positive and negative: you have done something shameful only because you have failed in the positive aspect, in modesty and decency. Out of *entrope* a Greek avoids saying things and doing things which would reflect on the *philotimo* of himself, his family, his country. For example, the self-made man in Greece does not boast of his rags-to-riches progress. This would expose the poverty of his village, the inability of his family to help him, the fact that his uncle or his godfather could not or did not do his duty by him; it would expose much that should remain decently covered, and would further prove him to be lacking in *philotimo.*[5]

Dr. Lee then goes on to explain that the essence of philotimo is inviolability and freedom and that the sense of inviolability makes a Greek extremely "touchy." An offended philotimo leads to retaliation, not self-reproach. She writes:

To suggest to a Greek that he needs aid in raising his standard of living because his ways are backward is to violate his *philotimo* as a person and as a Greek. There is need for aid now because of acts of God, not because of personal failure or Greek inadequacy. . . .

One may well ask how this trait of self-esteem is related to a sense of community. The connection is twofold: first, the adult member of the community participates as a free agent and as an expression of his own individuality; he can cooperate because he feels free, and by the same token he can refuse to cooperate. But the second connection makes him think seriously before refusing to cooperate, for he would be shaming himself and others if he let his village down. Yet the sense of community need not be limited to formal cooperation; it can be a state of mind as well, a feeling of loyalty one carries about, and a deep psychological identification with the village where one was born and in which one grew up.

A common living space. One writer attributes the unity of the Greek village to the residents' dependence upon their physical environment:

First, the people are directly dependent on the land, hence their interests are all one. Second, the village owns grazing lands and meadows used in common by the farmers. Third, the people are highly interdependent in respect to water supply. Thus a sense of cooperation pervades the village. Fourth, the people of the village are limited in their actions by the very village's physical structure; the width of the streets, the pavement or lack of pavements, and degree of crookedness of same. Lastly, the whole physical lay-out is such that ceremonials and rituals as repeated year-in and year-out by slow processions, must change even if the ceremonials were to become mechanized.[6]

An earlier chapter on the village setting has discussed this factor, which must be taken into account in considering the identification people feel with their village. People develop a "sense of belonging" with those who walk the same village lanes, send their animals to the same community pastures, draw water from the same wells or fountains, and share the same living space. This propinquity does not necessarily produce a liking for everyone frequently encountered, but it calls for the recognition that these neighbors or fellow villagers must be dealt with in solving many of the ordinary affairs of life.

Shared institutions. Partly related to the physical pattern of the village are the church, the school, and the office of the local government, whose very structures are visible and concrete signs of the institutional complex which they embody. But these institutions are more than a material expression; they are also the focal points of the values which the people inherit and pass on to their children. On the basis of these, people ascribe rank to each other; on the basis of these, people make decisions relative to what activities are most worthy and which are least worthy. Community life, as well as individual life, has its evaluative mechanisms which are brought into play in problem solving. The local institutions, described so fully in previous chapters, either have certain kinds of problems which they are supposed to treat, or the institutional leaders are sometimes called in to help deal with situations too grave for any single institution to handle. Again, the sense of community which a Greek villager develops is based in part not only upon sharing with others the activities which these institutions perpetuate, but also in knowing that he and his family are dependent upon them for meeting many of life's basic needs and aspirations.

The introduction of formal organizations into the Greek village, although they may accomplish certain specific goals, can also have the net effect of introducing new cleavages. The local institutions as described have been inclusive in that almost everyone in the village who wanted to could participate in them, with some allowances made for sex and age differences. But organizations bring in the idea of members and nonmembers. Some belong; others do not. Where membership is interpreted as signifying that the member is superior to or better than the nonmember, it causes resentment within that village where organizations are relatively new and not much appreciated. This may even run counter to the local value system. Yet experience in other societies, and even in the urban sectors of Greek society, has shown that economic development — which many peasants ardently desire — is based on specialization. This, in turn, is promoted by organizations which encourage and sustain this specialization. Society, even in the village, becomes more heterogeneous as the level of living rises, as the number of alternative choices (occupational, recreational, and such) increase, and as greater reliance is placed upon the individual.

Therefore, in understanding the traditional sense of community one must see the countervailing tendency to organize along specialized lines and to promote individual rather than community interests. In an industrialized society this means that a new kind of solidarity, based on functional interdependence, replaces that solidarity based on homogeneity and a common view of world and work.[7] Very often in the shift from the traditional to the more complex type, individuals and communities experience disorganization which, in time, leads to a reorganization better adapted to new needs. Closely related to the degree and type of disorganization is the system of social control and how it operates.

Social control. In Greece, as elsewhere, the most effective social controls are built into the personality structure of a person as he grows up. He learns what his society considers to be morally right and wrong and, if "well brought up," does not question these standards and, more often than not, abides by them; he also learns what is appropriate and inappropriate behavior at given times and places; he knows, too, that in a particular situation some people (say, the oldest men present) behave differently from others present, for there are prescribed roles that go with the position one holds at a given time. Social control tends to enforce the playing of these prescribed roles and to discourage the highly individualistic variations to which others are not prepared to respond.

Without attempting to trace the complete system of operating controls in a Greek village, I shall mention some of the methods encountered as supplements to many already dealt with in earlier chapters.

The most far-reaching controls have to do with the taking of human life. Today in most parts of Greece this has passed into the hands of the police and the legal system, but some generations ago it was common for family members to think that they themselves should deal with anyone who killed a kinsman.

From time to time, I would ask in a village whether any serious crimes had been committed and would hear of an isolated case — such as the woman who, a few years ago, as the result of a boundary dispute, had picked up a stone and killed a man, thereafter being put in jail for a year or so. Usually, people said, the relatives help settle disputes.

Or, when I asked what would happen locally if a person were caught stealing, I was told: "We don't have such people here. If anyone did steal the villagers would exclude him; they would ostracize him so he couldn't stand it. They would also take him to court."

But for most villagers the controls deal with behavior which is not considered criminal. Photiadis shows one way in which this operates:

The father is the leader, and family members want to please him, and he in turn takes care of the whole family. If a mother sees her adolescent daughter mingling with boys more than is expected, she will reprimand her by saying "you are ridiculing your father," or "the men at the coffeehouse will laugh at you." [8]

He contends that the coffeehouse operates as a social control over the family through the father, "who is confronted directly by the opinions of the cliques that form it and operate as reference groups for the rest of the population in the village." It is also true that social control operates in much the same way for the women through the neighborhood "gossiping groups."

Even in Athens one is aware that the social controls from the village still pursues the individual. A Greek friend asked her dressmaker why she did not wear dresses with short sleeves and was told that she could not. "But don't you get hot?" "Oh, I would rather get hot," replied the dressmaker, "than have people gossiping about me in the village."

A group of village girls in a special course at Pierce College near Athens, when asked what the people of their communities would do if anyone went counter to prevailing norms, compiled this list:

The people speak against the person.

If a woman gossips, people ignore her.

If a man drinks too much, they beat him.

People give advice, for there are usually two or three older people who have the role of advisers and to whom people turn.

Sometimes the solution is by means of knives.

The village people threaten the person who does not conform and may drive him out of the village.

They may take the person to church and make him say special prayers.

They may take revenge on the person by injuring his animals, or by burning his house if his conduct is too much of a threat to the rest.

This last item illustrates that at times the people can behave cruelly to other villagers who threaten the safety, morality, or even reputation of the village. Individuals as individuals seek personal revenge, but much of the time such an action is collective, discussed by several leaders in advance, and carried out with dispatch by a group.

Apparently, living in a Greek village is a great deal like living in a gold-fish bowl. One writer comments of his village:

Here in our village one has no secrets from the others. Someone asks about something and we reply. Even if we want to hide something we cannot. Everybody knows about it. . . . We say: "The whole world announces it with drums, while we think it's a secret." [9]

But the sense of community grows not only out of the acceptance of the same "thou shalt nots" but also is related to the systems of rewards held out by the community to those who conform. This is the positive side of social control. To have the esteem of the villagers is to enhance one's own self-esteem, to win an election because others think well of you, to be sought out when others need advice, to have your sons or daughters considered as good "catches" for marriage, all indicate that one has conformed to the code of accepted behavior. It may also mean that one has used individual initiative in behalf of the community when situations arose for which the code gave no specific prescription.

One villager summarized the sense of community well when he pointed out that people were loyal to their village because they lived there and their interests were connected with it, adding, "one is loyal to whatever is close to one's birth certificate and death certificate."

Although the life of the villager centers in most details upon the settlement where he lives, his range of interests may go far beyond it. True enough, he is apt to be loyal to his village; but he is also loyal to his region. Those who come from Arcadia, whether they are residing in Athens or in the United States, feel a close bond with the others who come from Arcadia. They form societies to continue this association and to give an opportunity to dance and sing the folk arts of that region.

A Greek villager is, moreover, a Greek. Villages can be uprooted and destroyed, their families dispersed, but Greece goes on as a living spirit and as a mighty cultural heritage. The fact that so many Greek families have relatives living in other parts of the country, including Athens, means that they keep in fairly close touch with the body politic. They are not merely dependent upon what some village notable or visiting politician tells them; they can hear directly from their relatives just what the state of affairs really is. This means that kinship plays a part in the communication network on which the national community rests. In conclusion, it is important to look briefly at the role of the villager in the total society, taking our eyes from the village scene and viewing the larger picture. This is necessary if one is to understand the Greek village of the next few years — the one which is emerging — because the changes being introduced come for the most part from outside the village. They are promoted to a considerable degree by national authorities or impersonal forces over which the peasants have relatively little control.

··❦[Part Five]❦··

Change

··❧[XVI]❧··

Social Change in Rural Greece

The Greek social spectrum, the rainbow in the rock, is losing some of its
hues today. This occurs as regions of Greece, despite their traditional social
differences, adjust to common changes engulfing the whole country. The fact
of change is accepted by all, but the evaluation of specific kinds of change
(in family life, economic development, political trends) varies with the
position of the person passing judgment. For most villagers, changes — at
least those they want — are not occurring fast enough. When I had sorted
out and studied their comments, which usually dealt with some facet of
change, past or present, I found that the experiences they related could be
grouped under three general types: the *cataclysmic* change caused by some
great social or natural upheaval; the changes resulting from *social drift,* or
the slower spread of unplanned change as new ways moved from town to
village; and the *planned* change, most frequently sponsored by government
agencies in an effort to raise the level of living in the villages.[1]

CATACLYSMIC CHANGE

Almost every generation of Greeks has experienced some social dislocation accompanying a war or, at least, armed encounters. The present adult
population has had more than its share. While the country was busy with
the tasks of assimilating the northern provinces, wrested from Turkey in

the First Balkan War (1913), and of recuperating from the First World War, the Greek forces, with the permission of the Great Powers, occupied an area around Smyrna, Turkey. Then they pushed inland in 1921 to attack the Turkish forces under Kemal Pasha in the hope of occupying the part of Turkey peopled by many Greeks. The highly nationalistic Turks, following the defeat of the Greeks, rose against the Greek-speaking residents of Asia Minor as well as the retreating Greek army.

In the Treaty of Lausanne (January 1923) Greece and Turkey agreed to exchange their populations then living under the control of the other, as a result of which over a million Greeks migrated from Asia Minor to Greece proper and over 400,000 Turks left Greece for Turkey. In addition, exchanges of 46,000 Greeks from Bulgaria and 53,000 Bulgarians from Greece [2] followed the Treaty of Neuilly, which dealt with Bulgaria for her participation with the Central Powers in World War I.

In my various visits to Northern Greece, I had difficulty in fully appreciating the immensity of the impact of these refugees upon Greek national life. I could try to imagine what it must mean for any country, especially one as deficient in natural resources as Greece was in the 1920s, to have 22 percent of its total population made up of recently displaced persons, many of whom were widows and children whose husbands and fathers had perished in the ordeals of Asia Minor. It was as though the United States, which consisted of about 110 million at that time, were to receive over 24 million immigrants in a three- to four-year period, as compared with the figure of just over a million, representing the largest number to arrive in any previous year.

As I listened with interest to the involved story of a single family's flight and their subsequent difficulties, I could comprehend, at least in part, what this experience had meant to them.[3] Or I could follow the complaints of the leaders of a community, such as those in Thomai, Thessaly (Chapter 4), who, as late as 1953, were talking of how much better off they had been when living in caves in Turkey with all the land they wanted to cultivate. Yet, when I tried to multiply these experiences of a few to those of a thousand displaced people, with all of their pent-up emotions and problems, I had to stretch my imagination to the fullest and admit the futility of trying to multiply this thousand by another thousand if I were to seek to encompass the totality of the refugee problem in Greece in the 1920s. No wonder the League of Nations stepped in to render assistance, as did philanthropic groups in the United States and elsewhere.

What happens to a nation when it receives newcomers up to one fifth of its total number? What complications arise when these refugees come from different geographic and cultural areas, bound together only by the sense that their families were Greek in origin? By 1952-53, most of these settlers had adjusted to their new conditions and were making significant contributions to their homeland. Enough time had passed to enable many of them to assess the impact of their encounter with Greek national life, for numerous changes had followed their arrival.

Their resettlement had, in the first place, brought about a national unity not heretofore possible, since Turks and Bulgarians had left Greece (with the exception of the Turks in western Thrace who were permitted to remain because Greeks were allowed to stay in Istanbul), and the Greeks from Asia Minor were now collected in metropolitan Greece. With the exception of Cyprus and perhaps northern Epirus, there was now little ground for irredentism, which has so consistently plagued each of the Balkan states since their creation as independent political units.

A second effect of the refugees' arrival was the improvement of agriculture, especially in Northern Greece, where the refugees chiefly settled, as well as in Crete, where they improved the vineyards. Because they had been uprooted, the newcomers were much more ready to adopt modern farming methods, to use fertilizer and improved seed. They even introduced new crops to the mainland of Greece. This readiness for change at times contrasted sharply with the more apathetic and conservative native villagers.

The refugees, in the third place, helped create a public health service. Many of them settled in the marshy deltas of the rivers emptying into the Aegean Sea, where malaria — to which they had developed no immunity in Asia Minor — wiped out whole villages. Being desperate, they cooperated to the fullest with authorities who were draining the swamps and inaugurating malaria-control measures.

Even more important was the refugees' role in creating new industries, such as rug weaving, especially in urban centers. They brought in skills, including entrepreneurial ability; even the untrained represented a willing labor pool. They had to rely on their wit and skill to survive in this new environment. The same held true for the fishing industry, which at best was at a primitive level in Greece before the coming of the refugees.

One nomarch, long-familiar with the refugee problem, summarized his observations as follows:

At the time of their coming, we looked upon these refugees as a terrible burden. But they did bring a creative and civilized element. Here in Macedonia, the refugees are a progressive element: in industry, commerce, and agriculture. They are progressive because they have had so many hardships that they are like iron which has gone through fire and become more malleable. Most of the refugees think they have a better life here than they had in their former homes.

This cataclysmic event, resulting from the disastrous Asia Minor campaign by the Greeks, brought not only a large population increase; it also introduced a social transfusion which all observers agree led to a more progressive spirit in Greece.

World War II and the guerrilla war which followed constituted another major social upheaval. Whereas the Nazi forces often wreaked vengeance for sabotage upon settlements close to the main thoroughfares, the Communist forces stayed away from the main highways and brought disaster to mountain villages, such as Valtetsi in the Peloponnesos (Chapter 6). All countries occupied by an enemy suffer social as well as economic disorganization, but the case of Greece was aggravated by the nature of the guerrilla war. In order to protect the exposed rural people and to curb the unwilling (and sometimes willing) support of the Communist forces by the villagers upon whom the guerrillas descended for food and supplies, the central government in Athens removed a number of villagers, estimated at from 700,000 to 750,000, from their homes to quarters near some town or city. Because this was a temporary resettlement, most of the villagers did not become incorporated into the local economy, which was not able to utilize such a volume of labor; instead, these migrants were supported by government subsidy which provided a bare minimum of services. But, as earlier chapters have shown, this exposure of from one to two years to the city had a profound psychological impact upon the women and young people. The women learned that there was an "easier" life; the young people got many new ideas about dress and beauty aids, entertainment, types of indoor jobs, and patterns of greater independence from their parents. One girl who had worked in a factory in Salonica felt ashamed to carry water when she went back to her village, and moreover she wanted a regular income.

According to a prominent Greek child-welfare worker, the changes following the guerrilla war ranged from shifts in such basic values as virginity, with this being less highly esteemed than before the war, to the presence of bobbed hair and permanents in villagers where they had never been seen before. Before the war, such changes had been gradual; now they came suddenly. George Sakellopoulos, the inspector of agriculture in Ioannina, summarized very clearly the impact of this population displacement for his area:

During the guerrilla war the people had to go to the towns. They lived in homes much better than they had known before. They learned to wash themselves, which many had not done before. When they were persuaded to go back to their villages, they took back the changes they had seen. Many of them went back reluctantly. While they were refugees they had a subsidy. When that was cut off, they could no longer remain in the town house, for they could not pay the owner, who could kick them out. A free distribution of flour was made in the village, and not in the town, so they had to go back to the village to receive it. Then the tractor operators said they would plow only the fields of those who were actually in the village; even the army helped with the plowing. At first, there were some who stayed behind in the towns because their children were in school, but eventually the families were brought together again in the village.

Whereas the effect of the coming of the Asia Minor refugees was to increase the population and heighten the economic activity of the country, the effect of the stay of these northern villagers in town was to loosen somewhat the social cement that holds the kinship group and the village community together. It set in motion more perceptibly in Northern Greece what has long been characteristic of Central Greece and the Peloponnesos: the urbanization of the countryside, in the sense of the spreading influence of urban ways.

War is not the only source of cataclysmic change. Devastating earthquakes sometimes destroy densely populated areas. In 1953, shortly after we left Greece, earthquakes created havoc on the islands of Cephalonia and Zante. My former interpreter, Bessie Adossides, described this in a revealing letter:

As soon as these earthquakes started, Mother and I presented ourselves to the Greek Red Cross and volunteered to go either to Cephalonia or Zante. Thus on August 13th we left via Patras for Zante. Mother was heading a group of eighteen volunteer nurses and, when we arrived at our destination, the whole town was still in flames and the place smelled of burned flesh. The disaster in the town of Zante was complete; only one church, a school, and a bank were standing. The panic, suffering, and agony of the population were indescribable. We found on our arrival that nurses from Patras had set up a provisionary tent hospital, but as there was not sufficient place for all the wounded and sick, these were being shipped to Patras. For two nights we stayed awake as the fire came very near the hospital and we had to be ready to carry everybody on board a ship in the harbor. Luckily this did not happen.

Although this letter describes the efforts of a few individuals, the whole Greek nation was asked to contribute to the reconstruction of these destroyed island communities. International agencies also helped. Such a catastrophic experience, with its rupturing of some social bonds and the forging of new ones, has brought about social changes in the areas affected. The economic drain resulted in readjustment of the government's plans for economic development, since substantial material resources had to be routed to this area of dire need. A few years before, the city of Volos in Thessaly had been badly affected; earlier it had been Corinth.

No matter what type of cataclysm occurs, when governmental authorities have to step in and assist in reconstruction, there is always the tendency — as expressed by one nomarch — for people to take "distribution of clothing, food, and medical care for granted, hoping it will go on forever." The fact that they have suffered entitles them, so they think, to continued support even after reconstruction days are past.

Social Drift

Even in a country as subjected to catastrophe as Greece, individuals decide whether or not to try new ways which they have seen or about which they have heard. Many of these are not forced on the villagers, nor even urged upon them, but have some appeal which causes men, women, and young people to experiment with them. If they give satisfaction, then they become incorporated in the general social patterns. To trace these changes due to social drift would be a review of what has been written so far, yet the comparison of the descriptions by adults of life in their villages when they were young with what one observes there today indicates that over a period of time innovations, both social and technological, reached these villages, were adopted by the bolder individuals, and were imitated in time by others. Within recent years the tempo of change in rural Greece has been speeded up. The Bishop of Messenia, already referred to in the discussion of religion, observed:

People have now raised their standard of living well above their possibility to pay. They want running water in their home, city clothes, and modern furniture. They don't go into debt necessarily to obtain these things, but they have stopped saving as they used to do. When they have money, they spend it; they don't save it. They have made very great strides in education. They all want a road right up to their village so automobiles can reach them; they all want electricity. The changes which would have normally taken fifty years are now compressed into ten.

Greece, therefore, is a good example of the rising level of expectations going on among rural people the world over. Through the "percolation" of ideas and impressions into the rural areas, many people are demanding what the city person has long taken for granted: education, a road to one's door, electricity, and running water.

Many factors enter into the decisions by village people to do something new. Population increase or decrease affects life in rural areas. With an increase, the father has to divide his patrimony among more children, with the result that farms get smaller, less efficient, and people approach the poverty line if offsetting measures are not found. With population loss, those who are left have to make many new adjustments.

A study made by two Dutch geographers, de Vooys and Piket, during April and May 1957, of two villages in the Peloponnesos showed the connection between population (viewed as labor supply) and social change. The residents of one community, on the edge of the Argos Plain, produce tobacco, olives, and grain, and also raise sheep. The economy is thus transitional, between the economy of the plains and that of the mountains. After analyzing the labor requirements of this community and weighing the gains from introduction of modern farm technology, the geographers conclude:

A burning question in the under-developed countries is how to *increase prosperity*. As a matter of course, enlargement of the very small holdings would be considered the solution where the agrarian sector is concerned. But even if a part of the peasant population could be successfully transferred elsewhere, this would merely cause a shortage of labour in the fields under the present system of exploitation. A great part of the cultivated area would remain fallow and only be used for grazing. . . . In the tobacco villages the problem would be the reduction of the labour peaks in the spring and summer: these require all the labour available and even cause a fairly extensive seasonal migration. Mechanization might bring about some decrease in the April and May peaks. The result would be that more seasonal female labour would be needed for tobacco planting. The labour peak in August is caused by the tobacco harvest and this work cannot be mechanized or simplified. If the holdings are enlarged, more female labour would have to be attracted; on the other hand, however, the production per farm unit of the cash crops tobacco and wheat . . . would be augmented, thus increasing local prosperity.[4]

In the second village studied, one located in the Megalopolis Basin, de Vooys and Piket were impressed by its remarkably deserted appearance. Many houses were unoccupied, abandoned terraces betrayed former vine growing, and bushes had grown up on formerly tilled fields. Why has this come about in a country where land is so scarce?

The agricultural unit was originally based on two cornerstones: growing grain and keeping sheep. Self-sufficiency was remarkably developed; only the sale of surplus products — derived from the sheep — supplied a scanty money income. When finally a money economy penetrated here, the inhabitants reacted to it by mass emigration: especially the younger generation moved away. At first this lightened the population pressures, but when the migration process persisted, it soon became clear that the consequences were serious. The older people eventually died and the land was left to descendants who lived elsewhere. When these heirs lived far off, either in Athens or abroad, they had little interest in such legacies. They neglected the land and permitted the other villagers to use it as common pasture.[5]

The writers conclude that only a radical change in the labor processes (mechanization and simultaneous enlargement of the holdings) and changes in the attitude of the peasants (enabling the founding of cooperative societies, together with the immigration of young families into this region, will turn this area around Megalopolis into a prosperous one. Thus we see the close connection between population shifts, economic trends, and social change.

Another factor affecting change in the village is the family head's economic ability to make the changes he would like. The Greek peasants, though numbering more than half (55 percent) of the total population, receive about 45 percent of the total national income.[6] The per-capita income of the 900,000 farm families runs lower than the national average of $185 per year, a figure permitting only minimal improvements, no matter how strong the desire.

Closely related to a family head's economic predicament is the demand for, and therefore the price of, the cash crops that he grows. The tobacco farmer of Northern Greece, the peasant growing olives on Mount Pelion near Thessaly, the apple grower in western Macedonia around Phlorina, and the producer of currents in the northern Peloponnesos are familiar with the ups and downs of the world markets. When he shifts from wheat to cotton or rice, the farmer makes more than an economic decision; he also determines much about family relationships in his home. Growing wheat calls for a very different participation of the woman than does the cultivation of rice in irrigated fields. In the latter case, the farmer also has to submit himself to the organizational control that the use of irrigated water necessitates, being ready to divert the stream into his own fields when his neighbor has used the allotted time for watering his fields. With his neighbors, too, he must cooperate to keep drainage ditches clear, unless this can be turned over to some governmental agency. Or, if a family shifts from sheep raising to settled farming, the fate of the children is apt to be different. In caring for sheep the children are an important economic asset, which keeps them away from the house for several hours during the day and even away from school for two or three years.

Social change of the drifting, unplanned sort can be observed among the young people as well. On a Sunday afternoon a young man recently returned from the army may go up to a young woman in the promenade on the village square and ask if he can walk with her. This may be the first time that any young man has made this maneuver in this village. The other young people watch with almost unbelieving eyes and, if they see that no serious social consequences are visited upon the innovator, may eventually themselves get around to pairing off. Village opinion, too, may be in for a start when a father and his grown son, perhaps because they want to continue the discussion of some economic transaction in which they are involved, go to sit together in a coffeehouse where it has never been customary before for sons to sit with their fathers. Indeed, as pointed out earlier, the practice may be that sons are not even to enter the coffeehouse where the fathers go. Now and then, particularly in the past, innovators of this sort have experienced unpleasant social pressures of many kinds, which may even have stopped them from trying to change local customs. Today, there is such social ferment, such a mixing of traditional and modern roles, that much more individual variability is permitted.

Several times I asked Greek friends who were familiar with village life whether the villager was more apt to imitate what he saw in Athens or what he saw in a provincial town. In other words, I wondered if the changes emanating from the city were mediated by the townspeople who lived nearer the villager and in whose community the villager felt more at home. These observers did not agree on this matter, nor was I able to conduct detailed studies; nevertheless, I gained the definite impression that what counted was not the size of the city so much as the location of family members who had sought work away from the village. They were often influential agents of change with their relatives back home. This has been more recently confirmed by the investigations of Ernestine Friedl in a Boeotian village:

Considerable social mobility exists in Greece . . . but this mobility does not come at the expense of kinship ties. The family remains a strongly functioning unit in spite of the fact that its members may occupy different social positions and may live in many different communities — in villages, towns and cities. . . . Therefore, it is often the upwardly mobile members of his own family who link the villager to the national culture and the national social structure of Greece. As a result, not only are cultural and social changes expected in the village, but continuing urban influence is an integral part of village life.[7]

She then shows how the grown children, even though living in the city, still have some rights over the father's real property back in the village; the same applies to a son-in-law living elsewhere, because of his vested interest in the dowry in land which his wife brought to him and which is located back in the wife's village and perhaps farmed by one of her brothers living there. Dr. Friedl cites four mutually reinforcing patterns of Greek culture which make possible the continuing involvement of the members of the dispersed kinship group in matters of common concern: first, the amount of time that the Greeks spend in reaching a major decision. It will not be arrived at in a hurry and may take as much as a year or two of discussion. Second, Greeks consider visiting between country and a city kin a highly favored form of recreation for both parties. Third, this visitation is made possible by the willingness of the Greeks to double, triple, or quadruple up, sleeping on pallets when beds are insufficient. Fourth, the fact that the rural and urban people involved are kin to each other keeps down much of the suspicion and jealousy that rural people might have of the urban person, thus facilitating continuing interaction.

In personally witnessing this process I have wondered, but never investigated, whether those villagers most vigorous in their denunciation of Athens and city life were those who had no urban relatives.

But one should not overlook the influence that a change in one village has upon those in nearby villages. If the people of one community decide to put a neglected cemetery in order, then those elsewhere will say, "don't you think we had better do something about our cemetery?" and take steps accordingly, while trying to keep the fact that they are imitating the other village from being obvious. There is, thus, some competition among Greek villages, not an intense rivalry but a desire by those in one village to have what they see that other communities have. Nothing is more irksome to those in one village than to be refused electricity from a power line passing close by when the current is made available to other villages in the region.

Most of the time, unplanned social change takes place as a response by villagers to forces from outside the village which impinge on their way of life. The response may be one of solid resistence to certain types of innovation, even though some individuals are for the change but unwilling to take the necessary social risk of advocating it. At other times, a selective change occurs when villagers choose some new items while rejecting others. They may welcome a new opportunity to send their sons away for more education, but demur at letting their daughters pursue a similar advantage. Now and then, the villagers may accept a new practice and give it a local twist not contemplated when the practice originated elsewhere. Women, for instance, have been given the right to vote, but how they exercise this prerogative depends much on local village opinion and the authority of the male family heads. Women who vote just as their husbands tell them to vote, a phenomenon common in many countries other than Greece, are not following the independence of thought and the privacy of ballot which supposedly accompanies the free citizen. But they do vote, which testifies to the fact that an innovation of radical proportions has been accepted.

This interaction between outside forces and the willingness or reluctance of local people to change are best brought into focus in the consideration of planned programs of change, which are confronting the villager on every hand.

PLANNED CHANGE

Immediately after the end of the guerrilla war, programs of welfare and reconstruction were energetically initiated in rural areas which had suffered most. These were designed to help the villagers rebuild their houses and schools, replace draft animals or depleted flocks, obtain implements and seed. Food staples were also provided where needed. The orphans or otherwise dependent children were brought into special child villages, set up by the Queen's Fund for care and education, until old enough to go out on their own. But these measures, planned chiefly for rehabilitation, also carried with them implications for change. In doing so, they were following a trail previously blazed.

Americans past middle age, who contributed to the Near East Relief at the end of World War I, may or may not know that the funds donated so generously at that time were being put to good use long after the immediate relief needs had been met. Its successor, the Near East Foundation, chose Greece as one of its main arenas of operation. The attempts at rural reconstruction, or village improvement, by this organization in cooperation with the Greek government in the 1930s have been fully described by the educational director, H. B. Allen, in his book *Come Over Into Macedonia*. This program also trained Greek personnel, who were later to play important roles in the rural rehabilitation of Greece. With the coming in, under the Truman Doctrine and Marshall Plan, of the American Mission to Greece, staffed and financed to deal with rural problems on a tremendous scale, the Near East Foundation decided about 1953 to end its Greek program in order to concentrate on assisting Near Eastern countries not receiving the support which was being officially extended to Greece by the American government. But one of its final achievements was the elementary, but nevertheless very useful, series of village studies conducted by its staff, to which frequent mention has been made in this book. The Near East Foundation was also instrumental in bringing the first Fulbright professor to Greece — Howard W. Beers, who taught the first courses in rural sociology to be given in Greece (at the Superior School for Agriculture, Athens) and who initiated the village studies just mentioned.

Several references have also been made to the American Farm School of Salonica, which celebrated its fiftieth anniversary in 1955. Founded by Reverend John Henry House, and continued by his son, Charles, and daughter-in-law, Ann, the school has been a vital force in the improvement of agriculture in many sections of Northern Greece. Bruce Lansdale, who succeeded Charles House as director, is also seeing to it that the school, through a community-development program, extends its influence even more directly to the villages. One of its activities is to offer short courses for groups of village leaders — priests, community presidents, and others — who come in to discuss how they can improve life in their communities.

Before World War II, the cooperative movement — described in Chapter 10 — sought to raise the economic conditions of the villages. The Food and Agriculture Organization Mission, viewing the prewar record of the cooperatives, cited in its 1946 report that these organizations had pioneered in the development of bucket pumps, tobacco water-storage tanks, and, through financial aid, the development of improved farm practices. Also, the national government had agricultural specialists who advised villagers on farm problems, but the success of these individuals was minimal as compared to postwar developments.

A survey of prewar programs of planned change, therefore, would indicate that either they reached only special areas where pioneering measures were being tried by private agencies or that they covered the country generally but relatively ineffectively through cooperatives and officials of the Ministry of Agriculture. This is not to imply that rural Greece was static during this period; only that it was not yet receiving the impact of planned change that was to characterize the years following World War II.

In turning to these postwar efforts, a selection has to be made from a wide variety of endeavors. The United Nations, for instance, helped in several ways, and one of the most interesting impacts this body made upon the villages was the program promoted by one of their officials, Glen Leet. It was termed *pronoia dia tes ergassias,* often translated "welfare through employment," which made it possible for villagers to work on some useful community project and be paid minimal wages for their labor. This not only brought some much-needed cash into poor areas but resulted also in actual physical accomplishments which people could see and in which they could take pride. This program, of course, was supplementary to the customary "voluntary" or unpaid labor (*prosopike ergassia*), usually ten days, which able-bodied villagers are supposed to contribute to the community upon call of the community council.[8]

Mention has already been made of a few efforts of the American Mission to Greece — whether called Economic Cooperation Administration (ECA), Mutual Security Administration (MSA), Foreign Operations Administration (FOA), or International Cooperation Administration (ICA). One of these was the attempt to set up radio receiving sets in the most isolated Greek villages so the people there would feel in touch with the outside world; another was the vast road-building program which has left its mark not only upon the Greek countryside but upon the Greek social structure as well. Physical isolation has been broken down on a scale not dreamed possible in the prewar years.

The American Mission is also largely responsible for the speeded-up mechanization occurring in Greek agriculture in the 1950s. The same holds true for greatly expanded drainage and irrigation projects which increased the production of cotton and rice. To credit the American Mission with these and other developments does not reflect upon Greek ingenuity and desire for progress, for all of these programs were carried out by Greeks and through Greek agencies, but the outside financial and technical assistance had to be present for any large-scale success. A sober evaluation of American aid to Greece is found in a book by that title, written by A. A. Munkman, who was chief of Audits and Surveys of the United States Economic Mission to Greece.[9] While citing the positive achievements, he also inquires into how the two billion dollars supplied could have been better used for the benefit of the Greek people. He deals none too gently with some of the administrative weaknesses and concludes pessimistically that Western influence is steadily losing ground, because the ordinary Greek peasant or worker feels that it promises far more than it fulfills. This goes back, he thinks, to the fact that public opinion is poorly informed about the mechanics of aid.

Without necessarily taking issue with Munkman's conclusion, it is important to point out that, by their very nature, programs of planned change invariably raise peasant expectations beyond the sponsors' ability to satisfy. This need not be a negative fact if the dissatisfaction can be channeled into increased economic activity and not become a disturbing political force. A further fact is the peasant's chronic tendency to assume that he is not getting a square deal, or everything that is due him, because throughout his memory and that of his forebears he has been used to what he considers exploitation by a government or those from the city who would take advantage of him. No aid program can ever create a contented peasantry. Yet it is fair to ask what is being done in Greece today to help the individual villager solve the problems of immediate interest to him. The brightest hope, and one recognized by Munkman, is the creation of the Agricultural Extension Service, so organized as to take advantage of the long American experience in this field, the lessons learned by the Near East Foundation in Greece, and the application by dedicated Greeks of these lessons to contemporary conditions. A comparison between what is now available to the farmer and what was available before the war shows a tremendous gain in his behalf. To be sure, the peasant does not apply all that he is taught by the extension worker, and now and then administrative decrees (such as cutting from the budget the transportation item) limit the effectiveness of the extension worker. But in every part of Greece trained personnel are visiting the villagers and, as never before, showing an interest in their welfare and helping them think through their economic problems. Home-economics workers, working with the farm women, are also making considerable headway.

When I investigated social changes occurring between 1952-53 and 1959, those whose knowledge of Greek village life I have found to be most accurate said, "Certainly the greatest change you will find is the development of the agricultural-extension program and the service it is rendering." In other words, the central government is sending "change agents" [10] throughout Greece to help initiate improvements in farming and homemaking, and it is not waiting for the peasants to journey to Athens for answers to their problems. There are limits to what any professional staff can do, but to the extent that these extension workers, both men and women, receive necessary support, to that extent one will find rapid change in the countryside.

Mention has already been made, in Chapter 15, of the organizations being set up in Greek villages by the extension service as well as by the Queen's Fund. This fund concentrates primarily upon Northern Greece and through its village welfare centers seeks to raise the educational, cultural, and economic level of the villages. The King's Fund is interested in the villager. In September 1959 I visited near Athens the handsome Community Development Training Center, financed by this fund, where I met with a group of about fifty teachers who had been invited there, with all expenses paid, to study how teachers can be agents of community improvement. When I joined the group, they were listening to a lecture on scientific beekeeping so that they could talk intelligently on this subject to their pupils and the pupils' parents.

During this same September 1959 visit I had occasion to review, as on a previous occasion, the community-development program of the Save the Children Federation, an American organization. It contributes its funds, set aside for community development, only if the adults of the community agree to make contributions of their own (labor, materials, money) to the construction of a better school, the installation of a public water supply, the planting of a school orchard, or the construction of a dock to bring economic advantages to an otherwise bypassed coastal village.

Anyone trying to cover completely the numerous programs designed to change village life for the better would find them springing up in a variety of places. The official government programs, each under one of the ministries, cover a wide range of activities. Agriculture is more adequately represented than health, education more than social welfare, and economic programs more than recreational programs. But this emphasis is not unexpected in a rural setting. All official American programs, being governmental, work through the Greek ministries and agencies. Next, in drawing up a comprehensive list, one could chronicle the quasi-governmental programs such as those embodied in the King's Fund and the Queen's Fund, the Volunteer Nursing Corps, and similar bodies. In addition to these, there are numerous groups started and managed by public-spirited Greek citizens interested in rural improvement. These range from agricultural education to reforestation to preservation of the folk arts. To those already found could be added the programs of a variety of international agencies, such as UNICEF, the Food and Agriculture Organization, the World Health Organization, UNESCO, and the Secretariat of the United Nations, as well as the very active International Red Cross. Finally, one could include a large assortment of private efforts sponsored by organizations from several European countries as well as Canada and the United States. Such organizations might be religious in nature, strictly welfare, or a combination of both.

No wonder, then, that the Greek villager becomes confused about who promises what and fails to deliver, or whom to thank for a bundle of clothes received in the mail. No wonder that he sometimes is nonplussed about what government official to wait upon. If he is a community president, he will probably visit his nomarch, but the chances are that the nomarch is not altogether versed in the number of programs intent upon effecting change in the villages under his supervision.

More than ever before, the Greek villager's way of life has become a target of change. In this sense, he typifies efforts being made in other countries and on other continents to move people from an archaic to a modern style of life, and to help them realize expectations and hopes of which they are only now becoming aware.

··◦[XVII]◦··

Social Consequences of Foreign Aid

This excursion through the Greek countryside should have shown that all change, whether in the guise of foreign aid or not, has definite social consequences. Social relationships as well as economic sectors are affected. Nor are these social consequences simply political in character; they go much deeper into the social structure. This should not seem mysterious, although it is often overlooked, for any program of economic development or political reconstruction has to work through people, through their social organization as it exists or as it is being fashioned anew. Despite this truism, and the fact that the economic and political aspects of foreign aid have been dramatically debated and ably analyzed by competent scholars, the social consequences are still *terra incognita* to many American specialists abroad. Furthermore, foreign aid, by its very nature, is designed not to maintain the status quo but to promote social change.

FOREIGN AID MEANS SOCIAL CHANGE

For anyone who is thinking through a philosophy of social change, the Greek experience is significant. It was a battleground between Western and Communist ideology and between conflicting loyalties. Here, through the Truman Doctrine, the United States intervened to influence the outcome, and succeeded. But the military defeat of the Communist-led guerrilla forces was not enough: American dollars and American specialists came into the country — one might almost say they inundated the country — to improve health programs, statistical services, transportation routes, agriculture, homemaking, educational facilities, social welfare, foreign trade, and industry. Some idea of the extent of the financial cost is gained from a simple calculation: if Greece had received one million dollars a year since the time of Alexander the Great, the amount received would not quite equal the approximately two and one-half billion dollars received since World War II. Greece is often cited as the prize exhibit of the United States in the cold-war struggle. While such a presentation often overlooks the great contribution that the Greek people themselves made to their own recovery, as well as the help received from Britain and numerous international agencies and organizations, Americans were indubitably the chief agents of change in the sense of providing specialized knowledge about many facets of life. From Greece, many of these same specialists went on to Taiwan, Viet Nam, and other underdeveloped, or formerly colonial, areas where American technical assistance was in demand.

This is not surprising, nor was it entirely a matter of choice. The United States and other Western societies are forced into being agents of change by at least two major features of our way of life: one is our dynamic Western economy, which can no more operate effectively within a political boundary than spilled water can be contained by lines drawn on a table; the other feature is the explosive quality of the political and social ideas which we have inherited from our founding fathers and which we have implemented sufficiently to show the great promise which their further realization would bring. Around the world, words such as democracy, equality, freedom, brotherhood, progress are magic symbols to peoples awaking from centuries of life in a traditional mold and now part of the great "revolution of rising expectations." Our businessmen, financiers, and industrialists are developing world-wide economic perspectives, not because they necessarily want to but because they have to. They also know that in their foreign operations whatever location they choose, what they manufacture or extract from the earth, how they organize the activity, training, and benefits they give their workers, how much they contribute in taxes to local governments — all of these considerations and many more make them agents of change and, in that sense, constitute interference.

As for the revolutionary ideas now spreading to many shores, we can identify many of them as American or Western and should be deeply concerned with the interpretations that they receive. These interpretations go back to a foreign society's immediate experience with our armed forces abroad, the older teachings and examples of Western missionaries, the educational and cultural exchanges which expose future leaders of other countries, often while immature, to the good and bad points of our way of life.

Abroad, our movies, international radio transmissions, and printed material also contribute to the interpretation given to democracy, our economic system, and our social institutions. These facts alone indicate the deep involvement of the United States in the problem of change; but the urgency for a careful reconsideration and a more effective discharge of this involvement is driven home hard by the alternatives for change which the Soviet bloc offers to the new countries grappling with the problems of becoming part of the modern world.

In the face of this challenge, we of the Western world are coming more and more to recognize that the task of our generation is to serve as agents of international social change. Even though as individuals we stay at home, we still play some part in initiating change in many parts of the world through our government and the many private organizations which we support. For Americans this is inevitable, whether or not we like it. It is hard to see that we are all responsible for great changes in Asia or Africa; yet this is grim reality. In a sense, this is what people from many countries mean when they say that the United States must assume more actively its role of world leadership, for they are suggesting that this nation fit itself and assert itself more fully to guide and, at times, even set in motion social, economic, and political change among many peoples. Those urging this position, if one listens carefully, usually qualify their comments by pointing out that there are "right and wrong" ways of exercising this leadership, mistakes to be avoided, and a strong possibility that such a channeling of energies will not necessarily help the United States win a popularity contest, though it may greatly increase respect for this country.

Such a call to leadership is sufficient to make many Americans recoil in horror at the thought of playing the role of some global master-minder, Santa Claus, or do-gooder. And as they pull back, they drop the rational approach with which they face certain aspects of their lives and fall into a much more comfortable emotionalism absolving them from some of the disagreeable consequences of facing facts in today's world. They, as well as the rest of us, need to think through some philosophy of change compatible with democratic ideals and more in keeping with a world moving fast toward the twenty-first century. One of the first requirements is to accept change, rapid and dislocating as it often is, as one of the paramount traits of our times.

The Greek village, chiefly on the receiving end of change, can provide us some clues as to what happens when comparatively isolated villages begin to swing in the orbit of a town or city, or when archaic agricultural practices give way to modern farming. Statistics can tell about the increases in production, but one will have to rely on general observations to discern what such changes bring to social life. We are responsible as American citizens for helping bring about this social redesign in Greek life. What have we done, and what are we doing in other countries? Our society is so urbanized that we have to make a real effort, use all possible clues, to understand that what we are doing abroad is to move great masses of rural people toward the type of urban life which they know little about.[1] Three considerations shed light on this general problem: how a peasant is changed into a farmer; what happens when a villager moves to the city or accepts city ways in the village; and how a subject is changed into a citizen. These considerations do not add up to a full picture of rural change, but they provide useful guides for further thought. They also demonstrate that most foreign-aid programs are inevitably agencies for social change.

From Peasant to Farmer

In order to feed the people of the cities and to raise the living standards in the villages, the leaders of developing countries are sponsoring programs of agricultural improvement in a variety of forms. The basic purpose of these programs, when viewed in human terms, is to change the peasant into a farmer. In Greece today one finds very conservative peasants as well as those who have become farmers in the most modern meaning of the term, although most rural Greeks fall somewhere in between these extremes. To understand the effects of social change we might examine, one at a time, some of the more prominent traits of the peasant way of life and contrast these with the traits found among farmers in the more industrialized societies.[2]

Perhaps the most striking difference between the two types of farming is the peasant's self-subsistence as contrasted with the farmer's production for a market. In the traditional, relatively isolated peasant village, there are only a few wants which cannot be supplied locally. Because people expect little in the way of material goods, they get along with what they have, buying or bartering a few necessities (nails, salt, kerosene) from outside. The family head, however, thinks in terms of producing enough to feed his family, provide seed for harvest, and have sufficient surplus to sell for cash with which to pay taxes and buy the necessities. His choice of crops and the amount of land devoted to them are determined by family needs, not usually calculated in rational terms but by following customary practices which have seen the family through from one year to the next.

On the other hand, the modern farmer produces for the market. He may even grow very little of his food, preferring to put his energies into growing crops which can be sold at good prices. The income is used to buy a much larger volume of purchases than the peasant would ever dream of. The peasant may be price-conscious at the time he is ready to sell his few bushels of wheat or quintals of rice, but the modern farmer tries to anticipate the price as he plans the next year's production.

It follows from this that the peasant has less need for money than the commercial farmer. To be sure, the peasant does use some money, and some colonial powers in the past have found that the way to persuade "natives" to grow cash crops that the authorities wanted for export was to require that taxes be paid in money rather than in kind. To get the money, the peasant had to put in some cash crop, and he eventually moved toward commercial farming. Both types of farmers periodically become involved in debt: the peasant because he wants to spend an extravagant amount on some village festival, wedding, dowry, pilgrimage, or other noneconomic expenditure, whereas the modern farmer — though he also may try to keep up with the Joneses — goes into debt to buy machinery and other capital equipment. The peasant in earlier days went to the village moneylender, whose rates were oppressively high since he as a debtor could give little collateral, but now under government auspices credit cooperatives are moving out to the villages to provide loans to the villager on his livestock or an expected harvest. The modern farmer uses the financial institutions which are an integral part of a complex economy.

The production for a market highlights another difference. The peasant is primarily oriented toward the present; the modern farmer thinks of the future. The peasant, because he has had little economic margin with which to experiment or accumulate, tries to get through one crop year at a time. He may think vaguely about the future in terms of the hopes he has for his children, but seldom in hardheaded economic terms. When he begins to put out vines, to plant olive trees, or to make capital investment connected with agricultural production, the peasant is changing into a farmer — in this one trait, at least.

Both the peasant and the farmer operate in terms of what they consider to be their own self-interest, but they differ in their conceptions of what their self-interest is. The so-called obstinacy of the peasant is not just irrational opposition to change for the sake of holding back progress; it arises from his refusal to believe that the innovation suggested is to his own self-interest. Many times the peasant shrewdness shows up when some new scientific practice fails because of the soil and weather conditions of a given area. Demonstration, rather than talk, works more effectively with the peasant. The farmer, on the other hand, is more willing to take the word of the agricultural specialist, whether spoken or written, and may even do some experimenting on his own. If he is moderately successful, he has a margin for experimentation, whereas the peasant's food supply or source of the cash that he needs would be jeopardized if the innovation proved unsuccessful. Rather than fly to evils that he "knows not of," he sticks with the ways that have helped his people survive through the centuries.

This same conservatism shows up in the peasant's attitude toward his land. The peasant prizes land above all else, whereas the farmer views it as a commodity to be bought and sold. Land has been the peasant's security; if he has a few acres available to him he knows that he can put in a crop and maintain life; without land he is helpless. That is why many peasants will insist on buying more land when they get a sum of money. The modern farmer, on the other hand, views land as only one of the factors of production. He can be quite impersonal toward particular patches of land, whereas in some countries the peasants feel closely attached to family acres handed down through two, three, or more generations. Peasant fathers, too, feel a strong sense of obligation to pass on to their children the patrimony of land intact, if possible. At times, this is even more important than providing the children with an education or a respectable dwelling. The modern farmer may feel much more security in the cash balances in the bank or in the improvements made on the land he has rather than the acquisition of more land simply for the sake of adding acreage to his estate.

Perhaps the most visible contrasts, as one passes from a peasant farming belt to one of modern farms, is the presence of machinery in the latter. The peasant relies on family labor to help not only with ordinary daily tasks but as much as possible to meet the needs at peak periods, such as harvest time. Any money given to outsiders who help is that much taken away from the family exchequer. This means that a peasant with many children is considered blessed over one with few, for the many sons especially are economic assets, though daughters help until they are married off as members of their husbands' family labor reserve. As Chapter 5 has shown, the purchase of a tractor by a Greek farm family ushers in numerous changes. Arthur Mosher, who is familiar with agriculture both in the Far East and in Latin America, points out the following consequences of shifting from family labor to machinery.[3] First, by reducing the labor requirements it frees members of the family for work in the city and may even necessitate their search for employment away from the village — a fact which introduces change into what may have been a closed family circle. Second, there is sometimes a change in status of the sons and younger men of the family who, unlike the older men, know how to operate the newly acquired machine. In peasant families, where the word of the older people, especially the father, has been law and where there is supposed to be unquestioned obedience to his directives, the emergence of a new technical "authority" in the family is bound to produce changes in the family relationships. A third effect of mechanization treated by Mosher is the creation of greater socioeconomic disparity between large and small farms, since mechanization is usually more economical on large farms. This tendency of the rich to get richer and the poor to get poorer is sometimes offset, however, by the poorer farmers pooling their resources and setting up a small joint-ownership group, similar to some of the threshing "rings" of the American Midwest a generation or so ago. Or the small farmers may get the advantages of mechanization if the machines can be rented to them when needed, or if plowing and other operations can be performed on contract. In any event, the introduction of the type of machinery which reduces labor requirements is apt to send people off the farm, whether from the family acquiring the tractor or the poorer farmers who rent their land to a machine owner looking for a larger area to farm.

Another feature mentioned by Mosher is a further distinguishing trait between the peasant and the farmer: namely, the greater dependence of the farmer upon the town. The peasant makes occasional trips to a market town, often as much for the excitement of a change as for the economic benefits he derives. If it were necessary, he could postpone such trips almost indefinitely, particularly if there were other villagers who would buy his surplus crop or a calf or who would purchase for him some necessities from outside. But the man with a machine of a complex sort is dependent upon the repair shops of the town; moreover, he has bought the machine there and is financially tied to the town. To the extent that his children pursue a secondary education, he also develops interests in the center where the school is located. If good roads are built, and automobiles or cheap bus transportation become available, he may even seek recreational outlets in the town.

As the rural people become familiar with town ways, they shift from peasant dress to the more uniform and less colorful urban clothes. It is no longer possible to look at a Greek farmer in town and tell what village or immediate area he is from by the characteristics of his costume; he becomes anonymous and nondescript, indicating the beginning or even culmination of a psychological break with peasant life. Money which would have formerly been spent in other ways now goes for modern goods and garments; more cash becomes necessary to maintain the changing standard of living, and alternative sources of employment have to be found to supplement the income from the farm.

This increased exposure to town usually carries with it heightened exposure to various communication media. In the past, the village has been the peasant's universe; the main currents of city or national life passed him by. But as he becomes a farmer, he visits the supply store in town to hear about prices, new fertilizers, new types of seeds, new insecticides. At the same time, he hears about many other things going on in the world. With the coming of radio to his village, and the occasional newspaper, his distance from town is minimized, but learning from these sources is not quite the same as talking to individuals in the town who claim "to be in the know," whether as well-informed officials or individuals recently returned from the capital city. He also brings back some reading material to ponder over when work is slack. His former mental isolation breaks down.

Such exposure to town influences, along with whatever he learns about government agricultural policies, increasingly involves the peasant in political life. Traditionally, the peasant was interested in visible benefits from the government: a bridge, an all-weather road, a new school building, a better priest, or a drainage project. But the farmer moves in his thinking from concentration on single projects to the more confused level of governmental policies. He has learned that such policies affect him just as definitely as some local measure, and he reacts accordingly. In some countries, peasant parties arise, chiefly under the instigation and leadership of urban intellectuals who see a discontented segment to weld into a political force. Such movements help transform the apolitical peasant into a partisan, a condition which increases his acceptance of the traits of the modern farmer.

One could continue the listing of these traits, one set characterizing the peasant at one extreme and the commercial farmer at the other extreme. Perhaps it will suffice to conclude with a brief examination of some of the less tangible and noneconomic consequences of shifting from a peasant to a farmer.

The first of these is a new attitude toward nature. The peasant, depending upon the philosophical tradition of which he is a part, may submit and resign himself to the vagaries of nature, or he may actively adjust, fighting flood and drought as best he can. With the technology available to him, however, he is at a great disadvantage. The farmer, on the other hand, has moved toward an attitude of mastery over nature, although he never completely approaches this. It is more than a partnership since the farmer is constantly trying to do something to nature: fertilize the soil, put up trees as shelter belts, tile a field to give proper drainage, spray crops to kill insects and eliminate plant disease, and apply contour plowing.

A second subtle, though no less real, attitudinal change deals with the growth of individualism. This occurs as the young people tend to liberate themselves, in some ways at least, from the authority of their parents. They begin to express their own personalities, to stand on their own feet, not as a reflection of a family group but as individuals in their own right. It also means that a farmer, in determining a new course of action, is much less inclined than the peasant to wonder what the neighbors would think; instead, he tries to calculate the economic return, the saving in labor, or the greater productivity. Peasants know that if they depart too far from the accepted practice, they are considered disruptive and may wake up one morning to find their haystack burned down as a sign that they had better conform. The open-field system and communal nature of much of peasant life leaves little room for too many exceptions to the general rule. On the other hand, when local villagers have been persuaded that a new practice is desirable, it can be carried out much more quickly and effectively than if every family head had to be contacted as a separate individual. The informal channels of communication in a village are amazingly fast and, when public opinion has been structured to favor a course of action, it is hard for recalcitrant individuals to hold out for long.

A third attitudinal shift might be characterized as that from the sacred to the secular. In social science, these terms have their specialized meanings. A sacred society, such as an extreme peasant type is supposed to be, relies almost entirely on custom and tradition as the guide to what is right and wrong, proper and improper. The elders are respected, for they are the repositories of wisdom from the past and can interpret to others what should be done, whether in the family circle or in communal affairs. The modern farmer, on the other hand, lives in a secular society in the sense that the rational, scientific test is applied to his economic choices. He does not ask at what stage of the moon's cycle he is supposed to put seed potatoes in the ground, but uses other criteria for determining this. Furthermore, if a young man knows more than an older man about a matter of concern to him, the older man will listen just as eagerly to the young man.

Finally, the peasant's feeling of security, based almost entirely on kinship and the mutual aid of neighbors, gives way to the farmer's reliance on his own efforts plus an organized system of crop and fire insurance, governmental pension plans, and membership in associations and cooperatives of various types which help him weather whatever economic storms he encounters. This leads to much greater social interdependence, which carries with it possibilities both for good and for difficulty. Once there is any breakdown in the social network, the price mechanism, or the system of delivery of which the farmer is a part, he is at the mercy of forces which he as an individual cannot control. At the same time, when these forces do work well, he is assured of a level of living far beyond the peasant's fondest dreams and a sense of participation in an ever-expanding social universe.

Anyone who has read through the book thus far is familiar with the wide range which different regions of Greece represent on this peasant-farmer continuum. Even more important, the following of any single Greek villager through his daily rounds would indicate that no villager holds to these peasant traits in their entirety, nor have any of them moved to commercial farming to the extent represented by much of American agriculture. One thing is certain: those that have been primarily of the peasant mold are moving from many of these traits into those more closely approximating the modern farmer. This movement goes on at an uneven rate and points up much inconsistency in village behavior. But social change inevitably works itself out at this uneven tempo, and planning from on high in Athens seems to do little to smooth out the jagged course of modernization. Recent trips to Greece reinforce my earlier impressions that farming in the Greek countryside is becoming much more scientific because of the very successful programs of planned change previously described, as well as because of the dynamic quality of the Greek villager himself. The Greek peasant is rapidly becoming a farmer. But what about those who leave the village, displaced by the machine or attracted by opportunities elsewhere? What transformation do they have to go through if they are to adjust to urban and industrial life?

From Villager to Urbanite

Although this study of Greek life has concentrated upon the village, some observations about villagers transplanted to the city have relevance to foreign aid as a force for change. If farm workers are displaced by the machine, they tend to gravitate toward population centers where they hope to find work as general laborers or to follow some small skill they may have acquired. The coming of factories usually means some migration of labor, much of it frequently stemming from the rural areas. In fact, in the Western sense, to industrialize means to de-ruralize.

Any foreign-aid program, therefore, which creates new urban centers or leads to the movement of rural people to older centers in search of jobs is introducing not only a type but a tempo of change that must be taken into account in the allocation of economic resources. Some funds will undoubtedly have to be used to ease the transition for those making the move if they are not to become a discontented proletariat. This becomes more evident when we see what happens when a villager becomes an urbanite.

One of the first effects is for the villager to find himself immersed in a much more heterogeneous society. Occupations are more numerous, specialization is greater, and social extremes — the rich and the very poor — are more pronounced than anything he had experienced in the village. There is an intoxicating excitement in the possibilities that seemingly lie before him, although he realizes early in his stay that lack of training and insufficient income limit the realization of many of the more desirable alternatives. He comes face to face with people deriving from different cultural backgrounds, encounters different religious and ethnic groupings, and can participate in recreational pursuits not known in his native village. This richness, this complexity of urban life often calls for living techniques not acquired in the village. As a substitute, therefore, those recently arrived from rural areas may live with others of their kind in a semifolk environment in parts of cities where they are to some degree insulated from the total impact that the city might make upon them.

A second effect of migration to the city is that life becomes job-focused. One's fortune rests not only on the kind of job one has but frequently upon the mere fact of having a job or not. As a peasant back on the farm he had many tasks to perform, but these varied with the season and could often be done at a time of his choosing, within limits. But as an employee, whether a general laborer on a construction project or a worker in a factory, he moves into a different way of life. He must subscribe to a new type of authority — the boss. With some of the younger migrants, the boss may become a father-surrogate; for others, he may represent a challenge to their independence.

Furthermore, a job-focused life means a regimented routine, particularly if fellow workers in an assembly line are dependent upon one's own performance. In such cases, others make decisions which one has to carry out. Along with this, a time consciousness, not necessarily present in the village, has to develop, particularly if factory managers are Western-trained. To live by the clock instead of by the sun calls for a major psychological orientation for many villagers.

Also inherent in this arrangement is the fact that the individual and not the family becomes the economic unit. To be sure, different family members may bring their earnings to a common family purse, but they each must go out to tasks over which the family as a group has no control. And as the individual becomes economically more prominent in his environment, he finds his security increasingly in the skills which he possesses. Industrialization and urbanization, therefore, work out part of their changes simply because jobs loom large and life becomes focused on them.

The villager while changing into an urbanite may need welfare and housing programs, largely governmental in origin. He may try to maintain connections with others in the city who have come from his same area; he may have relatives nearby upon whom he can depend in times of emergency; he may never completely cut off his ties with his home village; but he quite often stands in need of unemployment compensation, his wife may need maternity care in a government-run maternity home, and his children may need shots to protect them from diseases. A foreign-aid program which finances factories but gives little consideration to the welfare needs of the people moving into these factories is overlooking an important social dimension. The developing countries also need help in learning effective welfare and health practices as well as in mastering machine technology at the management level.

For the transplanted villager mass organizations may possess some attraction. He may be persuaded to join a labor union without fully realizing what membership involves; he may be talked into participating in a political-action group with no knowledge of the ideology behind the action; or he may content himself simply with belonging to some regional association made up of people from his own native area. One can safely predict that most villagers will not actively seek out the mass organizations but that many of them will get caught up in them with no clear picture of their nature. Should they find the leaders of these groups voicing their own aspirations or resentments, then the new urbanites gain a sense of belonging in an otherwise alien world. Although not touched upon in preceding pages, the work of the labor specialists in the American Mission to Greece deserves special commendation. They provided for the Greek labor leaders a type of training which not only made them more effective officials but which also instilled a sense of responsibility in many of them. A similar type of training was not held for the new managers of industries being created with funds furnished by the United States.

Finally, the newcomer to the city has to develop a self-discipline which was not necessary in a village where intimate social controls were so permeating. To hold a job, one must live by certain rules and routines; to keep out of trouble with the police or with neighbors in a workers' apartment house, one must respect the rights of others; to receive promotions, one must add to one's knowledge and skills or else win the favor of those in positions of superiority. It is in these connections that adult-education courses or people's universities (for the working class) serve a useful purpose, even though reaching only a fraction of the eligible population. To visit these classes and to watch daily laborers, some born in the city and others in the villages, strive for more education makes one aware of the changes being ushered in on every hand in these developing countries.

FROM SUBJECT TO CITIZEN

Almost every developing country has within its recent memory the fact of liberation from some outside power. The more than four centuries of Turkish rule have left their imprint on Greek local government, as have the heroic episodes connected with the Greek war of independence. Other countries, more recently liberated, have even more vivid memories of what it means to be a subject whose political fate is decided at the seat of an empire far removed from the subject's homeland.

One purpose of our foreign-aid program, at least as enunciated by some of the most authoritative American spokesmen, is to help establish democratic forms of government wherever people can be found who are receptive to this development. But democracy as we conceive it calls for an enlightened citizenry, conscious of the fact that much sovereignty resides in its hands and that regularly scheduled elections provide an opportunity to express its will. It also assumes that governmental leaders will be aware of and responsive to the rise and fall of public opinion about crucial issues.

It is appropriate to ask, therefore, what the necessary conditions are for the shift of an individual from the position of a subject to that of a citizen. Once this is understood, its connection with a foreign-aid program becomes apparent. Again, observations of the Greek scene help us to understand other areas.

The first condition which usually, though not invariably, comes about is the rise of nationalism and the identification of an individual with a larger political entity. Any study of village life will reveal the parochialism of many villagers, which in the developing countries means that they are not bound by any loyalty greater than that to their family and their village. Whether through a highly virulent nationalism or a growing sense of participation in a multinational state, the individual — to change from a subject to a citizen — must expand his circle of loyalties to encompass the larger political unit of which he supposedly is a first-class citizen.

A second condition, tied in with the first, is the growing sense on the part of the villager that the central government is concerned with his welfare. Without this, the necessary loyalty will not develop. Villagers need both physical manifestations of governmental activity in their behalf (new schools, roads, bridges) and expanding economic opportunities. To some extent, foreign-aid programs can help in this area, particularly in seeing that the benefits are not all concentrated in the cities and mushrooming towns but that even remote sections gain some sense of benefit.

A third corollary is the necessity for widespread education. In the developing countries, the young people with the most education are often viewed as the troublemakers, so much so that some observers may even question the assumption that stable democratic government depends on a highly literate and educated electorate and point out that some of the most educated people, such as the Germans, have moved on occasion whole heartedly into totalitarianism. They argue that a little education is a dangerous thing politically. But it seems clear that the alternative of holding back educational programs is fraught with even more political danger if truly democratic regimes are to become established. Since every regime has to think about ways and means of staying in power, it is all too tempting to promote only that kind of education which most benefits the regime and to forget future needs. Studies of the experiences of many new nations would probably show that education and economic opportunity need to go hand in hand if serious dislocations are to be avoided. Increased income among the uneducated is socially unproductive, and an educated segment with no suitable employment possibilities leads to political discontent. It is also true that a people lacking the basic reading and mathematical skills cannot achieve modern economic development. Thus, if a subject is to become a citizen, he needs to receive an education that fits him not only to perform as an economic producer but also to play his part in the political process.

Since democratic governments depend upon active political organizations — such as parties — the villager must learn how to participate in formal organizations. As pointed out in Chapter 10, the Greek villager does not think in terms of formal organizations to the same extent as the Western European or American. He uses the direct personal approach rather than relying upon organized joint action to gain his goals. In this sense, the rural Greek is much like villagers throughout the world. To take part in a democratic government, therefore, he must gain experience in organizational behavior which will keep him from being merely manipulated and through which he can make many of his own wishes known. From a sociological standpoint, this lack of organizational skill is a crucial variable in the failure of democratic forms to emerge and maintain themselves. The subject who becomes a citizen can learn how to deal with political parties as he gains experience in other large-scale organizations, such as the cooperative movement, labor unions, and in some cases religious groups. One might draw the analogy that a true citizen of a political unit is much the same as the active member of a large organization. Neither is indifferent or uninformed, and each knows the organizational mechanics open to him to checkrein activities of which he does not approve.

A further condition required for the shift from a subject to a citizen is a growing tradition of efficient public administration. Many of our foreign-aid programs have dealt with the need for training local people in systems of taxation, public financing, more streamlined bureaucratic procedures. Connected with these changes in practices, there must be an accompanying shift in attitudes on the part of the officials toward the people they are paid to serve. If the representatives of the central government continue to treat villagers like subjects, the villagers will continue to act like subjects; if they are treated as citizens, with dignity and fairness, then the villagers can much more easily make the shift to true citizenship. Local officialdom is apt to present one of the greatest difficulties, and any foreign-aid program which fails to change traditional official attitudes is probably making only a small contribution toward political stability.

To draw up a complete list of the attributes of an ideal citizen would move far beyond the possibilities that can currently be realized in most developing countries. Enough of the conditions for the citizenship role have been mentioned to show the connection between foreign-aid programs and this kind of social change. It is only reasonable that one test of any program in which the United States has invested is to ask to what extent this program advances and encourages, and even makes possible, the shift from a subject to a citizen.

SOCIAL DIMENSIONS OF AID

Anyone familiar with the Greece of the early 1950s (or with the Viet Nam or Laos of the early 1960s) knows what it is like to have hundreds of Americans, civilian technicians and military specialists, busily carrying out their official duties. These hundreds quickly grow into thousands as dependents arrive from the States, and the equivalent of an American suburb springs full blown with all of its attendant recreational facilities, transportation service, food-distribution system, and educational program. Such an occurrence is inevitable when Americans become involved in any program of foreign aid sponsored by our government; nor would we expect it to be otherwise. We are committed to giving our technical knowledge, through the use of specialists, even ranking this in importance with providing capital funds; nevertheless, American specialists will not absent themselves for long from their families, for our pioneering heritage depended upon moving in family groups even before the days of the covered wagon; nor will any American specialist want to see what he considers the health or educational progress of his children jeopardized by insufficient provision. Furthermore, under some circumstances, wives and children can prove effective agents of social change along with the specialists.

But perhaps the most significant aspect of the whole problem of aid to Greece, or elsewhere, is not the fact of introducing change but, rather, the way in which it is introduced and carried out. At times, but certainly not always, careful planning can help cushion the shock of certain kinds of change. We know, for instance, that mechanization in agriculture will affect the labor supply and we can even predict what kinds of workers will be displaced. Making provisions for them early in the process can cut down much human wear and tear. Our foreign-aid programs, to the extent that they represent the genius of American traditions, should always keep sight of the human element in change; those administering these programs should continue to remind themselves and the local leaders that these changes are designed to help people and that people do not exist merely to carry out changes. Unless the sense of individual worth is reinforced by the aid programs, they will prove poor seed beds for the democratic types of government which many expect to grow to full bloom in the countries receiving aid. Foreign aid that is impersonal, merely materialistic and gauged in readily obtained statistics, can frequently play into the hands of calculating leaders whose interest lies in self-perpetuation in power rather than in promoting the general welfare of the people subject to them.

Heavy investments in programs of foreign aid call for comprehensive evaluation, such as that represented by the various studies commissioned from time to time by our own Senate Committee on Foreign Relations. The study of Greek village life, as well as evidence from many countries elsewhere, indicates that the evaluation of social consequences, especially for rural people, receives scant attention. This is due in part to the preoccupation with the pressing military and political considerations which have a direct, immediate bearing upon national safety; it is also due to the fact that specialists who make the evaluations do so in terms of their own specialties, which seldom include the sociological viewpoint. An even greater difficulty is presented by the methodological problems of evaluating intangibles for which no simple social yardsticks can be devised. This is no place to work through such methodological considerations, but one can assert that the social-science techniques are rapidly developing to the point that an increasing number of "intangibles" are being subjected to a kind of measurement which — if not altogether exact — certainly is more useful to those responsible for foreign aid than the guesswork or impressions which often underlie much policy formation. Most of us accept as a goal the idea of "open societies." Do our representatives and specialists abroad know what are the processes and structures, forces and tensions in any society? How can we move toward a world of open societies if we make no effort to understand? It is like saying that we want good health for all people without stopping to ask if the profession of medicine exists to help.

Since any society is complex, it is possible to draw up an almost unlimited number of social dimensions. But for the purposes of examining the ways in which foreign-aid programs may be serving the goals which are prompting these programs, we might look at three such dimensions, remembering that these are illustrative and not necessarily the most important under all conditions.

Changes in the class system. Certainly, if we are to try through foreign aid to assist in the development of newly emerging nations, one of our purposes should be to try to reduce the disparities between the élite and the average people. In essence, this is saying that foreign-aid programs should be concerned with the kind of class system which they are helping to create. If all of the money channeled into a country goes into the hands of the élite and is used by them to entrench themselves, then their political loyalty may be bought for a time, but the social conditions for sound development are not being laid. An effective test of this social dimension is to ask whether or not a middle class is coming into existence and to what kind of an ideology it subscribes. The purpose of furthering the growth of such a middle class is not merely an imitation of our own social system, but because in the world in which we want to live we find that a middle class, firmly rooted, is a safeguard of social stability. Aristotle pointed out that the states consisting of the very rich and the very poor are the most unstable.

Implementing such aims immediately involves one in crucial choices, but they are choices which should be made. In some countries a land-reform program would be indicated if foreign aid is to prove helpful, but this is not an invariable rule. Other factors, such as capacity to service and educate those peasants who get their own land, must be present if this is to be a sound move. A further question revolves around the effect upon the landholding élite. The Communists simply eliminate them as a social class, even though they may spare their lives. But Western nations, which work within a different political and moral framework, must see to what an extent such an élite — or members from it — can provide the transitional leadership in a period of such drastic change. What must be avoided where possible is the creation of a social vacuum as in Cuba, into which can flow revolutionary movements, commanded by a small well-organized cadre, resulting in the substitution of one élite for another with little thought of moving the general populace along the road to political freedom and economic stability.

In several countries, such as Japan or India, perhaps, there already exists what seems to be an oversupply of intellectuals, university graduates whose training has not fitted them for the kind of work (technological, financial, developmental) which is most needed in their country. A foreign-aid program should take into account the contributions or handicaps that such an unassimilated social segment can introduce.

When a foreign-policy administrator asks himself, "what impact is my program having upon the class structure of the host country?" he is dealing with an important social dimension. He finds that he also needs to know the extent to which the program contributes to social mobility, an essential ingredient in the kind of economy and society that is compatible with the assumptions on which the Western world is based. Can those of low birth rise through individual merit and initiative to a higher social status? Is the foreign-aid program tending to close the avenues rather than to open them? Part of the answer to this question lies in the type of concentration of economic and political power which the aid program by its very nature is supporting or changing. Certainly, if the whole Marxist ideology is based on a theory of the class struggle, it is mandatory that any program designed to counterbalance such an ideology seriously examine its own impact upon the class system. Otherwise, it might unwittingly be furthering the Marxian hypotheses by bringing into being just those conditions which Marxists predict will occur when those engaged in a free-enterprise approach involve themselves in the development of non-Western countries. One might win the economic battle, as represented by increased income and production statistics, and yet lose the social battle — which really means losing out in the political struggle. This social battle is the one most overlooked in Latin America.

Potentiality for orderly social change. A second dimension also calls for an over-all look at the social system brought into being and particularly at its potentiality for orderly social change. In many parts of the world, the traditional way to effect change of a planned sort is through a *coup d'état*. The net effect of this is often to crush or eliminate much of the progress made up to that point simply because the progress is associated with the ruling group that is thrown out of power. The essence of orderly social change is its cumulative quality, so that the gains of one generation can be passed on to another generation for adaptation to the new conditions which arise.

Any social system at a given time possesses overt or latent conflicts which may be stimulating certain kinds of change while holding back programs of planned change. (The drive for civil rights and racial integration in the United States is a good illustration close at home.) These points of conflict for a given society should be well known to those responsible for the general outlines of an aid program. In order to accomplish certain desired results, it may be necessary to exacerbate certain types of conflict since there is no altogether placid way of initiating and carrying through social change; yet some foreknowledge of what the sore points are apt to be helps one deal with them in as constructive a manner as possible. The conflicts alluded to here may be generational (parents and youths), religious (Hindu and Moslem), social class (élite and *fellahin*), political (subversive groups), and economic (agriculturists and industrialists). Many others could be cited, but those considered significant should be viewed in the light of changes to be promoted by the foreign-aid program.

To ask that one gauge the contribution a foreign-aid program is making to the development of potentiality for orderly social change is to require an analysis of the dominant social institutions of a country and to relate various phases of the aid program to the institutions affected by it. If the religious bodies have been the main force in keeping change orderly and cumulative, how does the building up of the nonreligious sectors of the society (economic and political) affect the hold of religion? Is this why the youth of Japan is inclined to extremes? If the grip of religion weakens because of the increasing secularization of life which attends industrialization, are other ways being found for building into the growing institutions the techniques of adapting to changing conditions?

This view suggests that what the foreign-aid program should impart to leaders of a given country is not a rigid blueprint to follow but rather a set of operating principles, consonant with the social realities or possibilities which they face, and of the type that enhance human dignity, respect for law and justice, and an appreciation of the capability for liberating man inherent in mechanization, where the machine is used to serve man.

Changes in social values. A third dimension is attitudinal and deals with the value system of a society. Every society that is reasonably integrated possesses a set of values about which its members have a fair degree of consensus. These serve as social cement, for people understand that they are important and need to be supported. These values vary from country to country. Those of Burma differ in many ways from those of Greece; those of Ghana from those of Argentina. One of the most far-reaching effects of any foreign-aid program is the attitudinal change it brings about toward what have been the traditional values of the society. For a hardheaded administrator to deny this is softheaded thinking; for a person intent on changing the economic system to disclaim any responsibility for changing values is to overlook some of the more obvious cause-and-effect relationships of our time.

Many projects which are integral parts of aid programs inevitably affect the changing status of women, as the Greek village will attest. This leads to shifts in family relationships with the attendant modifications of values and behavior. A glance back through American history from the days of the Industrial Revolution on down shows how economic change has wrought changes in social values. Yet many host countries hope to telescope into a relatively few years all of the economic changes which have extended over two centuries in the West. Anyone interested in foreign aid might well ask whether there is the recognition that the people will have to change their value systems just as rapidly if serious social dislocation is to be avoided. This is not to deny that such shifts are possible, but rather to urge that changes in values be taken into account in assessing the impacts of a foreign-aid program. Again, there are social-science techniques which can give an approximate picture of the changes in values which have occurred or which are under way.

But why are values important? The ultimate aim of conscientious foreign-aid programs should be to help developing countries move toward full participation in a world order based on law. Law, whether international or domestic, is a set of values which have been enunciated and codified. Those values which contribute most to an international order, however, are in "the process of becoming" since most nations, including the Western powers, still think primarily in national rather than international terms. Whether the developing countries will have to pass through a national period before they can behave internationally is still a moot question; but certainly they will move toward contributing to the international sphere if their people have strengthened those inherent values which lead to world order and if foreign-aid programs unwittingly do not obliterate these basic values by stressing shallower ones.

Epilogue

What of the Greek villager and his relation to the social changes that foreign aid introduces? There in his village lanes, on his way to the fields, he is the object of foreign aid. It is his way of farming, of caring for children, of thinking about his government, that foreign-aid programs invariably affect. New textile factories produce fabrics which he can buy more cheaply and may even provide employment for his son or daughter; new highways bring a bus to his village for the first time and help him get perishable goods to market; radio programs make his wife urge him to do something about getting running water in the home; and the agricultural-extension agent urges him to stop raising so many sheep and shift to dairy cattle. To the extent that we keep the villager in focus, to that extent we emphasize the human element in foreign aid, not in a maudlin, sentimental fashion, but in the concrete, hardheaded analysis of the relative effects of various alternative programs upon his way of life. The analysis should move, if the Greek villager has anything to teach, from the economic effects to the political and social effects. Do these expensive undertakings really lead toward the kinds of regimes ready to cooperate in a world order based on law? Much of that answer is found not merely in the diagnosis of political institutions themselves, but in the larger question of the degree to which social stability is brought about or undermined. Any widespread technological development, as we have seen in the case of the spread of tractors and combines in Greece, calls for social readjustment. When this occurs, social policies, carefully developed, can prevent large numbers of villagers from being cut adrift from their past or forced from their farms to search unsuccessfully for urban employment, with political alienation the net result. If their children have a chance to get educated and rise in the social scale, if one segment of the society is not seemingly fattening itself with aid funds at the expense of the rest, if locally acceptable services become established in the rural areas to assist villagers in achieving common goals — then the peasants will have hope for the future.

To most of the Greek villagers, foreign aid was intervention, but welcomed intervention. It changed the face of the countryside and the ways of many villages in a short period of time. It brought social consequences, many unanticipated, with which the villagers are having to learn to live. How they evaluate and what they do about these social effects, whether in the village or at the national political level, is the real final test of the American program of aid to Greece.

Each age creates its own mythology and writes its own legends, even rewriting the legend of the Rainbow in the Rock. The version of the first half of the twentieth century would tell of the rise of modern man, fit for the times in which we live. His activity would be centered upon the Rock, for it is tangible, specific, and its secrets point to a mastery of nature. Things and knowledge of things have accumulated in keeping with man's belief that they lead to health, comfort, and happiness. If pure water, abundant crops, attractive schoolbooks, well-paying jobs, and adequate housing came into being, then mankind would come into his rightful heritage.

But contemporary man is being rudely awakened to the fact that the Rock is never sufficient without the Rainbow. Things, and programs for things, in themselves are sterile, neutral, cold, and hard. It is as people give them use, clothe them with meaning, and fit them into humane purposes that they contribute to man's happiness.

This story of rural Greece has shown that village people can be as durable as the Rock itself. It has shown, too, that programs of aid must take into account the invisible but omnipresent qualities of the Rainbow as well as the visible realities of the Rock.

·∘] Bibliography · Notes · Index [∘·

Bibliography

The works below relate to mainland Greece and not to the islands. They deal with some aspect of rural life, though not exclusively. Omitted are many interesting travelers' accounts from the past century, as well as all publications in Greek. Where such sources have been used in a direct way, however, they have been cited in the notes.

BOOKS

Abbott, G. F. *Macedonian Folklore*. Cambridge, Eng., 1903.

Alderfer, Harold F. *I Like Greece*. State College, Pa., 1956.

Allbaugh, Leland G. *Crete: A Case Study of an Underdeveloped Area*. Princeton, 1953.

Allen, Harold B. *Come Over Into Macedonia*. New Brunswick, 1943.

Anthony, Anne. *Greek Holiday*. Athens, 1957.

————— *Meet the Greeks*. Athens, 1950.

Bardis, Panos D. *Ivan and Artemis*. New York, 1957.

Beza, Marcu. *Heritage of Byzantium*. London, 1947.

Boyazoglou, Alexander J. *Contribution à l'étude de l'économie rurale de la Grèce d'après guerre*. Paris, 1931.

Chaconas, Stephen G. *Adamantios Korais: A Study in Greek Nationalism*. New York, 1942.

Cvijic, Jovan. *La Péninsule Balkanique: géographie humaine*. Paris, 1918.

Dalven, R., trans. and ed. *Modern Greek Poetry*. New York, 1949.

Dawkins, R. M. *Modern Greek Folktales*. Oxford, 1953.

Eddy, Charles B. *Greece and the Greek Refugees*. London, 1931.

Eliot, Sir Charles. *Turkey in Europe*. London, 1908.

Fermor, Patrick Leigh. *Mani; Travels in the Southern Peloponnese*. New York, 1958.

Ferriman, Z. Duckett. *Home Life in Hellas, Greece, and the Greeks*. London, 1910.

Forster, Edward S. *A Short History of Modern Greece, 1821–1940*. London, 1941.

Gomme, A. W. *Greece*. London, 1945.

Gregoire, H. *Dans la montagne grecque*. Bruxelles, 1947.

Halliday, W. R. *Folklore Studies: Ancient and Modern*. London, 1924.

Hamilton, M. *Greek Saints and Their Festivals*. Edinburgh, 1910.

Haralambides, Theodor. *Die Schulpolitik Griechenlands: Studie zur Kulturgeschichte Neugriechenlands von 1821–1935*. Berlin, 1935.

Höeg, Carsten. *Les Saracatsanes: un tribe nomadique grecque*. Paris, 1925.

Kitto, H. D. F. *In the Mountains of Greece*. London, 1933.

Kolisevski, Lazar. *Macedonian National Question*. Belgrade, 1959.

Kousoulas, Dimitrios G. *The Price of Freedom: Greece in World Affairs, 1939–1953*. Syracuse, 1953.

Ladas, Stephen F. *The Exchange of Minorities; Bulgaria, Greece and Turkey*. New York, 1932.

Lawson, John C. *Modern Greek Folklore and Ancient Greek Religion: A Study in Survivals*. Cambridge, Eng., 1910.

Lee, Dorothy Demetracopoulou. "Greece," in *Cultural Patterns and Technical Change*. Paris, 1953.

McNeill, William H. *Greece: American Aid in Action, 1947–1956*. New York, 1957.

Mariolopoulos, E. G., and A. N. Livathines. *Atlas climatique de la Grèce*. Athens, 1935.

Mears, Eliot G. *Greece Today; The Aftermath of the Refugee Impact*. Stanford University, 1929.

Megas, George A. *Greek Calendar Customs*. Athens, 1958.

―――― *The Greek House: Its Evolution and Its Relation to the Houses of the Other Balkan Peoples*. Athens, 1951.

Miller, William. *Greek Life in Town and Country*. London, 1905.

Moore, W. E. *Economic Demography of Eastern and Southern Europe*. Geneva, League of Nations, 1945.

Morgenthau, Henry. *I Was Sent to Athens*. Garden City, 1929.

Munkman, C. A. *American Aid to Greece: A Report on the First Ten Years*. New York, 1958.

Philippson, A. *Der Peloponnes*. Berlin, 1892.

―――― *Zur Ethnographie der Peloponnesus*. Petermanns Geographische Mitteilunger, 1890.

―――― *Das Klima Griechenlands*. Bonn, 1948.

Polyzos, N. J. *Essai sur l'émigration grecque*. Paris, 1947.

Rodd, James Rennell. *The Customs and Lore of Modern Greece*. London, 1892.

Saloutos, Theodore. *They Remember America*. Berkeley, 1956.

Sanders, Irwin T. "Selection of Participants in a Mutual Aid Group in Rural Greece," in J. L. Moreno, ed., *Sociometry and the Science of Man*. New York, 1956.

Schultze, Joachim H. *Neugriechenland; eine landeskunde Östmakedoniens und Westthrakiens mit besonderer berucksichtigung der geomorphologie, kolonistensiedlung und wirtschaftsgeographie*. Gotha, 1937.

Servakis, Georges, and C. Pertountzi. "The Agricultural Policy of Greece," in O. S. Morgan, ed., *Agricultural Systems of Middle Europe*. New York, 1933.

Smith, Ashley, *Greece: Moments of Grace*. London, 1943.

Smothers, Frank, William Hardy McNeill, and Elizabeth Darbishire McNeill. *Report on the Greeks: Findings of a Twentieth Century Fund Team Which Surveyed Conditions in Greece in 1947*. New York, 1948.

Spencer, Floyd A. *War and Postwar Greece. An Analysis Based on Greek Writings*. Washington, D. C., 1952.

Stavrianos, L. S. *Greece: American Dilemma and Opportunity*. Chicago, 1952.

Stephanides, Theodore Ph., and George C. Katsimbalis. *Modern Greek Poems — Selected and Rendered into English*. London, 1926.

Sweet-Escott, Bickham. *Greece. A Political and Economic Survey, 1939–1953*. New York, 1954.

Weber, Shirley H. "Greece and the Greeks of Today," in George H. Chase, ed., *Greece of Tomorrow*. New York, 1943.
Wogasli, D. K. *La Solution de la Question Agraire en Grèce*. Athens, 1919.
Zotiades, George B. *The Macedonian Controversy*. Thessalonike, 1954.

ARTICLES

Adossides, Andreas. "The Shepherds of Greece," *Geographical Magazine* (London), XVI (September 1943), 217–225.
Aghnides, T. "What Ancient Greece Means to the Modern Greek," *John Rylands Library Bulletin* (Manchester), XXVII (June 1943), 260–270.
Alderfer, Harold F. "Modern Greek Government I," *Journal of Central European Affairs*, XII, 4 (January 1953), 331–345.
——— "U. S. Aid at the Grass Roots," *National Municipal Review*, XLII, 4 (April 1953), 168–172.
Angel, J. L. "Social Biology of Greek Culture Growth," *American Anthropologist*, no. 48 (October 1946), 493–533.
Bardis, Panos D. "The Changing Family in Modern Greece," *Sociology and Social Research*, XLI, 1 (September–October 1955), 19–23.
Beers, Howard W. "Survival Capacity of Extension Work in Greek Villages," *Rural Sociology*, XV, 3 (September 1950), 274–282.
Bent, J. Theodore. "Greek Peasant Life," *The Fortnightly Review*, August 1886, pp. 214–224.
Codellas, P. S. "Modern Greek Folklore: The *Smerdaki*," *Journal of American Folklore*, no. 58 (July 1945), 236–244.
Delivanis, D. "Balkan Economic Developments," *Balkan Studies* (Thessalonike, 1960), pp. 1–18.
Dulakis, C. C. "Klephtic Folk Songs of Modern Greece; with English Text of Aretousa; Sailor's Last Farewell; Song of Demos," *Poet Lore*, LIII, 3 (1947), 222–231.
Evelpidis, C. "Some Economic and Social Problems in Greece," *International Labour Review*, no. 68 (August 1953), 151–165.
Friar, Kimon. "New Greek Poets, an Anthology and Commentary," *Poetry*, LXXVIII, 3 (June 1951), 145–184.
——— "Greek Poems of the Twentieth Century," *Poetry*, LXXVIII (June 1951), 154–183.
Friedl, Ernestine. "Dowry and Inheritance in Modern Greece," *Transactions of the New York Academy of Sciences*, ser. 2, XXII (1959), 49–54.
——— "Hospital Care in Provincial Greece," *Human Organization*, XVI (1958), 24–27.
——— "The Role of Kinship in the Transmission of National Culture to Rural Villages in Mainland Greece," *The American Anthropologist*, LXI (1959), 30–38.
Gallop, Rodney. "Folk-Songs of Modern Greece," *Musical Quarterly*, XXI (January 1935), 89–98.
Hadjimichali, Angheliki. "La Maison grecque," *L'Hellénisme contemporain* (1949), pp. 169–190, 250–265.
Harrison, Catherine. "Epirus, the Greek Province with a Bad Name," *Geographical Magazine* (London), XI (September 1940), 348–359.
Lee, Dorothy D. "Greek Tales of Priest and Priestwife," *Journal of American Folklore*, no. 60 (April 1947), 163–167.

Lee, Dorothy D. "Greek Accounts of the *Vrykolakas*," *Journal of American Folklore*, no. 55 (July 1942), 126–132.

———— "Greek Personal Anecdotes of the Supernatural," *Journal of American Folklore*, no. 64 (July 1951), 307–312.

Levy, Harry L. "Property Distribution by Lot in Greece," *Transactions of the American Philological Association*, LXXXVII (1956), 42–46.

Mirambel, A. "Blood Vengeance in Southern Greece and Among the Slavs," *Byzantion*, XVI (1943), American series, II, 381–392.

Ogilvie, Alan G. "Physiography and Settlements in Southern Macedonia," *Geographical Review* (New York), XI (April 1921), 172–197.

———— "A Contribution to the Geography of Macedonia," *Geographical Journal*, LV (1920), 1–34.

Pepelasis, A. A. "The Image of the Past and Economic Backwardness," *Human Organization*, XVII (1958–59), 42–46.

Roucek, Joseph S. "Economic Geography of Greece," *Economic Geography* (Worcester, Mass.), XI (January 1935), 91–104.

Sanders, Irwin T. "The Nomadic Peoples of Northern Greece: Ethnic Puzzle and Cultural Survival," *Social Forces*, XXXIII, 2 (1954), 122–129.

———— "Research with Peasants in Underdeveloped Areas," *Social Forces*, XXXV, 1 (October 1956), 1–10.

———— "Village Social Organization in Greece," *Rural Sociology*, XVIII, 4 (December 1953), 366–375.

Stephanides, C. S. "County Agent in Greece," *Foreign Agriculture*, XV, 8 (August 1951), 168–169.

Stroup, Herbert. "Social Changes in Greece," *Sociology and Social Research*, XXXIX (July–August 1955), 387–394.

Stycos, J. M. "Patterns of Communication in a Rural Greek Village," *Public Opinion Quarterly*, XVI, 1 (1952), 59–70.

Valaoras, Vasilios G. "A Reconstruction of the Demographic History of Modern Greece," *Milbank Memorial Fund Quarterly* XXXVIII, 2 (April 1960), 115–139.

———— "Some Effects of Famine on the Population of Greece," *Milbank Memorial Fund Quarterly*, XXVII, 3 (July 1946), 215–234.

Varvaressos, A. "Land Ownership in Greece," *Foreign Agriculture*, XIV, 8 (August 1950), 180–183.

Vouras, P. P. "Greece's Major Problem: Too Many People," *Ohio Journal of Science*, no. 54 (March 1954), 131–134.

———— and A. Taylor, "Greece — A Land of Small Farmers," *Focus*, no. 7 (February 1957), 1–6.

Whipple, Clayton E. "The Agriculture of Greece," *Foreign Agriculture*, VIII. 4 (1944), 75–96.

MISCELLANEOUS

Coutsomaris, George. "Possibilities of Increasing Economic Efficiency in Greek Agriculture." Unpublished master's thesis, University of Chicago, 1952.

Photiadis, John D. "The Coffee House and Its Role in Stavroupolis, Greece." Unpublished master's thesis, Cornell University, 1956.

Stephanides, Charalambos. "A Sociological Sketch of the Village of Megali Vrisi, Greece." Unpublished master's thesis, Cornell University, 1941.

Theodore, Chris Athanasios. "Demographic Aspects of the Greek Economic Problem." Unpublished doctoral dissertation, Boston University, 1951.

Valassis, Vlassios Thomas. "The Living Past and Technical Change." Unpublished master's thesis, University of Maryland, 1956.

Kingdom of Greece, National Statistical Service. *Statistical Yearbook of Greece, 1958.* Athens, 1959.

Library of Congress, Division of Bibliography. *Greece: A Selected List of References.* Washington, 1943.

National Bank of Greece, Foreign Trade Dvision. *Greek Production and Exports in Figures.* February 1959; 2nd ed., February 1960.

United Nations, Food and Agriculture Organization. *Report of the FAO Mission for Greece.* Washington, March 1947.

Varvaressos, Kyriakos. *Report on the Greek Economic Problem at the Request of the Government of Greece.* Mimeographed, Washington, 1952.

Notes

CHAPTER I. THE PEOPLE OF GREECE

1. This version of the legend was told by an old shepherd to a hunting party which had taken refuge in his hut from a storm brewing over Lake Stymphalia in the northern Peloponnesos. Mrs. Bessie Adossides, who served as my interpreter, had been in the party and told the story to me. For a less colorful version, see A. W. Gomme, *Greece* (London, 1945), p. 11.

2. A prominent subgrouping running through these three divisions is that of the Asia Minor and other refugees who were settled in Greece in the 1920s. Also, divisions among the city Greeks appeared following the French Revolution, when commercial opportunities opened up, creating a new merchant bourgeoisie in contrast to the "old patriarchal class whose members were the political administrators of the Sublime Porte and whose strength lay in landed wealth and special prerogatives." See S. G. Chaconas, *Adamantios Korais: A Study in Greek Nationalism* (New York, 1942), p. 38.

3. S. Manolas, in a personal conversation, pointed out three factors accounting for the settlement in cities of Greeks coming to America: as "late" immigrants, there was little land available to them for homesteading; they came over individually — not as families — and could not run a farm; they were not here to work the land, for Greece was still their home. They wanted to make money and go back, staying on here to take care of "one more dowry, one more acre to buy." For many, time ran out and they did not go back. To these one might also add the Greek's unfamiliarity with the mechanized agriculture found in the United States and the greater ease with which he found employment in the cities.

4. This point of view is borne out in an article by Anton-Hermann Chroust, "Treason and Patriotism in Ancient Greece," *Journal of the History of Ideas*, April 1954: "The democrats, like the oligarchs, bore their native city a quite strange kind of love: the desire to dominate it completely and, if necessary, to exterminate their political antagonists. . . . It would be difficult, indeed, to find a prominent Athenian politician, irrespective of his political persuasion, whose public actions were not motivated by partisanship or loyalty to some faction or club within the city rather than by true patriotism," p. 287.

5. The books dealing with the history of Albania, Bulgaria, Serbia, and Rumania usually discuss the role of the Greek clergy in the spread of Greek culture. As one example, see N. Forbes and others, *The Balkans: A History of Bulgaria, Serbia, Greece, Rumania, Turkey* (Oxford, 1915).

6. A good characterization of the city Greek by Dorothy Lee appears in Margaret Mead, ed., *Cultural Patterns and Technical Change* (Paris, UNESCO, 1953), p. 79: "The city Greeks consider themselves very different from the peasants. There is a vogue for peasant handicrafts but not for peasant attitudes. Urban Greeks like to take on the ways of foreigners, to use the products of technology, even the processed foods of technology. Many French and English words are used in their speech.

They take on the attitudes of the Western World, using clocked time in business and living a life relatively pressed for time, adopting to some extent the Western scientific approach and objective external limits, instead of the more animistic approach and the body-patterned limits of traditional Greek culture."

W. Miller, in *Greek Life in Town and Country* (London, 1905), gives a penetrating description of Greek urban life fifty years ago.

7. Robert P. T. Coffin, *Hellas Revisited* (Athens, 1954), p. 35.

8. Bruce Lansdale, director of the American Farm School of Salonica, maintains in a letter that the qualities I have set forth for the city Greek hold for the villages as well: "Almost any villager can give you some very sound ideas on how the Greek government should be run as well as how the American, the Russian, the British, and any government in the world should be run. I remember hearing from villagers at the time of the Dewey-Truman election campaign that they were quite sure that Truman would win the election, which in fact he did. I would furthermore say that the intellectual curiosity of the villager is every bit as great if not greater than that of the urban Greek. This is in part because he does not have the pseudo-sophistication of the urban Greek."

9. For an anecdote illustrating the Athenian attitude toward the peasant, see H. D. F. Kitto, *In the Mountains of Greece* (London, 1933), pp. 138–139.

10. One Greek friend, well known for his frankness and objectivity, reacted to my characterization of the city Greeks as follows: "I, as a Greek knowing my Greeks, would add that he is a spendthrift, since a great percentage of the Athens families are living beyond their income; he is an individualist; he is suffering, and has since his appearance, from megalomania which pushes him into starting to build marvelous things without funds."

11. For further information about the islanders, see Andreas Adossides, "Fishermen of the Aegean," *Geographical Magazine* (London), XIV (1941), 86–91. One of the most complete studies in English of the folklore of any Greek island is that by Philip P. Argenti, *The Folk-Lore of Chios,* 2 vols. (Cambridge, Eng., 1949). See also J. Theodore Bent, "On Insular Greek Customs," *Journal of the Anthropological Institute,* XV (1885–1886); and Nikolas G. Chaliores, *Hydreika Laographika* (Concerning the Folklore of the Island of Hydra (Hydra, 1931), chiefly a collection of customs surrounding the engagement, wedding, pregnancy and childbirth, death, the church, holidays, the sea, and the building of a house. Peter Gray's *The People of Poros* (New York, 1942) is a highly entertaining account of a sojourn just prior to World War II on this attractive island southeast of the Peloponnesos. See also Osbert Lancaster, "The Island Greeks," *Atlantic Monthly,* CLXXXII (1948), 59–64; and H. F. Tozer, *The Islands of the Aegean* (London, 1890).

12. Of course, many areas and even villages on the mainland have special characteristics for which they are noted and which have developed through long years of relative isolation. The Maniates from Mani in the southern Peloponnesos afford one such example. See P. L. Fermor, *Mani: Travels in the Southern Peloponnese* (New York, 1958).

13. By far the most helpful book on Greek peasant life was written by Rennell Rodd, *The Customs and Lore of Modern Greece* (London, 1892). It has proven a bench-mark against which to gauge my own impressions sixty years later.

Jacques Ancel is one of the few historians writing about the Balkans who takes the peasant into account. See his *Peuples et nations des Balkans* (Paris, 1926), pp. 107–114. Considerable insight into the nonmaterial culture of the mountain people of Thessaly is gained from A. Hadjigakis, *T 'Aspropotamo Pindou* (The Village of Aspropotamo in the Pindus Mountains), 3 vols. (Trikkala, 1946–1950). See also V. Valaoras, "To Helleniko Chorio" (The Greek Village), *Ellin-Ellinitha* [sic] (Hellenic-American Monthly Review), VII (1956).

14. No purpose would be served in a book of this sort in trying to trace the controversy and weigh the arguments for and against the Greek claims of direct descent from the ancient Hellenes. On the one hand, we have the extreme (and today unaccepted) view of Jacob Philipp Fallmerayer that Slavic invaders from the north

completely replaced any Hellenic stock. His *Geschichte der Halbinsel Morea Während des Mittelalters* (History of the Peninsula of Morea in the Middle Ages) (1830) is one of his important works. This has been refuted by Karl Hopf, who claimed that Fallmerayer used documentary evidence which was proven false.

Other works dealing with this question are those by George Finlay, *History of Greece from its Conquest by the Romans to the Present Time*, 7 vols. (London, 1877); Rodd, *Customs and Lore;* and J. C. Lawson, *Modern Greek Folklore and Ancient Greek Religion: A Study in Survivals* (Cambridge, Eng., 1910).

A detailed analysis of the problems would involve two separate investigations: (1) that from the standpoint of physical anthropology to determine the biological resemblances of the modern Greeks to those living in classic times; and (2) the survival of the cultural traditions, including the Greek language, from the days of early Grecian greatness to the present. After these investigations have been made there remains the even more difficult — and perhaps impossible — task of relating point one — the biological — to point two — the cultural. But the reader is entitled to the interpretation given by educated Greeks to the presence in Greece of different-language-speaking groups. According to Ph. Annino Cavalierato, former Counsellor of the Royal Greek Embassy in Washington and now in the Foreign Office in Athens:

"The Albanian and the Vlach dialects, spoken in some areas, denote a foreign influence on a segment of the Greek people rather than the existence of a racial minority. The same could be said about the Heptanesian dialect, a blend of Greek and Venetian Italian. These dialects, Albanian, Vlach, Heptanesian, tend to disappear, and this is another proof of their superficial character: had they been truly the national feature of a minority, they would be perpetuated by education and culture. Being, instead, a passing historical accident, people care little about them and allow them slowly to disappear.

"As for the 'Macedonian' dialect, it should be noted that a 'Macedonian' dialect and a 'Macedonian' nation are both a fairly recent political invention. According to most linguists, 'Macedonian' is just a Bulgarian patois. During the days of the Ottoman Empire, the province of Macedonia was inhabited by Turks, Greeks, Serbs, and Bulgars, the three latter ethnic elements being denser in areas closer to the respective countries. At the outcome of the Balkan Wars (1912–13) and of World War I (1914–18), this province was distributed among Greece, Serbia and Bulgaria. A wide exchange of populations followed, as a result of which each individual was free to resettle in the country he considered his own. It is reasonable to assume, then, that those who remained in each country consider themselves as nationals of that particular country. There is only one explanation for the fact that Bulgarian is still spoken by some Greeks of Western Macedonia, while Greek, that was widely spoken in Southern Bulgaria, for example, has completely disappeared from that area. The reader will easily find explanation for this.

"Turkish is the only foreign language spoken in Greece by a minority in the true sense of the word. This Muslim minority, living mainly in Western Thrace, was not exchanged in 1923, as were other Turks living in Greece, because the Greek minority of Constantinople was also allowed to remain in their homes."

CHAPTER II. MOUNTAINS, PLAINS, AND THE SEA

1. The artist is Mrs. Maria Alexandrakes, who has also been connected with the Local Government Division of the American Mission. She helped us gain many revealing insights into Greek Life.

2. For two Greek sources on the habitat, see George Megas, *Geographia tes Ellados* (Geography of Greece) (Athens, 1958); and George Kolias, *Historike Geographia tou Hellenikou Chorou* (Historical Geography of the Greek People) (Athens, 1948). For especially useful sources in English, see *A Handbook of Greece* (London,

the British Admiralty, 1930); and M. L. Newbigin, *Southern Europe: A Regional and Economic Geography of the Mediterranean Lands* (3rd ed., London, 1949).

3. One still finds many similarities between the peasants of Hesiod's time (see his "Works and Days") and those of today.

4. Many allusions to nature are found in the passionate novel about the Communist guerrilla war by Panos D. Bardis, *Ivan and Artemis* (New York, 1957).

5. "The Holy Virgin's Hand" is mentioned on p. 123 of G. F. Abbott, *Macedonian Folklore* (Cambridge, Eng., 1903). This book gives a number of examples of the peasants' use of and adaptation to nature.

6. For a delightful essay on the flowers of Greece, see "Flowers of Ancient Greece," *The Christian Science Monitor*, April 23, 1954.

7. For an earlier account of peasant cosmological beliefs, see the article by N. G. Politis in *Attikon Emerologion* (1882); also G. Kapsalis, "Meteorologikes paroimiakes Phraseis" (Meteorological Proverbial Phrases), *Laographia*, XIII (1950).

8. One of the most authentic documents on Greek village life came into my hands through a mutual acquaintance of T. K. Papaspyropoulos, the author. This account is in Greek typescript, from which the passages used in my book have been translated with the permission of the author. Mr. Papaspyropoulos teaches singing in one of Athens' secondary schools and has specialized in folk music. I accompanied him on a visit to his village, where I had a chance to observe at first hand many of the sights he so colorfully describes.

9. A very common phrase among the peasants is *Ean theli o Theos* (If God is willing), to which one replies *Vevea, prota o Theos* (Yes, of course, first God).

10. Interesting observations on the use in Homer of the ancient Greek terms *atē* (divine temptation or infatuation, cause of irrational actions) and *moira* (portion or lot) are found in E. R. Dodds, *The Greeks and the Irrational* (Berkeley and Los Angeles, 1951).

11. The facts and figures used in this section are taken in large part from *Report of the FAO Mission for Greece* (Washington, 1947), and *Story of the American Marshall Plan in Greece, July 1, 1948 to Jan. 1, 1952*, Press Release No. 1300, MSA (Athens, July 20, 1952).

12. For the problem of soil erosion, see Constantine I. Nevros, "Soil Erosion in Greece," *Soil Conservation*, VI (1940), and F. G. Renner, "Erosion, Trojan Horse of Greece," *National Geographic*, December 1947. For forestry, see W. Miller, *Greek Town and Country Life* (London, 1905), pp. 229–232.

13. E. G. Mariolopoulos and A. N. Livathinos, in *Atlas climatique de la Grèce* (Athens, 1935), give a good description of the Greek climate.

14. For two views on the sun (Helios) and St. Elias, see the articles by N. G. Politis in *Laographika Symmikta B'* (1921), and E. Rein, "Zu der Verehrung des Propheten Elias bei den Neugriechen," *Ofversigt af Finska Vetenskaps-Societetens Förhandlingar*, XLVII (1904–1905).

15. Percy F. Martin, *Greece of the Twentieth Century* (London, 1913), pp. 267–68, discusses the company-tenant relations worked out at Lake Kopais as of 1913.

16. One friend wrote in 1959: "Fresh fish has always been expensive. Earlier this winter there was a sudden 50 percent price rise. We ourselves cannot afford fresh fish and buy frozen fish brought in by Greek boats from the Atlantic, which is now available in many parts of Greece. It is a scandal that abundant fresh fish at reasonable prices is not available to the Greeks."

17. This gorgon is really a sea nymph or mermaid (*gorgona* in modern Greek) and not one of the classical gorgons of terrifying aspect (Medusa and her sisters).

18. Elias Venezis, *Aeolia*, trans. from the Greek by E. D. Scott-Kilvert (London, 1949), p. 94.

CHAPTER III. THE VILLAGE SETTING

1. Sir Charles Eliot, *Turkey in Europe* (London, 1900), p. 333.

2. In a village of Central Greece (Schematari), for instance, where the people number about 1800, I found in 1953 four small grocery stores, four coffeehouses (any one of which might also serve as a tavern), one bakery, one post office, one elementary school and one secondary school, one church, one motor-driven mill for grinding corn and wheat. There is one telephone, no electricity, four or five battery radios.

3. Numerous references are made throughout this book to information taken from thirteen Greek village studies conducted by the Near East Foundation for the Greek Ministry of Agriculture and the United States Economic Cooperation Administration. The studies were made in 1951 and 1952 and issued in Athens in mimeographed form, first in Greek and later in English. The first seven were directed by William J. Tudor and the last six by E. J. Kilpatrick. A general summary of content and complete bibliographical data may be found in my article, "Village Social Organization in Greece," *Rural Sociology,* December 1953, pp. 366–375. In most cases this series will be referred to here collectively as "village studies," but the individual titles are as follows: "A Village in Central Greece" (19 pp.), "A Village in the Arta Plains" (8 pp.), "A Macedonian Village" (14 pp.), "A Village in the Agrinion Area" (16 pp.), "A 'Control' Village of the Mesolongi Area" (12 pp.), "A 'Control' Village in Macedonia" (14 pp.), "A Village in the Serres Plain" (9 pp.), "A Mountain Village, Grammos Area" (16 pp.), "A Mesolongi Village (Irrigated)" (19 pp.), "A Tobacco Village in Xanthe Nomos" (17 pp.), "A Mountain Village, Lamia Area" (13 pp.), "A Livestock One-Half-Irrigated Village" (15 pp.), and "A Village in the Plain of Veria" (14 pp.).

4. T. K. Papaspyropoulos, "Ta Laographika tes Kleitorias" (Concerning the Folklore of Kleitoria), unpublished ms., no date.

5. UNNRA, *Greece, Ripe for Improvement* (Washington, D.C., 1946), pp. 9–10.

6. Henry Morgenthau, *I Was Sent to Athens* (Garden City, 1929).

7. H. D. F. Kitto before World War II commented on the peasant's strong desire for good roads: "The village of Proussos is large, but not prosperous, in spite of the fertility of the soil. The only shop contains next to nothing; even the lemons were scraggy. Time after time we were told: 'If only we had a road! Then we could send our stuff away.' Eight hours by mule — transport is slow and expensive, and for the fruit which Proussos produces in profusion, nearly useless." From *In the Mountains of Greece* (London, 1933), p. 43.

In 1952 Pierce College students working in their adopted village in Northern Greece invited the Presidents of ten nearby village councils to come to a meeting in the adopted village. They arrived with difficulty, and most complained because their villages were off the road where people didn't see them.

8. *Medical and Sanitary Data on Greece,* revised by Public Health Division, Mutual Security Agency Mission to Greece (Athens, June 1952), mimeographed, pp. 12–13.

9. A report prepared by an American engineering firm for the Greek government on a proposed hydroelectric project points out: "The rural villages obtain their water from artesian wells, drilled or driven tube wells, springs and streams. In most of the villages the water supply is both inadequate and subject to contamination. As none of the villages have standard pressure distribution systems, much time and labor is expended in carrying water from wells and springs. Most of the rural homes are small and poorly lighted, and sanitary facilities are primitive."

10. *Medical and Sanitary Data on Greece,* p. 25.

11. Useful works on the Greek house are: K. Doxiades and others, *Dodekanesos: to oikistiko kai plastiko provlema* (The Dodecanese: The Problem of Housing from the Point of Design) (Athens, 1950); D. Loukopoulos, *Aitolikai oikesseis, skeve kai trophai* (Aetolian Housing, Tools, and Food) (Athens, 1926); D. E. Kalitsounakes,

"Oikismos-astyphilia" (Housing and Urbanism), *Megale Hellenike Enkyklopaideia* (Large Greek Encyclopaedia), X (Athens, 1934), 412–413; and Angelike Chatze-michale, "Architektonike" (Architecture), *ibid.*, pp. 826–827. See also G. A. Megas, *The Greek House. Its Evolution and its Relation to the Houses of Other Balkan Peoples* (Athens, 1951).

12. Papaspyropoulos, "Folklore of Kleitoria."
13. Megas, *The Greek House,* pp. 6, 8.

CHAPTER IV. LAND AS A BIRTHRIGHT

1. Figures for size of farm are taken from *Statistical Summary of Greece, 1954.* These figures differ somewhat from those quoted in *Greece Today* (August 1954), which is published monthly by the National Bank of Greece and Athens. The latter places 27 percent of the farms at less than 2.5 acres and 57.5 percent between 2.5 and 12.5 acres. See also *Labour Problems in Greece: Report of the Mission of the International Labour Office to Greece,* Oct.–Nov. 1947 (Geneva, 1949).

2. Anyone familiar with Greek mythology will find it tempting to try to link the peasant's present attachment to his land with the folk beliefs about "the mistress of the world," which J. C. Lawson, in his *Modern Greek Folklore and Ancient Greek Religion: A Study in Survivals* (Cambridge, Eng., 1910), links with Demeter or Kore, or both. "She is a real person, not the personification of any natural force. The tiller of the land foresees his yearly gain from cornfield and vineyard; the shepherd on the mountainside expects the yearly increase of his flock; but by neither is any principle inferred therefrom, much less is such a principle personified; the blessing which rests on field and fold is the work of a living goddess' hand" (p. 89). Even more to the point may be the early belief in the earth as the mother because she is the fruit bearer. See J. E. Harrison, *Themis: A Study of the Social Origins of Greek Religion* (Cambridge, Eng., 1912), pp. 166–167.

Conceivably, these cultural survivals could explain part of the hold on many peasants of the belief that land is sacred, that it should be kept as a family heritage, that it is the source of life's security; but this would not help us understand the regional variations in Greece today or the differing points of view between the older and younger generations within the same region. Obviously, economic considerations are greatly altering the picture.

3. Another point needing further study in the Greek villages is the degree to which the seeming attachment to the soil is really that or, instead, a strong sense of localism, an attachment to a *place.* The travelers for generations through Greece have commented on this localism, which found its early expression in the city-state as opposed to an over-all *imperium.* It is possible that with many Greek peasants this localistic spirit, such as that noted for Epirus, is based on psychological attachments to things and persons quite apart from the soil.

4. See Panos D. Bardis, "The Changing Family in Modern Greece," *Sociology and Social Research,* XL (1955), 19–23.

5. Bruce Lansdale reminded me that the farmer who puts in a vineyard is probably thinking in terms of his children more than himself and that the man who puts in an olive tree is probably thinking in terms of his grandchildren. In certain areas of Greece it is customary to plant a tree for the dowry of the daughter. There are also differences in attitudes toward land between the native peasant and the refugee from Asia Minor, for many refugees do not yet have the actual deed to their land.

6. What happened in Epirus under the Turks must have occurred in many parts of Greece. When the Turks first overran Epirus, the villages were independent, but the Turkish government placed a Turkish military protector in charge of a locality. This official said: "In order for us to keep you secure, you have to pay 10 percent in kind." Then it rose to 15, 20, and even up to 33 percent. When the peasants could not pay these high taxes, the officials took over the land and became large land-

owners, even having the power to keep the peasants off the land they formerly owned. In Epirus, land redistribution in the 1920s involved finding out who the former Greek owners had been or still were, once the land had been appropriated from the Turks with an indemnity payment. In Thessaly, however, there were no former Greek peasant owners to locate, so the large Turkish-owned estates were merely redistributed to peasants who had worked them as hired workers or tenants.

7. The quotation about the sixth century B.C. comes from *The Cambridge Ancient History*, V, 12.

8. Most of the information on which the description of land tenure in Attica is based comes from P. J. Iliopoulos, *L'Attique au point de vue physique et économique* (Athens, 1951).

9. For a discussion of agrarian conditions in the Byzantine Empire in the Middle Ages, see the chapter by that title in *The Cambridge Economic History*, I.

10. See K. D. Karavidas, *Agrotika* (Athens, 1931), whose sections on the *tsiflikia* and *kephalochoria* proved particularly helpful in an effort to gain a proper background. In a private conversation, Mr. Karavidas pointed out that some acute problems arose when the tsiflikia were broken up and distributed to the former tenants. Under the landlord, the workers were forced to keep irrigation ditches clear, but when redistribution occurred in 1923 nobody worried about the maintenance of such ditches. Trees fell into them and they became stopped up.

11. *L'Attique*, p. 115.

12. One of the best short descriptions of land ownership in Greece is an article by that title in *Foreign Agriculture*, August 1950. The article is adapted from the book by A. Varvaressos, *The Fulfilment of the Agrarian Reform* (Athens, 1949). Another useful account of land reform in Greece is found in W. E. Moore, *Economic Demography of Eastern and Southern Europe*, appendix 3. D. K. Wogasli wrote extensively on questions of land reform, publishing in 1919 a work entitled *La Solution de la question agraire en Grèce* (Athens, 1919). He also wrote a work in Greek on the agrarian question in Thessaly and especially in the prefecture of Trikkala.

It is interesting to contrast Thessaly of today with that described by Leon Heuzey, *Excursion dans la Thessalie Turque en 1858*. Of the village of Vloko, he writes: "Là, je me renseigne comme à l'ordinaire, sur la condition des paysans. Le propriétaire, Hassan-bey, les déplace à sa volonté, bien que lui-même, à l'heure actuelle, tienne un homme en prison pour avoir cherché à quitter son tchiflik. Malgré les nouvelles lois, le régime de la glèbe existe encore, mais ce n'est pas toujours dans les conditions d'équité qui pourraient le rendre tolerable pour le cultivateur" (p. 76).

13. A common practice on the part of a landlord was to transfer title to various parts of the estate to close relatives, who permitted him to continue to operate the farm as one unit.

14. The Agricultural Section of the United States Mission to Greece and officials of the Greek Ministry of Agriculture have given much study to the problem of consolidation of scattered strips. The great amount of time required for surveying even one village for this purpose is hard to believe. At least twenty villages have been surveyed by Dr. Kypriades and attractive picture displays prepared to show what can be done when consolidation is carried out.

15. For more on the domka system, see O. S. Morgan, ed., *Agricultural Systems of Middle Europe* (New York, 1933), chapter by Georges Servakis and C. Pertountzi entitled "The Agricultural Policy of Greece." On the problem of scattered strips, see the *Report of the FAO Mission for Greece* (Washington, D.C., 1947), in which Recommendation 71 deals with consolidation and land redistribution.

16. UNRRA, *Greece, Ripe for Improvement: A Study of Marginal Land Farming in Greece* (Washington, D.C., 1946), p. 9.

17. Frederick Strong, *Greece as a Kingdom* (London, 1842), pp. 163–164. But in 1914 Lucy M. J. Garnett, in *Greece of the Hellenes* (London, 1914), wrote as follows: "It is . . . foreign emigration that is robbing Hellas of her hardy peasantry. and this constitutes one of the most serious problems with which the Hellenic Gov-

ernment is at the present confronted. For Greece *has no surplus population,* and, if the country is to prosper, the services of every able-bodied man and boy are needed for the proper development of its natural resources. Weekly emigrant steamers carry large numbers to Western lands and bring but few back . . . with the consequence that many agricultural districts are left without labourers to till the soil" (p. 133).

For more on this emigration, see Theodore Saloutos, *They Remember America: The Story of the Re-Patriated Greek-Americans* (Berkeley and Los Angeles, 1956); and Henry Pratt Fairchild, *Greek Immigration to the United States* (New Haven, 1911).

18. The figures used in this presentation of land use are taken from *Greece Today* (August 1954); from Bickham Sweet-Escott, *Greece: A Political and Economic Survey, 1939–1953* (London, 1954); and from data supplied by the United States Department of Agriculture. In these three sources the years differ, as do some of the categories of land use, but the details prove interesting.

19. The study on idle lands made by the American Mission for Aid to Greece appeared in mimeographed form in 1952 and was based on detailed reports turned in by the field representatives of the Civil Government Division of the Mission. The report was issued by William M. Tait, who was then deputy director for field service. Other informants point out that in Epirus, and probably elsewhere, thousands of acres are owned by Greek-Americans in the United States, and Greek villagers do not feel free to make use of such idle lands.

20. For a discussion of these exports, see E. J. Bell, "Greece, Exporter of Farm Products," *Foreign Agriculture,* March 1958, pp. 5–6.

21. The use of lots in dividing up a patrimony among brothers in a Boeotian village is described in an article by Harry L. Levy, "Property Distribution by Lot in Greece," *Transactions of the American Philological Association,* LXXXVII (1956).

Chapter V. The Peasant at Work

1. The unpublished manuscript from which this comes is "Ta Laographika tes Kleitorias" (Concerning the Folklore of Kleitoria).

2. UNRRA, *Greece, Ripe for Improvement: A Study of Marginal Land Farming in Greece* (Washington, D.C., 1946), p. 8.

3. Robert P. T. Coffin, *Hellas Revisited,* p. 14.

4. Dr. Charles House, former director of the American Farm School in Salonica, played a great part in preparing the way for mechanization in Northern Greece, since the students at this school were taught how to operate and repair tractors long before they began to appear in so many villages. He said that one argument for the use of the tractor in preference to the draft animal was the fact that the animals ate up too much of the farm produce.

5. For the full World War II picture, see C. S. Stephanides, "Agricultural Machinery in Greece," *Foreign Agriculture,* XII (November 1948), 250–253.

6. Supplementary labor is an important element in the economy of many families and even whole villages. In the Peloponnesos people from the mountain villages can harvest olives and help with the pressing of the oil, receiving pay in kind. When they help with the vineyards they are paid in money, as they are in Macedonia when they help plant tobacco. Near Ioannina there are villages specializing in certain crafts from which many men go during the winter to ply their trades.

7. "A Tobacco Village in Xanthe Nomos," (1952, mimeographed), prepared by A. Argyropoulos. One of the village studies conducted by the Near East Foundation for the Greek Ministry of Agriculture and the United States Economic Cooperation Administration. The following comment about this village (Dafnon) by John D. Photiadis is helpful: "I have served as a county agent in that area and I think that Dafnon is not a representative village. It is considered the poorest village in the area and the most stricken by the reduction of prices of Turkish tobacco. This is because

tobacco is the only product they can raise due to the lack of additional land. I think this is the reason why the Mission sent somebody to do a study of the village in 1952" (personal communication).

CHAPTER VI. THE CHANGING LIFE OF THE SHEPHERD

1. It is of interest to note the breakdown by products on a percentage basis for the total income from sheep. Figures for Greece are taken from C. S. Stephanides, "Sheep — Man's Best Friend in Greece," *Foreign Agriculture,* XII (July 1948), 153–155, as is the quotation about the characteristics of the Greek sheep used in the text of this chapter. Kentucky figures are from C. D. Phillips and J. L. Pearson of the University of Kentucky College of Agriculture.

	Greece	*Kentucky*
Milk and milk products	45.10	
Mutton	14.26 ⎤	
Lamb	24.77 ⎦	84.00
Wool	8.68	16.00
Hides	7.19	
	100.00%	100.00%

2. Although this chapter is primarily concerned with some of the human factors in the small livestock industry, the table below will give some basic information for those interested in livestock numbers and products. These data are based on official Greek Ministry of Agriculture figures.

Total Number of Sheep and Goats, Greece (In Thousands)

Period	Sheep	Goats
1935–38 (average)	8,304	5,111
1938	8,139	4,356
1945	6,262	3,066
1946	7,228	3,462
1949	6,785	3,629
1954	8,738	4,643
1957 (estimate)	9,300	4,900

3. See P. J. Iliopoulos, *L' Attique au point de vue physique et économique* (Athens, 1951). Three other studies that deal with sheep production are: P. H. Kontos, *Dase kai ktenotrophia eis ten Hellada apo oikonomikes kai politikes apopseus* (Forestry and Livestock Production in Greece from the Economic and Political Aspect) (Thessalonike, 1932); G. D. Kyriakos, *E Ktenotrophia mas* (Our Livestock Industry) (Athens, 1941); V. Handziolos, *To Provlema tes ktenotrophias en Helladi* (The Problem of the Livestock Industry in Greece) (Athens, 1941).

4. The description of the three systems of grazing practices (Vlachs, village ranchers, and village farmers) is taken from the American Embassy, Athens, Report No. 1056 (February 29, 1952), p. 13.

5. The study of transhumance as a habitat adjustment is almost a field in itself and will not be tackled here. Suffice it to say that I recognize the difference geographers make between transhumance and nomadism. Nevertheless, in the next section on the "nomads" of Epirus, I have followed conventional practice in thus alluding to these people, although most of them may actually be practicing transhumance rather than nomadism.

6. An interesting source in this connection is Jovan Cvijic's *La Péninsule balkanique, géographie humaine* (Paris, 1918). This was published in French before it

appeared in Serbo-Croatian, the author's mother tongue. In 1922 the first volume entitled *Balkansko Poluostrvo i Južnoslovenske Zemlje: Osnove Antropogeografije* (418 pp.) appeared in Belgrade. Volume two (254 pp.) appeared in 1931 with the subtitle *Psihičke Osobine Južnih Slovena* (Psychic Characteristics of the South Slavs). The connection between Cvijic's work and the present study is the interesting map facing p. 282 of volume one, which shows the migration patterns of the various shepherd groups throughout the Balkans. Any thorough study of shifting migration habits would have to take Cvijic's work as a starting point at least, although this would not imply accepting all of his generalizations about the effect of the physical environment upon social life.

7. Although no attempt has been made to cover the literature dealing with sheep production in the Peloponnesos, I have noted in passing that Z. Duckett Ferriman, in *Home Life in Hellas: Greece and the Greeks* (London, 1910), tells of the pastoral pursuits of those living near the site of ancient Sparta early in this century: "Pastoral occupations become a necessity where tillage is impossible, and in every land the wildest districts are the domain of the shepherd, who is the most uncultured element of the population, and also the hardiest. The youths of Sparta were not kept in the valley, but sent up into Taygetus to acquire the training which they turned to account against the Messenians of the plain. . . . And so, today, the Arcadian mountaineers are noted for their strength and hardihood, and are perforce shepherds. Every cottage has its flock, tended during the day by children, elusive, faun-like beings, who manifest neither pleasure nor discontent nor surprise at the presence of the stranger, so unlike in this to the inquisitive, obtrusive Greek child of the towns and villages of the lowlands. At sunset they are relieved of their task by their fathers, who keep watch by night against wolf and robber. At the end of October all the livestock is moved to the plains, marching in solid phalanx, goats in front, sheep in the middle, mules and donkeys behind, the well-armed shepherds and their fierce dogs on either flank" (pp. 28–29).

Another interesting source is volume one of *Travels in the Morea* (London, 1830), by William Martin Leake. Interesting information about sheepraising in the western Peloponnesos is found in K. N. Eliopoulos, "Poimenika tes Eleias" (Pastoral Life in Elis), *Laographia*, XII (1938), 253–285.

8. Many travelers to the Balkans come into contact with these nomads and write about them. M. E. Picot, *Les Roumains de la Macédoine* (Paris, 1875), analyzes all of the source material available to him, and prior works need not be cited here. Lucy M. J. Garnett, *Greece of the Hellenes* (London, 1914), devotes a few pages to pastoral life, stressing particularly the appearance of a Vlach encampment and the authority of the Vlach chieftains. Sir Charles Eliot, *Turkey in Europe* (London, 1900) makes this interesting comment on the Vlachs in Macedonia: "They remind one of those ingenious pictures in which an animal or a human face is concealed so as not to be obvious on first inspection, though when once seen it appears to be the principal feature of the drawing. In the same way, one may live and travel in the Balkan lands without seeing or hearing anything of the Vlachs, until one's eyes are opened. Then one runs the risk of going to the opposite extreme and thinking, like Roumanian patriots, that most of the inhabitants of Macedonia are Vlachs in disguise" (p. 409).

Andreas Adossides, "The Shepherds of Greece," *Geographical Magazine*, September 1943, pp. 217–225, gives a vividly written account.

Jovan Cvijic, "The Geographical Distribution of the Balkan Peoples," *The Geographical Review*, V (June 1918), 470–482, estimates the number of Arumani (or Vlachs) at about 150,000 to 160,000 scattered individuals. He points out that during the Middle Ages they were very numerous and constituted the majority of the population in Thessaly and in Aetolia, two areas respectively called Great and Little Vlachia.

V. T. Vikas, "Ethima para Vlahophonois," (Customs of the Vlach-Speaking People), *Laographia*, VI (1917), 169–188, is chiefly a description of holidays and recreation.

G. F. Abbott, *The Tale of a Tour in Macedonia* (London, 1903), gives evidence of the degree of Hellenization of the Vlachs fifty years ago.

H. N. Brailsford, *Macedonia: Its Races and Their Future* (London, 1906), devotes a whole chapter to the Vlachs, beginning with the description of Pisoderi, which he considers a typical village. He also, contrary to Abbott above, foresees a weakening of connection between the Vlachs and the Greeks.

Rennell Rodd traces the derivations of the word Vlach and provides some historical background in his book *The Customs and Lore of Modern Greece* (London, 1892).

9. This is a thoroughgoing study of their migration practices, costumes, birth, marriage, burial customs, intervillage relationships, the distribution of the Vlachs, the Vlach language, and the history and origin of the Balkan Vlachs. Full citation is: A. J. B. Wace and M. S. Thompson, *The Nomads of the Balkans: An Account of Life and Customs Among the Vlachs of Northern Pindus* (London, 1914).

Without attempting to cover the references to the Vlachs in other Balkan languages, I might mention one in Serbo-Croatian, entitled *O Cincarima* (Concerning the Cincari), by D. J. Popovic (Beograd, 1937). These Tsintsars are Serbized Vlachs, who have also become urbanized. Th. Capidan, himself a Koutso-Vlach who studied and lived in Roumania, has written very extensively about these Balkan nomads, primarily with the purpose of showing that all of them, even the Greek-speaking Sarakatsani, were originally Koutso-Vlachs. See his *Les Macédo-roumains. Esquisse historique et descriptive des populations roumaines* (Bucarest, 1937).

10. See Carsten Höeg, *Les Saracatsans, une tribe grecque* (Paris, 1925), for an excellent linguistic study. D. J. Georgacas, in his "Peri tes katagoges ton Sarakatsanaion kai tou Onomatos Auton" (Concerning the Origin of the Sarakatsani and Their Name), *Archeion Thrakikou Glossikou kai Laographikou Thesaurou*, XIV (1948–49), 193–270, argues against Höeg's theory that the Sarakatsani derive from an ancient nomadic tribe and claims that they did not become nomadic until the late Middle Ages.

11. This work of Demosthenes Sirakes is the best Greek source on the nomads. It discusses almost every possible aspect of their life, particularly in the economic sphere, and tries to indicate how the nomadic livestock producers can best be settled. Although the figures quoted here are old, they are probably as reliable as most estimates would be today. Full citation of the article is: "Orismos nomadikes, monimou kai georgikes ktenotrophias e e nomadike ktenotrophia en Helladi," *Georgikon Deltion tes Hellenikes Georgikes Etaireias* (Agricultural Bulletin of the Greek Agricultural Society), XII (1925), 651–777.

12. Z. Duckett Ferriman, mentioned in note 7 above, has even more to say about the undesirable qualities of the nomads (see pp. 45–54). He calls the reader's attention to the shepherds' dogs as follows: "We are apt to associate the name of sheep dog with collie. That graceful and sympathetic member of the canine family is far removed from the savage cerberi who guard the folds of Greece. Huge and powerful mastiffs, with heavy jowls and ensanguined eyes, they are no doubt valuable auxiliaries in the presence of marauding wolves. But, like their master, they are of low intelligence, and they take everyone except their masters for a wolf" (p. 52).

13. The work by K. Koukkides, *To pnevma tou synergatismou ton neoteron hellenon kai t'Ambelakia, o protos synetairismos tou kosmou* (Athens, 1948), is a splendid source for the study of patterns of mutual aid.

14. It is of historic interest to note that many of these chief shepherds became important klephts during the days of Turkish rule over Epirus and Northern Greece. If the klepht was friendly to you, he was known as a guerrilla leader; if he opposed you, he was a bandit. It was ever thus in the Balkans.

15. For a scholarly treatment in Greek of the tselingata, one should consult K. Karavides, *Agrotika* (Concerning Rural Life) (Athens, 1931). He analyzes for the rural Balkans as a whole four major forms of economic organization: the tselingata, the feudal tsifliki (estate), the patriarchal family which he associates with the zadruga, and the kephalochoria, or independent village where the peasants were their

own proprietors even under Ottoman rule. Also see D. Loukopoulos, *Poimenika tes Roumeles* (Pastoral Life in Roumele) (Athens, 1930).

16. Some of the references to particular villages are taken from the village studies of the Near East Foundation, the Mutual Security Administration, and the Greek Ministry of Agriculture (mimeographed, 1951, 1952).

An account of some shepherd festivals is found in an article by K. Marines, "Vlahopanegyria," *Nea Estia,* XI (1932), 586–590. Although this work deals only with the mainland of Greece, some readers interested in the islands may wish to consult the following representative studies of sheepraising there: For Chios: Philip P. Argenti and H. J. Rose, *The Folk-Lore of Chios,* 2 vols. (Cambridge, Eng., 1949); G. Madias, "Oi Poimenes en Kardamylois" (Life of the Shepherds in Kardamyla-Chios), *Laographia,* VI, 225–226. For the Dodecanese: K. Doxiades and others, "Dodekanesos: Genike perigraphe" (The Dodecanese: General Description), *Ministry of Reconstruction Series,* no. 21 (Athens, 1947), 109–117; An. G. Vrontes, "E melissokomia kai to mandradorema ste Rodo" (Beekeeping and Sheepraising in Rhodes), *Laographia,* XII, 209–228. For Karpathos: M. G. Michailides-Nouaros, *Laographika symmikta Karpathou* (Folklore Miscellany for Karpathos), (Athens, vol. I, 1932; vol. II, 1934). For Lesbos: D. Ch. Eleftheriades, "Ktenotrophia" (Livestock Industry), *Lesviakon Emerologion* (Lesbian Almanac), 1950, pp. 281–282. For Skyros: Nike Perdika, *Skyros: Entyposeis kai perigraphai, historika kai laographika semeiomata, ethe kai ethima, mnemeia tou logou tou laou* (Skyros: Impressions and Descriptions, Historical and Folklore Notes, Manners and Customs, Glossary of Popular Speech) (Athens, 2 vols., 1940 and 1943 — pp. 157–165 deal with the major occupations, including that of shepherd; also see V. Antonakes, "E Poimniovoske mas" (Our Sheepraising), *Skyros,* 1948, pp. 112–114.

Chapter VII. Woman's Work Is Never Done

1. In any account of family life in Greece, some mention should be made of the family system among the Turks who live in western Thrace. When visited in 1953 and 1955, their daily lives were not too much affected by the Turkish-Greek controversy over Cyprus. Like other Greek citizens, the Turkish men must perform military service according to the law, but, since they are not considered very reliable soldiers, they are permitted to pay the fixed sum which exempts them. One of the problems in the last war was the inability of the Greek officers to command non-Greek-speaking Turks.

Much of the family life of these Turks centers about the farm and strict religious observances. To visit Turkish homes during Bairam, at the end of their month of fasting, makes one feel that he is in the interior of Turkey, although Greek place names and Greek officials bring one back to reality.

For two days at the time of Bairam the men do no work in the fields and are glad to spend leisurely hours with strangers interested in their way of life. They invite the guests to their homes which have been newly whitewashed for the holidays. The Turks remove their sandals or shoes at the bottom of the stairs leading to the main room, but non-Turkish visitors are not expected to follow this practice. There in a carpeted room the guests are seated on the few chairs, while the Turkish men squat cross-legged on the floor. A rich meal of *dolmades* (grape leaves stuffed with ground meat and rice), chunks of veal, dark bread, and a dessert of dripping sweet baklavas served with black coffee proves very filling. No women make their appearance, and men do all of the serving. Women are very much in evidence throughout the villages of western Thrace because they have many different tasks to perform, but they do manage to keep their faces partly covered by their veils when they see strangers approaching.

Marriage arrangements among the Muslims we visited are under the control of the Mufti in Xanthe. Polygyny is not very common, according to the Greek officials.

Turks do not receive dowries from their brides but have to pay a deposit in advance for the wife-to-be. When a divorce occurs, the wife's family keeps the money if the man is to blame, but is supposed to give the money to the man or his family if the woman is to blame.

2. See "Women in Greece Demand Equality," *New York Times,* August 22, 1954. Some indication of the changing status of women, particularly in the cities, is found in the periodical *Hellenia: The Voice of Greek Women,* published in English in Athens by four of the leading women's organizations: National Council of Greek Women, Lyceum Club of Greek Women, Hellenic Association of University Women, and Hellenic Girl Guides Association. Also see Panos D. Bardis, "The Changing Family in Modern Greece," *Sociology and Social Research,* XL (1955), 19–23.

3. See K. M. Kalyves, *Laographika Kymes Euboias* (Concerning the Folklore of Kyme, Euboea) (Athens, 1938).

4. Occipital flattening occurs in Epirus. This shape is not particularly sought, according to informants in Ioannina, the provincial capital, but results because the Epirote mother does not take the time to change the child from side to side so that the different parts of the head press against the cradle board. They go about their work and leave the child to cry for hours. Epirote men also seem to prefer the type of haircut that accentuates their particular headshape. It was interesting to find that many educated Greeks in Athens thought the Epirote head an inherited biological trait and not the result of child-care practice.

5. D. Lee, "Greece," in *Cultural Patterns and Technical Change* (Paris, 1953), p. 87 (Mentor edition).

6. UNRRA, *Greece: Ripe for Improvement* (Washington, D.C., 1946), p. 10.

7. Z. D. Ferriman, *Home Life in Hellas: Greece and the Greeks* (London, 1910), pp. 181–82.

8. Kitsos A. Makres, *Pelionitikes Phoresies* (Volos, 1949). He has made a special study of the art themes on the heads of shepherd crooks: ram's heads, dove feeding a snake, various sitting figures, to mention a few.

9. Angelique Hadjimihali, *L'Art populaire grec* (Athens, 1937). See also her article in the *Megale Hellenike Enkyklopaideia,* X (1934), 827–844.

10. See also D. Loukopoulos, *Pos hyphainoun kai dynontae oi Aitoloi* (How the Aetolians Weave and Dress) (Athens, 1927).

11. Throughout Greece there are various customs related to "feeding the fountain." Women may bring cheese, butter, bread, to leave at the fountain and say, "As the water runs, may animals and crops be abundant and prosperous."

12. Economic Cooperation Administration Mission to Greece, *The I.K.A. Insurance Population,* November 1951 (mimeographed).

13. J. C. Lawson, *Modern Greek Folklore and Ancient Greek Religion: A Study in Survivals* (Cambridge, Eng., 1910) p. 21.

14. D. Loukopoulos, "Symmikta laographika en Aitolias" (Collection of Folklore Materials about Aetolia), *Laographia,* XII (1938), 7–11, 47–61. The Spetsai materials came from personal interviews with Chrysoula.

15. Mutual Security Agency Mission to Greece, *Medical and Sanitary Data on Greece,* June 1952.

16. Ernestine Friedl, "Hospital Care in Provincial Greece," *Human Organization,* XVI (Winter 1958), p. 25.

17. *Ibid.,* 26.

CHAPTER VIII. COURTSHIP AND MARRIAGE

1. K. M. Kalyves, *Laographika Kymes Euboias* (Concerning the Folklore of Kyme, Euboea) (Athens, 1938), pp 27–30.

2. Panos D. Bardis, "Main Features of the Greek Family During the Early Twentieth Century," *Alpha Kappa Deltan,* Winter 1956, p. 17. Indicative of this double standard is prostitution, which is found in the town or city, although no houses of

prostitution are found in villages. One or more women with "loose morals" may live in the village and be visited by the men. In the town or city the person who introduces village girls into prostitution is apt to be a fairly young widow who seeks this as a means of support.

3. William Miller, *Greek Life in Town and Country* (London, 1905), p. 93.

4. Around Phlorina, in western Macedonia, boys marry older girls, since fewer women are available. This is a Slavic-speaking area where the women work more in the fields. In most Greek villages it is considered undesirable for a man to marry an older woman.

5. In one group of twenty-five soldiers from different villages, six reported that there was no promenade in their village, although each of the six knew of its existence elsewhere. The remaining nineteen said that they had the promenade.

6. Matchmakers, the proxenetres, still exist today, according to a clipping from the *Athens News,* November 23, 1952: "Athanasia Markou arranged marriages. That is to say, she was what they call a 'proxenetra.' A short time ago she had as a client one Irene who wanted to get her first cousin, Maria, married. Markou undertook to find a husband, and introduced Irene's cousin Maria to her own brother. The marriage took place, but the agreed fee to the 'proxenetra' was not paid, and Markou tried to dissolve the marriage out of anger."

7. A statement of the connection between dowry practices, attitudes toward land tenure, and the status of a son-in-law living in his wife's paternal home is found in Ernestine Friedl, "Dowry and Inheritance in Modern Greece," *Transactions of the New York Academy of Sciences,* XXII, ser. 2 (November 1959).

8. One important reason why a young woman prefers a shopkeeper or artisan from a town or city is the fact that she will be relieved of the drudgery of farm work.

9. Bardis, "Main Features of the Greek Family," pp. 17, 20.

10. D. Loukopoulos, *Laographia,* XII (1938).

Chapter IX. Ceremonies and Holy Days

1. See D. Loukopoulos, *Laographia,* XII (1938).

2. See William Miller, *Greek Life in Town and Country,* p. 96.

3. Miller, *Greek Life,* p. 73, correctly points out that the strong particularism, or local loyalty, found in Greece is often given expression in the local saint's day which heightens clannishness.

4. Agnes Diamantopoulos, "Greek Dances of Today and the Dances of Ancient Greece: A Comparison," *Hellenia,* XXI (January–March 1953), 9. On Easter Tuesday the people of Megara dance the *trata,* an ancient dance depicting the motions of the fishermen hopefully hauling in their nets.

5. *Ibid.,* p. 8.

6. After this material had been written, there appeared a volume in English by George A. Megas under the title *Greek Calendar Customs* (Athens, 1956). It is a valuable source book for anyone wishing to understand the rural customs associated with various holidays. For an interesting description of the holidays in a village of Central Greece, see V. G. Valaoras, *E laographia tou choriou mou: Perista, Navpaktias* (The Folklore of My Village: Perista, Naupaktias) (Thessalonike, 1939).

7. See Anne Anthony, *Meet the Greeks* (Athens, 1950), for an excellent description of holidays of particular interest to the foreigner living in Athens. This small book is a most useful orientation to Greek life.

8. These facts about specific holidays are taken from St. P. Kyriakidis, "Erotimata dia ten laiken latreian" (Questions Concerning Popular Worship), *Laographia,* XI (1937), 659–677. Although I have not personally witnessed all of these customs in Greek villages, I have seen almost every one of them observed by other nationalities of the Orthodox faith.

9. For further details about the kallikantzari, see G. F. Abbott, *Macedonian Folk-*

lore (Cambridge, Eng., 1903), pp. 73–76; Anthony, *Meet the Greeks*, pp. 135–39; A. Triantaphyllidis, "Christmas Customs and Folklore," *Hellenia*, III (December 1948), 2–3; and Kyriakidis, "Erotimata."

CHAPTER X. MUTUAL AID AND COOPERATIVES IN RURAL GREECE

1. One article has been particularly helpful in providing details to supplement actual field observations. It was written by D. A. Petropoulos under the title, "Ethima synergasias kai allelovoetheias tou hellenikou laou" (Customs of Collaboration and Mutual Aid of the Greek people), *Epeteris laographikou archeiou* (1943–44), pp. 59–85. Anyone wishing to find out the actual Greek terms for various kinds of arrangements in different regions of the country should consult this article. Petropoulos also quotes many of the proverbs in full and is the source of those used here as well as the statement on the nychteria.
2. This is taken from "Ta Laographika tes Kleitorias" (Concerning the Folklore of Kleitoria), unpublished manuscript by T. K. Papaspyropoulos.
3. For a detailed account of Ambelakia, see Elias P. Georgios, *Historia kai synetairismos ton Ambelakion* (History and Association of Ambelakia) (Athens, 1951). In 1875, François Boulanger published a book, *Ambelakia ou les Associations et les Municipalités Helléniques . . .* (Paris). F. C. H. L. Pouqueville, according to his *Voyage de la Grèce* (2nd ed., Paris, 1826), found in the early nineteenth century that the town consisted of 460 families. The people were proud of their past, but had little to show for it. E. S. Forster mentions Ambelakia in his *A Short History of Modern Greece, 1821–1940* (London, 1941), p. 6.
4. See Civil Affairs Handbook, "Greece" (Section 7: Agriculture), *Army Service Forces Manual* (Washington, D.C., November 16, 1943), pp. 48–51. For the pre-World-War-II situation, see also Banque Agricole de Grèce, *Statistique des Associations Cooperatives Agricoles de Grèce* (Athens, 1937).
5. See Bickham Sweet-Escott, *Greece: A Political and Economic Survey, 1939–1953* (London, 1954), p. 142. Sweet-Escott also calls attention to the ILO report on *Labour Problems in Greece* and writes: "In addition, the principle of the consumers' cooperative has been applied extensively since the war, especially in the towns. By October 1947 no less than 5,390 urban cooperatives had been registered, including cooperatives formed by small tradesmen for production, for example, of furniture, and many consumers' cooperatives."
6. Food and Agriculture Organization of the United Nations, *Report of the FAO Mission for Greece* (Washington, D.C., March 1947), pp. 46–51.
7. Robert Hewlett, "Agricultural Cooperation in Greece," *World Agriculture,* October 1954, writes: "There is nowhere any binding engagement on the farmer-member to deal with his cooperative, or on the local cooperative to deal with its regional or central organization. Such an obligation would be contrary to Greek law. It may be argued that this is a severe handicap to cooperative development. It is certainly true that the element of compulsion in business relations between member and society is found in a number of countries where farmer cooperation is most advanced, and that many leaders in those countries consider it has been decisive, even if it no longer is so important today. It seems unlikely, however, that the mere inclusion of a compulsory delivery clause in the agreement between the farmer and his marketing cooperative of itself achieves very much. Such clauses are often difficult to enforce at law and no cooperative relishes the prospect of a series of legal actions, even if successful. What gives the contractual obligation real binding force is the climate of opinion among the members."
8. Memorandum from A. W. Willis to Brice M. Mace, Jr., "1953–54 Marketing and Distribution Analysis and Justification," Mutual Security Administration in Greece, May 22, 1953.
9. These figures are from the *1958 Statistical Yearbook of Greece*, p. 209.

10. Print Hudson, *1952 Agricultural Report — Greece* (American Embassy, Athens, Dispatch No. 771, January 3, 1953), comments: "The foundation of the cooperative movement is the 8,700 village cooperatives (including fishing and forestry as well as farm coops). The total membership was 684,000 at the beginning of 1952. In each Nomos is found a Union of the Cooperatives of that region. This organization supplies the village cooperative with production credit obtained from the Agricultural Bank. In some districts more than one Union may be found, with the total for Greece being over one hundred. Most of the Unions belong to the Panhellenic Confederation of Unions of Agricultural Cooperatives with headquarters in Athens. Those in control of this Federation so centralize and direct the program of Agricultural cooperatives that it often works to the disadvantage of the movement by eliminating farmer participation. . . ." In addition to the geographical organization of the cooperatives, described above, there are several commodity cooperative associations. These include:

1. *KYDEP.* The Central Organization for the Administration of Indigenous Products. It collects quite a number of products under the Government's price support program. During 1952 it collected only wheat and rye.
2. *SEKE.* The Association of Tobacco Growers' Cooperative Unions, Ltd.
3. *KSOS.* The Union of Sultana Growers' Cooperatives. In 1952 this organization collected nearly 7,000 tons of sultanas (grapes).
4. *ELAIOURGIKE.* The Central Union of Olive Oil Producers.

It often happens that the village cooperatives indicate a certain degree of dissatisfaction with the commodity associations, particularly because of their high costs in handling the products.

CHAPTER XI. THE VILLAGE COFFEEHOUSE

1. Near East Foundation, *et al.*, mimeographed village studies, "A Village in the Arta Plain" (Athens, Spring 1951).
2. *Idem,* "A Mountain Village, Grammos Area" (Athens, March 1952).
3. *Idem,* "A Village in the Serres Plains" (Athens, December 1951).
4. *Idem,* "A Macedonian Village" (Athens, May 1951).
5. Chester Bowles, *Ideas, People and Peace* (New York, 1958), p. 86.
6. John Democritos Photiadis, "The Coffee House and Its Role in Stavroupolis, Greece" (unpublished master's thesis, Cornell University, 1956).
7. Near East Foundation, *et al.*, "A 'Control' Village in Macedonia" (Athens, November 1951).
8. *Idem,* "A Village in the Agrinion Area" (Athens, October 1951).

CHAPTER XII. LOCAL GOVERNMENT

1. United States Economic Cooperation Administration, Civil Government Division, *Facts on Greek Local Government: A Preliminary Outline* (Athens, December 15, 1950), p. 2 (mimeographed).
2. K. Koukkidi, *To Pnevma tou Synergatismou ton Neoteron Hellenon kai t'Ambelakia, o Protos Synetairismos tou Kosmou* (The Spirit of Cooperation of Modern Greeks and Ambelakia, the First Cooperative of the World) (Athens, 1948).
3. *Ibid.*, p. 46.
4. United States Economic Cooperation Administration, *Facts*, p. 7.
5. United States Economic Cooperation Administration, *Revitalizing Greek Local Government: Special Supplement,* Report 67, p. 3 (mimeographed).
6. Frank Smothers, William Hardy McNeill, Elizabeth Darbishire McNeill, *Report on the Greeks: Findings of a Twentieth Century Fund Team Which Surveyed*

Conditions in Greece in 1947 (New York, 1948), p. 111. For a report done ten years later for the same sponsor by one of the earlier authors, see William Hardy McNeill, *Greece: American Aid in Action: 1947–1956* (New York, 1957).

7. See the mimeographed village studies done by the Near East Foundation, *et al.*, "A 'Control' Village of the Mesolongi Area" (Athens, October 1951).

8. John D. Photiadis, "The Coffee House and its Role in the Village of Stavroupolis, Greece," p. 25.

9. United States Mutual Security Agency, *Report on Greek Local Government, 1952* (Athens, Civil Government Division, 1952), pp. 16–17 (mimeographed).

10. An excellent statement of the problem is found in United States Mutual Security Agency, *Report on the Decentralization of Greek Government Services* (Athens, Civil Government Division, June 1953), mimeographed.

11. C. A. Munkman, *American Aid to Greece: A Report on the First Ten Years* (New York, 1958), p. 254. Munkman served for four years as chief of a unit in the United States Economic Mission to Greece which had the responsibility for investigating the effectiveness of expenditures in our aid program.

12. Photiadis, "The Coffee House."

13. Three documents which proved particularly helpful were prepared by O. F. Traylor, Local Tax Specialist, United States Mission: Economic Cooperation Administration, *The Financing of Greek Local Government: Special Supplement*, Report 70 (mimeographed, n.d.); *Summary Analysis of New Interim Local Finance Law* (E. L. 1910/1951, Official Gazette 221), memorandum to Director, FP Division (typed), August 10, 1951, 14 pp.; *Significance of Survey of Turkish Local Finance . . . for Financing Greek Local Units of Government*, memorandum to Joel W. C. Harper, Chief, Public Finance Section, FP Division (mimeographed), September 12, 1951, 18 pp.

14. One of the most penetrating analyses of Greek governmental administration and its problems was made by a Greek at the request of the Greek government: *Report on the Greek Economic Problem*, by Kyriakos Varvaressos (English translation, Washington, D.C., February 12, 1952, mimeographed). He cites five characteristics of the administration: excessive number of employees, particularly in the center; indifference to public interest; lowered standards through appointments of unqualified personnel; narrow bureaucratic spirit; total incapacity and willingness to meet responsibilities imposed on it by the granting of foreign aid. In fairness to all concerned, however, it should be pointed out that this was written in 1952, when Greece was trying to recover from the wounds of war.

15. These are excerpts appearing in the *Athens News*, September 17, 1952. For those preferring a happier note, the following *New York Times* item, December 12, 1955, will prove of interest:

Athens, Dec. 11. Premier Constantin Karamanlis has announced a plan by which free medicines will be made available to 4,000,000 Greek peasants. The plan is expected to become effective at once.

Mr. Karamanlis also announced that his Government had decided to compensate peasants whose beasts of burden had been requisitioned by the State for war purposes since 1942.

The Premier said 120,000,000 drachmas ($4,000,000) had been earmarked in the 1955–56 budget for this ambitious welfare plan. Other Government decisions announced were to increase allocations for land improvement projects; to put aside larger amounts for middle-term loans to the peasantry; and to install a cotton press in Salonika.

16. An account in *Harper's Magazine* in 1872 on "Political Characteristics of Modern Greeks" has a most up-to-date ring. Charles Cheston, in his *Greece in 1887* (London, 1887), points out traits which survive to the present, as does William Miller in *Greek Life in Town and Country* (London, 1905). Especially appropriate are the comments by Henry Morgenthau, *I Was Sent to Athens* (Garden City, 1929), in the section on "The Greatness of the Greeks."

Chapter XIII. The Village School

1. See Dorothy Lee's section on Greece in *Cultural Patterns and Technical Change* (Paris, 1953).

2. "Ta Laographika tes Kleitorias" (Concerning the Folklore of Kleitoria), unpublished manuscript.

3. A. H. Sassani, "Education in Greece," *College and University*, XXVII (1952), 295.

4. *Athens News*, October 10, 1952.

5. United States Mission to Greece, Field Service Report 601, July 7, 1952, Athens (typescript).

6. These 1956–57 figures are from the *Americana 1958 Annual*.

7. See Archie W. Johnston, "Plan for Depressed Villages," Mission Field Services, Report 70, to William M. Tait, January 22, 1953.

8. From Near East Foundation, *et al.*, village studies (Athens, 1951–52).

9. Kristine Konold, "Brief Survey of Elementary and Educational Institutions in Greece," November 18, 1952, United States Information Service (typescript) .

10. *Programmata Analytika kai Orologia ton Demotikon Scholeion* (Program Analysis and Horaria of the Public Schools) (Athens, 1946), p. 1.

11. Accompaniments to K. Konold report. See note 9 above.

12. More information about this and other American educational institutions in Greece is contained in various chapters of this book. Anatolia College in Thessalonike, like others mentioned, has a program of village community service. Athens College students also contribute time and money to such endeavors.

13. Adapted from a paper entitled "Classic and Modern Greek," by Ph. Annino Cavalierato, given at the Foreign Language Conference, University of Kentucky, 1954.

14. The word "pure" is not an accurate translation of *katharevousa*, since *kathara* means "pure." *Katharevousa* implies a certain striving, a certain effort toward the pure, or "purist."

15. Kimon Friar, "New Greek Poets, An Anthology and Commentary," *Poetry*, LXXVIII (1951), p. 151.

16. *Greece: Geographical Handbook* (Naval Intelligence Division, British Admiralty), I, 297.

17. *Ibid.*

18. Floyd A. Spencer, *War and Postwar Greece: An Analysis Based on Greek Writings* (Washington, D.C., 1952), p. 154. This is an excellent treatment of Greek works dealing with educational problems.

19. Friar, "New Greek Poets," p. 152.

Chapter XIV. Religion and the Greek Peasant

1. See a classic work on the subject by John C. Lawson, *Modern Greek Folklore and Ancient Greek Religion: A Study in Survivals* (Cambridge, Eng., 1910).

2. William Miller, *Greek Life in Town and Country* (London, 1905), p. 73.

3. Marcu Beza, *Heritage of Byzantium* (London, 1947), p. 89.

4. See also B. P. D'Estournelles, "The Superstitions of Modern Greece," *The Nineteenth Century*, no. 62 (April 1882).

5. Thanassis Aghnides, "What Ancient Greece Means to the Modern Greek," *John Rylands Library Bulletin*, XXVII (1943), 263–64.

6. Harold F. Alderfer, "Greece and the West Today," ECA Memorandum, Athens, April 13, 1951, p. 8. Also see Alderfer's *I Like Greece* (State College, Pa., 1956), chap. 10, "The Church Is the Foundation."

7. Floyd A. Spencer, *War and Postwar Greece: An Analysis Based on Greek Writings* (Washington, D.C., 1952), p. 153.

8. Alderfer, "Greece and the West Today," p. 8.

9. For observations on the village clergy, see Sir Charles Eliot, *Turkey in Europe* (London, 1908), and H. D. F. Kitto, *In the Mountains of Greece* (London, 1933), p. 16.

10. See Dorothy D. Lee, "Greek Tales of Priest and Priestwife," *Journal of American Folklore*, April–June 1947, p. 163. This article contains nine stories about the priest and his wife, some of them Chaucerian in tone. He is either interested in an attractive parishioner whose husband eventually deals drastically with him, or his wife is involved with a lover whom the priest may or may not outwit.

11. Angelike Chatzemichale made this observation.

12. The material for this whole paragraph is adapted from Anne Anthony, *Meet the Greeks* (Athens, 1950), pp. 37–41.

13. D. Lee, "Greece," *Cultural Patterns and Technical Change*, p. 84.

14. One of the most vivid accounts in English of the prominent role of the priest is found in Nikos Kazantzakis, *The Greek Passion* (New York, 1954), a fictionalized account of what happened in an Asia Minor Greek community when some of its characters in a passion play began to play their roles seriously in real life.

15. D. A. Petropoulos, "Ethima synergasias kai allelovoedeias tou hellenikou laou" (Customs of Collaboration and Mutual Aid of the Greek people), *Epeteris Laographikou Archeiou* (Yearbook of the Folklore Archives), 1943–1944, p. 71.

16. *Ibid.,* p. 84.

17. See W. M. Leake's account of his explorations for the River Styx in chap. 26 (vol. 3) of his *Travels in the Morea,* 3 vols. (London, 1930).

18. From D. Kontogannis, *Sylloge demotikon paradoseon* (Collection of Popular Traditions) (Athens, 1920), p. 60.

19. Rennell Rodd, *The Customs and Lore of Modern Greece* (London, 1892), p. 120.

20. Kontogannis, *Sylloge,* p. 60.

21. D. Loukopoulos, "Symmeikta laographika en Aitolias," *Laographia,* XII (1938), 20–21.

22. Rennell Rodd, *Customs and Lore,* p. 129. See also Baron P. D'Estournelles, "The Superstitions of Modern Greece," *The Nineteenth Century,* no. 62 (1882), p. 590, who points out quite correctly that these dirge singers are frequently professionals employed to render this service. Lady Verney in an article on "Songs and Legends of Modern Greece," *The Contemporary Review* (1875), describes funeral customs which survive today: "The myriologia, or funeral songs, are always sung and composed by women . . . and are uttered first immediately after the death takes place. Next, when the body is laid on a bier, dressed in its best clothes, the face uncovered, turned to the east, the arms closed over the breast, the nearest relation begins her lamentation, and is followed by the more distant in blood; then the friends and the neighbors. Often messages are sent to those who have died previously; flowers and small presents for them are thrown on the body, which is entreated to carry them to the next world. . . . Hired mourners are often brought in to sing to the honour of the dead, as in the funeral of Hector, when Achilles has given up the body to his father."

23. Loukopoulos, "Symmeikta," p. 20.

24. G. F. Abbott, *Macedonian Folklore* (Cambridge, Eng., 1903), p. 208. He has an excellent chapter on funeral rites.

25. V. T. Valassis, "The Living Past and Technical Change" (unpublished master's thesis, University of Maryland, 1956), pp. 13–14.

CHAPTER XV. THE VILLAGE COMMUNITY

1. The best study of these Greek-American returnees is found in Theodore Saloutos, *They Remember America* (Berkeley and Los Angeles, 1956). H. D. F. Kitto,

in his *In the Mountains of Greece,* has mentioned that he found only one village in the Peloponnesos which did not produce an English-speaking inhabitant.

2. These references are to John D. Photiadis, "The Coffee House and Its Role in the Village of Stavroupolis, Greece," (unpublished master's thesis, Cornell University, 1956) p. 41.

3. See Near East Foundation, *et al.,* village studies (Athens, 1951–52).

4. Photiadis, p. 42.

5. This description by Dorothy Lee will be found in Margaret Mead, ed., *Cultural Patterns and Technical Change* (Paris, 1953), pp. 60–61 (Mentor edition).

6. V. T. Valassis, "The Living Past and Technical Change," (unpublished master's thesis, University of Maryland, 1956), p. 16.

7. The reader familiar with contemporary social theory will quickly note the extent to which these observations derive from Emile Durkheim and those sociologists who work in his tradition.

8. Photiadis, p. 84.

9. From the village study by T. K. Papaspyropoulos, "Ta Laographika tes Kleitorias" (Concerning the Folklore of Kleitoria), unpublished manuscript.

CHAPTER XVI. SOCIAL CHANGE IN RURAL GREECE

1. The three types of social change used here are adapted from N. F. Washburne, *Interpreting Social Change in America* (Garden City, 1954).

2. See Stephen P. Ladas, *The Exchange of Minorities; Bulgaria, Greece, and Turkey* (New York, 1939).

3. In almost every one of my hundreds of interviews during an eleven-month period in Greece, I touched on the topic of social change. In a country such as Greece, one cannot understand the present without a knowledge of what has changed. A summarizing chapter such as this cannot fully convey the deep emotional overtones surrounding the discussion of what it was like to flee as a child from Asia Minor, to have one's village occupied by an Axis army, or to experience the fury of Communist guerrillas on the run.

4. A. C. de Vooys and J. J. C. Piket, "A Geographical Analysis of Two Villages in the Peloponnesos," *Tijdschrift van het Koninklijk Nederlandsch Aardrijkskundig Genootschap,* LXXV (1958), 44–45.

5. *Ibid.,* p. 51.

6. This figure is much more favorable to the villagers than that prevailing between the two world wars. In the Balkans generally during that time, the proportion of peasants was higher and their share of the total national income lower than the figures here cited in the text.

7. Ernestine Friedl, "The Role of Kinship in the Transmission of National Culture to Rural Villages in Mainland Greece," *The American Anthropologist,* LXI (1959), 31.

8. An excellent though brief description of some of the most important programs of planned social change in rural Greece through the 1950s is found in the mimeographed paper entitled "Community Development Programs and Policies in Greece," prepared for the Eastern Mediterranean Study Tour on Community Development (Athens, 1955). Among other things, it tells of the merger into a Small Common Utility Projects program of four previous programs: the Agricultural Land Improvement Program, the Small Sanitary Projects Program, the Relief through Employment Program (under the Ministry of Welfare), and the Small Community Projects Program (under the Ministry of Interior). The third program particularly has created much international interest. See Glen Leet, "Greece Finds One Key to Development," *United Nations Bulletin,* X (1951); Paul H. Guenault and Howard W. Beers, *Community Development Programmes in Greece with Special Consideration of Welfare Through Employment* (New York, United Nations, 1953).

9. A. C. Munkman, *American Aid to Greece* (New York, 1958).

10. The term "change agent" is employed by Western students of social change to designate those professionals whose primary efforts are directed toward the initiation and implementation of planned change. See Ronald Lippitt, Jeanne Watson, and Bruce Westley, *Planned Change: A Comparative Study of Principles and Techniques* (New York, 1958).

CHAPTER XVII. SOCIAL CONSEQUENCES OF FOREIGN AID

1. Fortunately, many studies are appearing which seek to explain what happens to an agrarian society when it moves toward industrialization. One of the best single sources for the study of this kind of change is *Economic Development and Cultural Change,* a periodical now in its tenth volume, published at the University of Chicago. See also Charles P. Loomis, *Social Systems: Essays on Their Persistence and Change* (Princeton, 1960).

2. See Irwin T. Sanders, "Characteristics of Peasant Societies" (chap. 4) and Carle C. Zimmerman, "Euro-American Rural Society" (chap. 10) in E. deS. Brunner. Irwin T. Sanders, and Douglas Ensminger, *Farmers of the World* (New York, 1945). See also Robert Redfield, *Peasant Society and Culture* (Chicago, 1956).

3. A. T. Mosher, "Interrelationships Among Agricultural Development, Social Organization, and Personal Attitudes and Values," in Irwin T. Sanders, ed., *Interprofessional Training Goals for Technical Assistance Personnel Abroad* (New York, 1959).

Index

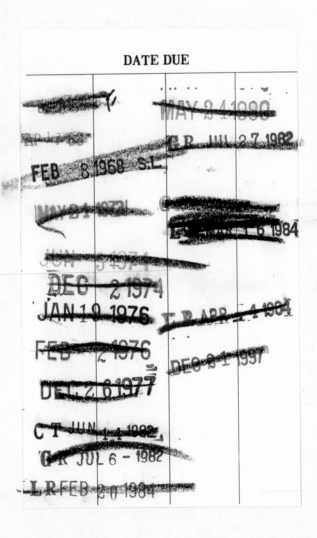